W9-DID-761

DATE DUE

BIRTH CONTROL, SEX AND MARRIAGE IN BRITAIN 1918–1960

Birth Control, Sex and Marriage in Britain 1918–1960

KATE FISHER

OXFORD
UNIVERSITY PRESS

63395769   11-8-07

OXFORD
UNIVERSITY PRESS

Great Clarendon Street, Oxford OX2 6DP

Oxford University Press is a department of the University of Oxford.
It furthers the University's objective of excellence in research, scholarship,
and education by publishing worldwide in

Oxford New York

Auckland Cape Town Dar es Salaam Hong Kong Karachi
Kuala Lumpur Madrid Melbourne Mexico City Nairobi
New Delhi Shanghai Taipei Toronto

With offices in

Argentina Austria Brazil Chile Czech Republic France Greece
Guatemala Hungary Italy Japan Poland Portugal Singapore
South Korea Switzerland Thailand Turkey Ukraine Vietnam

Oxford is a registered trade mark of Oxford University Press
in the UK and in certain other countries

Published in the United States
by Oxford University Press Inc., New York

© Kate Fisher 2006

British Library Cataloguing in Publication Data

Data available

Library of Congress Cataloging in Publication Data

Data available

Typeset by Newgen Imaging Systems (P) Ltd., Chennai, India
Printed in Great Britain
on acid-free paper by
Biddles Ltd., King's Lynn, Norfolk

ISBN   978–0–19–926736–1

Acknowledgements

My greatest debt is to the many people I interviewed in Blackburn, Hertfordshire, Oxford, and south Wales, on whose intimate recollections, thoughts and feelings this book is based. They shared their memories generously and unselfishly, even when they were painful, and their commitment, patience and good humour, gave me enormous inspiration and pleasure. The book is essentially theirs. I am also grateful to all the institutions, care organisations and individuals who not only allowed me to make initial contact with interviewees, but also encouraged participation within supportive environments, and provided invaluable practical help.

I am very grateful for the assistance of the librarians and archivists at the Wellcome Library for the History and Understanding of Medicine, the Mass-Observation Archive at the University of Sussex and the British Library Department of Manuscripts. As this work has developed over many years, I have accumulated debts to many individuals, in particular to the supervisors of my original Oxford thesis, Jane Lewis and Richard Smith, and also to its examiners Angus McLaren and Megan Vaughan. I have benefited from various intellectual environments; the Wellcome Unit for the History of Medicine in Oxford, the colleges of Wadham and Wolfson in Oxford, the Cambridge Group for the Study of Population and Social Structure, and most recently the University of Exeter, where my colleagues have offered unfailing kindness and support.

Both the Wellcome Trust and the ESRC have provided me with generous funding over many years: Wellcome supported my doctoral work with a studentship; and my part in the ESRC-funded project originally granted to Simon Szreter has also been aided by a Wellcome fellowship and further grant; I am also grateful to Wellcome for the strategic award recently made to the Centre for Medical History at Exeter. Simon Szreter has been endlessly generous in allowing me the time and space to work on this book alongside our shared project, which will shortly result in a joint publication on 'Sexuality, Love and Marriage in England, 1918–1960'. Our fruitful and stimulating collaboration has contributed greatly to my own work, and I am delighted to have been able to draw here on material which will receive more detailed and extensive treatment in the joint work currently in preparation.

For transcription of oral history interviews and archival assistance, I am grateful to Jenny Attoe and Lindsay Marks, respectively, and others. Several interviews were expertly conducted by James Mark and Simon Szreter. Adrian Haddock, Pete O'Neill and Matthew Wright proofread the manuscript. I also thank Janet Yarker for her work on the index. Anne Gelling, Janet Moth, Ruth Parr, Samantha Skyrme, Zoe Washford and their editorial colleagues at Oxford University Press have been most helpful throughout.

I am especially grateful to all those who have given so much of their time to improving the text of this book. Nic Bilham, Lesley Hall, James Mark, Barry Reay, John Tosh and my parents, Nick and Sarah Fisher, read many drafts assiduously, and discussed them with intelligence and sensitivity. Rebecca Langlands was supportive both in our shared teaching work and in the writing process. Other specific debts are acknowledged in footnotes throughout the text.

For all the roles they fill in my wonderful home and home-from-home environments, I thank my parents, my brother Matthew and sister Rebecca, all my Ashburton friends, Kate Austin, Nic Bilham, Steph Cragg, Rebecca Lemon, John and Frances Williams and, above all, James Mark. Our first son Edmund brought discipline to the writing process, and his brother Isaac has had the sensitivity not overly to disrupt the final stages.

Too many other friends and colleagues to name here have provided both intellectual stimulation and practical and emotional support - they are all deserving of my heartfelt thanks.

Contents

Abbreviations

A & M	Archives and Manuscripts Collection at the Wellcome Library for the History and Understanding of Medicine
A&M: GC/105	Television History Workshop, 'In the Club: Birth Control This Century' (1988) transcripts
A&M: PP/HRW	Helena Wright Papers
A&M: PP/MCS	Marie C. Stopes Papers
A&M: SA/FPA	Family Planning Association Papers
BL Add. MSS	British Library Additional Manuscripts
BMJ	*British Medical Journal*
CBC	Society for Constructive Birth Control and Racial Progress
NBCA	National Birth Control Association
NBCC	National Birth Control Council
NVA	National Vigilance Association
PIC	Population Investigation Committee
SPBCC	Society for the Provision of Birth Control Clinics

Introduction

Well some people have big families and that generation didn't seem to have big families—my generation—none of my friends had big families—I mean, my sister only had two, I only had two, my other sister had 'bout four or five girls, but not big families, you know . . . just one of them things, you know, just that was it—careful I suppose—we never used nothing, no . . . Still he was a pretty good chap. I think him being brought up in big family, and me in big family it's just how it worked out. Funny though, I've thought about that myself, you know, my sister only had two and I only had two and my brothers had about three.[1]

From the end of the nineteenth century marital contraceptive practice changed dramatically. The first half of the twentieth century saw increased numbers of married couples using birth control with ever greater consistency, and a concomitant sharp and sustained decline in average family size, which reached its nadir in Britain during the 1930s. The rapid decrease in marital fertility across most of Europe and North America from the end of the nineteenth century onwards is frequently termed 'the fertility decline'. Birth rates rose during and after the Second World War, but the extremely large families of the Victorian period did not return.

The massive increase in the use of birth control and the sharp and sustained decline in average family size has long been subject to academic investigation. Demographers and demographic historians have produced a large body of literature attempting to explain this major transformation in the European population.[2] More recently, the development of social history, and the interest of historians in family, gender, and sexuality, have provoked a new focus on the increased availability of contraception, in changes in family forms, and in developments in sexual behaviour.[3]

The changes in contraceptive behaviour during the course of the twentieth century are seen as revolutionary: 'This change in reproductive behaviour is undoubtedly the most dramatic in human history and merits the designation

---

[1] Hilda, bc3ox#5. All names are pseudonyms.

[2] This literature is discussed in e.g. van de Kaa, 'Anchored Narratives'; Szreter, *Fertility, Class and Gender*, 7–65; Greenhalgh, 'The Social Construction of Population Science'; and Friedlander, Okun, and Segal, 'The Demographic Transition Then and Now'.

[3] See e.g. Banks, *Prosperity and Parenthood*; Brookes, *Abortion in England 1900–1967*; Davey, 'Birth Control in Britain during the Inter-War Years'; Gittins, *Fair Sex*; Ittman, *Work, Gender and Family in Victorian England*; McLaren, *A History of Contraception*; Porter and Hall, *The Facts of Life*; W. Seccombe, *Weathering the Storm*; Weeks, *Sex, Politics and Society*.

"fertility revolution".'[4] The enormous contrast between generations is also stressed: 'fertility regulation within marriage was established as a mass practice', the suddenness of which change meant 'there was evidently widespread discontinuity between the generations—daughters and sons breaking radically with the sexual mores of their mothers and fathers'.[5] There is seen to be a wide chasm between the values, ideals, and beliefs of pre-transition and post-transition families, such that, as Ettienne van de Walle claims, 'it is as hard for contemporary Western laymen to understand that fertility was unlimited among their ancestors as it is for couples in a natural fertility regime to understand that family size can be an object of conscious choice'.[6]

Indeed, 'the fertility decline' is seen as integral to the development of modern societies. The decline in average family size is portrayed as a revolutionary moment in family forms, revealing a radical shift in the nature of marital relations and individuals' expectations of the future, hopes for their lives, and desires for their families. Birth control use distinguishes the modern family from the traditional one: 'In traditional societies fertility and mortality are high. In modern societies fertility and mortality are low.'[7] The mass use of birth control is linked with the onset of 'modern' ways of thinking such as the separation of sex from reproduction, the perception that the future can be controlled and planned, the reconfiguration of gender relationships along a companionate model, and the readjustment of gendered power relations within marriage. In sum, the fertility decline is seen by almost all commentators to represent a 'profound' change in 'ideas, aspirations and attitudes'.[8]

The aim of this book is to examine these changes from the perspective of individuals involved in the later years of this transition. It is a much more systematic social history of birth control practices than anything yet published and aims to explore, in detail, the ways in which individuals negotiated and maintained the small family that had become the norm by the 1920s and 1930s.[9] Recent demographic history has drawn attention to the need for such a micro-level

---

[4] Easterlin and Crimmins, *The Fertility Revolution*, 3.

[5] W. Seccombe, 'Starting to Stop', 153, 156.

[6] van de Walle, 'Fertility Transition, Conscious Choice, and Numeracy', 489. See also Cleland and Wilson, 'Demand Theories of the Fertility Transition', 29, who warn against 'underestimating the fundamental nature of the change from reproduction without conscious control to a regime of deliberate regulation of births within marriage'.

[7] Paul Demeny, quoted in Coale, 'The Demographic Transition Reconsidered', 64. Despite the discrediting of 'modernization' theory, Susan Greenhalgh demonstrates its unshakable dominance in discussions of fertility decline and demographic theory in 'The Social Construction of Population Science'.   [8] Pollak and Watkins, 'Cultural and Economic Approaches to Fertility', 469.

[9] In this book I shall use the terms 'birth control' and 'contraception' very broadly to denote all possible methods by which fertility might be reduced. It should be recognized that individuals do not always share these definitions: withdrawal in particular is frequently not considered a form of 'birth control' or 'contraception'. During interviews particular care was taken when framing questions to avoid any confusion on this point and various means of describing contraceptive options were used to explore different understandings of family limitation methods.

approach using data based on individual behaviour. David Levine, for example, recognized that a 'consensus is emerging that if we want to study the ways in which large-scale social processes are refracted, through the prism of personal experience, into changing strategies of reproduction, then we have to adopt a micro-level mode of analysis'.[10] There is, however, little detailed qualitative material about individuals' contraceptive use in the documentary record. Information on individual behaviour is confined to such evidence as the findings of a few inquiries into contraceptive use, data collected at birth control clinics, material such as letters written to birth control campaigners for contraceptive advice, and occasional accounts in private, literary material. Of central importance are the letters written to Marie Stopes, the reports and notes from various birth control clinics, the inquiry into contraceptive use undertaken by E. Lewis-Faning for the Royal Commission on Population (1949), and material collected by Mass-Observation between 1937 and 1944.

It is striking, given the chronic paucity of existing evidence, that our understanding of marital contraceptive practices has not been enriched by any systematic oral history. Where previous oral histories have considered such issues, their interest has only been marginal—such as in Elizabeth Roberts's oral history of working-class women in Barrow, Lancaster, and Preston—or based on a small sample size, such as Diana Gittins's interviews with twenty-seven people as part of her study of changing family size.[11] Even oral histories dealing with sexual cultures, such as Steve Humphries's *A Secret World of Sex*, tend to ignore contraception, particularly that practised within marriage.[12]

The research conducted for this book represents, therefore, the first substantial and systematic use of oral history to study contraceptive behaviour and the dynamics of family formation. Detailed and in-depth interviews were conducted with 193 people within two major research projects. The first group of interviews, undertaken as part of a D.Phil. thesis on marital contraceptive practices, involved fifty-eight people from south Wales (thirty-nine women and nineteen men) and forty-six (twenty-nine women and seventeen men) from Oxford.[13] The second, part of a wider investigation of sexual beliefs and practices, was conducted both under an ESRC project grant and a Wellcome project grant.[14] Thirty-eight individuals from Hertfordshire (twenty-one women and seventeen men) and fifty-one individuals from Blackburn (thirty-five women and sixteen men) were

[10] Levine, review of Michael Teitelbaum, *The British Fertility Decline*, 720. On new approaches to the issues see also Kertzer, 'Political-Economic and Cultural Explanations of Demographic Behaviour'.
[11] E. Roberts, *A Woman's Place*; Gittins, *Fair Sex*. See also Williamson, ' "Getting Off at Loftus" '; Higgins, 'Changing Expectations and Realities of Marriage'.
[12] Similarly, his and Pamela Gordon's oral history of parenting does not examine parents' deliberations about the timing of pregnancy, nor their family limitation strategies and attitudes towards birth control: *A Labour of Love. The Experience of Parenthood in Britain, 1900–1950*.
[13] Fisher, 'An Oral History of Birth Control Practice, c. 1925–50'.
[14] Szreter, 'Marriage, Fertility and Sexuality 1900–1950'; Fisher, 'Sexuality, Marriage and Family 1918–1960'.

interviewed. Most were widows or widowers. There were twenty-one interviews with couples: five in South Wales, eight in Oxford, four in Hertfordshire, and five in Blackburn.[15] Dates of birth ranged from 1899 to 1931, and dates of marriages from 1918 to 1958, with the vast majority of marriages clustered in the mid- to late 1930s (see Appendix).[16]

This book will use spoken testimony in conjunction with contemporary historical evidence to explore hitherto neglected aspects of birth control practices. These narratives provide rich and extensive material on areas of contraceptive knowledge and behaviour rarely glimpsed in the available historical record. In-depth oral history interviews have provided unprecedented evidence on the methods of birth control couples used during the course of their married lives, where information about birth control was obtained, and what criteria framed method choices. In addition, testimony describing intimate details about sexual practices, respondents' own understandings of their sexuality, the process of decision-making, and gender differences in attitudes towards or roles undertaken in negotiating contraceptive practice reveal the intricate relationship between cultural codes, norms and values, and lived experience.

The evidence from both oral testimony and existing accounts challenges earlier historians' understandings radically. Interviewees' rationales for birth control use contrast starkly with a depiction of 'rational' contraceptive behaviour in which couples make deliberate and calculated choices about the number of children they desire, based on a clear assessment of the costs and benefits of childbearing. Testimony reveals actors, making contraceptive choices at the very end of the process of fertility transition, who do not look like the products of a revolutionary period of social change. Far from distancing their approach to family-building from that of their parents and their grandparents, they stressed the continuities. For them, as for previous generations, family size was deemed unpredictable, uncontrollable, and contingent. Far from adopting a 'new' mentality towards conception, and seeking out and experimenting with new reproductive technologies, they saw little shift in consciousness between themselves and their parents.

Those who were using birth control, at the very end of what has been characterized as a sustained period of revolutionary change, did not fulfil the criteria usually deemed necessary for successful family limitation. Instead of people who sought out the most effective types of contraception, we find individuals who claimed not

---

[15] One Blackburn couple had only married in the preceding year; their material relates to their previous marriages to other people.

[16] The social and economic positions of respondents varied. Those from south Wales were predominantly 'working-class' as were the majority of those from Oxford. A concerted effort was made to locate individuals from a broader social spectrum in the Hertfordshire and Blackburn samples. Class is not a particular focus of this book. Although some significant class differences emerged from the research, a systematic analysis of these can be found in Szreter and Fisher, 'Sexuality, Love and Marriage in England, 1918–1960'. Here the striking similarities in aspects of birth-control practices revealed by both oral history respondents and contemporary archival documents from a variety of class backgrounds will form the basis of the analysis.

to know about any form of birth control. Rather than planning their future, discussing how many children they wanted, and acting accordingly, they denied having been in a position to plan their families and claimed not to have cared exactly how many children they had or when they had them. Most couples made uncertain choices and mild resolutions based on a perception of limited options and vague desires. Such deliberations also challenge the model of extensive conjugal communication often depicted as a necessary prerequisite for successful birth control use. Couples did not discuss family planning, and responsibilities emerged only gradually and implicitly. Women do not appear to have regarded birth control as a great personal benefit which reduced the fear of pregnancy and divorced sex from reproduction; many wives shied away from the issue, leaving responsibility for birth control in the hands of their husbands. In contrast to the widespread assumption that women were at the forefront of birth control practices, respondents asserted that they valued male responsibility for and authority over contraception. Instead of an increasing reliance on modern methods of birth control and dissatisfaction with older 'inefficient' methods, we find withdrawal, abstinence, and abortion remaining popular. Despite the development of new reproductive technologies, notably the female cap and the latex condom, contraceptive practice in the early twentieth century did not reflect a revolution in contraceptive methods. Rather, the absence of information about birth control was highlighted and the appeal of traditional methods, above all withdrawal, was revealed. Behind all of this were gendered attitudes towards sex, in which male prerogatives in sexual knowledge, decision-making, and practice were paramount. Women were not in the vanguard of changing contraceptive practices; instead they sought to preserve themselves in a state of naivety and passivity.

It is in this context that this book seeks to explain how small families were negotiated and maintained. There are four main areas of enquiry: the extent and nature of contraceptive knowledge; the processes of contraceptive negotiation and decision-making; the methods of birth control adopted and the criteria behind method preferences; and gendered patterns of practice within the context of conjugal roles and models of masculinity and femininity.

Birth control was increasingly visible from the end of the nineteenth century onwards. Books and pamphlets were produced and sold. Birth control organizations and clinic campaigners turned the subject into a topic of major public and national debate which was frequently discussed in local as well as national newspapers. Sex and marriage manuals, many of which provided detailed information about contraceptive methods, became best-sellers during the inter-war period. Contraceptive appliances were sold in chemists, barbers, rubber and hygienic stores, pub toilets, on market stalls, and by mail order companies. By the Second World War, venereal disease campaigns brought information about prophylactics into posters, films, and public lectures.

Many historians have seen the increased awareness of the possibility of family limitation and the spread of knowledge about the means to achieve this as crucial to the reduction in family size.[17] At the same time, it is widely acknowledged that many remained ignorant of contraceptive technologies, and historians have emphasized the social silence on issues of sex and birth control in many communities throughout the nineteenth and early twentieth centuries.[18] The extent of knowledge of various forms of birth control during the twentieth century thus remains unclear, and there is an unresolved tension between evidence revealing the rapidly increasing prevalence of sexual material and widespread contemporary assertions of the inadequacy of sexual education and the scarcity of reliable or comprehensible material on birth control methods. It is only through investigation of the ways in which birth control material was received and the role such information played in the formation of sexual identities that this tension can be understood and resolved. The first chapter explores the nature and availability of information about ways of limiting family size, where it circulated and the contexts in which individuals came into contact with it. Assertions of ignorance are shown to have operated as a shorthand for the muddle and confusion that surrounded the acquisition of such information and the difficulties experienced in making sense of the puzzle. Secondly, reference to ignorance served as a rhetorical strategy intimately tied to highly gendered modes of self-representation. For women, being ignorant was central to their identity and was a state of consciousness which many actively sought to preserve.

The deliberations and negotiations behind the decisions to use contraception are extremely difficult for historians and demographers to reconstruct. Most of the available material provides information about the outcome of behaviour (fertility statistics or the birth dates of children) from which motivation has to be surmised. Such inferences have employed simplistic formulations of the family-building process and the nature of the 'decisions' that accompanied birth control

---

[17] Much of the demographic literature on declining fertility and fertility transitions is polarized between economic and cultural models of change, the latter focusing on the spread of values, ideas, and information about the limitation of the family; see Kertzer, 'Political-Economic and Cultural Explanations of Demographic Behaviour'; Some demographers have explicitly focused on what has become known as 'diffusion': the spread of ideas about the practice of fertility regulation across communities. See e.g. W. H. Beveridge, 'The Fall of Fertility among the European races', *Economica*, 5 (1925), 10–27, discussed in Szreter, *Fertility, Class and Gender*, 13; Himes, *Medical History of Contraception*, ch. 10; Banks, *Prosperity and Parenthood*; Himes, 'Charles Knowlton's Revolutionary Influence on the English Birth-Rate'; Fryer, *The Birth Controllers*; Knodel and van de Walle, 'Lessons from the Past'; E. Rogers, *Communication Strategies*; Lesthaeghe and Surkyn, 'Cultural Dynamics and Economic Theories of Fertility Change'; Lesthaeghe, 'On the Social Control of Human Reproduction'; Montgomery and Casterline, 'Social Learning, Social Influence, and New Models of Fertility'; Woods, *The Demography of Victorian England and Wales*, 149; Cook, *The Long Sexual Revolution*; and Garrett and Reid, 'Thinking of England and Taking Care'. See also Kohler, *Fertility and Social Interaction*. However, 'economic' models do not discount the relevance of the spread of information. Many who explicitly reject diffusion in fact draw upon its arguments, while 'economic' models frequently incorporate 'cultural' costs into their utilitarian arguments, arguing that the spread of information about birth control into communities might provide couples with rational reasons for adopting it. See Greenhalgh, 'Anthropology Theorizes Reproduction'.

[18] See e.g. Cook, *The Long Sexual Revolution*, ch. 7; Sutton, 'We Didn't Know Aught'.

use. A fundamental distinction is drawn between those who used birth control (with little recognition that such use might have been irregular, ineffective, or unsustained) and those who did not (who are sometimes assumed to have found the very notion of family limitation inconceivable). In such literature a sharp divide is drawn between 'pre-transition' communities before 1870 and subsequent generations who used birth control.[19] The fertility decline is presented as a 'rapid break from natural fertility to family limitation'.[20] Robert Woods argues that 'The very question, "how many children should we have?" was new to most Victorians.'[21] Whether the use of contraception is characterized as an 'innovation' (new family size ideals or new methods of contraception) or an 'adjustment' (a response to changing economic imperatives), almost all studies of changing contraceptive practice rest on the claim that those who used birth control had a particular, mindset distinct from those living in times of high fertility.[22] Such literature places considerable emphasis on the necessity of communication between husband and wife in achieving smaller families. Explicit, detailed, and rational discussion between partners is seen as key to the successful use of birth control. Thus, for many, the increased use of birth control is correlated with the rise of more egalitarian unions in which couples openly articulated and shared decision-making about a range of domestic and family issues.[23]

Chapter 2 challenges the dominant idea that decision-making about family size was necessarily both revolutionary and calculated, and that the widespread use of contraception indicates a dramatic change in consciousness which served to 'break the unquestioned assumptions that automatically lead to patterns of natural fertility'.[24] Indeed, the use of the vocabulary of conscious, explicit, and rational calculation in much demographic literature masks the complexities of the decision-making processes in ordinary families.[25] Patterns of birth control changed during the course of a couple's childbearing years. Couples switched methods, and used birth control with shifting degrees of regularity according to varying levels of determination.[26] First, couples did not consciously plan their families. They did not generally decide, either upon marriage or later, exactly how many children they wished to have or when to have them. Birth control was used, but not always conscientiously, in such a way that the frequency of births was

---

[19] Ariès, 'On the Origins of Contraception in France' and id., 'An Interpretation'; van de Walle, 'Fertility Transition, Conscious Choice, and Numeracy', 496, 495.
[20] Reay, *Rural England's Labouring Lives*, 102, challenges this view.
[21] Woods, *The Demography of Victorian England and Wales*, 169.
[22] Carlsson, 'The Decline of Fertility'.   [23] Gittins, *Fair Sex*, 156.
[24] Woods, *The Demography of Victorian England and Wales*, 168.
[25] Some literature is beginning to recognize the limitations of language predominantly used. Antony Carter sees the 'concepts of agency . . . employed in theories of fertility change' as 'unworkable', and rejects the standard alternative which sees individuals as unconscious and passive duplicators of cultural values: see 'Agency and Fertility', 56.
[26] See Mundigo, Phillips, and Chamratrithirong, 'Determinants of Contraceptive Use Dynamics', 10.

systematically reduced, but the timing of pregnancy remained unpredictable. Secondly, couples rejected the idea that they should take a calculating approach to the building of a family, and positively embraced an alternative strategy. They frequently chose a fluid and contingent approach which preserved a veneration of the providential intervention of nature, God, or biology, and prevented family planning from appearing to be a cold or calculated exercise in hubristic control. Thirdly, couples rarely communicated openly or directly about family-planning matters. Many couples did not talk openly about sexual matters, and issues of childbearing and family limitation skirted very close to these sensitive areas. Many women chose to keep discussion unspecific, leaving the nitty-gritty details of exactly when birth control was used and what method was chosen to their husbands. Only in cases where the urgency of restricting births increased was explicit planning or debate necessary.

Improvements in technology and its availability are assumed to have immeasurably improved individuals' ability to control their fertility.[27] It is generally agreed that, by the inter-war period, appliance methods of contraception were gradually replacing 'inefficient', 'unreliable', and 'unpleasant' traditional forms. Whereas withdrawal and abstinence were predominantly used by those limiting the size of their families in the late nineteenth century, a shift towards condoms and caps is in evidence from the beginning of the twentieth. Wally Seccombe has concluded that 'the decisive shift . . . from "natural" to "appliance" methods occurred in the 1920s', a time when, he also notes, 'people were deluging Marie Stopes with letters pleading for contraceptive information'.[28] Such a shift is seen as having dramatically reduced the incidence of accidental pregnancy caused by both an 'understandable' reluctance regularly to employ abstinence or withdrawal as well as the inherent fallibility of these strategies.

The shift towards appliance methods of birth control in the twentieth century, and especially the eventual incorporation of the Pill into practice, is frequently presented as one of the developments of twentieth-century history that can retain a Whiggish narrative of progress. Hera Cook has written that 'the introduction of reliable contraception' was a 'substantial improvement, amounting to a transformation, in the lives of English women over the past two centuries'. It 'increased the control of fear, and allowed a greater experience of pleasure and increased emotional aspirations'.[29] While for considerable numbers of women the Pill was perceived and experienced as liberating, emancipatory, and exciting, no particular experience of sex should necessarily be associated with any specific contraceptive method.[30] The Pill is not inherently liberating and withdrawal is not intrinsically

---

[27] van de Kaa, 'Anchored Narratives'; Gittins, *Fair Sex*, 162–3; Szreter, *Fertility, Class and Gender*, 412, 435–6; Langford, *Birth Control Practice and Marital Fertility*, 88–9.

[28] W. Seccombe, 'Starting to Stop', 167.   [29] Cook, *The Long Sexual Revolution*, 8.

[30] Hera Cook testified to her own personal appreciation of the sexual freedom provided by the Pill, an experience which avowedly and directly frames her interpretation of the sexual and reproductive lives of women during the nineteenth and twentieth centuries; Cook, *The Long Sexual Revolution*, 1.

frustrating; perception of methods is historically contingent, and we cannot assume that attitudes towards methods remain constant or that there are any 'natural' or obvious responses to birth control techniques.[31] Diverging from the advice given in family planning, sex and marriage guidance manuals of the period, and in opposition to the assumptions of demographers and historians, the majority of those questioned had positive reasons for preferring to use 'traditional' methods of birth control, notably withdrawal. The views and experiences of many couples marrying between the 1920s and the 1940s bear little relation to the opinions of those authoring marriage manuals despite the fact that these individuals were restricting their families to between one and three children following forty years of progressive and sustained fertility decline. Where one would expect to have found a relatively 'advanced' and 'modern' repertoire of contraception we find a continued reliance on 'natural' methods such as abstinence, abortion, and withdrawal, and a positive dislike of their modern alternatives.

Chapter 3 reveals that, although appliance methods were increasingly used from the inter-war period, such use did not initially signal a transition away from the use of traditional methods. Traditional methods frequently continued to be used some of the time by couples who turned to modern methods on other occasions. Chapter 4 examines the reasons behind individuals' choice of method. Female caps were generally disliked and frequently rejected in favour of traditional methods. It has been suggested that, when withdrawal was chosen, it was only for negative reasons: lack of knowledge of alternatives (although withdrawal was indeed the best-known method); moral or religious objections to the use of birth control (although abstinence, rhythm, and withdrawal were the methods primarily used by those who opposed contraception on principle); or the effort, cost, and embarrassment involved in obtaining modern methods (though withdrawal was perceived as conveniently cheap, easy, and private). Far from it—withdrawal also had a number of key positive attributes, while its supposed defects were seen to be shared by its alternatives.

The importance of looking at gendered roles in contraceptive strategies has been increasingly recognized.[32] Wally Seccombe castigates the 'unacceptable naivety' of the 'standard models of fertility regulation' which are 'formulated at the level of the reproductive couple taken as a unified subject' and thus assume 'the perpetual existence of harmonious needs and aligned interests between husbands and wives with regard to childbearing, sex and contraception'.[33] Studies of contraceptive behaviour have concentrated attention on female roles, and have paid particular attention to women's employment patterns, women's education, and women's knowledge networks, on the assumption that women were more

---

[31] See Risman and Schwartz (eds.), *Gender in Intimate Relationships*; Gamson, 'Rubber Wars', 263.
[32] Folbre, 'Of Patriarchy Born'; Watkins, 'If All We Knew About Women'; Mackinnon, 'Were Women Present at the Demographic Transition?'; Riley, 'Research on Gender in Demography'.
[33] W. Seccombe, *Weathering the Storm*, 157.

concerned than men to reduce family size, and that this was their responsibility.[34] Very little work has been conducted on men's attitudes.[35] The assumption that changes in birth control practices primarily reveal changes in women's position, influence, or attitudes is not new: much of the primary source material available to historians also reflects this focus.[36] Birth control campaigners between the wars certainly believed that birth control was largely of interest to women and, moreover, were anxious to promote 'female' methods of birth control, such as the cervical cap. Most other sources of direct testimony, such as sociological surveys of sexual behaviour and birth control practices, have also tended to question only women.[37]

The concentration on women by those studying fertility behaviour is characteristic of more recent surveys too: 'men are rarely interviewed in fertility surveys of any kind'.[38] That 'attitudes of men regarding family planning are negative' is 'a misperception that has persisted in the face of contrary research conducted on

[34] See e.g. Brookes, 'Women and Reproduction 1860–1939'; Davey, 'Birth Control in Britain'; Faulkner, ' "Powerless to prevent him" '; Gittins, *Fair Sex*; Ittman, *Work, Gender and Family in Victorian England*; Mason, *The Making of Victorian Sexuality*; McLaren, *A History of Contraception*; E. Roberts, *A Woman's Place*; ead., *Women and Families*; E. Ross, *Love and Toil*; W. Seccombe, *Weathering the Storm*; id., 'Starting to Stop'; Crafts, 'Duration of Marriage, Fertility and Women's Employment Opportunities'. Joseph and Olive Banks' influential account is the exception. They explicitly reject the idea that women played a role in family planning processes and argue that the desire for small families reflects increasing economic and social pressures on middle-class men to invest sufficiently in their children, especially in the education of their sons. They have rightly been criticized for an account which dismisses women's roles altogether. However, we should not invert the error by focusing solely on women: Banks, *Prosperity and Parenthood*; Bank and Banks, *Feminism and Family Planning in Victorian England*; Banks, *Victorian Values*; McLaren, review of J. A. Banks, *Victorian Values*.

[35] This complaint is made by Susan Cotts Watkins, who points out that any reader of fertility literature might 'wonder about the absence of data on men': 'If All We Knew About Women', 560. It would also be interesting to examine the roles of other individuals in fertility decisions, such as children or wider kin relations.

[36] Mass-Observation toyed with the idea of testing assumptions about gendered roles with regard to birth control. Tom Harrisson suggested that the 'family questionnaire' conducted in 1944 should ask: 'Who should have the final say about family planning? Husband or wife?' These crucial questions, however, were not added to the interview schedule. Mass-Observation, TC Family Planning 1944–49, TC3/1/J.

[37] Lewis-Faning, *Report on an Enquiry into Family Limitation*; Enid Charles rejected all forms filled out by husbands: *The Practice of Birth Control*, 21. See also McKee and O'Brien, 'Interviewing Men', 147; Langford, 'Birth Control Practice', table 3.1 and pp. 60–1. The Population Investigation Committee's survey of 1959–60 was the only one which interviewed men when examining methods of birth control within marriage: Pierce and Rowntree, 'Birth Control in Britain', Parts I and II. Some surveys on sexual behaviour in general (rather than specifically on birth control), did involve male respondents: Slater and Woodside, *Patterns of Marriage*; M. Schofield, *The Sexual Behaviour of Young People*; Gorer, *Exploring English Character*; Chesser, *The Sexual, Marital and Family Relationships of the English Woman*. These include much less detailed treatments of marital contraception, however.

[38] Oppenheim-Mason and Taj, 'Differences between Women's and Men's Reproductive Goals in Developing Countries', 620. One project—a notable exception—interviewed men in Pittsburgh in 1971 on the grounds that 'all family planning services, educational programs, research and advertising seems to be directed at women': Spillane and Ryser, *Male Fertility Survey*, p. vii. This survey attempted to 'obtain relevant fertility data from a sample of urban married men' and found that contraceptive use and choices were dominated by men's concerns for the health of their wives (p. 74).

men since 1967'.[39] Susan Cotts Watkins has criticized both her own research and that of her colleagues: 'My friends and I believed that women had more reason than men to be concerned with the consequences of childbearing, and we took it for granted that their husbands simply would not co-operate.'[40] Gigi Santow has asked whether we 'are correct . . . in believing that men are always less concerned than women with the limitation of their families'.[41] Recent work (influenced in part by the argument that in many developing countries a failure to consider male perspectives on contraception impeded the successful implementation of family-planning programmes) has begun to advocate the incorporation of investigations into men's attitudes as part of the understanding of gendered roles in birth control strategies.[42]

Material produced by social and cultural historians on masculinity is also remarkably silent on men's reproductive roles.[43] Even studies of sexuality or fatherhood frequently leave birth control out of the analysis.[44] A recent oral history of masculinity, family life, childcare and sexual behaviour by Steve Humphries and Pamela Gordon, for example, contains virtually no information from male respondents on contraception or family-planning decisions.[45] Men

[39] Swanson, 'Men and Family Planning', 27. Myra Woolf revealed in her 1971 study *Family Intentions* that they had decided to interview married women only about family size and intervals between births 'on the assumption that they would be the individuals likely to have the most valid knowledge of past, present and future events in this subject area'. She acknowledges, however, that 'this initial assumption may be questionable since it could be that husbands are the final arbiters of the sizes of their families'. Nor did the follow-up survey, five years later, introduce interviews with men into the sample, even though the initial survey had indeed suggested that a significant number of women, particularly in the oldest cohorts (couples married before 1940), felt that the avoidance of pregnancy ought to be the husband's responsibility: Woolf, *Family Intentions*, 4, 75–7; Woolf and Pegden, *Families Five Years On*, 7.   [40] Watkins, 'If All We Knew', 557.

[41] Santow, 'Coitus Interruptus in the Twentieth Century', 769. See also Karen Seccombe's conclusion that 'For too long, data on men have been ignored because of the presumption that women are responsible for fertility decisions': 'Assessing the Costs and Benefits of Children', 201. Sally MacIntyre charges herself as having been 'as remiss as most other sociologists in assuming that marriage and childbearing are primarily of importance to women rather than to men, and hence neglecting men in the research design': ' "Who Wants Babies?" ', 5.

[42] As early as 1973 Everett Rogers concluded that it was a mistake for family planning programmes to concentrate on providing advice to women: 'It is usually assumed (implicitly) by program officials that women are the decision makers about such female methods . . . Yet several recent researchers [indicate] that "*Husbands are much more important than wives in decisions to adopt family planning method* . . . Husbands are involved jointly or unilaterally in almost all family planning decisions; very few such decisions are made by the wife alone" ': Rogers, *Communications Strategies*, 309–10. On male roles, see also the articles in Harcourt (ed.), *Power, Reproduction and Gender*; Angin and Shorter, 'Negotiating Reproduction and Gender During the Fertility Decline in Turkey'; Dudgeon and Inhorn, 'Men's Influences on Women's Reproductive Health'; Hollos and Larsen, 'Which African Men Promote Smaller Families and Why?'; Rosen and Benson, 'The Second-Class Partner'; Dodoo, Luo, and Panayotova, 'Do Male Reproductive Preferences Really Point to a Need to Refocus Fertility Policy?'; Mundigo, 'Re-conceptualizing the Role of Men in the Post-Cairo Era'.

[43] Roper and Tosh (eds.), *Manful Assertions*; Pendergast, *Creating the Modern Man*; Lunbeck, 'American Psychiatrists and the Modern Man'; Crotty, *Making the Australian Male*.

[44] Gillis, 'Bringing Up Father'; Brod (ed.), *The Making of Masculinities*; West, *Fathers, Sons and Lovers*; LaRossa, *The Modernization of Fatherhood*; La Rossa and Reitzes, 'Gendered Perceptions of Father Involvement in Early Twentieth Century America'. L. Hall, *Hidden Anxieties*, is the exception.

[45] Humphries and Gordon, *A Man's World*.

had much greater access to birth control information, and male methods of contraception (condoms and withdrawal) were far more frequently used than female methods (caps, pessaries, and abortion). Moreover, male methods were largely preferred precisely because they put the onus on the husband. The sexual dynamics of marital relationships were the crucial factor in the construction of gender roles in birth control behaviour. Negotiating birth control practice involved not only issues of having children and family size but also of sex and sexuality. Men had much greater access to sexual information (hence superior contraceptive knowledge), were much more at ease discussing sex (this was itself evidenced in interviews), and were expected to initiate all sexual encounters. Women preferred using birth control methods which did not place them in the position of having to negotiate, anticipate, or prepare for sexual activity. This testimony radically challenges earlier historians' understanding of the impact of gendered roles on birth control use, although in fact closer analysis shows that it is supported by much of the existing historical evidence.

The final chapter will examine why men saw it as their role to implement and manage a contraceptive strategy and why women were keen to preserve this state of affairs. It will explore the relationship between contraceptive practices and the fluctuating balance of power in marriage, the capacity of each partner to achieve his or her reproductive objectives, and the cultures of masculinity which framed men's dominant contraceptive role. A simple dichotomy between old-fashioned 'inconsiderate' men unprepared to use birth control and 'companionate' husbands who had been persuaded of its expediency and its benefit to their wives is simplistic and unconvincing. Debates about marriage are shown to have provided men with a range of models of masculinity around the polarized opposites of companionate and patriarchal. In all these models, however, contraception was seen as a male prerogative and duty. Those men who saw themselves as authoritarian thought it was their role to use birth control just as much as those who saw birth control use as a benefit to the wife. Fundamentally, there was not a radical difference in the extent to which, in most of the marriages observed, male authority was broadly accepted. Male use of contraception was deemed considerate to the wife, but nevertheless placed men in a position of power. That this power was not challenged reveals simultaneously the importance to women of remaining divorced from the explicit discussion of sexual matters and their confidence that most men would concur with the need to keep one's family size relatively small.

AN ORAL HISTORY OF BIRTH CONTROL: CONTEXT AND APPROACHES

Although this book uses documentary material alongside oral history, the majority of the evidence is provided by spoken testimony. It is easy to see the benefits of using this method to investigate a subject such as birth control behaviour, where little material on the details and meanings of everyday practices, choices, preferences, and beliefs exists in archival sources. Moreover, where individuals do appear in written sources it is frequently in a snapshot of their lives framed by others' concerns at a particular point in time, such as birth control clinic material which used horror stories of traditional methods to reinforce campaigns for new clinics and new appliance methods. Oral history, by contrast, allows the historian to examine birth control practices from within the context of a whole life and on the interviewee's own terms. Robust defences of the methodology over the last thirty years have largely replaced academic scepticism about the historical validity of oral testimony.[46] However, the fact that the interviews focused on sexual issues raised particular methodological questions. First, it might be questioned how far interviews which proceeded successfully, and from which the evidence is therefore drawn, reflect only the attitudes of the minority prepared to talk about sexual issues, rather than the experiences of the population more generally.[47] Secondly, one might doubt the likely veracity of responses on such a sensitive topic, and suspect that elements of behaviour have been concealed or deliberately misrepresented.[48] Thirdly, it is justifiably assumed that the changing and intricate details of one's sexual history are difficult to remember and reconstruct accurately, while changes in sexual cultures and ideologies during the twentieth century are likely to introduce considerable retrospective overlay into the construction of life stories.[49]

Two responses to such problems have been adopted. On the one hand, sensitive and painstaking procedures were implemented to ensure that as wide a range of participants as possible was chosen, that interviews were conducted with care and rigour, and that testimony was verified and cross-checked for internal consistency. On the other hand, one can legitimately claim that the perceived limitations of oral history—small sample size, lack of representativeness, the erosion of memory, and the impact of external influences on the construction of material—should not be viewed so negatively. The creation and use of oral history testimony is subjective, yet this is a strength of the methodology. Particularly when investigating sexual subjects, where behaviour is intimately bound to individuals' identities, the intrusion of the subjective into testimony can be highly revealing. Interviews were not conducted with the sole purpose of minimizing the extent to which the material was 'compromised' by issues arising from its sexual subject matter. Nor did subsequent analysis concentrate exclusively on ascertaining the truthfulness of testimony or on weeding out instances of poor recall, exaggeration, concealment, or post-hoc revision. The complexity of oral interviews, and in particular the forms,

---

[46] A particularly succinct defence is found in Thompson, 'Oral History and the Historian'. See also Thompson, *The Voice of the Past*; Portelli, 'The Peculiarities of Oral History'; Popular Memory Group, 'Popular Memory'; Portelli, *The Battle of Valle Giulia*. On the institutional prejudices and disadvantages faced by oral historians see Grele, 'Movement Without Aim'.

[47] Moser, *Survey Methods in Social Investigation*, 127–44; Porter and Hall, *The Facts of Life*, 248; Humphries, *A Secret World of Sex*, 10–11; R. Lee, *Doing Research on Sensitive Topics*, 60.

[48] Dare and Cleland, 'Reliability and Validity of Survey Data on Sexual Behaviour', 95.

[49] Cuttler, 'Accuracy in Oral History Interviewing'.

structures, and narratives that frame the presentation of life stories, should not be seen as a barrier that the historian tries to break down to view the underlying truth. Rather, they are key indicators of the meaning of experience. These subjectivities form the analytical focus of this book.

[It's] very difficult to talk about . . . there's going to be a lot of sex in your book, isn't there? That's all you've asked me today—sex, sex, sex.[50]

It may perhaps be feared that research on sensitive topics might mean that only those comfortable discussing delicate issues—a self-selecting minority with special characteristics—would agree to be interviewed. Methods were adopted that minimized such a possibility.[51] Advertising in local or national newspapers was avoided. The majority of interviewees were selected through contacts with local authority-run day centres and community groups (social clubs, bingo halls, working men's clubs, and coffee mornings). They provided an ideal forum for potential interviewees to examine the researchers, ask questions, and decide at their leisure whether or not to be interviewed.[52] The research was then presented in a sensitive way; in day centres, group discussion and reminiscence workshops were used to introduce potential respondents to the interviewer and the project's themes. Subsequently, each individual was invited to take the discussion further in the form of a private interview in his or her own home. This procedure proved an ideal way of ensuring a potential interviewee had developed a relationship of trust with the interviewer prior to letting him or her into the home, provided a forum in which to discuss the issues, and illustrated to each individual how much they had to contribute. The success of such a strategy was illustrated by one woman who happily agreed to an interview despite having refused, on a previous occasion, to co-operate in a survey questionnaire which arrived through the post and asked: 'how many men she had been with', 'whether she'd ever had an affair', 'what methods of birth control she used', and 'how often she and her husband had sex'.[53]

---

[50] Felicity, msf/kf/bl/#37. No attempt has been made to tidy up the spoken English when transcribing it into text. Every effort has been made to reproduce faithfully the subtlety of language and dialect expressed by respondents, without obfuscating the content of the material.

[51] R. Lee, *Doing Research on Sensitive Topics*, 71.

[52] To a lesser extent, contact was made either through local authorities' home help systems or by visiting interviewees in their residential care homes.

[53] Tact also has to be exercised when explaining the research to potential interviewees in social settings; I did not wish to embarrass potential respondents by discussing the research too explicitly in front of their peers. In other instances, despite explaining the research in full, it proved relatively diffi-cult to ensure that respondents fully understood the nature of the research topic and the outcomes of the analysis before arranging an interview. Some ethical guidelines suggest that information sheets are provided to interviewees prior to an interview to ensure that interviewees are fully appraised of the nature of the questions, and some require a consent form to be signed at this stage. Yet asking an interviewee to sign a document saying they agree to be interviewed places power in the hands of the interviewer. However the pre-interview consent form or information sheet is worded, however clearly it states that signing it does not commit the subject to co-operate and does not bind them to answering all questions, the very act of signing a form places pressure on a respondent to continue to participate. It is essential that interviewees feel in control and able to back out at any time or to avoid answering

However, as others conducting sex surveys have also discovered, it is a mistake to assume that many would not want to be involved because of the sexual themes of the research.[54] When people expressed reluctance to be interviewed, it was usually before the nature of the research was revealed. In fact, many respondents were keen to tell representatives of a younger generation about the sexual cultures of their youth. The chance to contrast their past lives with modern sexual cultures was appealing and meaningful. The very fact that many had not talked about sex before itself provided a rationale for participation. A number of interviewees explicitly saw contemporary ignorance about past sexual cultures as detrimental to members of younger generations. They decided to break their cultural silence in order that a modern youth might understand the benefits of their own sexual culture, and hoped that through talking about their sex lives the privacy that they valued might be reclaimed. Through a combination of conscious strategy and potential interviewees' openness about sexual issues, there was little danger of only a self-selected minority agreeing to take part; indeed, over 90 per cent of those whom I approached, and talked to in reasonable detail about the research, agreed to be interviewed.

In order to ensure that a wide range of voices is heard, it is also important not to select out weak oral history material once it is garnered from a respondent. It is especially tempting for the oral historian to discard material from untalkative, hesitant, or inarticulate people in favour of those who are enthusiastic, energetic, sharp, have time to spare, and are open and discursive about contraceptive practices. However, I did not reject or cut short interviews conducted with less talkative people, those who were more frail, or those who were rather inarticulate. Interviews with people who were hesitant in revealing details of their sexual behaviour were not removed from the study, as they were frequently representative of wider silences within their culture.

In order to obtain high-quality oral history material on sexual issues, I adopted an unstructured interview technique which was flexible enough to accommodate respondents who held differing ideas about the appropriateness of talking about sexual issues with a relative stranger. It is widely acknowledged that 'when the

certain questions. This is made much easier if respondents do not feel they have formally agreed to anything before the interview begins. So signing a pre-interview consent form has the potential to be disempowering rather than protective. We have to recognize that it is very difficult for respondents to grasp before an interview exactly what they might be asked. Consent to be interviewed has therefore to be interpreted as consent on the interviewees' own, as yet undefined, terms, and during the interview careful attention must be paid to the possibility of discomfort or dissatisfaction on the part of the interviewee. For ethical codes of practice in presenting research to respondents, see Morton-Williams, *Interviewer Approaches*, 33. On explaining the sexually explicit content of interviews to potential respondents see Holland and Ramazanoglu, 'Power and Interpretation in Researching Young Women's Sexuality', 138 and 142.

[54] Little difference in response rate has been found between sex surveys and those on apparently more 'neutral' topics. See e.g. England, 'Little Kinsey', 589; Dare and Cleland, 'Reliability and Validity', 94.

survey subject is complex or emotional, it may be that the greater flexibility of an informal approach succeeds better than set questions in getting to the heart of the respondent's opinion'.[55] 'Many topics—especially of a sensitive kind—remain ill-suited to study by means of the survey. In these circumstances, a preference has commonly been voiced for the use of unstructured or "depth" interviewing.[56] An unstructured, open-ended interview strategy was thus adopted which gave wide licence to respondents to present their memoirs and stories at length, independently of the interviewer's analytical agenda.[57] The way in which sensitive questions were phrased also varied significantly: some people spoke about sexual issues without prompting; others were initially hesitant, and in such cases each instance of discussion of sex and birth control was kept short. The subject was changed to allow them some respite, and returned to later in the interview.[58] The same question with a slightly different wording often produced more detailed answers, and the use of localized phrases and euphemistic descriptions also triggered high-quality responses.[59] This approach also allowed great flexibility. Interviews could be adapted and expanded as major research themes emerged.

Strategies were adopted to create an environment which minimized the possibility of deliberate misrepresentation. First, all respondents were guaranteed anonymity (although many did not request this), to minimize the desire to conceal embarrassing, regretted, or shameful experiences. Secondly, interviews were frequently long and detailed. Despite the assumption that many individuals would lie about the sexual aspects of their lives, significant or deliberate distortions are difficult to maintain for many hours, particularly on more than one separate occasion, unless they have already been incorporated into an interviewee's personal life story and sense of self. Many interviews involved several visits (especially those in Hertfordshire and Blackburn due to the scale of the research agenda), and interviews varied in length, each session generally lasting between two and four hours.[60] Such interviews allow the historian plenty of scope to assess testimony for internal consistency;

---

[55] Moser, *Survey Methods in Social Investigation*, 204–5.

[56] R. Lee, *Doing Research on Sensitive Topics*, 103. See also Lees, *Sugar and Spice*, 11. Janet Finch noted the 'stilted' and 'grudging' answers a researcher obtained using a questionnaire, as opposed to the 'relaxed', 'private' confessions she was provided with by the same respondent when using an unstructured, in-depth approach: Finch, ' "It's great to have someone to talk to" ', 73. The opposing view, that 'censored behaviour' is more willingly revealed in 'self-administered questionnaires than in face-to-face interviews', is maintained by Dare and Cleland in 'Reliability and Validity', 101.

[57] On the disadvantages of structured interviews about contraception, see Busfield and Paddon, *Thinking about Children*, 84–5.

[58] See Beed and Stimson (eds.), *Survey Interviewing*, especially the chapter by C. F. Cannell, 'Overview Response Bias and Interviewer Variability in Surveys' (pp. 1–23), for a summary of possible interview techniques and strategies of asking 'embarrassing questions in non-embarrassing ways'. See also Schuman and Presser, *Questions and Answers in Attitude Surveys*.

[59] Elliot Mishler argues that 'variability in how interviewers ask questions is the key to good interviewing': Mishler, *Research Interviewing*, 22.

[60] Barbara Laslett and Rhona Rapoport stress the 'inter-interview dynamic', seeing the period of time between the first and second interview as crucial. During this gap feelings about the research and

suppressions or inventions often produce contradictions and anachronisms.[61] Far from giving the reader grounds for suspecting significant deliberate omissions or distortions of fact, the testimony obtained was remarkable for its apparent frankness. Many spoke openly about the process of revelation. Gill's comment that 'I may say that's the first time I've ever told anybody what I did . . . to make sure that we . . . don't have any more [children]' was common.[62] Many took their role as participants in academic history seriously, endeavoured to be honest, and apologized when unable to remember a specific detail. Hubert was typical in commenting, 'Well I hope it does some good, said I tried to be as honest as possible.'[63]

Some, however, were hesitant in revealing sexual practices and some were evasive in their responses, or omitted to mention certain practices until very late in an interview.[64] Such diffidence might be seen to cast doubt on the ability of oral history to obtain entirely truthful depictions of contraceptive behaviour. However, such issues should not necessarily be seen as barriers to discovering truths of experience; rather, the variety of ways in which respondents discussed sex—the hesitations and pauses, giggles and leers, coyness and suggestion, fumblings and eloquence—was very revealing of underlying opinions, attitudes, and practices. What interviewees did not say is just as revealing as what they did; indeed, the silences surrounding sex are crucial to the themes of this book.[65] For example, that men often provided more detailed and articulate accounts of sexual practices, and that women found difficulties in articulating details of their sexual behaviour, should not be seen as problematic but rather revealing: the capacity of individuals to express ideas about sex was a crucial indicator of the extent to which they had assumed sexualized roles and identities within marriage.

Many women lacked fluency in discussing family-planning practices. Their vocabulary was much less sophisticated, and many faltered when trying to describe practices for which they lacked the words:

If they stop before it—the main thing happens . . . That's right, you just gotta trust that them not finish properly, then—Just get away before the seed starts.[66]

the interviewer are developed, as well as attitudes towards and opinions about the material, resulting frequently in a second interview which reveals a more complete depiction of a life: 'Collaborative Interviewing and Interactive Research', 973–4. On the other hand, Julia Brannen advocates the use of the 'one-off interview' in her research on marital difficulties, as she found that respondents valued the anonymity and one-off nature of single research encounters: 'The Study of Sensitive Topics', 559.

[61] Thompson, *The Voice of the Past*, 239.

[62] Gill, msf/kf/bl/#48. On the difference between rehearsed and non-rehearsed narratives see Askham, 'Telling Stories', 559.

[63] Indeed after the interview he wrote me a letter outlining the further memories and thoughts that had come to him after I had left. Hubert, msf/kf/ht/#32.

[64] On the importance of repeating themes and expecting different answers to materialize at different stages of an interview see Briggs, *Learning How To Ask*, 91–111.

[65] Kerry Daly is clear that whatever research techniques are used to invade 'the private spheres of families, there will be secrets and loyalties that remain inaccessible'. She insightfully realizes, however, that any avoidance of sensitive topics reveals 'rich data' about 'disclosure limits and the norms of social acceptability': Daly, 'The Fit Between Qualitative Research and Characteristics of Families', 5.

[66] Phyllis, bc3ox#17.

'Well, I don't know how I can tell you that, it's a bit awkward, I don't know if you know anything about sex, I suppose you do . . . Well, I suppose you just—when you feel something climax, you just part innit? It's the only thing I can explain.[67]

Men, by contrast, fluently described intimate aspects of birth control:

Course as used to have tablets then, you could put them in a girl's fanny in them days.

Oh yes, tell me more about them.

Oh, buy them in the box and, er, if you were getting a little bit—'how are you'—we used to reach for one and you would have to put it in her fanny and you wait for a few minutes and then you would put your willy in and then you could let it go.[68]

The silences of oral testimony should be seen as highly revealing rather than methodologically irritating.[69] While the men were generally more forthcoming, frank, and confident, the women were much more laconic, hesitant, and evasive, less expansive and more uncertain. This difference draws attention to gendered approaches to the issue of birth control. Women claimed that they did not discuss sex, had no access to birth control information and left such issues up to their husbands. Such claims were reinforced by the narrative structure of testimony. Embarrassment and a lack of verbal fluency in themselves lent force to the central points made by women in their material: that they did not discuss sex or contraception, did not have a wide circle of information networks about sex and birth control, that they did not even talk to their spouses about the issue, and that they left responsibility in the hands of their husbands.[70] Men's lack of embarrassment and eloquence also underscored their greater desire to be seen as informed about contraception and as having greater exposure to sexual information through crude homosocial sexual banter.

The effect the interviewer has on the willingness of a respondent to divulge personal details might also be questioned, particularly the age and sex of the investigator. However, the relationship between the interviewee and the interviewer should also be seen as productive rather than as distorting. I collected the vast majority of interviews for this work. I was at the time in my twenties, unmarried, and childless. Some, however, were done by a man, Simon Szreter, who was married, in his forties, and had three children, and a few by another man, James Mark, in his twenties, unmarried, and childless.[71] The standard view in sociological

---

[67] Beatrice, bc3sw#5.

[68] Charlie, bc2#25. Note also his involvement in a 'female' method, explained perhaps by the clear associations it had with 'sex' and the presentation of pessaries as a method *he* used/inserted.

[69] Anderson and Jack, 'Learning to Listen', 23.

[70] Such narratives are also illustrative of gender identities. In declaring that they did not discuss sex or take the initiative in implementing the use of birth control women defined what they saw as appropriate female behaviour and demarcated the boundaries of community respectability. On the use of language to frame gender identities see Graddol and Swann, *Gender Voices*, 65.

[71] Those wishing to know the identity of interviewers should examine the interview codes: *srss* in any code refers to interviews conducted by the married male Simon Szreter; *jm* to those conducted by

literature is that women talk more openly to other women and that men respond best to male interviewers, but that women make the best general investigators.[72] However, all researchers found their age and gender gave them certain advantages and disadvantages when interviewing both men and women. An interviewer who had had children was able to use the perception of common experience as a means of empathizing with respondents and encouraging the disclosure of information. As Sherna Gluck argues, 'likeness can generally promote trust and openness, whereas dissimilarity reinforces cultural and social distance'.[73] However, the absence of shared experiences could equally be exploited by interviewers: it served to explain and justify interest in the past and to excuse the persistent questioning about certain topics. For one man, such distance was certainly the motivation behind his agreement to be interviewed:

I find it interesting to talk to you for one reason, that—that I don't think you, you really understand how we lived.[74]

In particular, young interviewers could exploit their apparent inexperience to obtain further information. I found the assumption of naivety particularly fruitful in obtaining clarifications of euphemisms and more detailed descriptions of sexual practices:

A lot of people have spoken to me about 'being careful'.
Yes.

But I don't really know what that is . . .
Well, 'being careful' is, um—well, do you know when you're having sex? Well, before you come like, innit?—Well draw back. That's what being careful is, yes. It's being careful, yeah. But, um—you didn't know what that was? No, well you wouldn't, would you? (laughs) But there's a lot of ways you could avoid children.[75]

The effect of the interviewer on the production of material should not be over-stated. For instance, it is frequently assumed that male investigators would not be given reliable or frank accounts of abortion.[76] However, the following example, in which the same respondent was interviewed twice, once by the author and once by the younger male researcher, indicates the high-quality material obtained by both. Felicity was interviewed initially by the author, with whom she had a

the childless, unmarried male interviewer James Mark; *kf* to those conducted by the author Kate Fisher. Any interview code without one of these initial identifiers was also conducted by the author.

[72] See e.g. Cartwright and Moffett, 'A Comparison of Results Obtained by Men and Women Interviewers in a Fertility Survey'. They saw little difference in the material obtained by male or female interviewers and decided in subsequent work to 'use only women interviewers' when interviewing 'both mothers and fathers' (p. 322).

[73] Gluck, 'What's So Special About Women?', 227. See also Baber, 'Studying Women's Sexualities'; P. Green, 'Taking Sides'.   [74] John, bc3ox#33.

[75] Aileen, bc3sw#14.

[76] See e.g. Padfield and Procter, 'The Effect of Interviewer's Gender on the Interviewing Process'.

discussion of abortion which focused on the back-street practices resorted to by unmarried acquaintances:

So what could women do if they did get pregnant and didn't want to be pregnant?
Well, there were these women that did illegal abortions with knitting needles. But there weren't a lot that did. The ones that did got married usually.

And did you ever hear about anyone going to woman with a knitting needle?
. . . Well, there were somebody in our street which—she was always like a bit of tart, and they said that—and she died and they said she'd been having an illegal abortion.

And what do you mean by 'a bit of a tart'? What sort of girls were . . .?
Well all lipsticked up and . . . always out with men, different men. And she got pregnant and it killed her.

And? Did you know her?
Not personally, I knew who she was. Didn't know her to talk to.

She showed no reluctance to talk to a man about abortion. Indeed her response to his questions arguably produced more interesting testimony focused on first-hand experiences more than hearsay:

Did you ever hear of anybody bringing on a period?
Yes, Pennyroyal. Yes, I heard about it but I didn't do it.

Where did you hear about it?
Well, a friend that I had in the Wrens—by now she was married and she didn't want a baby at that time and she thought she was having one, and she wrote to me to see if I could get some at a local druggists. But I wrote her back and said no, if she wanted it she must get it herself.[77]

The gendered interaction of the interview itself frequently illustrated a respondent's sexual identity and was thus a useful analytical tool, rather than merely a methodological hindrance that had to be accounted for. For instance, some men debated the propriety of talking about sex to a young female interviewer:[78]

What sort of things can you talk about as men that you can't talk about if there were women there?
(laughs) That's not fair.

It is (laughs).
No, it's not (laughs).

(laughs)
That's not a fair question.

---

[77] Felicity, msf/kf/bl/#37. Both these stories were told towards the end of interview sessions when a range of other sexual matters had already been discussed; neither story was juxtaposed with an obviously related topic. It is difficult to discern what triggered the recollection of each particular story at that precise moment in the interview.

[78] Interviews conducted by men were not noticeably more frank, bawdy, or revealing. Nor were the interviews conducted by men with women significantly less informative.

Why not?

Just because it's not . . . It's not fair to tell you because you're a young lady. I'm old enough to be—be your grandfather.

So you'd tell a man, would you?

Oh yeah.

Oh well, I'll have to get one of me men-friends to come in and talk to you then.

Well, you wouldn't expect me to tell you would you?

Um, I don't see why not.[79]

The reluctance of the interviewee to talk with a young female researcher about sexual issues, rather than being a drawback, was in fact highly revealing of how Merlin had communicated with his wife about contraception. This exchange backed up his earlier assertions that women ought to be protected from 'crude discussions', that he therefore did not talk with his wife about birth control, and that he silently managed their contraceptive strategy.

The effect of the relationship between interviewer and interviewee on the testimony obtained is further compounded when interviewing couples. The orthodoxy is that couples should be interviewed separately; husbands and wives cannot be expected truthfully to represent the details of their sexual lives when together.[80] This approach was used initially, but proved unsatisfactory.[81] Some houses and flats were small, which made it difficult to send a partner away for any length of time, allowing only brief, rather rushed, individual interviews. Moreover, it was difficult to engineer separate interviews without implying that an aim of the research was to play each partner off against the other. Arthur and Dorothy did not object to being interviewed separately, but they specifically compared the research methods to the television programme *Mr and Mrs* whose purpose is to test couples' knowledge of each other's idiosyncrasies and preferences.[82] Because of these practical and ethical considerations the strategy was subsequently abandoned, and in later interviews couples were kept together. In a few cases, such an approach limited what couples would reveal in front of each other. Doreen, for example, was uncomfortable explaining marital disputes in front of her husband:

Why didn't you want her to go out to work?

LARRY   Well, I felt as though I could keep her. And I did.

DOREEN Yeah, but it was tight . . . I wanted go teaching you see, I were capable. And, er, he objected to that. I think it was because he thought it would be higher thing than being a builder.

Tell me about that.

---

[79] Merlin, msf/kf/bl/#35.   [80] Brannen, 'The Study of Sensitive Topics', 557–8.

[81] One survey of birth-control practices concluded that it was necessary to conduct interviews in the presence of family or friends. Pierce and Rowntree 'Birth Control in Britain, Part I', 7.

[82] Arthur and Dorothy, bc3ox#30.

DOREEN   Well, I can't in front of him, but, er—caused a lot of friction.
          And how did you feel?
DOREEN   Frustrated. I'm still frustrated about it.[83]

For this reason considerable care was taken during interviews with couples to examine and explore the extent to which a reluctance to discuss certain topics or emotions was induced by the presence of a disapproving spouse. This could then be followed up or explored in an additional separate interview. In the above case, Doreen herself requested a further interview on a day when her husband would be out.

Yet such examples were the rare exception. Most interviews with couples were remarkable in the extent to which, far from telling a sanitized, consensual version of their past, husbands and wives openly revealed differences of opinion, challenged each other, and revised each other's memories. In this way, far from impeding the research, interviewing couples together provided a rare opportunity to view a relationship in action. Couples frequently flirted with each other, teased one another, and relived old arguments. The finding that men and women avoided talking to each other about sexual matters and that women frequently deferred to their husbands' views with regard to contraceptive use and family planning was reinforced by the marital dynamics displayed during interviews. Cecil and Wyn, for example, asserted that he made all contraceptive decisions. For example, he forcefully rejected the idea that she might have tried to engineer a spell of abstinence when keen to avoid pregnancy:

> *And were there any times in your marriage when, in order not to get pregnant you had less sex, or you even stopped having sex for a while?*
> CECIL   No. None at all. I wouldn't—I wouldn't have allowed that. No.
> WYN   What? Wouldn't have allowed what?
> CECIL   You to say no, I—in case I—in case we have a child.
> WYN   Oh.
> CECIL   No, I would say no.[84]

His dominance during the interview lent further force to this claim. Cecil dominated the conversation, and seemed to want to exercise control over the interview, frequently interrupting his wife in order to tell her stories 'properly'. Wyn was complicit in this interaction and in her own silencing. She allowed him to speak for her, apologized to him on the few occasions when she interrupted him (even when she was correcting his presentation of her actions and feelings), and put herself down as less intelligent:

> CECIL   Of course, that's been one of the main problems I've found is the emancipation of women, it's altered married life, hasn't it?

---

[83] Doreen and Larry, msf/kf/bl/#20.   [84] Cecil and Wyn, bc3ox#40.

In what ways? Tell me.

CECIL   In what way? Well (clears throat) women have careers now; which in those days they didn't, they just—all they wanted to do was just get married, have children, and look after a husband. So they were always at home, looking after the children. But now, life is quite different. I mean, men go out to work, women go out to work, sometimes they have 'house-husbands', which was unheard of in those days, er, and vice versa. Sometimes it's the wife that's at home, sometimes it's the husband, and sometimes neither, the children are being cared by child-minders and that sort of thing. And I think that sort of, er, makes married life much more difficult than it was in the olden days when you had a set pattern that you kept to all the time. And, well I dare say it, because I've been married to her a long time, but, the man was always the governor,

WYN   (chuckles)

CECIL   but now of course he's not, he's, er

WYN   (laughing) Pardon me, but piffle.

CECIL   But that is the case, you see, that—er, life has changed so much in, er—married life has changed so much. (pause)

So you were going to object when he said that he was the governor.

WYN   What? What was I going to say?

I don't—you were about to say something when he said that he was the boss in the house.

WYN   Was it 'piffle', or something else? (laughing)

CECIL   Yeah, 'piffle' is a favourite sort of, er—well I suppose you can use it as an adjective—piffle is when I say something she doesn't agree with, she says 'piffle'.

WYN   (laughing)

(To Wyn) So did you think you were the boss?

WYN   Me the boss? No, no, no, we don—he is a bit bossy, actually, but um (laughs), he knows it. He's cleverer than me.[85]

Interviews conducted with both partners present thus provided analytically significant illustrations of marital dynamics. Rather than focusing on what couples said in each other's absence, the interviewer sought to make the most of this interaction.

Various problems face the oral historian analysing material regarding individuals' sexual behaviour over fifty years ago. First, there are issues associated with the accurate recollection of information on sex lives which are constantly evolving and difficult to recall in their complexity. Secondly, given the massive changes in sexual cultures in Britain since the inter-war period, it is likely that new ideas about sex will have affected, and possibly significantly reformulated, individuals' representations of their sexual behaviour. Although the oral historian must be aware, and often critical, when analysing distortions in testimony, these mis-rememberings, clichés, and post-hoc rewritings can be very useful in understanding respondents' sexual identities.

---

[85] Cecil and Wyn, bc3ox#40.

It is undeniable that it is difficult for individuals to remember precise details of contraceptive choices, debates, and practices so long after their childbearing years.[86] Many respondents struggled to remember certain details:

You can't always remember just what you said or did fifty years ago when you were—you were just beginning to enjoy your married life . . . Things may have been said [about birth control clinics] but I can't remember whether fifty years ago somebody said to me something that you are now asking me, because if they did, oh, they'd be out of me mind after twenty-four hours.[87]

Moreover, the changing nature of sexual discourses in contemporary Britain is also likely to have had an impact on the testimony received.[88] People often reappraise their past in the light of modern interpretations, particularly since the advent of modern media and the prominence of living history on television.[89] The assumption that the sexual activity of modern societies far outstrips that of previous generations in its frequency was widespread and clearly had an impact on the presentation of oral testimony. The majority assumed that they were 'undersexed' in comparison with modern custom. Allusions to abstinence sometimes served to create distance between past and present cultures rather than to indicate the avoidance of coitus to prevent pregnancy. When I asked Gladys how often she and her husband had sex when they were first married she emphasized its relative absence:

I didn't—never did like that side of married life . . . he wasn't very—not bad, fair play, he wasn't bad. Not like—did you see that *Vanessa* yesterday on the TV? . . . There was a man in his sixties, he couldn't leave the women alone—there was another couple on—they'd been married forty years, and, she said 'He's like a magnet, I've only got to look him in the eyes, even in car parks, in the back of a car'—the police caught them once in the back of their car, and they're married forty years. Dewdew, I must have missed out a lot! (laughs)
So with you . . . was it?
Couple of times a week.[90]

---

[86] In response to the problem of the deterioration of memory, many oral historians claim that there can be as much conflict of memory hours or days after an event as years later, or that the reliability of memory is not too great a problem for the social historian studying everyday events, routines, and attitudes that are likely to have been held for a long time. It is argued also that in later life many people go through a period of 'life review' in which early memories are remembered with renewed clarity. Thompson, 'Oral History and the Historian', 26; Slim and Thompson, *Listening for a Change*, 140; Yow, *Recording Oral History*, 19; Coleman, 'Ageing and Life History', 120–43. As one interviewee commented: 'the sort of older you get um, you know the more you, you sort of remember', Peggy, msf/srss/ht/#20.   [87] Bernard, msf/jm/bl/#45.
[88] See Leydesdorff, Passerini, and Thompson (eds.), *Gender and Memory*, 13.
[89] This point is largely missed by one study of oral testimony and the mass media which mainly champions oral history as a counterbalance to universalizing and simplistic media messages: Ferrarotti, *The End of Conversation*. Alistair Thomson found Anzacs presenting scenes from the film *Gallipoli* as part of their own personal histories: 'Putting Popular Memory Theory into Practice in Australia', 301.
[90] Gladys, bc3sw#28; 'Dewdew': a Welsh phrase, translatable as 'Good God'.

Perceptions of contemporary sexual mores have a strong influence on reports and interpretations of sexual frequency, yet access to such contemporary values are usually highly sensational, clichéd, and fanciful. In this context assertions of comparative continence cannot be seen as empirically literal. Nonetheless, assertions of sexual passivity, sexual restraint, and indifference, particularly among women, testify to the sexual identities adopted. First, the fact that sexual frequency itself was not prized or seen as a symbol of the strength, power, or value of the marital relationship is likely to have had a direct effect on the dynamics of sexual relationships and the frequency with which intercourse took place. Secondly, such narratives illustrate women's attitudes towards sex, the sexual roles they adopted, their approach to contraception, and the roles undertaken in negotiating sexual practices. Ambiguous narratives about sexual frequency may tell us little about the actual incidence of coitus but much about women's roles and attitudes.

The analysis of oral history material in this book rarely takes testimony at face value. This is not because of suspicions of the validity or accuracy of oral history material, but because testimony is thick with layers of meaning and significance which demand meticulous and intricate dissection. Thus, this book is concerned not only with the factual truth of the stories presented but with why these accounts constitute the memory of the respondent, why certain memories are retained, and what role they play in the historical consciousness of the respondent. The imperative is to analyse how interviewees' tales are structured and how meaning is conveyed.[91] The focus is on how oral respondents have decided to organize and present their memories as a means of elucidating the subjective meaning and cultural significance that they attach to their lives. As Ashplant realizes, the advantage of oral history testimony lies 'not only in the discrete facts it may yield, but also in the interpretation of lived experience'.[92] Individuals' comments on their perceptions of changes in sexual beliefs and practices occurring in their lifetime dominated testimony, and are important in providing insight into the ways in which members of societies define themselves.[93] We will learn as much about the dynamics of birth control use from the context of description as from the depictions themselves. Above all, oral history material provides insight into the identities which informed and determined contraceptive practices.

---

[91] See e.g. Featherstone, 'Jack Hill's Horse'; see also Tonkin, *Narrating Our Pasts*; H. White, 'The Value of Narrativity in the Representation of Reality'.

[92] Ashplant, 'Anecdote as Narrative Resource in Working-Class Life Stories', 99.

[93] On collective memory see Halbwachs, *The Collective Memory*; Connerton, *How Societies Remember*; Gedi and Elam, 'Collective Memory—What Is It?'; Popular Memory Group, 'Popular Memory'; Fentress and Wickham, *Social Memory*; Samuel and Thompson (eds.), *The Myths We Live By*; Crane, '(Not) Writing History'; Hamilton, 'The Knife Edge'; Portelli, *The Death of Luigi Vastulli*; Perks (ed.), *The Oral History Reader*.

1

'What've a boiling kettle got to do with a baby?'[1]

The Maintenance of Ignorance

When Marie Stopes wrote *Married Love* in 1918 she professedly did so as a result of her own ignorance of sex upon her marriage in 1911, which was annulled in 1916 on the grounds of non-consummation. The purpose of her book, as stated in the preface, was to prevent any other woman suffering 'such a terrible price for sex-ignorance'; to replace 'blind questioning in the dark; with enlightenment.'[2] The response to her book suggests that her experiences were not isolated. Letters poured in from men and women, testifying to their own ignorance and asking for information.[3] Diaries, surveys, letters, reports and the calls of the burgeoning sex reform movement all suggest that both formal and informal sex education in Britain in the first half of the twentieth century was meagre. Schools and parents avoided the issue, and many saw innocence as a form of protection, particularly for girls. Even friends, siblings, or workmates were apparently reluctant to talk about such matters. Lesley Hall concludes that 'those who wrote to Stopes were only the determined and literate tip of an iceberg of bewilderment about sexual phenomena'.[4]

Yet, paradoxically, the first half of the twentieth century was also the period during which information about birth control increased considerably and, moreover, was the time when the birth rate fell most dramatically. For some historians it has been difficult to accept that extreme levels of ignorance could possibly have been as widespread as the record suggests. Thomas Laqueur was puzzled by women who 'report not knowing where babies came from': 'It is odd that in such a print saturated culture such ignorance was so widespread'.[5] To understand this apparent contradiction, it is important to recognize that ignorance was as much a

---

[1] Edna, bc3sw#16.   [2] Stopes, *Married Love*, p. xvii.
[3] See e.g. R. Hall (ed.), *Dear Dr. Stopes*; Stopes, *Mother England*.
[4] Porter and Hall, *The Facts of Life*, 247.
[5] Laqueur, 'Simply Doing It' (review of *The Facts of Life*), 12; Hera Cook sees such 'scepticism' as the outcome of 'unexamined assumptions' based on Freudian notions of the centrality of the sex drive to human behaviour: Cook, *The Long Sexual Revolution*, 167. I shall argue below that there is a genuine tension between the discourses on sex and birth control and the testimony of ignorance

state of mind as a quantifiable level of understanding. Knowledge was not an objective set of facts waiting to be received. Narratives which focused on the absence of knowledge were not exaggerated or fallacious; the nature of the information obtained meant that many continued to feel ignorant. Despite the existence of a wide selection of birth control methods, information about which was accessible in a variety of contexts, individuals experienced difficulties in interpreting the information they received and remained painfully aware of continued gaps in their understanding. Gender differences in knowledge acquisition meant that women experienced comparative ignorance in relation to their male counterparts. Moreover, being ignorant was also an important identity for many; women in particular sought to preserve and maintain a state of naivety in defiance of the spread of information. Ignorance implied moral purity, innocence and respectability.

'SOLD IN SLOT MACHINES AND HAWKED ROUND FROM DOOR TO DOOR':[6] THE SPREAD OF INFORMATION ABOUT BIRTH CONTROL

From the mid-nineteenth century, publications aimed at providing birth control advice and information to the general public were increasingly widespread. Between 1830 and 1877 various freethinkers and radicals published tracts on the importance of family limitation and details of methods such as coitus interruptus; the 'safe period'; sponges, douches, and spermicidal treatments; condoms; and 'occlusive pessaries' which covered the cervix.[7] Francis Place's propaganda is thought by Michael Mason to have been the most widely available: he estimates that tens of thousands of handbills were distributed in working-class communities between 1823 and 1826, particularly in Scotland and the north of England.[8] Such material increased after the trial of Charles Bradlaugh and Annie Besant in 1877 for publishing Charles Knowlton's *Fruits of Philosophy*, a tract on family limitation methods first available in the 1830s.[9] H. A. Allbutt's *The Wife's Handbook*, for example, published in 1886, had sold over 250,000 copies by 1900 and more than

---

(especially since those who report their own ignorance also provide details of contraceptive awareness and use). I am, however, not 'sceptical' of the honesty of such claims, but rather aim to show how analysis of such narratives reveals the complex impact of various sources of information on individuals and the social function of sexual innocence.

[6] Joyce Daniel report to Margaret Pyke, on Merthyr Tydfil, July 1938: A&M: SA/FPA/A11/76. Margaret Pyke was the secretary of the National Birth Control Association (NBCA), which became the Family Planning Association in 1939.

[7] These are discussed in McLaren, *A History of Contraception*; Wood and Suitters, *The Fight for Acceptance*; Himes, *Medical History of Contraception*.

[8] Mason, *The Making of Victorian Sexual Attitudes*, 181.

[9] See the accounts in Himes, 'Charles Knowlton's Revolutionary Influence on the English Birth-Rate'; Bland, *Banishing the Beast*, 191–4; D'Arcy, 'The Malthusian League'.

half a million by the inter-war years.[10] The trial itself received widespread popular coverage and was thought by Sidney and Beatrice Webb to have had a significant impact on the decline in fertility.[11] For many, including H. G. Wells, Havelock Ellis, and Ethel Elderton, the notorious trial 'revolutionised the sexual habits of the English people', transforming the bearing of children from an involuntary to a voluntary condition.[12] One miner wrote to Bradlaugh and Besant in 1877 of his avid reading of *Fruits of Philosophy* which proved a 'blessing to me and my wife'.[13] The advertising and distribution of such works also expanded.[14] Michael Mason estimates that sales of the *Fruits of Philosophy* before the trial stood at about 1,000 copies a year, advertised in comic weeklies such as the *Penny Satirist* and the *Fly*. By the 1870s 'literature was pressed on married middle-class women by a 'respectably-dressed woman' in the Tottenham Court Road, and mailed to every girl seeking a post as a barmaid in the *Morning Advertiser*'.[15]

Following the Bradlaugh–Besant trial, the Malthusian League was formed in 1877 to continue to campaign for information about family limitation; it produced a monthly journal and various pamphlets, and gave public lectures. Before 1913 it cautiously avoided providing specific advice about methods, but by 1900 they were receiving over 2,000 requests each month for appliances advertised in its journal, *The New Generation*.[16] In 1912 the League gave public meetings in poor areas of south London, and in 1921 began 'an intensive campaign of canvassing and outdoor and indoor meetings'. It distributed 10,000 'Practical Leaflets' a week, and doctors were on hand to teach the use of methods to women.[17]

As the birth rate continued to fall, public discussion of family limitation became yet more widespread. Serious concern at the size and quality of the population was expressed by the popular press, as well as in specialized journals and academic literature, particularly following the report of the Committee on Physical Deterioration occasioned by the scandalous condition of the troops enlisting to fight the Boer War.[18] During the First World War, the 'ignorant poor' were said to 'flock to see' a film produced by the National Council of Public Morals, *Where Are My Children?* condemning abortion and birth control for

---

[10] H. A. Allbutt was struck off the medical register for publishing this book. The first edition has many illustrations and advertisements expunged from later versions. Himes, *Medical History of Contraception*, 251.

[11] Sidney and Beatrice Webb, *Industrial Democracy*, 638; Soloway, *Birth Control and the Population Question*, 53.

[12] Elderton, *Report on the English Birth-Rate*, pp. viii, 234–7; Soloway, *Birth Control and the Population Question*, 53.

[13] Mason, *The Making of Victorian Sexual Attitudes*, 183.

[14] On the spread of information about sex through a range of methods see Cocks, 'Saucy Stories'.

[15] Mason, *The Making of Victorian Sexual Attitudes*, 187.

[16] Soloway, *Birth Control and the Population Question*, 326 n. 37. See also How-Martyn, *The Birth Control Movement in England*; D'Arcy, 'The Malthusian League'.

[17] SPBCC, *Birth Control and Public Health*, 2.

[18] Soloway, *Birth Control and the Population Question*, 119; National Birth-Rate Commission, *The Declining Birth-Rate*.

creating a dangerously low birth rate.[19] The eugenics movement succeeded in placing population anxieties at the forefront of national debates and allowed proliferation of material about birth control to be discussed as part of the question of national deterioration and the concept of 'racial health'.[20] Popular books on sex education were focused on ensuring that young girls and boys grew up not so much 'informed' about sexual practices, but rather aware of the relationship between sex, health, and fitness.[21] Norah March's guide for parents, *Towards Racial Health*, and her later *Sex Knowledge, with a Special Chapter on Birth Control*, presented the prudent use of family limitation measures as a central element of preserving 'racial health'.[22]

From the end of the First World War lectures and leaflets were supplemented by an attempt to establish specially equipped and staffed birth control clinics. Throughout the 1920s various voluntary clinics were set up. The first was Marie Stopes's Mothers' Clinic for Constructive Birth Control in London, closely followed, also in 1921, by the Walworth Women's Welfare Centre, initially run by the Malthusian League and then by the Society for the Provision of Birth Control Clinics, which had, by 1932, set up sixteen other clinics in various parts of the country.[23] Marie Stopes opened a further five centres and also had a travelling caravan clinic which sought to provide information in communities where clinics did not exist.[24] The first regional tour of the caravan clinic was to south Wales (it later went to the north of England). Scheduled to stay only three months, 'the demand for its services is so great and the interest shown so continuous' that it spent a year between May 1929 and June 1930 travelling around south Wales.[25] There were additionally, perhaps, other voluntary clinics run outside the auspices of the major birth control organizations, about which less is known.[26] When Marie Stopes's clinic moved to new premises off the Tottenham Court Road the existing clinic was taken over by a private firm.[27] The *New Generation* reported, in 1924, that

[19] Soloway, *Birth Control and the Population Question*, 118. On the plot and reaction to this film in the USA see Eberwein, *Sex Ed.*, 53–4.   [20] Porter and Hall, *The Facts of Life*, 228.

[21] See e.g. Baden-Powell, *Rovering to Success*; Scharlieb and Sibly, *Youth and Sex*; Schofield and Vaughan-Jackson, *What a Boy Should Know*.

[22] March, *Towards Racial Health*; ead., *Sex Knowledge*.

[23] These were situated in Walworth, north Kensington, Wolverhampton, Cambridge, Manchester, East London, Glasgow, Aberdeen, Oxford, Birmingham, Rotherham, Newcastle upon Tyne, Exeter, Nottingham, Pontypridd, and Bristol: SPBCC, *Birth Control and Public Health*. On the various types of clinic, see Florence, *Progress Report on Birth Control*, 13–17.

[24] Leeds and Aberdeen in 1934, Belfast in 1936, Cardiff in 1937, and Swansea in 1943.

[25] 'The Welsh Tour', *Birth Control News*, 8/10 (Feb. 1930), 154. Marie Stopes later boasted that the caravan had been in Wales for three years: 'Behind the Scenes', *Birth Control News*, 16/5 (Dec. 1937), 54.

[26] See Norman and Vera Himes, 'Birth Control for the British Working Classes', 582; Himes, *Practical Birth-Control Methods*, appendix A, 216–24.

[27] I am very grateful to Lesley Hall for this information. She speculates that this clinic may have been run by Lamberts, who initially supplied Stopes with contraceptive appliances. For Stopes's fraught correspondence with Lamberts, see the Marie C. Stopes Papers in the Department of Manuscripts at the British Library, BL Add. MSS 58638.

Nurse E. S. Daniels had set up one clinic in Cardiff.[28] She was found, in addition, by one of Marie Stopes's spies to be providing birth control advice in a chiropodist's in Crouch End.[29] In Yorkshire, a Mrs Ellen Waddington set up clinics in her own home, and that of her nurse, in Mirfield and Goole.[30] In 1930 the government conceded that birth control advice might be given out by local authorities if they wished to do so. By 1939, 284 local authorities had acted, forty-eight setting up birth control clinics;[31] thirty-one providing birth control advice at gynaecological clinics; twenty-one hiring premises out to (and sometimes also funding) a National Birth Control Association clinic; twenty-three contributing a block grant to a voluntary clinic; ninety-eight referring cases to voluntary or municipal clinics or private doctors, paying fees and/or expenses in almost all cases; and sixty-three authorities authorizing their medical officers to give advice without necessarily providing special arrangements to help or encourage them to do so.[32]

The clinic movement successfully repositioned birth control information as part of a debate about the needs of working-class mothers and the reduction of maternal mortality.[33] In 1928 the *New Generation* provided five reasons why it supported birth control. First and most prominent was 'the suffering of the mothers' for whom 'motherhood is a very dangerous occupation'.[34] The assertion that motherhood was more dangerous than mining was frequently repeated in left-wing circles.[35] More pervasive still was the rhetoric which from the 1920s placed birth control at the centre of a successful and harmonious married

[28] Nurse Daniels had gained notoriety when she was dismissed in 1922 for telling women who came to the Edmonton Maternity and Child Welfare Clinic where they could receive birth-control advice. Her clinic is mentioned in the *Daily Herald* and in *The New Generation*. I have not come across any mention of it when looking at local newspapers. There is no indication of how long it lasted or how successful it was. See *Daily Herald*, cutting in A&M: PP/MCS/C.15; *The New Generation*; 3/10 (Oct. 1924), 111.

[29] Nurse E.A.J., letter to Dr Marie Stopes, 13 Jan. 1924, BL Add. MSS 58596. The letters she wrote to Norman E. Himes confirm the existence of her own private clinic and chiropody practice in London. I am grateful to Lesley Hall for this information.

[30] Robinson, *Seventy Birth Control Clinics*, 22; 'A New Clinic in Yorkshire', *The New Generation*, 3/9 (Sept. 1924), 101.   [31] Sixteen clinics closed that year, however.

[32] NBCA Annual Report 1938/9, A&M: SA/FPA/A11/21. The NBCA was the amalgamation of various birth-control organizations: the Workers' Birth Control Group, the Birth Control Investigation Committee (which had merged with the NBCC in 1930), the Society for the Provision of Birth Control Clinics and the Birth Control International Information Centre (in 1938). The Society for Constructive Birth Control and Racial Progress under Marie Stopes briefly amalgamated with the NBCC before returning to independence. Lella Secor Florence noted that the extent to which instructions from local authorities regarding birth-control advice were implemented depended on the 'presence of individuals who are eager and willing to undertake the tasks involved' and that many initiatives fell victim to 'pressure of other work, or lack of interest, or fear of disapprobation': *Progress Report on Birth Control*, 28–9). On the establishment of clinics and the difficulties in assessing the realities of clinic provision in the absence of detailed local studies, see Fisher, ' "Clearing Up Misconceptions" '. One additional local study is Grier, 'Eugenics and Birth Control'.

[33] Lewis, 'The Ideology and Politics of Birth Control in Inter-War England', 42.

[34] 'Why We Advocate Birth Control', *The New Generation*, 7/1 (Jan. 1928).

[35] See e.g. the debate at the annual Labour Party conference of 1927 discussed in L. Hoggart, 'The Campaign for Birth Control in Britain in the 1920s', 148.

relationship. The published works of Marie Stopes and the other marriage manuals focused on birth control as essential to sexual compatibility, happiness, and in particular female fulfilment. Marie Stopes's *Married Love* was perhaps the most influential such work. Selling 2,000 copies during its first two weeks, it was reprinted seven times in its first year.[36] It was quickly followed by a range of others, in particular *Wise Parenthood* and *A Letter to Working Mothers*, designed to provide the detailed information about birth control methods only alluded to in *Married Love*. Marie Stopes supplemented her books with regular articles in working-class newspapers such as *John Bull* and *Penny Magazine*. A supreme publicist, she ensured she was rarely out of the newspaper headlines for several decades. She bombarded local and national newspapers with information about her activities, especially her struggles with the Catholic Church, and wrote bitter letters if she felt unfairly represented or worst of all ignored, frequently threatening legal action.[37] In 1922 she filed a libel suit against Dr Halliday Sutherland, deputy commissioner for Tuberculosis Medical Services in England and Wales, and a Catholic, who had charged her clinics with experimenting on poor women. Stopes was found to have been 'unfairly' defamed, but nevertheless libel was not proved. The confused decision was reversed on appeal, and the whole affair provided an enormous amount of publicity about both Marie Stopes and birth control.[38]

Stopes became a household name. Many oral history respondents from all backgrounds, but especially the middle classes, knew something of her general message without having come across her books or clinics:

Marie Stopes was a big—what you call it—of birth control, wasn't she? And she wasn't very popular. I can't remember a lot about her, but I remember her name and she was all for birth control, wasn't she? . . . She was all for controlling sex and that, you know.[39]

Others came across her books. Ernest, a fishmonger from south Wales, 'must have read Marie Stopes when I was about nineteen, you see she gave you the knowledge to prevent having babies to start with'.[40] Sam, an articled clerk who grew up in Northumberland, remembered the 'dirty books . . . that went the rounds of the fellas', one of which was by 'somebody called Marie something'.[41] Tim, who was born in 1917, found his parents' copy of *Married Love* and remembered many of the details of her message:

she wrote a book called *Marry in Love* didn't she? . . . Well, I found this book at 'ome . . . Me parents' book . . . it was in, eh, one of the drawers in the upstairs—in their room. It wasn't locked up or anything . . . Funnily enough I 'aven't read it since, but I remember it pretty well, it's contraception isn't it? And, eh, use-using the Dutch cap method mostly, inn't it? Yeah, and, eh, it caused a bit of an uproar at the time I think 'er book didn't it?[42]

[36] Soloway, *Birth Control and the Population Question*, 211.   [37] Ibid. 221.
[38] June Rose, *Marie Stopes and the Sexual Revolution*, 163–75; Soloway, *Birth Control and the Population Question*, 246–7.   [39] Dilys, bc2#13.
[40] Ernest, bc3sw#2.   [41] Sam, msf/srss/ht/#28.   [42] Tim, msf/srss/bl/#19.

Marie Stopes was not the only figure writing practical advice books for married people which included information about birth control.[43] Notable were *Wise Wedlock* (1922) by G. Courtenay Beale (accused by Stopes of plagiarism); Herbert Gray's *Men Women and God* (1923); Isabel Hutton's *The Hygiene of Marriage* (1923); and Theo van de Velde's *Ideal Marriage* (1928; it was claimed by Eustace Chesser, author of several sex surveys and founder of the Marriage Guidance Council, that this was given to young husbands in the same way and as often as Mrs Beeton was given to brides).[44]

'BEWILDERED BY THE WEALTH OF CONDOMS, CAPS, PESSARIES, FOAMS, SPERMATICIDES AND OTHER APPLIANCES . . . SHOWERED ON THEM':[45] ADVICE ON BIRTH CONTROL METHODS

This literature provided in-depth information about a range of contraceptive options. Abortion was rarely recommended; in fact, most contraceptive advice manuals were vehemently opposed to any attempt to control fertility after conception may have taken place. Yet such discussion drew attention to its alleged prevalence. Moreover, newspapers were full of carefully worded adverts, promising to provide relief to women with irregular menses, to restore missed periods, or to remove 'obstinate' 'obstacles' preventing menstruation:[46]

Good God, penny royal, Dr Patterson's female pills—and they used to—in the newspapers—used to give you a write up what to do if you were pregnant . . . things like this would be in the newspapers.[47]

Marriage manuals generally also condemned withdrawal, though most included a long description of it and devoted chapters to detailing its unreliability, and the effect it had on pleasure and on physiological and mental health. Yet Dale Owen's *Moral Physiology* recommended it above all other methods.[48] Much contradictory information was written about the points in the menstrual cycle during which it was thought safe to have sex. Maggie thought sex was safe 'a week before my period came. About a fortnight in between I'd let him have a go.'[49] Most

---

[43] An early work, which focused on birth control rather than marriage, was G. Hardy, *How to Prevent Pregnancy*.

[44] See Porter and Hall, *The Facts of Life*, 212. On sex manuals see Cook, *The Long Sexual Revolution*, pt. II, 165–260.

[45] Mass-Observation, DR 3338, reply to April 1944 Directive.

[46] See McLaren, ' "Not a Stranger: A Doctor" ', 271; Brown, 'Female Pills and the Reputation of Iron as an Abortifacient'.   [47] Elizabeth, bc3sw#12.

[48] See Cook, *The Long Sexual Revolution*, 40–61.

[49] Maggie, bc2#21. It was not until 1929 that ovulation was no longer equated with oestrus in mammals and thought to coincide with menstruation: Szreter, *Fertility, Class and Gender*, 409.

authors in the twentieth century condemned such methods, however they were formulated. In 1933, four years after Knaus and Ogino published their research declaring mid-cycle to be women's most fertile period, Leonora Eyes warned readers not to place any reliance 'on a supposed safe time in between the monthly period'.[50]

Some writers (albeit cautiously) advised women to avoid having an orgasm in order to prevent fertilization. Van de Velde and Haire both felt that orgasms increased the chances of women conceiving. Moreover, van de Velde and Marie Stopes both argued that certain positions during coitus would also reduce the possibility of pregnancy. Stopes suggested 'sitting upright the moment after ejaculation had taken place and coughing violently or taking some other exercise to contract the pelvis' while van de Velde suggested positions in which the penis was angled away from the cervical os.[51] Angus McLaren argues that the 'Galenic' idea that 'female seed' was essential to conception continued in the popular imagination long after its supposed elimination from medical knowledge.[52] While most evidence suggests that women were aware that they could get pregnant without experiencing orgasm, many women nevertheless felt that 'holding back' was a fertility limitation strategy worth trying. One woman, for example, informed Marie Stopes that before writing to her, 'restraint at the critical moment' was her only means of avoiding pregnancy.[53] Iris's two children were seen as evidence of her experience of sexual pleasure by maternal welfare clinicians in Pontypridd:

I've never, not even once, been interested in sex, it has never worked. I told them that in the clinic and she said 'Well you've had two children', I said 'I don't care if I've had twenty-two I don't have a climax as you say, never'. They laughed at me.[54]

In this story her anecdotes about sexual disinterest were countered by 'medical' voices linking pleasure to pregnancy and conception. Here we see folk beliefs and community jokes coexisting with, rather than coming into conflict with, medical knowledge.[55]

Most birth control and marriage manuals sought to dissuade couples from abstaining. Indeed the books provided information on birth control methods in

[50] Eyles, *Commonsense about Sex*, 94.

[51] Van de Velde, *Fertility and Sterility in Marriage*, 298–9; id., *Ideal Marriage*, 186; Stopes, *Contraception*, 138–9, 61–3.

[52] McLaren, *Reproductive Rituals*, 13–29. See also Laqueur, *Making Sex*. Estelle Cohen similarly challenges the claim that medical discourse shifted uniformly away from Galenic ideas about reproduction during the eighteenth century and stresses the continuities and ambiguities in medical knowledge: ' "What the women at all times would laugh at" ', 127 n. 15, 139.

[53] Quoted in L. Hall, 'Marie Stopes and her Correspondents', 31; E. S. Daniels also regarded this as a common misunderstanding on the part of working-class women in the 1920s: see *The Children of Desire*, 34.   [54] Iris, bc2#8.

[55] Barbara Brookes found that 'germ' theory supplemented rather than replaced 'humoral' ideas about the body in early twentieth-century New Zealand: Brookes, 'Hygiene, Health and Bodily Knowledge, 1880–1940'.

order that such 'drastic' action might be avoided.[56] Weatherhead described abstinence as a 'form of torture'; by practising birth control, 'young couples in such circumstances' could avoid the resultant 'strain, friction, irritability and bad temper'.[57] Yet, as Hera Cook points out, abstinence is mentioned as a 'widely recommended approach' which it is assumed the 'readers might well be using'.[58] Moreover, restraint and moderation were valued by some manuals, especially those written from an explicitly Christian or religious standpoint. Eyles emphasized the dangers of too frequent intercourse: 'most people tire of a thing that is too easy, too accessible. But if a man will trouble to make love each time, and to make each union a thing of perfection, he will not be tempted to do it too often, nor will he tire.'[59]

Above all the marriage manual literature promoted female methods of contraception, and in particular caps and diaphragms (also frequently referred to as pessaries), which covered the woman's cervix. Initially made of metal and cellulose, by the 1920s they were constructed out of rubber. Some advised leaving caps in place for days, even weeks; others, especially after 1930, advised inserting the cap when necessary and removing it soon after.[60] Various birth control organizations recommended various forms of cap or diaphragm. Stopes had her own, called the 'pro-race': small, domed, and held in place by suction, it had to be fitted to each individual so that it perfectly covered her cervix. She rejected her competitors' brands, such as the diaphragm which was fitted between the cervix and the pubic bone by means of a spring; she claimed that some caused cancer, while others might be dislodged by female movement during intercourse or would stretch the vaginal walls.[61] Some intra-uterine devices were also discussed. Haire described a 'wishbone pessary', which involved a v-shaped spring that was pushed into the vagina and held against the cervix by a metal plate, while the spring expanded into the uterus. Marie Stopes initially rejected the device before recommending it in certain cases in the 1920 edition of *Wise Parenthood*.[62]

Various chemicals were observed to have spermicidal properties, and manufacturers advertised a range of products: spermicidal tampons which dissolved in the vagina; jellies to be inserted; or recipes for solutions to be made at home and applied by a douche or syringe. Rendall's was perhaps the oldest, most familiar brand of pessary, consisting of quinine and cocoa butter. Nineteenth-century birth control campaigners such as Annie Besant and Francis Place suggested using

---

[56] See e.g. Eyles, *Commonsense about Sex*, 90.   [57] Weatherhead, *The Mastery of Sex*, 85.
[58] Cook, *The Long Sexual Revolution*, 110.   [59] Eyles, *Commonsense about Sex*, 68.
[60] Stopes's uncertainty on this question was damaging during her libel trial. See June Rose, *Marie Stopes and the Sexual Revolution*, 167–8.
[61] Stopes, *Contraception*, 162. On the relationship between birth-control methods and cancer see also Drysdale, *The Small Family System*, ch. 5, 'Do Preventive Methods Cause Cancer?' (pp. 72–82); O. C. Beale, *Racial Decay*.
[62] Cook, *The Long Sexual Revolution*, 131. Debate between Haire and Stopes on the suitability of the 'gold-pin' pessary occurred at the Halliday Sutherland libel trial: June Rose, *Marie Stopes and the Sexual Revolution*, 168–9.

a sponge, placed over the cervix and sometimes soaked in a form of spermicide.[63] The sponge continued to be recommended: Norman Haire cautioned users to get the right size, recommended artifical rubber sponges rather than sea sponges for ease of sterilization, and the use of lactic acid jelly as a spermicide. Stopes advised coating a sponge with olive oil.[64]

Information about various types of sheaths and condoms was widely available; all birth control books and marriage manuals mentioned them. They were sold in chemists, sometimes mentioned by the barber, and provided by the army. Various types were marketed: reusable sheaths, made out of vulcanized rubber, and from the 1930s, more expensive latex versions, some of which were disposable. Female condoms were also available, as were unisex ones. A brochure from Charles & Co. Ltd, Manufacturers, West Green Road, London dating from the late 1930s or early 1940s recommended the *ladies own sheath* or *capote Anglais*:

This ingenious contrivance for FEMALE use. In reality it is a Female Sheath made of finest cut sheet rubber. NO difficulty is experienced in fitting as with the Check Pessary. Will last for years.

Also advertised was:

The combined pessary and sheath . . . which . . . can be rolled up into the shape of a Check Pessary, and can be so used by the wife [or] . . . used unrolled as a Sheath by the husband, and will be found one of the most convenient and reliable articles for this purpose.[65]

One supplier of the 'pessarie capote' or 'complete protector' for female use noted in 1921: 'We have made these for years, but the sale is comparatively small'.[66]

Advertisements for condoms from hygienic stores and mail-order companies were widely reproduced in newspapers and magazines, local as well as national.[67] Dilys, a postman's wife from Swansea, remembered such advertisements:

It's drugs and condoms now, before they used to advertise them . . . as French letters, French ticklers—I've seen some ads for French ticklers—that's years ago . . . and one lady I knew, and this is true, I knew her personally, and she didn't want any more children, she sent away to . . . newspaper,—how to avoid having children. It was only 7/6 then to send. And she had a . . . leaflet back: 'Now keep Toby out'.[68]

Ethel Elderton's 1914 survey reported that birth control material was advertised all over the north of England. In Durham, for example, books on

---

[63] Place also argued that sponges could be substituted with 'lint, fine wool, cotton, flax or what may be at hand', quoted in Mason, *The Making of Victorian Sexual Attitudes*, 182.

[64] Annie Besant, The Law of Population', 188; Himes, *Medical History of Contraception*, 214–18; Stopes, *Wise Parenthood*, 56–8.

[65] Mass-Observation, TC Sexual Behaviour 1939–50, TC12/16/B.

[66] Mr Lambert to Marie Stopes, 16 Dec. 1921, BL Add. MSS 58638.

[67] On the commercialization of contraceptive devices and abortifacients in America (despite the Comstock Laws which made such trade illegal) see Tone, 'Contraceptive Consumers'.

[68] Dilys, bc2#13.

family limitation were sold on market stalls, and appliances had, until recently, been openly sold by men and women who 'stood like cheap-jacks on platforms'. In Huddersfield, 'small bills in urinals' advertised 'appliances for limitation of the family' and 'the announcement of a birth in a newspaper [brought] "literature" on the limitation of the family from firms who manufacture and sell preventative appliances'.[69] *The Lancet* observed in 1917 that rubber goods companies were in the habit of sending out circulars to parents after the birth of a first child and that even in small rural areas shop windows openly displayed birth control devices.[70] A GP in London told the 1904 Committee on Physical Deterioration, 'You cannot go into a single public urinal without seeing an advertisement [for condoms] which has been gummed up there.'[71] By the 1930s there were condom-vending machines in pubs.[72]

Posters, lectures, and films such as *Where Are My Children?* and *Damaged Goods* were also widely shown.[73] For example, in 1920 the Preston Branch of the National Committee for Combating Venereal Diseases arranged for educational films such as *The End of the Road, How Life Begins*, and *The Shadow* to be shown along with lectures to mixed audiences and parents' conferences at which sex education in schools and homes was discussed.[74] Some such films were remembered by oral history interviewees from Lancashire. Mrs Peterson, born in 1899, remembered a film shown during the First World War which revealed VD patients as 'cripples and all sorts. I thought it was terrible.'[75] Daphne remembered seeing posters in nearby Great Harwood, 'when you went in the public toilets . . . about venereal disease . . . taking care . . . your hygiene and that sort of thing'.[76] By 1925 the National Vigilance Association felt that the information about sex and birth control was dangerously widespread, with American magazines 'entirely occupied with sex' reportedly on sale in Woolworths.[77] Condoms and prophylactic ablutions were also recommended by those fighting the spread of venereal disease. Most men who spent time in the army would have been exposed to information

[69] Elderton, *Report on the English Birth-Rate*, 106, 181.

[70] 'Annotation on "Birth Control"', *The Lancet*, 2 (1917), 207–8, quoted in Porter and Hall, *The Facts of Life*, 258.

[71] Dr Lewis Hawkes, 'Report of the Interdepartmental Committee on Physical Deterioration', quoted in E. Ross, *Love and Toil*, 103.

[72] Joyce Daniel report Aug 1938, A&M: SA/FPA/A11/76. The location of vending machines was controlled by the Local Government Act of 1933, section 249. Some birth-control campaigners sought to have such machines removed by local police forces under the 'suppression of nuisances' clause, seeing them as contributing to an image of contraception as sordid and illicit and not for use by respectable couples. They had little success in this, however. On the laws concerning the display of contraceptive material see e.g. Latham, *Regulating Reproduction*, 25.

[73] See Kuhn, *Cinema Censorship and Sexuality, 1909–1925*, chs. 3 and 4.

[74] 'Report of the Medical Officer of Health on the Health of the Borough for the Year 1920', quoted in Beier, ' "We were as green as grass" ', 472.   [75] Ibid.

[76] Daphne, msf/jm/bl/#38.

[77] NVA, Box 10–7, Objectionable Literature, 88E, 1925, cited in Porter and Hall, *The Facts of Life*, 258.

about VD, and, by the Second World War, provided with a source of condoms. Walter spread a bunch of blown-up condoms all around the army canteen:

I remember in Germany when I was in the army I found a big box of them, big as this table, full of them, so of course . . . I blew all these French letters up in the canteen, you've never seen anything like it in your life, there was French letters everywhere![78]

When Felicity was a Wren she would have to 'pull [her] pants down' because 'they used to always be doing these free from infections inspections because er, they'd want to keep everybody healthy'. She also saw 'big adverts on the wall warning you not to be promiscuous. And at the bottom it told you where to go at the hospital'.[79]

'I WONDERED WHATEVER WAS WRONG WITH ME':[80] NARRATIVES OF SEXUAL IGNORANCE

Despite the proliferation of information about birth control, both contemporary voices and retrospective accounts claim that very little information was available, that they felt confused and unable to make informed birth control choices. Stories of ignorance dominate the historical record. Almost all aspects of sex are reported as having been mysterious. Many accounts focus on adolescence; women in particular revealed themselves as unprepared for the corporeal changes associated with puberty, and the shock of such developments.[81] One respondent, who grew up in care in Cardiff, had a particularly traumatic experience of menarche, but the horror of suddenly finding oneself bleeding was common:[82]

Eleven years of age I was and the foster mother said 'Somebody have wet their knickers', she said 'Is it you Mary?' 'No miss, not me.' 'Well who is it? Well if nobody will own up', she said 'get in a line yeah'—we had just come home from school—'get in the line, you', she said 'and give me your knickers'. And we was all in this line now and I looked at mine and there was blood on mine, so I was in the queue now and I started to cry and then Miss Jenkins, the maid . . . 'What are you crying for?' 'I didn't do it I don't know where it come from, I didn't do it' (laughs). 'Get back over there', she said to me, and she took me to the linen cupboard and she said to me 'Don't be so silly', she said 'you've become a woman', she said to me, I said 'I don't know where it come from'. 'Now let me show you',

[78] Walter, bc2#20.   [79] Felicity, msf/jm/bl/#37.   [80] Bertha, bc3ox#41.
[81] Clephane, *Towards Sex Freedom*, 232; Chesser, *Love without Fear*, 12; Tait, *Diseases of Women*, 51–5; Bertrand Russell, *Marriage and Morals*, 58; M. Davies, *Maternity*. See also e.g. Sutton, 'We Didn't Know Aught', 22–7, 33–50; E. Ross, *Love and Toil*, 100; E. Roberts, *A Woman's Place*, 15–19; ead., *Women and Families*, 59–62; Williamson, ' "Getting Off at Loftus" ', 9–10; John Burnett, *Destiny Obscure*, 26–31; Anon., 'Reflections of an Abortionist', 116–17; Chinn, *They Worked All Their Lives*, 143–4; Alexander, 'The Mysteries and Secrets of Women's Bodies'; Klein, *Samples from English Cultures*, i. 65.
[82] On the traumatic onset of puberty for girls see e.g. Humphries, Mack, and Perks, *A Century of Childhood*, 157; Strange, 'The Assault on Ignorance', 251–2.

and she gave me a linen bag and there was six towels in there and they were terry towelling, and there was a loop on each end of the terry towelling—you fold it up, and she gave me a belt, and 'You will loop this loop onto the belt, back and front', and she said 'wear that', she said, and she said 'Change it', she said 'night and morning'. And 'You're to have a bucket to wash them all out after (pause). Terry towelling, and hang 'em on the line out the backyard'. Oh, I'll never forget. It frightened me to death when I saw that—'cause we were lining up because somebody smelt knickers—they'd peed their knickers—and there was this blood on mine! God, I'd just come home from school. I never forgot it. We were really innocent in them days—they didn't tell you—teach you sex or nothing in the schools, in them days, no—so she had me in the linen cupboard and she told me all about it, she said 'Don't talk, don't talk to any boys and keep away from the boys, and don't tell the girls what you—what's the matter with you', she said. She said 'but you keep these six terry towels in this little linen bag and', and she said 'when you come from home from school', she said 'wash them out and put them on the line'. I had to boil them in the bucket and all . . . yeah, on the stove, oh God . . . aye. I thought I was going to have a hiding![83]

Men also frequently remembered the lack of information available to them as teenagers. William, son of a deep-sea diver, born in 1902, recalled that: 'nobody told me anything . . . your parents never told you nothing like that years ago. That was a topic that was taboo. Nature come, just the same.'[84] Stan Dickens's autobiography recalled that his father, like most,

could not bring himself to tell me anything outright about the subject . . . He tried to tell me there were certain habits cultivated by sinful boys that must be avoided at all costs lest I end a physical or mental wreck . . . My father never warned me about girls . . . had he done so it would have involved him telling me about physical relationships between the sexes, and most parents shied from such embarrassing talk . . . some boys waited in fear and trepidation for what might follow from fumbling a girl.'[85]

Narratives of ignorance also frequently claimed that bewilderment might last long after the initial stages of puberty up to and including marriage itself:

I didn't know where a baby come from, I didn't, and I didn't know what had to happen before you had the baby. My husband knew most of it, and then he had to tell me and that was it.[86]

A pharmacist in Torquay also recalled having to provide basic information to honeymooning couples: 'I have advised many a person about when they have come down on honeymoon to Torquay, what to do. Remarkable! People would come down, and they didn't know what the devil it all meant.'[87] Nicky Leap and Billie Hunter's oral history interviews with midwives and nurses found that stories of ignorance dominated personal accounts despite the chosen profession of the respondents. One nurse contrasted her ignorance of sex and pregnancy with the

[83] Elizabeth, bc3sw#12. She grew up in a children's home in Cardiff.
[84] William, bc3ox#37.   [85] Dickens, *Bending the Twig*, 119–20.   [86] Eileen, bc2#22.
[87] S. Anderson, ' "The most important place in the history of British birth control" ', 24.

responsibility she was given to look after a girl who was in labour:

This story will make you laugh! It was about 1924. I was on night duty . . . I had no idea where a baby came from. I was twenty-one. I had no idea where a baby came from or how it got there, or anything! I mean, I just thought they came! Any rate Sister came back, and she said, 'Well, I'll show you what to do to get her ready to have her baby' . . . It's interesting because when I saw that baby coming, I really couldn't believe it. You know, I thought, 'Oooh, I wonder how it comes out of there?' . . . So that was the first baby I saw being born and I was ever so interested. But I couldn't work out how it got there even then! When I think of how daft I was! I really was silly, you know! But then, if you don't really know about men and boys at the time, well, then you don't really know, do you? Well, at the time I thought that they must have been kissing and cuddling. Well, that's OK. I don't see how that's going to bring a baby![88]

The evidence for ignorance does not only come from memoirs and oral histories. It is also a feature of contemporary sources, diaries, surveys, and observations. As early as 1880 the *British Medical Journal* decried the 'complete ignorance regarding the sexual organs and sexual functions' deliberately inculcated among young people and called for sex education in schools.[89] Similar anxieties about the paucity of reliable information fuelled education movements throughout the first half of the twentieth century (and continue today).[90] Letters to women's magazines revealed the frustrated attempts women made to acquire knowledge: one reader reported that her mother, in response to a request for information, 'was very shocked indeed, and told her that those things were not spoken about' leaving her in 'UTTER IGNORANCE'.[91] Simon Szreter calculates that 12 per cent of the 160 working-class women's letters published in 1915 in Margaret Llewellyn Davies's *Maternity* professed complete sexual ignorance at marriage.[92] Mass-Observation found that the majority of those surveyed were 'left to stumble for themselves upon the 'facts of life' and that 'prolonged ignorance' was not 'by any means rare'. Extreme ignorance, such as the 'discovery of sex facts by getting married' was mentioned by one in every twenty. This was mainly a feature of less well educated women from the older cohorts, such as a 39-year-old grinder's wife (born *c*.1910) who 'didn't know until I was married—all my mother said was 'behave yourself' and none of the details'.[93] Yet ignorance was not by any means confined to the working classes or to older respondents. One woman reported that a young woman of 25 had just come to her 'in a very tearful state' not knowing how her baby was to be born, 'whether it was going to come out under her arms or what'.[94] Another middle-class teacher from Watford had not been told

[88] Leap and Hunter, *The Midwife's Tale*, 79–81.
[89] *British Medical Journal*, 2 (1885), 303–4, quoted in Porter and Hall, *The Facts of Life*, 226–7.
[90] See e.g. Gallichan, *A Text-Book of Sex Education*; Bibby, *Sex Education: A Guide*; Campbell, *Sex Education Books*. On the 'inadequacy of school sex education' in contemporary Britain see e.g. Holland, Ramazanoglu, and Sharpe, *Wimp or Gladiator*, 7–8.
[91] *Woman's World: The Favourite Paper of a Million Homes* (weekly, 2d.), 17 Jan. 1925, quoted in Porter and Hall, *The Facts of Life*, 238.   [92] Szreter, *Fertility, Class and Gender*, 396.
[93] Stanley, *Sex Surveyed*, 83.   [94] Ibid. 82.

anything as her mother 'believed that sex was a dirty subject . . . would not have it mentioned'.[95]

In this context it is not surprising that birth-control knowledge, like information about sex, was also presented as having been hard to come by, both before and after marriage. Mass-Observation's 'Little Kinsey' survey concluded that 'many people are still either ignorant or inadequately informed about birth control', particularly women and those who left school before the age of 14.[96] In 1944 Mass-Observation specifically asked its panel of respondents, 'What is your personal attitude to the dissemination of birth control information and the availability of contraceptive appliances?' The replies from men and women, of various (though predominantly middle) classes from all over Great Britain frequently called for more information to be made available. A statistician and housewife born in 1916 commented that: 'At the moment the whole business is conducted in an "under the counter" manner, and sources of information and appliances are not available for the poorer and less educated people. I don't see how the present problem of the distribution of the birth-rate can be solved without general knowledge of birth control.'[97]

Those campaigning for birth control clinics also saw ignorance as a critical cause of the higher birth rates in working-class communities. In 1927 the annual meeting of the Malthusian League reported that 'millions of poor women still had no idea of how to control conception safely and reliably'. What the movement needed, it was argued, was 'more practical leaflets and clinics'.[98] *The New Generation* ran article after article on the extent of ignorance and need for birth control information, particularly in deprived working-class industrial areas. Miners had the largest families; articles with headlines such as 'Huge Miners' Families', and 'Teach the Miners Birth Control' reported that 'the Miners' wives are desperately anxious to avoid having more children, if only they knew how'.[99] A number of prominent birth control campaigners such as Stella Browne, Frida Laski, and Richard Pennifold toured the country providing lectures on birth control methods to large and receptive audiences at which the ignorance and demand for information was reported as critical. A mother told Stella Browne: 'You've come too late to help me, Comrade, but give me some papers for my girls. I don't want them to have the life I've had', and Richard Pennifold was told: 'We wish you had come years ago.' An elderly woman said: 'I have had nineteen children: six are

[95] Mass-Observation, DR 1048, reply to April 1944 Directive.

[96] Those conducting this survey were particularly concerned about the use of the term birth control, thinking that some of those who may have had some knowledge of family limitation practices answered negatively, as they did not understand the term or use it to describe contraceptive behaviours. Stanley, *Sex Surveyed*, 95–7.

[97] Mass-Observation, DR 1346, reply to April 1944 Directive.

[98] 'Report of the Annual Meeting', *The New Generation* (Jan. 1927), 3; *The New Generation* (Apr. 1927), 45, both quoted in Soloway, *Birth Control and the Population Question*, 205–6.

[99] *The New Generation*, 6/12 (Dec. 1927), 133; *The New Generation*, 8/4 (Apr. 1928), 38; *The New Generation*, 8/1 (Jan. 1929), 1; *The New Generation*, 8/3 (Mar. 1929), 25.

living; I buried eight with consumption. I wish I had only known of birth control before; I would not have had them, and been a better woman for it.'[100]

Oral history testimony confirms this image of contraceptive bewilderment. A great many respondents presented themselves at the start of the interview as having been ignorant of any method of birth control or any means by which their fertility could be reduced. Almost all, in fact, during the interview revealed the nature of the contraceptive behaviour actually practised. This emphasis on ignorance varied in degree among interviewees but was exhibited by the great majority. Some spent much of the interview denying all knowledge of family limitation practices before finally revealing relevant actions they had taken. Others simply emphasized what they did not know about, rather than mentioning the practices they were familiar with. Some were forthcoming with information about some methods, and failed to mention other methods that were known about and/or used until much later in the interview. Beatrice, who worked behind the bar of a pub, and her husband Jack, who was a miner, emphasized that birth control methods were not known to be available:

So what could you do to make sure you didn't get pregnant again?

Didn't do anything. Wasn't like it is today, is it? There was no pills about, no contraceptives was there? . . . No, I was rather ignorant those days, not like they are today, mind.

I find it amazing you managed to have such a small family, if you say you didn't know anything like they do today.

Oh, Jack didn't have such knowledge them days as they have today, the kids can tell you more than you know, now.[101]

Phyllis presented herself as ignorant of most methods of birth control; even those she had heard of were mysterious and unfamiliar to her at that time:

Did you try to have more children?

Well, we didn't take any precautions, 'cos we didn't know anything in them days, just had what came . . .

I think it's very interesting, the way people started having smaller families.

(pause) Yeah, I, well I don't know why, because I'm sure they didn't know an—well, I don't know. We were never told how not to have them like they are these days. I mean—not to have the Pill, and—what's the other thing they use? (pause) Condoms. That's it. I mean I didn't know what—well, I don't think any of 'em did.

Did you know about French letters?

I'd heard of them, but I didn't know what they were. (laughs) I don't think my husband even did at the time. N-now I have heard of them, but, we didn't bother . . .[102]

---

[100] Stella Browne, 'My Tour in Monmouthshire', *The New Generation*, 3/1 (Jan. 1924), 8; Richard Pennifold, 'A Birth Control Mission', *The New Generation*, 8/5 (May 1929), 50.
[101] Beatrice and Jack, bc3sw#5.   [102] Phyllis, bc3ox#17.

Thus the overwhelming impression is that, for all sections of British society, throughout the first half of the twentieth century, information about sex was scarce and as a consequence practical knowledge of birth control methods was limited and difficult to obtain. During the first half of the twentieth century reports of naivety dominate narratives from all sources.[103] Despite the prevalence of this theme it is tempting to discount these accounts and conclude that knowledge is deliberately concealed by embarrassed interviewees, or that memories have been tainted by subsequent developments in sexual cultures, and that even contemporary stories were cherry-picked for a particular purpose, for example, to illustrate the need for birth control clinics. Given the actual extent of birth control use the conclusion that ignorance was exaggerated would appear irrefutable. However, while there is evidence to suggest that stories of bewilderment were sometimes exaggerated, it is important to recognize the truths that lay behind them. While ignorance was not always as complete as many claimed, a closer analysis of these stories reveals important aspects of the process of sexual enlightenment: in stressing ignorance respondents drew attention to the difficulties of obtaining, interpreting, and using the material which existed. Their ignorance might not have been literal, but their experience of ignorance was very real.

'SUPPRESSED AND HUSHED UP':[104] THE DIFFICULTIES OF ACCESSING BIRTH CONTROL KNOWLEDGE

Despite the apparent prevalence of birth control information, the proliferation of material does not mean that individuals found such material easy to get hold of. A range of practical problems prevented many from obtaining advice. In saying that they knew nothing about birth control methods, individuals drew attention to the obstacles between themselves and enlightenment.

Books about sex and birth control, even best-sellers such as Marie Stopes's *Married Love*, were not easy to buy. Ernest remembered that it was not on sale at W. H. Smith's and had instead to be obtained through mail order, sent in an unlabelled brown paper package.[105] As Lesley Hall notes, 'sex literature often had to be sought in sordid 'rubber goods' shops'.[106] Few libraries stocked sex and marriage manuals, and those that did frequently kept them off the open shelves, in the librarian's office.[107] By 1935, however, the nurse at the Aberdeen clinic proudly reported that Stopes's books were displayed in the window of the bookseller in the

---

103 Beier, ' "We were as green as grass" ', 475–8, argues that the amount of information about sex and birth control available to ordinary families changed dramatically after the middle of the twentieth century; Cook, *The Long Sexual Revolution*, 168–82, also concludes that information became more readily available, but asserts that ignorance was not differentiated by class or region.

104 Mass-Observation, DR 3587, reply to April 1944 Directive.   105 Ernest, bc3sw#2.

106 Porter and Hall, *The Facts of Life*, 257.   107 Ibid. 259.

main shopping street and that he had agreed to put the clinic 'cards on show right away'.[108] However, such books, even as they became more widely available in the 1930s and more likely to be sold by respectable booksellers, might remain prohibitively expensive. Eustace Chesser's *Love without Fear* was priced at 12s. 6d. in 1942 in order to 'keep it out of younger people's hands, such as typists and others'.[109] Hence most of those who recalled reading such works came across wellthumbed copies as they circulated in the workplace, barracks, or playground, or discovered them hidden in drawers and under beds. Such cursory and public perusal provided only a general awareness of the possibility of family limitation but did not necessarily help the reader discover necessary details about methods or where to obtain them. Some respondents had only had a brief look at such material:

I can't say I've ever read one. But I've—I've had a quick look through, and back again, you know, and put it—put it away.'[110]

[He] had a quick decco at it before he gave it to me . . . they did give me a bit of an insight, but as I say, I didn't go into it the way I should have done.[111]

Appliances themselves were also difficult to acquire. Although Ethel Elderton reported in 1911 that, in Accrington, 'appliances for the limitation of the family are displayed in the most barefaced manner on the counters of local chemists' shops so that no one can miss seeing them',[112] the majority of chemists or barbers kept their range of contraceptives out of sight behind the counter:[113]

They weren't openly on sale like they are now, I mean you have, er, probably go to the barber's or somebody like that, I mean get them underhand. Nothing was above board like it is today—you can go into the chemist's shop and there they are emblazoned—you—you pick what you want and that's it, but in those days, no, there wasn't anything like that.[114]

While some, like Rosie's husband, a miner, might go 'to the chemist . . . and talk to them privately sort of thing you know', others might find the chemist ill informed.[115] Sally, who worked at Boots in Blackburn, hadn't heard of Rendall's pessaries the first time she was asked for one:

Did you ever know about Rendall's?

I used to serve them.

Did you?

[108] Margaret Rae to Marie Stopes, 3 Feb. 1935, BL Add. MSS 58604.
[109] Porter and Hall, *The Facts of Life*, 262.   [110] Cecil, bc3ox#40.
[111] Sarah, msf/kf/bl/#30.   [112] Elderton, *Report on the English Birth-Rate*, 35.
[113] S. Anderson, ' "The most important place in the history of British birth control" ', 25. Until the 1960s Boots would not sell condoms, though pessaries were available.
[114] Richard, bc3ox#32.
[115] Rosie, bc2#2. Stuart Anderson interviewed chemists who reported their own ignorance of contraceptives and their inability to provide any advice to those with sexual problems: ' "The most important place in the history of British birth control" ', 24.

On the counter. I had to laugh, one time a girl came in, was a relative of my sister-in-law up Carrington Avenue. And she said 'Have you got any Rendall's?' Well, I thought she—and she said pessaries—I thought she said pastilles. I said 'No.' I said 'The only pastilles we have are barley sugar and lemon.' She said 'I didn't say pastilles.' I said 'What did you say?' She said 'Pessaries.' She was saying it quietly, you see. 'Oh,' I said 'No,' I said. They came to me for one I'd have to tell 'em to go to China or somewhere! (laughs)![116]

One woman wrote to Marie Stopes having written to 'several London chemists . . . but got no reply' and another 'applied at every Chemist in my district' for a Check Pessary as advised by her doctor but had not 'been able to buy one at all'.[117]

Birth control clinics were also poorly advertised and many people remained unaware of their existence. Sometimes innovative measures were taken to attract attention to them. In 1925 Marie Stopes wrote to Naomi Jones enclosing 'some *Chimes of the Times* which have just been published as Christmas cards and if you could get any Abertillery people to send them round, it might make a good form of propaganda'.[118] When clinic attendance dropped in Abertillery Nurse Jones had 6,000 pamphlets printed and 'went from house to house . . . I walked miles and distributed them myself also Cwm, Ebbw Vale, Beaufort, Blaina, Nantyglo and as far down as Newport'.[119] The nurse in charge in Aberdeen urged Stopes to invest in 'a good advertisement in our local front page of the evening paper', 'or even a slide in one of our local cinemas' as 'Aberdeen people are slow'.[120] Such action was rarely taken. Marie Stopes informed Nurse Gordon of Cardiff that 'We simply cannot afford to advertise.'[121]

Local authority clinics were hampered from appearing to court all women in a community by Memo 153/MCW, which stipulated that only mothers whose poor health justified the use of birth control could be advised. Consequently, birth control clinics depended on local doctors and health visitors to inform patients of their existence. The clinic at Caerphilly was 'excellently attended', and this was largely because, as Joyce Daniel, the NBCA Area Organizer for South Wales reported, 'the co-operation of the Caerphilly general practitioners is stronger than that in any other place hereabouts, no less than nine having already sent us patients' (after only five sessions).[122] Margaret Pyke, Secretary of the NBCA, replied, over a year later: 'How very good that there are still so many patients. This

---

[116] Sally, msf/kf/bl/#31.　　　　[117] Stopes, *Mother England*, 48, 86.

[118] Stopes to Jones, 16 Dec. 1925, A&M: PP/MCS/D.16.

[119] Jones to Stopes, 14 Sept. 1926, A&M: PP/MCS/C.16.

[120] Margaret Rae to Stopes, 12 Oct. 1934, BL Add. MSS 58603.

[121] Marie Stopes to Florence Gordon, 7 Nov. 1937, BL Add. MSS 58624. After the Second World War *The Times* declined to advertise any of Marie Stopes's clinics or books: see Coldrick, *Dr. Marie Stopes and Press Censorship of Birth Control*, 12–13.

[122] Joyce Daniel report, April 1936, A&M: SA/FPA/A11/9. By contrast, Natalie Higgins has revealed that doctors in Birmingham interpreted the government guidelines narrowly; few women were referred to the established birth-control clinics in that city. Higgins, 'Changing Expectations and Realities of Marriage', 227.

just shows what can be done if local doctors are really helpful.'[123] However, many doctors throughout Britain were opposed to birth control and were unwilling to co-operate with the new clinics, or send patients.[124] Joyce Daniel complained about 'the apathy or antagonism of the local doctors'.[125] Many doctors shied away from providing practical advice to complement their admonitions to avoid pregnancy.[126] As Eva found: 'It took a lot of courage to even ask the doctor how to limit births. And the doctor was as embarrassed as I was. So I wasn't satisfied with what he told me, but I didn't have the nerve to go to another doctor or anything.'[127] In fact, many health professionals did not refer patients to clinics, as they remained unaware of local developments: Medical Officers of Health frequently failed to inform local doctors when a birth control clinic was set up in their district. Joyce Daniel reported, for example, in 1937 that 'the promise he [Dr Greenwood Wilson, of Cardiff] gave me last year to instruct his assistants to send suitable cases to Penarth Clinic was never carried out'.[128] In Monmouthshire the letter written by the Medical Officer of Health, Dr Rocyn Jones, who was adamantly opposed to birth control, explaining that birth control advice could be given out in 'dire necessity' at five designated ante-natal centres, was not received by many doctors.[129] Midwives were equally unlikely to provide information. Only in the 1960s did midwifery textbooks first include information on contraception, and the association of midwifery with illegal abortion meant many were anxious to distance themselves from all forms of fertility control.[130] Many couples remained unaware of clinics, even when one existed nearby. In Bolton during the 1930s, a birth control clinic opened at the end of the street where Sarah lived. Yet she remained unaware of its purpose and was 'left' to her 'own devices' by her nurses, doctors and midwives:

I didn't know much about it, even it was the end of our street almost, but I didn't know much about it . . . the nurses at the clinic, never pushed anything like that, and . . . they never mentioned the cap to us . . . They did not give you advice in those days. You were left to your own devices. It was only if, if you'd a bit more up here (points to her head) and you got a Marie Stopes book and you read the book that you got to know anything. They'd never the doc—the doctors, the midwives, they didn't advise you on anything. The only advice that you got . . . because they weren't very knowledgeable, was, how your baby was progressing.[131]

[123] Margaret Pyke to Joyce Daniel, 23 June 1937, A&M: SA/FPA/A11/9.
[124] See e.g. McLaren, *A History of Contraception*, 223; E. Roberts, *A Woman's Place*, 94.
[125] A&M: SA/FPA/A11/2.
[126] See also L. Hall, ' "Somehow very distasteful" ', 558; ead., *Hidden Anxieties*, 1–4; ead., 'A Suitable Job for a Woman'. [127] Eva, bc1#1.
[128] Joyce Daniel to Margaret Pyke, Oct. 1937, A&M: SA/FPA/A11/9.
[129] MAC: SA/FPA/A11/65. Joyce Daniel also reported that a woman sent by her doctor to one of these centres was 'laughed at' and turned away.
[130] Leap and Hunter, *The Midwife's Tale*, 90. Many health visitors were reluctant to become involved in contraceptive matters for similar reasons. [131] Sarah, msf/kf/bl/#30.

Aileen was surprised to learn that birth control advice, as well as maternity services, was provided in a chapel clinic in Caerphilly:

Well, I can't remember that, 'cos I would've gone there if I know. Yeah. Well, I never knew there was a birth control clinic at that time. Good Lord!

. . . There was a baby clinic there, 'cos I used to [take] our Jean there . . . I never knew it was a birth control there. Well, I mean if there was, they would've sent some of us there. Wouldn't they? . . . No! Well then, years ago love, the doctors never told you anything. Not the nurses, none of 'em told you anything.[132]

Thus clinic nurses reported the difficulties many faced in finding out about and locating birth control clinics. As Nurse Gordon told Marie Stopes: 'a patient who came this week had also searched for weeks and then her husband discovered it by accident'.[133] She lamented: 'It is a great pity that we cannot make it more widely known.'[134] Frequently, only chance and perseverance led to the discovery of birth control clinics:

We started hearing vague talk about family planning, and when they were having meal breaks where he worked sometimes they would talk about the babies, because they had babies about the same age as mine. And he came home one day, full of excitement, he said 'Well, I understand that there's a family planning clinic out in Splott and you can just go there—you don't have to be sent by the doctor or anything—you just go there.' So, we had a little talk about it, and I said 'Well I'll go out on the bike and scoot around', because it wasn't advertised in any way. And I went into Railway Street and went up and down and I did spot it.[135]

'WIDELY KNOWN EXCEPT IN VERY REMOTE DISTRICTS SUCH AS WE HAVE LIVED AT':[136] LIMITATIONS IN THE SPREAD OF BIRTH CONTROL

The spread of birth control information was concentrated in particular areas. Many, in stressing their own ignorance, sought to draw comparison with those they felt were better informed. The documentary record is full of complaints that working people were not provided with the knowledge or services easily obtained by the middle classes. 'Sources of information and appliances are not available for the poorer and less educated people' reported one Mass-Observation panellist;[137] another called for 'an increase in knowledge of birth control and biology' to

---

132 Aileen, bc3sw#14.
133 Florence Gordon to Marie Stopes, 18 Mar. 1938, BL Add. MSS 58625.
134 Florence Gordon to Marie Stopes, 5 Nov. 1937, BL Add. MSS 58624.
135 Eva, bc1#1, went to Stopes's Cardiff clinic in 1938.   136 Stopes, *Mother England*, 82.
137 Mass-Observation, DR, 1346, reply to April 1944 Directive.

'reduce the profligacy' of 'the least beneficial sections of the community'.[138] 'I am not being snobbish', wrote another, who worried that the 'disparity in knowledge about birth control' had resulted in 'the worst part of the population, the least valuable and intelligent' reproducing 'disproportionately'.[139] Another confessed 'blue blooded snob' presented the disparity more diplomatically: 'It would seem only fair that birth control knowledge should be available . . . to those unable to afford large families.'[140]

Working-class voices also called for the democratization of information: 'The upper class have had Birth control long enough', complained one 'working-class Mother'; another, a man, charged the 'wealthier classes' with oppressing the poor by putting birth control information out of their reach: 'I don't begrudge wealth but I do its value of knowledge.'[141] Oral history testimony similarly contrasted ignorance with that of the middle classes who possessed both the resources and the nous to obtain information:

Well, they seemed to know more about it, that's what I should say, they—they knew more about those kinds of things and uh, than—than us common working people . . . They read more books, they—they had the access, they—they—they were—they were more educated, that's all I can say, they were—they—they knew how to go about it. It was reading.[142]

We were ignorant to all that, you had to have money. We were working-class.[143]

Moreover, some contemporary observers suspected that, despite the fact that clinics were predominantly set up in working-class districts and targeted poor parts of the country, they were nevertheless disproportionately attended by better-off mothers.[144] Mass-Observation, however, argued that ignorance might equally be found among middle-class people, who did not have the benefit of local birth control clinics: 'the private middle-class clinic is more difficult to find than the public one'.[145] The need for more information for the middle classes was recognized by the Birth Control Advisory Bureau, set up in 1928 to provide birth control advice to 'middle-class women who, while not wishing to attend one of the free clinics for poor women at the same time do not wish to pay a Harley Street fee'.[146] Gerald and Esme also felt deprived of the knowledge available to those living in the poor districts of London who could go to birth control clinics:

ESME   I don't suppose they existed, er, I mean, apart from in the East End of London and that kind of thing, you know . . . I can't imagine birth control clinic in Cobham, can you? (laughs)

---

[138] Mass-Observation, DR, 2751, reply to April 1944 Directive.
[139] Mass-Observation, DR, 2770, reply to April 1944 Directive.
[140] Mass-Observation, DR, 2749, reply to April 1944 Directive.
[141] Stopes, *Mother England*, 82–3, 99.   [142] Sarah, msf/kf/bl/#30.   [143] Nora, bc2#1.
[144] See e.g. Charles, *The Practice of Birth Control*, 126.
[145] Mass-Observation, *Britain and her Birth-Rate*, 201.
[146] Hooper, *The Voice of Experience*, 9.

GERALD   No. (laughs)
ESME   No, I don't think so.
GERALD   Think of a very proper area and very posh houses and people a bit lah-di-dah
          and the nice avenues![147]

Those living in rural areas saw themselves as particularly poorly served by birth control propaganda. Ethel Elderton commented in 1914 that in towns, even among the poor, 'knowledge of preventive means is fairly well spread' whereas 'In rural areas knowledge is not so widely spread and opportunities for purchase are fewer'.[148] Joyce Daniel had to remind the NBCA committee that the narrow Welsh valleys meant clinics might be several hours apart despite their apparent geographical proximity.[149] A university student working as a farm labourer commented on the paucity of contraceptive knowledge and consequent need for birth control clinics 'in country districts' where 'so few of the people read and many hundreds and thousands will never have heard of Dr. Marie Stopes'.[150]

'WHO THE HELL IS HE WRITING TO IN FRANCE?':[151] EUPHEMISMS AND THE INTERPRETATION OF BIRTH CONTROL INFORMATION

The use of euphemisms was frequently cited as contributing to a continued sense of innocence. Obscure terminology hampered the comprehension of various forms of information about sex and birth control. Not only was word of mouth frequently euphemistic but so too were books, adverts, newspaper reports, and educative warnings against pre-marital pregnancy and masturbation. Thus, in part, the tendency of testimony to stress ignorance served to draw attention to the impact that a general sense of naivety and lack of basic sexual knowledge had on the absorption of birth control advice. Isolated moments when snippets of information about contraception were relayed were presented as confusing rather than enlightening. Such incidents were used to illustrate the realities of naivety. While silence was not absolute, for many, euphemisms remained oblique; without the context in which to decode it successfully, advice might remain indecipherable.

Scientific and encyclopedic references were frequently impossible to understand: 'Books! Scientific books . . . Words like fallopian tubes and spermatozoa—just words! I thought spermatozoa crept out and crept in while both parties were asleep!'[152] Literature and the Bible were equally confusing. As Jonathan Rose has

---

[147] Gerald and Esme, msf/kf/ht/#9.   [148] Elderton, *Report on the English Birth-Rate*, 34–5.
[149] 'A Daniel who fought for a family plan', *Western Mail*, 33356 (12 Oct. 1976), 4.
[150] Mass-Observation, DR 2699, reply to April 1944 Directive.
[151] Edward, bc3ox#15.
[152] Joan Grant, *Time Out of Mind* (Arthur Baker, 1956), 123, quoted in Cook, *The Long Sexual Revolution*, 198.

pointed out, 'the sexual themes' in some novels 'may seem obvious, but without the appropriate frame, the reader will not know how to decode the allusions'.[153] Mary Bentley's father confiscated her copy of *Jude the Obscure*. When she read it she still 'didn't understand', and Margaret Wharton read *The Well of Loneliness* 'without having the faintest idea what it was about'. Ethel Manin, despite having 'raked the Bible for information' and having 'made endless research' into 'encyclopaedias and home medical works' found that everything remained 'beyond our comprehension'. The Bible's description that 'Esau came forth from his mother's belly' was 'unspeakably dreadful'.[154] Even terms such as contraception and birth control were not commonly understood.[155] First used in America in 1886, contraception was not a widely used term in Britain until after the First World War and family limitation was more frequently referred to as 'pre-ventive checks', 'artificial checks', or 'Malthusianism'.[156] One interviewee, Sarah, whose mother was a weaver in Preston, 'ferreted' in her parent's drawers and found 'Aristotle's Works of Nature . . . tucked away amongst the towels'. She, however, 'didn't learn anything' despite the fact that 'it told you when what period of the month you could have it and have a child'. Instead she loved the pages which showed 'these babies curled up' although she 'didn't understand that they were babies in the womb' and 'tittered' over it with her friend. It provided no enlightenment because 'I wasn't serious enough to realize'; instead it was simply 'funny to me'.[157]

Leslie Paul's autobiography is especially eloquent on the oblique nature of sexual information. Living in such a 'curiously sexless world' meant that sexual material went unrecognized: 'I read about love in the romantic novels without ever suspecting it had anything to do with sex', and when a friend finally told him the mechanics of sexual intercourse 'the fantastic acrobatics' were disbelieved as ridiculous: 'beneath contempt'.[158] When he was warned by a preacher against 'great temptations and dangers' that would cause blindness, his friends were unsure whether they were meant to avoid telling dirty stories, going to the cinema, or smoking. Warnings against VD also confused Lyn, whose father was a herbalist. Taken by her mother to an educational film, in Blackburn, this rare example of a parent attempting some sexual education of her daughter was too isolated an incident to be useful. It instilled new anxieties about sexual relationships and a

---

[153] Rose, *The Intellectual Life of the British Working Classes*, 210.   [154] Ibid. 209–11.

[155] Of those surveyed by Mass-Observation in 1949, 29% did not know what the phrase 'birth control' meant, or gave a false definition: Stanley, *Sex Surveyed*, 95.

[156] Bland, *Banishing the Beast*, 191; Soloway, *Birth Control and the Population Question*, p. xiv.

[157] Sarah, msf/kf/bl/#30. In 1918 Sheffield Educational Settlement sought to investigate the cul-tural literacy of the working classes in Sheffield and surveyed a sample of 816 adult manual workers chosen as representative in terms of age, sex, and income strata: 20% recognized 'Aristotle' as the author of a work known as *Masterpiece*—which was an anonymous and oblique collection of infor-mation about pregnancy and childbirth, in wide circulation since the sixteenth century. See Jonathan Rose, *The Intellectual Life of the British Working Classes*, 206–7.   [158] Paul, *First Love*, 19–20.

misunderstanding of the dangers of kissing:

I remember my Mum taking me to lectures on venereal disease in King George's Hall until you even thought—you were frightened if you kissed a boy you'd probably—you would happen get venereal disease, as you really had quite a lot of fear put in you.[159]

Even an agony aunt, as late as 1930, responded euphemistically to earnest enquiries in the magazine, *Woman's Life*:

Readers often write and ask me, 'What does such and such form of love-making mean?' My dears, whatever it is beyond kissing, it means only one thing. It is just a step nearer the end nature had in mind when she made men and women. And that is why all such endearments should be kept until after marriage.[160]

Popular culture, while perhaps being cruder, was no more illuminating.[161] Popular songs were riddled with sexual jokes and innuendoes.[162] Cliff Edwards sang about 'giving it to Mary with love' and Billy Cotton lamented the loss of his yo-yo: 'the only thing which charmed his married life':

> I'm going to give it to Mary with love.
> I've got something that she's fondest of.
> Now I know that she, has had it before,
> and Mary's the gal that all the fellas adore.
> I'll let her take it, right in her hand,
> 'cos I know she'll stroke it so grand.
> Like Jack and Jill we'll both get a thrill,
> when I give it to Mary with love.[163]

> I had it when I left the house at half past ten,
> I had it in me hand all right.
> I showed it to a woman at the corner then.
> —it filled her with delight—
> The wife will want to play with it, when I get home,
> but I can't find it—oh! no!—
> She'll take the only course,
> and sue for a divorce,
> when she finds I've gone and lost me little . . . yo-yo![164]

---

159 Lyn, msf/kf/bl/#1. Julian Carter argues that American sex education literature similarly deliberately blurred the relationship between kissing and the spread of syphilis by hiding the key fact that one of the kissers had already to be infected. See 'Birds, Bees and Venereal Disease', 228–9.

160 Jordan, *Agony Columns*, 100–1.

161 Many presumably learnt to giggle knowingly at jokes and innuendoes without fully understanding their meaning. Such behaviour did not aid further elucidation or enlightenment.

162 Nott, *Music for the People*, 221–3. Some risqué songs were banned by the BBC, though they continued to be played in the cinema and in dance halls.

163 Cliff Edwards, 'I'm going to give it to Mary with love' (1933).

164 Billy Cotton and his band, 'I've gone and lost my little yoyo' (1932).

George Formby consistently made phallic allusions to his ukulele.[165] In 'With my little ukulele in my hand' (1933) the last section even uses the concept of sexual naivety to explain his mystification at the power of his ukulele to attract girls. Ignorance is used to describe his confusion at the 'come ons' of his girlfriend, his inability to learn anything more from a book, and his surprise when he begets a son endowed with his own ukulele:

> So with me little ukulele in me hand,
> I took a stroll with Jane along the sand.
> We walked along for miles without a single care or frown,
> but when we reached the sand hill she said, 'come on let's sit down'.
> I felt so shy and bashful sitting there.
> 'Cos the things she said I didn't understand.
> She said, 'your love just turns me dizzy, come along big boy get busy',
> but I kept me ukulele in me hand—Yes sir!—I kept me ukulele in me hand.
>
> Made up my mind that I'd get wed some eighteen months ago.
> I also bought a book about the things you want to know.
> But just about a week ago I got an awful fright,
> I had to get dressed quickly in the middle of the night.
> And with me little ukulele in me hand,
> I ran along the road for doctor Brand.
> It didn't take him long to get his little bag of tools,
> I held his hat and coat and let him have me book of rules.
> Out of the bedroom door he looked and smiled,
> Said, 'come inside and see your wife and child'.
> My heart it jumped with joy, I could see it was a boy,
> for he had a ukulele in his hand—oh baby!—he had a ukulele in his hand.

Information about birth control was just as euphemistically presented. Wyn, whose husband was a panel beater at the Morris car works in Oxford, remembered listening to her mother-in-law discussing a 'johnny': 'I thought that so-and-so was a man. Apparently (laughing) it was a condom'.[166] Many recalled the obfuscation caused by euphemisms and their initial inability to decipher the meanings behind the phrases used. Peter, who served with the Marines during the war, wondered 'what the Hell's a French letter' and why it would be sent 'through the post'; Edward, an engineer, also 'couldn't understand . . . the blokes talking' and wondered 'who the hell is he writing to in France'.[167] Phyllis, who was working as a bookkeeper, was warned that 'if you went out with an American they had the French letters . . . As I never went out with an American I never found out.'[168] Similarly Edna answered a question about the extent of her knowledge with a blunt statement that she didn't know anything. She illustrated this with an

---

[165] Nott, *Music for the People*, 214.   [166] Cecil and Wyn, bc3ox#40.
[167] Peter, msf/kf/bl/#26; Edward, bc3ox#15.   [168] Phyllis, msf/kf/bl/#5.

example of a woman who told her to 'take the kettle off the fire before it boils', a euphemism she did not understand:

So did you know of any means to prevent having children?
No, I didn't know. Huh! I remember coming up to tell the woman—I've forgotten who she was but—'Oh, look I've got this baby only seven months old or eight months' or something like that. And I said 'and now I'm gonna have another one'. 'Oh', she said, 'You want to take the kettle off the fire before it boils over', she said. I didn't know what she meant. Well, I never, or what—'What've a boiling kettle got to do with a baby?' And do you know it was months before I realized what it was she was talking about! (laughs).[169]

The great advantage, however, of euphemistic language was that it permitted and provided a humorous and inexplicit means of discussing family limitation. Withdrawal and condoms were by far the most commonly referred to methods of contraception, and, as will be explored below, were far the most likely methods to have been tried and regularly adopted. In part, the greater awareness of these methods can be attributed to the euphemistic terms which facilitated their widespread discussion. Eva, who worked in her husband's shoe-repair shop in Blackburn, did not mind talking about withdrawal—because to talk about 'being careful' was to discuss it 'in a nice way':

And so did you discuss it?
Yeah, uh, just in a nice sort of way, like, 'We'll have to be careful'. We always said that, you know, and we were—but, we—after nine years we were delighted when Sandra were come.[170]

The use of euphemisms, however, also blurred the distinction between types of method. Such euphemisms have puzzled historians attempting to work out which methods were used. It is likely that similar confusions plagued individuals seeking to decipher the meaning of coded references. The awareness that one could restrict one's family size by being careful, using restraint, using common sense, getting off early, tying a knot in it, or driving a car without petrol were suggestive of abstinence, withdrawal, rhythm methods, use of contraceptive appliances, and non-coital forms of love-making. Thus Eva described 'living very carefully' as both going 'without sex' and 'not going all the way'.[171] William, 'had to just be very very careful . . . had to have it at the right times' or withdraw.[172] By 'being careful' Catherine meant using 'French letters, or sometimes you perhaps wouldn't, actually have intercourse. You might do a bit of foreplay.'[173] 'Being careful' should perhaps be viewed not as a euphemism describing a specific birth control method, but rather a description of a contraceptive strategy, a term which encompassed a range of practices—it described a general carefulness in the approach to sex which could mean using withdrawal on certain occasions, thinking about the timing of intercourse at other times, or reducing its frequency overall.[174]

---

[169] Edna, bc3sw#16.   [170] Eva, msf/kf/bl/#9.   [171] Eva, msf/kf/bl/#9.
[172] William, msf/kf/ht/#24.   [173] Catherine, msf/kf/ht/#1.
[174] See Szreter and Fisher, 'Sexuality, Love and Marriage in England, 1918–1960'.

The euphemistic nature of sexual information meant that couples were left to interpret advice by themselves; facts about methods were insinuated and as a result individuals did not feel informed, despite being able to practise birth control. Ignorance was, therefore, quite justifiably recorded, despite exposure to a wide variety of information. Stressing ignorance was a convenient way of drawing attention to the difficulties of acquiring information from the euphemistic, coded, and even inaccurate sources available.

'THEY USED TO USE LEECHES TO GET RID OF THE BABY':[175] THE SPREAD OF FALSE INFORMATION

The spread of misinformation provides a further dimension to the experience of ignorance; without the ability to distinguish between truth and fiction, respondents quite justifiably did not know what information to trust and thus remained 'ignorant':

Oh, I think to start with it was sort of from one to the other in the school playground. You weren't told anything about—your mums never told you anything and you couldn't get hold of any books in any case. I think it was sort of, part truth, part distorted—as I found out when I was older—but that's how it all started, word of mouth in the playground.[176]

One woman wrote to Marie Stopes because 'people give you all kinds of advice until you don't know realy [*sic*] who to beleive [*sic*]'.[177] Information was sometimes clearly exaggerated or likely to be false. Gothic tales of dangerous abortions were particularly prevalent, especially among working class respondents from south Wales:

Two of my friends . . . took this Slippery Elm thing, and they were very ill after that. Yeah. It's like, um, it's like as if you're taking paraffin liquid, you know. It's a very thick and it were like green. But they call it Slippery Elm. What it was made out of I don't know. And there was a couple of my friends couldn't have children because they done that. Yeah. It must've done something to the lining of the womb.[178]

My one friend used to take gin with um something, and they used to put it in the oven and when it used to go down they used to drink it. It was like a sedative to make you go to the toilet and—used to get rid of it that way. Then there was slippery elm and the leech. The leech you'd put inside you and then it would attack the womb, and open the womb up, and of course you'd lose the baby then. I know one of my aunties done it.[179]

Slippery elm (which was not a vile green corrosive liquid paraffin, but a piece of bark) and gin were widely reported abortifacients. No other reference to use of the

---

175 Rosie, bc1#2.   176 Hetty, bc3ox#12.   177 Stopes, *Mother England*, 138.
178 Aileen, bc3sw#14.   179 Rosie, bc1#2.

leech has been found.[180] Given the range of methods, individuals faced with an unwanted pregnancy did not feel adequately informed about options with regard to abortion, despite having heard a considerable amount about the subject. The awareness that some methods were apocryphal and dangerous tainted all forms of information which might otherwise have been trusted.

The degree to which information was relayed through illicit, whispered, or anecdotal sources affected the extent to which they were trusted. As one of Stopes's male correspondents wrote of the information he had gleaned from the 'smutty talk' of army colleagues, 'I have grave doubts as to the advisability of making use of it.'[181] Another wrote to her directly 'to be sure it was your advice, as there are so many things advertised in the papers'.[182]

In this context, the contradictions between the various forms of information regarding contraceptive methods and devices should be seen as actively contributing to the continuation of confusion and ignorance. Messages about family limitation were not uniform. Rather, various forms of birth control information were forced to coexist uneasily, often in competition with each other. Most obvious was the opposition between the 'traditional' outlets of information—local abortionists, rubber shops, hygienic stores, and mail-order companies—and the new 'scientific' birth control advice manuals and clinics. Chemists and pharmacies occupied an uneasy position in between. Providers of birth control information attempted to give legitimacy to their own endeavours with reference to each other, and through the borrowing of particular vocabulary. Key words, such as scientific, hygienic, and racial, appeared within various forms of advice and acquired multiple meanings.[183] Material also consistently referred to the work of competitors: a rival's methods might be denigrated as dangerous, unreliable, or disreputable, or alternatively a spurious endorsement would be claimed from another authority. To Marie Stopes's annoyance, rogue traders peppered her name all over their products. For example, when she stationed her clinic in Bolton she complained to the police that a leaflet for aphrodisiacs and 'corrective medicines pour les dames' had printed her name on the top left-hand corner of the letter heading. 'This kind of thing has happened before', she wrote. 'These traders follow us with their objectionable literature.' She added that her project was to do 'all she can to get rid of this type of trader'.[184] She chastised the Medical Trading Company for allowing her name to appear on the same page as an advertisement for female pills and 'implying that I recommend the spring rim'. She insisted the advertisement was 'at once revise[d] so that it cannot be understood as if I recommend this particular article'.[185] She was also horrified in 1944 to discover that her preferred supplier of

[180] L. A. Parry claimed that it had been tried in France, without success: *Criminal Abortion*, 27.
[181] Quoted in Porter and Hall, *The Facts of Life*, 250.   [182] Stopes, *Mother England*, 12.
[183] See Blécourt, 'Cultures of Abortion in The Hague', 202.
[184] Marie Stopes & Co. to Bolton Police, 5 July 1932, A&M: PP/MCS/C.20.
[185] Marie Stopes to the Medical Trading Company, 11 May 1927, BL Add. MSS 58640.

caps also sold appliances to rubber goods shops, and 'use[d] the name "Pro-race" (which I had made world-famous in my writings and Clinics) for all sorts of things which I had not only *not* designed, but most actively disapprove'.[186] Stopes's own energies were frequently devoted to attacking the methods of other suppliers, thereby adding to the confusion; her comments, which professed 'to discriminate between the many unreliable and harmful Preventive Methods and those which are entirely safe and wholesome', in fact ignited a general fear that while some methods were safe many others were not.[187] The wrangling between birth control providers limited the ability of users to trust or accept any circulating information. A sense of ignorance would have been heightened for those who heard Marie Stopes declaring that cervical caps caused cancer, excepting her own 'pro-race' version.[188] Such information tended to taint all methods as risky or unreliable and suggested that considerable research was necessary to obtain sufficient knowledge to use contraception successfully and safely.

Advice was not only frequently known or suspected to be false, it was also likely to be incomplete. Information needed to use methods successfully was complex and not necessarily detailed in the sources available. Abortion again provides the clearest instance of this. A sense of ignorance was reinforced by difficulties in acquiring information about dose and preparation usually absent from euphemistic sources, such as carefully worded adverts or neighbourly recommendations. While many had heard that gin might induce a miscarriage, how much gin to take, whether or not a hot bath was also required, and whether the gin itself should also be hot remained a mystery. Similar doubts ensured that few felt fully informed about how to use penny royal, slippery elm, or quinine. Muriel was advised by her sister to take 'bitter something' and Widow Welch's pills; not knowing quite what to get or how much to take Muriel failed to induce a miscarriage: 'All I took was some Widow Welch's pills, 'cos they say they help to bring you on . . . but it didn't do nothing . . . I don't think I took enough really.'[189]

A close look at the extent of knowledge behind the assertions of ignorance reveals the complex relationship between the existence of information and the experience of innocence. During the first half of the twentieth century sex was not a taboo subject in popular cultural discourses—there was plenty of printed material about sex and popular entertainment; chat and jokes were often highly sexualized. Such material also regularly included references to birth control possibilities and practices. We should not therefore conclude that assertions of complete silence

---

[186] Marie Stopes to C. H. Birkitt, Chief Supplies Division, Rubber Control, Ministry of Supply, 26 May 1944, BL Add. MSS 58639.

[187] Medical Trading Company, *Supplement to Books on Birth Control*, 1927, BL Add. MSS 58640.

[188] Stopes, *Contraception*, 168–206; See also R. Hall, *Marie Stopes. A Biography*, 260. On Stopes's denigration of the methods recommended by rival birth-control providers see Neushul, 'Marie C. Stopes and the Popularization of Birth Control Technology'.

[189] Muriel, bc2#3. Widow Welch's pills had been sold since the eighteenth century. See Brown, 'Female Pills and the Reputation of Iron as an Abortifacient', 292–4. They probably contained iron and a purgative, such as aloes.

were precise or literal. However, by emphasizing 'silence' and speaking of taboos, the historical record draws attention to the ways in which individuals interpreted the information they received. Respondents, by stressing ignorance, emphasized the difficulties they had in deciphering and acting upon such information. The presentation of naivety reveals how individuals reacted to the euphemistic nature of available information; it highlights the contradictory messages and their underhand revelation and secretive exposition. The information available did have an influence on people's awareness of birth control, but its impact was not straightforward. Despite familiarity with contraceptive methods their experience remained one of ignorance. As one Mass-Observation panellist eloquently concluded, the information was there, but a sense of bewilderment was retained, together with confusion about how to act:

Your question goes on to imply that existing methods of birth control are available. Admitted, but how many young couples know of them . . . General information on the subject tends from my knowledge to be suppressed and all existing methods hushed up. With this state of affairs there [*sic*] efficiency can hardly be taken into consideration. I have little faith in existing methods for the simple reason that there is a lack of education and understanding and that what methods of birth control are implied only tend to be brought to nothing instead of budding fruition.[190]

Leslie suggested that, although he knew about contraceptives, his knowledge wasn't sufficient for him to think about using them when courting in the early 1930s in Pontypridd. The structure of his narrative illustrated the experience rather than the reality of ignorance. He initially suggested that he did not know how to avoid pregnancy. Realizing this was not quite true, he corrected himself and tried to convey his sense of ignorance; he 'didn't think of it' because he hadn't been sufficiently 'overwhelmed' by information:

Weren't you worried . . . that she might get pregnant?

No no, I wasn't, I didn't think of it—we didn't know—we never knew—we—we knew about it—conceptives, thing like that, but we wasn't overwhelmed with it—we didn't know—we knew about it—'bout children and things like that and where they come from and things like that, but we wasn't taught it in school—preventatives or nothing like that, or venereal disease—nothing like that in school then.[191]

'MEN KNEW ALL ABOUT THESE THINGS':[192] GENDER DIFFERENCES IN BIRTH CONTROL KNOWLEDGE

Assertions of ignorance were gendered. Far more women told stories of their naivety than did men, and such stories themselves frequently contrasted male and

---

[190] Mass-Observation, DR, 3587, reply to April 1944 Directive.   [191] Leslie, bc3sw#1.
[192] Doris, bc3sw#6.

female levels of awareness. Testimony from all sources suggests that knowledge about sex and birth control was circulated along gendered lines. Men's knowledge of birth control was far more extensive than women's, and men's networks of information about contraception were much more developed and varied than women's were. There were many more places and contexts in which men would and could find out about birth control. Men were far more likely to find out about contraception before marriage, and many more men discussed methods of birth control with friends or colleagues. Women, on the other hand, stressed their general ignorance of contraception. Contraception was something men were expected to know about and that women might remain ignorant about. When women talked about ignorance, in part they were contrasting their knowledge with men's and drawing attention to gender differences in the nature and extent of sexual discourses. Mass-Observation's 'Little Kinsey' survey found that 'women are worse informed than men' about birth control.[193] Men's contraceptive knowledge was presented by both sexes as having been far more extensive than women's:

So where did you first find out about condoms?
Good gracious me. It might be I was—I knew about them when I was a kid.[194]

Although many men also highlighted the difficulties they had in gaining information, nevertheless they presented themselves as having been curious and determined to find out about sex and contraception. Sexual and contraceptive knowledge was eagerly sought out:[195]

Self study really and reading and, and course you learn that off school kids ya know, but never—in those days it was a bit taboo amongst—parents, never, never, never discussed . . . ya 'ear kids talking about, ya know, the—boys do this and girls are like, yeah, yeah—and it suddenly struck me one day—'cos ya learn about umm, umm, ejaculation for want of a better word (sounds amused)—and it suddenly struck me, just like a flash of light: that's it, that's what does it.[196]

Some men perceived advantages in knowing about birth control and actively tried to decipher the information available. One of Jaclyn Gier's interviewees recalled, 'you went out with a Welsh man, they were out for it if they could get it'.[197] Knowledge of birth control was one way in which boys, such as this Welsh miner, thought they might increase their chances of persuading a girl to have sex:[198]

You'd hear somebody saying something and you'd go out and find somebody and try and experiment, that's the way you find out . . . You see there was lots of gossip around, them days, about what precautions and all that kind of thing—pessaries and French letters and

---

[193] Stanley, *Sex Surveyed*, 96.   [194] Arthur, bc3ox#36.
[195] In fact, Peter N. Stearns argues that boys during the first half of the twentieth century became keener than previous generations for sexual and contraceptive information because 'sexual criteria for manhood . . . gained in importance': Stearns, *Be A Man!*, 212.
[196] Tim, msf/srss/bl/#19.   [197] Gier, 'Miners' Wives', 98.
[198] See also R. Hoggart, *The Uses of Literacy*, 76–8; Mogey, *Family and Neighbourhood*, 52.

goodness know what . . . you'd find somebody selling them on the corner of the street, or, er, in a chemist . . . you used to try with a—when you met a girl, didn't you? Naturally— try to have sex. She didn't want it, well that was it. (pause) You could always find somebody that did.[199]

Indeed some, especially among the Welsh working-class sample, told stories of seeking information about birth control so that they could increase their chances of obtaining sexual experience. Walter and his 'pals, we used to always talk about' birth control, and they would tell him the 'best way to get round a girl'.[200] Hugh heard about withdrawal from 'the older men' 'talking at work'. 'They said "you wanna be careful. Or you'll be shoving her in a way, and then you'll have to get married".'[201] Men were more eager for sexual information and were far less sheltered from contexts in which sexual information was spread.[202] In all male groups talk frequently turned to sexual matters.[203] Some male subcultures of sex were crude, sometimes misinformed, but they were extensive. *Coal Is Our Life* stressed the prevalence of 'loose and unrestrained conversations about sex' among all-male groups of miners.[204] Ethel Elderton, despite stressing the importance of female communication networks, also revealed the variety and scale of birth control propagandism among men. Urinals were frequently posted with informa-tion, and 'preventives are hawked among the men leaving the North Eastern Railway Carriage Works' in York.[205] The 'Letters from Struggling Parents', a regular column in *The New Generation*, was dominated by earnest enquiries from men anxious to acquire better knowledge of birth control methods. Clinics reported that men frequently found out about them and sent their wives; one clinic put the large proportion of patients whose husbands were bus conductors and drivers down to the fact that one London bus route 'terminates directly in front of the clinic'.[206] In Aberdeen the notice in the window was seen by workmen who told their wives, while Nurse Gordon found in Pontypridd that 'the men seemed equally anxious to take our slips'.[207] When in 1945 a series of lectures on marriage and the physiology of sex and reproduction was provided as an experiment to British troops stationed in Baghdad, 'information was sought on the spacing of children' and on 'the best methods of birth control'.[208] Lesley Hall and Roy Porter point to the avid reading of Marie Stopes's *Married Love* in army barracks as evidence of the interest of men in the acquisition of birth control knowledge

---

[199] Tom, bc2#17.   [200] Walter bc2#20.   [201] Hugh, bc3sw#23.

[202] L. Hall, *Hidden Anxieties*, 46.

[203] See also N. Gray, *The Worst of Times*, 33, which claims that even though talk rarely turned to sex, 'dirty jokes' were obviously more prevalent. See also Williamson, ' "Getting Off at Loftus" ', 10.

[204] Dennis, Henriques, and Slaughter, *Coal Is Our Life*, 215. See also Frankenberg, *Communities in Britain*, 127.   [205] Elderton, *Report on the English Birth-Rate*, 140.

[206] Norman and Vera Himes, 'Birth Control for the British Working Classes', 603.

[207] Nurse Florence Gordon to Marie Stopes, 11 Feb. 1939, BL Add. MSS 58625; Margaret Rae to Marie Stopes, 12 Oct. 1934, BL Add. MSS 58603. Florence also comments on cases of men hearing about family-planning clinics from workmates: *Progress Report on Birth Control*, 68.

[208] A. J. L. Rogers, 'An Army Experiment in Sex Education', 184–5.

(either in spite of, or because of, masculine culture).[209] Rather than seeing use of birth control as likely to make 'men feel unmanned',[210] it is worth entertaining the possibility that the discussion of, and perhaps also the use of, contraception became a way in which men demonstrated their masculinity.

In this context it is men, in all classes, who were frequently cited as important if not sole repositories of birth control information.[211] Edith explicitly acknowledged that boys talked and girls did not:

I don't think the girls themselves knew so much—the boys I think used to do more of the talking and find out the right thing to do the right time, I mean, he knew exactly when my daughter was conceived, he knew straight away, he told me straight away that night.[212]

Wyn also presented herself as reliant on Cecil for much of her birth control education:

CECIL ... boys are much more er, they can express themselves better than girls. You, you don't agree with that; but I think so.[213] And I think that they're also more verbose: they can chatter to more than er girls. This is what I think. So that you gain a lot of information by talking, by conversing about things. And I think boys were more likely to talk about a subject like that than girls.
Wyn, I've heard a lot about how, how he found out about condoms, and withdrawal, and sex, but not a lot about how you found out things.

WYN Well I found out about 'em from Cecil . . . oh I er didn't know much about things really . . . I would think, um, boys probably chatted about it more than what, you know, er, girls did, because I think um, you know, there wasn't an awful lot of talk about it.. I don't think I had—knew anything until I met Cecil! (laughs)[214]

Most women cited their husband as the key provider of information and, indeed, to many women it was important that they could confidently rely on their husband to find out about available birth control options. Men were valued for their knowledge. Doris emphasized her husband's role in using French letters: 'Not me . . . that was up to him . . . oh, men knew all about those things long before they got married, don't worry.'[215] Catherine 'just left it to my husband':

You thought the man would do the necessary . . . you just thought he knew about these things and, yes, yes, you just had, you know, faith in a person but, um—you trusted the man—and they were going to look after you . . . I think in those days they used to leave it to the men, um—the women probably, you know, thought it was a v—a bit embarrassing

[209] Porter and Hall, *The Facts of Life*, 249.   [210] Stearns, *Be A Man!*, 91, 213.

[211] Studies of family-planning initiatives elsewhere provide interesting comparative examples. A recent study in Andhra Pradesh in India also found that men knew more about birth-control methods than women and that many women relied on male relatives or husbands to inform them. Karra, Stark, and Wolf, 'Male Involvement in Family Planning', 27.   [212] Edith, bc2#23.

[213] I did not consciously express my disagreement with his continual championing of male intellectual superiority. I am not sure whether this statement was prompted because I unconsciously and unintentionally betrayed such reactions, or he assumed that as a female 'writer and researcher' I would not agree with such a position.   [214] Cecil and Wyn, bc3ox#40.

[215] Doris, bc3sw#6.

to, (giggle) be thinking about that sort of—even thinking about having the sex (giggle) in a way. One didn't talk about it.[216]

Testimony is rich with similar examples of women, from all classes and all regions of the country, who presented themselves as having been almost entirely dependent on their husbands for birth control information. Most importantly, women deliberately relied on their husbands to obtain information as they would not investigate for themselves. One midwife working in Lambeth, who was born in 1894, remembered that mothers 'never asked me for advice' since that subject 'came on the man's side'.[217] Women deliberately sought to maintain their ignorance, aware that men frequently took on the inquisitive role:

Never asked. I wouldn't. (chuckle) I wouldn't. No. I wouldn't go and get 'em. No. No. Everything was so discreet in them days and that it er (pause)—and the married couples didn't talk about sex life. Men might do when they were in the pub. But women certainly didn't.[218]

Men were equally aware that their role was to obtain knowledge of birth control options. Gerald, who had been trained in mechanical engineering, knew the 'sniggery references' that informed him were unavailable to his wife. Before he got married, he purposefully set out to discover more information, anticipating that his fiancée would know nothing, and that it was his responsibility to be 'sufficiently equipped' so that his wife would not 'have babies year after year':

I did a lot of reading and, er, I managed to get hold of quite a library of books on the subject. I found a book in my father's bookcase . . . it was just entitled 'Marie Stopes'. So my eyes went as round as saucers and I sort of read all about her pessaries, all this kind of thing and um, so . . . these books um, really as it were took you through the whole business of marriage, sexual intercourse and so on and so forth. And I had read enough of this to be equipped sufficiently for us to meet up and get married and for you not to have babies year after year after year.[219]

Hugh, an electrical engineer, commented directly on his wife's ignorance, and she concurred that it was his copy of Marie Stopes that 'taught' her:

HUGH   'She didn't know anything about it when she got married, I didn't know about birth control, she wouldn't have known anything . . . I had the book Marie Stopes . . .

ANGELA   Well, I think that probably taught me, because I was very innocent.[220]

Recent oral history research into women's gossip networks in the US has found that, despite the existence of extensive and close-knit networks, women had difficulty finding out about birth control and did not discuss it. One woman claimed to have discussed 'everything and everybody', except birth control—'it seemed like it was private'. Husbands, on the other hand, were found to have used 'their

---

[216] Catherine, msf/kf/ht/#1.   [217] Leap and Hunter, *The Midwife's Tale*, 89.
[218] Grace, msf/srss/ht/#38.   [219] Gerald and Esme, msf/kf/ht/#9.
[220] Angela and Hugh, msf/kf/ht/#18.

own networks to provide information about birth control or to identify an abortionist'.[221] Clinics assumed that patients would inform their friends about clinics and that attendance would grow as a result. In fact, many women were unprepared to tell their friends if they discovered a birth control clinic.[222] Gender differences in sexual knowledge were acknowledged and promoted by the burgeoning sex education literature which consistently deemed it appropriate to tell male readers more than their female counterparts.[223]

The above stands in sharp contrast to the literature on declining fertility which sees women's knowledge of birth control and women's networks of information-sharing as crucial to the widespread use of contraception.[224] Information is thought to have been spread between neighbours and relations, especially in close-knit working-class communities where women spent a lot of time with other women, sharing experiences and assisting each other with various aspects of domestic life.[225] Female employment is also seen to facilitate the spread of knowledge of contraception, particularly in industries, such as textile factories, where women frequently continued (or returned) to work after marriage, which additionally provided greater economic incentives to limit family size, and a decreased emphasis on childrearing as the main focus of their lives and identities.[226] While the existence of close-knit, reciprocally helpful networks of women friends, both before and after marriage, is revealed by a range of sources, evidence suggests that among such groups sex, and therefore birth control, was one aspect of life that was rarely discussed:[227]

We would discuss our children. Some might bemoan their fate, that they didn't want any more, or that it would be damn hard luck if they did. But funnily enough, we never talked about how to restrict the children.[228]

Melanie Tebbut's study of working-class communication networks similarly found that 'personal' details were rarely discussed.[229] The influential argument which posits a relationship between women's employment, communication networks, and fertility change has been fuelled by the low fertility of the south

[221] Watkins and Danzi, 'Women's Gossip and Social Change', 475–6, 480.

[222] Florence, *Birth Control on Trial*, 49.

[223] See e.g. Schofield and Vaughan-Jackson, *What a Boy Should Know*; Scharlieb and Sibly, *Youth and Sex*; Gair, *Sexual Science*. See also Campbell, *Sex Education Books*.

[224] See e.g. Watkins and Danzi, 'Women's Gossip and Social Change', 469–90; E. Roberts, *A Woman's Place*; Gittins, *Fair Sex*.

[225] See e.g. E. Roberts, *A Woman's Place*, 183–201; E. Ross, *Love and Toil*. Maud Pember Reeves, by contrast, points out the loneliness of many working-class mothers imprisoned in the home under the weight of chores: Reeves, *Round About a Pound a Week*, 151.

[226] Many have focused on married women who worked, as women's employment opportunities after marriage were frequently a good indicator of low fertility. However, Diana Gittins argues that it was 'women's occupational experience before marriage' that was particularly significant: Gittins, *Fair Sex*, 186.

[227] Abortion may have been easier for women to speak about because it could be discussed without mentioning sex.   [228] Eva, bc1#1.

[229] Tebbutt, *Women's Talk?*, 88–9.

Lancashire cotton textile districts.[230] Ethel Elderton, for example, found in 1914 in Gorton that 'the subject is freely talked about . . . in the workshops where girls and young women work, and also during the dinner hour'.[231] However, Elizabeth Roberts's research found that weavers in Preston provide 'no evidence that women discussed sexual topics in the mill . . . there was still widespread ignorance and . . . textile workers were as likely to be ignorant as other sections of the population'.[232] Oral history suggests that working environments may have provided some opportunities for women to hear about birth control, particularly as such work brought women into contact with male networks. Nancy put her knowledge down to the fact that she was working in a laundry in Oxford with a lot of 'filthy-mouthed men'.[233] However, frequently such workplace interactions did not break down gender divisions in knowledge acquisition; indeed, gender distinctions might be artificially and carefully preserved.[234] Men censored or obfuscated their language in the presence of women, while women deliberately closed their ears. Many women knew that boys deliberately 'protected' them from sexual information. Marilyn's grandparents lived on a farm in Lancashire. Despite growing up around animals she claimed that she remained ignorant; euphemisms were used to discuss mating, and even boys of her own age prevented her from listening to some of their conversations:

there were a family . . . they had a farm, th—they'd three lads and I remember them talking about pigs. They had a pig and . . . they took it to a sow—took sow to a pig to be 'serviced'. But um—I know what they mean now, but didn't then, um. They were talking amongst themselves and they used to say, 'You're not to listen, it nowt to do wi' you'—they wouldn't let you listen.[235]

Dora, 'heard everything in the [London clothing] factory' but sought to avoid such knowledge:

I said to her, 'I don't wanna sit next door to you any more.' So she said 'Why not?' I said 'Well of course you're—you're talking about is—is disgusting.' And I asked to be

---

[230] Gittins, 'Women's Work and Family Size Between the Wars'.

[231] Elderton, *Report on the English Birth-Rate*, 61.

[232] Roberts, 'Working Wives and their Families', 154–5. See also J. Harris, *Private Lives, Public Spirit*, 49.   [233] Nancy, bc3ox#22.

[234] Comparisons might be drawn with research in other cultures. For example, in one North Indian village, family planning ideas were considered an indelicate topic. Whereas information about a new variety of wheat was spread rapidly and evenly among the villagers, 'family planning information, normally perceived as rather vulgar, spread along interpersonal channels in the village as would a dirty joke'. Such channels were restricted to male villagers of the same age and caste: 'a young Indian peasant was asked why he did not discuss family planning with other men in his family. He explained: "I might think about it in my own mind, but would not tell others. These are not the things to talk about to others in my family. We feel *sharam* (shame, or intense embarrassment) if it is brought into the open. We have to show respect for the others': quoted in E. Rogers, *Communication Strategies*, 36–7.

[235] Marilyn, msf/kf/bl/#7. There is some evidence to suggest that exposure to livestock was found to be informative. See for example the comment made by one woman from Scotland, born in 1911, 'Because I had been brought up on a farm, I knew a bit about the facts of life, so I wasn't as ignorant as some girls, married': Devlin, *Motherhood*, 41.

moved . . . I would never listen to anything filthy. And if I thought it was going to be naughty then I would walk away.[236]

The dominance of male networks of information about birth control was less marked among middle-class respondents and the youngest of those interviewed. While a number of middle-class women also saw knowledge of birth control as a male topic which they assumed their husbands would take full responsibility for, others saw it as their role to find out what they could. Ethel, for example, went with a female friend to a birth control clinic, where she was given a female method of birth control, probably a spermicidal pessary which she obtained regularly from the chemist:

I went to um, er—I think—I don't know what, um, she was professionally—but I went to somebody who advised about the anti, you know, anti—whatever you call them. I had a friend and we went together.[237]

Sarah was a working-class woman who joined a cycling organization and began to mix with a different class of people. She did not discuss birth control with her working-class female friends, though she did remember giggles about abortion: 'You'd get it in the girls' conversation . . . they'd had some Penny Royal and they'd had some Holland's Gin . . . it was jokey talk . . .', but with her new middle-class friends birth control was a serious topic worthy of intellectual debate:

We were quite serious, you know, it's [contraception] quite a serious topic of conversation, quite private . . . they seemed to know more about it . . . than us common working peo-ple. But you see, when I started cycling, I went with a different—a different crowd of peo-ple and I, I, uh (pause)—that sort of, continued my education.[238]

Abortion was an exception. Information about abortion was spread between women, and men knew much less about the practice than their wives. Some women recalled detailed incidents involving friends and relatives (as well as their own experiences) and many were familiar with the specifics of various methods or knew the addresses of abortionists. Men, in contrast, more frequently talked plat-itudinously about the operations performed by old women and ex-midwives. It was clear, when I discussed abortion with Ivor and Doris, who courted in Cardiff, that Doris knew much more than he did. He talked generally about illegal abor-tionists while emphasizing his ignorance, whereas she remembered hearing people talking about using slippery elm bark:

And were there abortions in those days?

IVOR   I can't remember any abortions, not in our day.

DORIS   Um, I can remember—nobody telling me—but I can remember two people talk-ing about bringing on their own, and losing them theirselves, and, not anyone else knowing, but down in the toilets. I've heard people talking about that . . .

What? How did they manage it, how did they do it?

---

[236] Dora, msf/srss/ht/#38.   [237] Emma, msf/kf/ht/#37.   [238] Sarah, msf/kf/bl/#30.

IVOR   Oh they used to have um in those days—you couldn't go in the hospital and have
         an abortion, you had to go a special woman—there was a woman and you had to
         pay her to have, er, in those days.
DORIS   No, they used to do it theirselves, and I heard talking.
IVOR   Yeah, some of it done it themselves, you know.
DORIS   There was a stuff that I remember 'em saying—slippery elm? That they used? To
         bring the abortions on, to lose the baby. And that's all I could hear—but never
         joined in anything like that—but I heard a lot of talk.[239]

Ethel Elderton's survey, which has been extremely influential in the development
of the thesis that birth control information was spread between women, in fact primarily attests to the spread of information about abortifacients rather than contraception.[240] That women's knowledge networks concerning abortion and induced
miscarriages appear to have been more extensive and less covert reveals the significance of a birth control method which could be discussed without mentioning sex
and without a woman needing to present herself as having any responsibility for
sexual activity. American research also found that 'women found it easier to talk
about abortion than about contraception'. As one American interviewee explained:
contraception was a 'secret . . . it was about intercourse. Abortion was different
because you might have learned about it because you knew someone was pregnant . . . birth control was too personal . . . Abortion was after the fact.'[241] Most
birth control knowledge was tainted by its association with sexual intercourse. The
attempt by those promoting scientific methods of contraception to realign birth
control as part of respectable political debate, public policy, and maternal health
was only slowly and partially successful. Abortion, by contrast, appears to have
occupied a different category. Although it was tarnished by its popular association
with pre-marital pregnancies, it could be discussed without mentioning sex.[242] As a
result women's discourses frequently avoided open conversation about contraception, but might include consideration of abortion.

Men, however, were not entirely ignorant about abortion and frequently
helped their partners obtain the necessary information to terminate a pregnancy.
Indeed, occasional male involvement in abortion provides further demonstration
of the importance of male knowledge networks. Leslie's detailed knowledge of
abortifacient methods attests to male cultures of information exchange:

And did girls ever have abortions in those days?
Oh yes, they had abortions, oh yes, oh yes . . . take a dose of gin and salts, got it now?
A nice, quart or half a bottle of gin and nearly half a bottle of salts and swallow that bloody

    [239] Doris and Ivor, bc3sw#29.
    [240] See also Gittins, 'Women's Work and Family Size'; McLaren, *Birth Control in Nineteenth
Century England*, 242–5.
    [241] Watkins, Spector, and Goldstein, 'Family Planning Patterns among Jewish and Italian Women
in the United States', 18, 29.
    [242] Most abortions appear, in fact, to have been sought by married women. However, popular
discourse and oral history testimony frequently associated abortion with pre-marital pregnancies.

lot down, then you'd haemorrhage—sometimes you'd haemorrhage with it—well you'd lose everything then . . . And another thing some used to take—that was a common thing again—was loose tobacco in a quarter of quinine, in a glass of quinine and they used to take that, and mix it all up and swallow it, then you'd spew.[243]

Use of and knowledge of abortion is usually seen as testament to women's power to avoid childbearing and of men's objections to fertility control.[244] While abortion was predominantly a method about which women knew more, men were neither opposed to it nor ignorant of it. Far from being a completely female-dominated endeavour, a number of men in both working-class and middle-class communities took a leading role in finding out about abortions.[245] Hubert's wife, who had been a nurse before marriage, 'urged me to do something about it when the third child was coming' and he 'made enquiries though I didn't like to'. Margaret's husband, who was a chef, went to the chemist, while Edith's, who was an unemployed builder, made an appointment with the back-street practitioner.[246] Men also wrote to Marie Stopes for advice about abortion. Lesley Hall has argued that such cases reveal the isolation of men from women's networks of knowledge; they were forced to try and get information from a nationally renowned figure. Men also sought advice when their wives were reluctant to find out themselves: 'My wife will not speak to anyone.'[247]

Women's assertions of ignorance, therefore, served to highlight gender differences in knowledge networks and sexual discourses. Excepting information about abortion, men knew far more about all methods of contraception than did women and, moreover, were actively involved in seeking out such knowledge. Although some women, particularly those involved in factory work, had access to information about birth control, some deliberately sought to remain distanced from such networks of information and would not take advantage of them. Instead women trusted the men they knew to obtain relevant information such that appropriate action could then be taken.

'SHUT MY EARS DOWN':[248] IDENTITY AND BIRTH CONTROL KNOWLEDGE

Women's determination to avoid direct sources of information about birth control methods draws attention to the role 'ignorance' played in both men's and women's self-identities. Not only did men claim to know more about birth

---

[243] Leslie, bc2sw#1. [244] See McIntosh, ' "An Abortionist City" ', 94.

[245] See Usborne, *Cultures of Abortion in Weimar Germany*.

[246] Hubert, msf/kf/ht/#32, Margaret bc3ox#18, Edith, bc2#23. Seven respondents could not remember whether or not they told their husbands about their abortion attempts. The other fifteen husbands all knew and four were involved in engineering its execution. See also Weir, 'Lay Abortionists', on the attempts made in the 1960s by men seeking abortions for their wives, girlfriends, or lovers. [247] L. Hall, 'Marie Stopes and her Correspondents', 35–6.

[248] Doris, bc3sw#29.

control than women, but, crucially, they presented themselves as having been eager for knowledge, while many women distanced themselves from information and the sources that might have provided enlightenment. Being innocent was presented as a crucial aspect of female identity, particularly among the working classes. Rather than being a simple description of the extent of their awareness, it was a declaration of their views about sexual knowledge and their approach to the subject. In representing themselves respondents sought to place their own particular histories both within what was expected socially and as part of a collectively resonant narrative. Women in particular experienced ignorance, despite having some sources of information. They felt uninformed due to the restricted, euphemistic, and confusing nature of available material, predominantly spread through male networks. Women further declared themselves ignorant because they were expected to be naive. Through stories of ignorance, women established that they had maintained a respectful distance from seedy sources of information and forestalled any allegation that they might have had pre-marital sexual experience. Men, by contrast, despite also revealing the challenges posed by obfuscatory sources, did not see total ignorance as valuable nor as a mark of honour.

Statements of ignorance were assertions of innocence. It was through stories detailing confusion and unawareness of birth control methods and sexual matters more generally that women indicated that they had avoided indulging in sex before marriage. The association between knowledge and behaviour was often indicated through juxtapositions within testimony. Gladys asserted that she knew nothing about birth control and immediately responded to a question asking about sexual ignorance with a statement that she was a virgin on marriage. For Gladys, a miner's wife from Merthyr Tydfil, ignorance of birth control was a crucial aspect of female identity and fundamental to proper pre-marital behaviour:

So didn't you know about anything to stop having children?
No, I got married, er—that's the truth—I mean, today, you're soon getting married in white and the children are bridesmaids! I was a virgin when I got married, I didn't know anything about anything, because the simple reason—if and when you'd be going in out . . . my mother'd say, 'now don't forget, lady, you bring any er trouble home here and you'll end up in the workhouse'—'till you were terrified to even go out with a boy. If you went to the pictures with a boy and he put his arms and you, you would never go out with him again, no fear. Phph! Too frightened to go with them.[249]

Thus many interviewees chose to present themselves as relatively innocent of sexual knowledge before marriage as a matter of personal and family honour. Sexual knowledge was more or less synonymous with sexual experience. It was not simply that to know about sex was to imply that one was experienced; rather, the very notion of knowledge was inseparable from practice. To have information about sexual matters, such as knowing details of birth control methods, tarnished one's

---

[249] Gladys, bc3sw#28.

naivety—one could not be truly inexperienced if one was aware of sexual facts. Such terms as 'carnal knowledge', 'sexual intercourse', and 'knowing' someone sexually draw out the semantic link between knowledge and practice, as does the term 'innocent', which suggests both a lack of awareness and a lack of experience. Women keen to preserve their 'innocence' sought to remain isolated from all forms of sexual conversation.

Being ignorant was a key element of female identity, closely connected to women's respectability and in particular their avoidance of illicit sexual behaviour prior to marriage. Laurence Housman, a founder of the British Society for the Study of Sex Psychology, reported the views of his stepmother, who claimed that women 'would not give up premarital ignorance'—because 'it's too attractive'.[250] Indeed, those who did know too much about contraception, or openly discussed their knowledge could be denigrated as loose, regardless of their behaviour. Sometimes women's sources of information were presented as marginal and originating from unusual types of people: from outsiders, or less respectable types. One, for example, remembered learning a good deal about sex and birth control from a 'sexy' adulterous woman from outside the community whom she described as 'daring' and 'man-mad'.[251] She presented her relationship to this friend and her knowledge in a very particular way, stressing that, despite the woman's promiscuity, she was a good friend and emphasizing that, despite associating with her, she remained 'innocent' and was not 'led off the path' by her friend:

I suppose I'm a bit um, how do you call it? Bit green, I suppose—innocent then, put it that way. I was really quite innocent—I learnt a lot from her, believe me.

What else did you learn from her?
Oh, all about sex and men and one thing and another—things I didn't know about—different ways of going about things, you know . . . but she was a daring woman, she'd try anything, you know, and yet, as I say she was a good friend to me, in spite of that—but I could never do the things that she done . . . . Oh she was a real daredevil. But as I say, for all that, she was good for me, a really good friend—but she had her ways, she liked men, and that was all there is to it—but she couldn't, she didn't lead me off the path, believe me, I wouldn't.[252]

In representing themselves women were keen to distance themselves from the less respectable women who knew too much about sex and birth control. One way in which a woman maintained her respectability was by remaining somewhat sheltered from sexual information; 'good girls were admired for their lack of sexual awareness'.[253] Not only was birth control rarely openly discussed, but many women in particular deliberately avoided contexts in which such topics might be mentioned and absented themselves if they found themselves in a situation where

---

[250] Housman, *The Unexpected Years* (London, 1937), quoted in L. Hall, 'Impotent Ghosts', 63.
[251] Doris, bc3sw#6.   [252] Doris, bc3sw#6.
[253] Judy Giles, ' "Playing hard to get" ', 181.

birth control knowledge was revealed. Mildred, who moved from South Wales to Huddersfield during her adolescence, avoided the girls in school who discussed abortifacients: 'I thought, I'm not in this position, so I don't want to know';[254] 'when other people talked about it', Doreen, who grew up in Preston, 'didn't go into detail finding things out';[255] and Edith, who lived in Penarth, was aware of the 'bad women in the road where we lived' but she 'kept away from them', thereby preserving her 'innocent' world in which 'people didn't do wrong' and 'didn't know what it was all about, until we got married' when 'it comes as a bit of a shock'.[256] Far from revealing a sorry state of ignorance, such a 'shock' was socially appropriate and important.

For men, stories of sexual ignorance were equally socially resonant; they shared the collective experience of ignorance, faced with scarce, euphemistic, and inaccessible forms of enlightenment. However, they did not seek to maintain their innocence. For most men feeling ignorant was not a socially desirable state. They did not hope to avoid knowledge, nor were their reputations potentially tarnished by the idea that they sought experience. Thus, they presented themselves as prepared to enquire after information. That men might, by revealing themselves to have had knowledge of birth control methods, imply that they were sexually experienced was evident, as it was for women. Indeed, some men regarded themselves as ignorant until they had experienced sexual intercourse. One could not be said to know about sex until one had done it. Dennis, an apprentice printer in London, did not find out about the facts of life: 'no, well I wasn't involved with anyone sexually before I met Eve'.[257] Fred, whose first job was in haulage, 'learnt a lot before I got to seeing my wife, like. Still, I was messing about when I was thirteen.'[258] Tom, a miner from Maesteg, 'found out by experiment', and Thomas, a pageboy, 'found that bloody thing out myself . . . up in London . . . I met her—park closed at midnight—I embraced her twice in 5 minutes, once without an overcoat [condom] and once with a bloody overcoat'.[259]

The crucial difference between men's and women's testimony, however, was the extent to which knowledge and experience were actively sought. Whereas women asserted their ignorance as a means of reinforcing their virtue, men presented their sense of ignorance as a problem to be overcome. Whether or not men had sex before they were married, they did not object to the notion that they might have wanted to.[260] Charlie sought sexual knowledge by trying to seduce the local 'servant girls' he would meet while delivering groceries to big houses in Penarth. He contrasted the lack of information about sex with his own eager experiments.

254 Mildred, msf/kf/bl/#41.   255 Doreen, msf/kf/bl/#20.   256 Edith, bc2#23.
257 Dennis, msf/kf/ht/#15.   258 Fred, bc2#14.   259 Tom bc2#17; Thomas, bc2#18.
260 Roughly three-fifths of oral history respondents denied having had sex before marriage. This amounted, however, to about 90% of middle-class respondents. More men in south Wales admitted pre-marital intercourse than women, but in other areas there was no gender difference in the reporting of such activity. Courtship narratives are explored in Szreter and Fisher, 'Sexuality, Love and Marriage in England, 1918–1960'. On pre-marital intercourse see also Slater and Woodside, *Patterns of Marriage*, 112.

For Charlie, knowledge was equivalent to experience. He also illustrated the importance of such experience for male identity. It was the acquisition of sexual knowledge through experience that marked the transition from boyhood to manhood, and thus a crucial element of masculinity was associated with the presentation of sexual awareness:

My parents didn't, we had to learn for ourselves: . . . you either put your hand on it or you didn't—so you found out, you became a man then . . . and you had to be very careful because you wasn't told anything about sex in them days . . . eventually you found out . . . it used to be nice then, but you always had to be careful.'[261]

Similarly John, in the absence of information at school, actively sought to educate himself through experience:

We was a bit raw in sexual—not like today, they're taught it all in school and all that—we had to find it out ourselves in our own little way like you know, just you know, put your hand around her shoulders for a start and things like that, then you get aroused like, then you find out—little thing 'ere, little thing there.[262]

This chapter has explored the disjuncture between assertions of ignorance and the proliferation of material about birth control methods. However ingenuous we judge statements of ignorance to be, more important is the recognition that, to use knowledge, one must be prepared to reveal that one has it. We do not need to accept women's statements of ignorance at face value in order to conclude that in practice they may frequently have behaved as if they knew nothing.

Indeed, some assertions of ignorance were probably exaggerated, or overplayed. First, testimony of ignorance is frequently comparative. Memories and oral history testimony are the product of a retrospective analysis, which in this case took place fifty or sixty years after the period being discussed, at a time when society is perceived to be saturated with birth control information. Extreme and vivid accounts frequently relied on contemporary comparison for effect:

Do you know, I didn't know, a couple of years ago—I didn't know what a French letter was! It was on the television about condoms, so I said 'what's condoms then?' and a man heard me and said, 'don't you know what they are?' and he said 'a thing a man puts over his penis'. Oh! I nearly dropped dead. I did, honestly. And I've never seen one in my life.[263]

The emphasis on the absence of communication networks was relative, and reflected an individual's attitudes towards contemporary society. An accountant's wife from Pontypool, Lilian's purpose in recalling her innocence was to criticize contemporary sex education practices:

I think it's wrong what they teach the youngsters today. I think it's all wrong. Like, like the nurse said 'What they don't know, they don't want to try'. But having been told, they want to try and experiment, and that's the cause of a lot of the trouble.

[261] Charlie, bc2#25.   [262] John, bc2#26.   [263] Ivy, bc1#2.

So when you were young what did they teach you?

Nothing. We had to learn it as we going along . . . I was really innocent when I was married. But, er, they wouldn't believe that today.[264]

Memoirs and autobiographies have a similar agenda. That one was not told about sex has become a cliché of the genre.[265]

Many contemporary accounts of ignorance were equally politicized. Marie Stopes's mission to educate and inform was fuelled by illustrations of the woeful ignorance of those who wrote to her for help. Lecture campaigns in distressed areas were used to impress the government of the need for birth control; meetings invariably resulted in 'a resolution calling for birth control instruction, in which the current state of ignorance would be pointed out, being 'passed unanimously' and sent to the Ministry of Health and/or the local M.P.[266] Sex reform radicals also told extreme stories to highlight their campaign for a more 'rational' approach to sex. Irene Clephane's demand for 'sex sanity' required that a 'child's innocent enquiries' be satisfied with 'honest' and 'unselfconscious' answers so that it was no longer possible for 'women with sexual experience [to be] still under the delusion that birth is effected by some natural equivalent of a Caesarean operation'.[267] The sex education movement similarly used accounts of ignorance to draw attention to its own drive for such information to be provided in schools.[268] Mass-Observation's enquiries also contributed directly to debates; it sought to find out how people 'found out about sex' and what they 'thought of sex instruction' precisely in order to shed further light on the 'essential' role of sex education for the development of 'normal sex attitudes'.[269]

Exaggerated stories of ignorance might serve to preclude the disclosure of embarrassing accounts of sexual discovery. Some, uncomfortable at being asked about their sexual awareness and knowledge of birth control methods, could hide behind assertions of ignorance. Many social surveyors have concluded that denying familiarity with certain birth control methods was a way of avoiding answering personal questions. For example, Rachel M. Pierce and Griselda Rowntree found that a significant number of interviewees (17.2 per cent of all informants married since 1930) denied knowing about or having used any form of birth control. Later on the questionnaire revealed that many such 'reticent users' in fact did know about and had used certain methods. Pierce and Rowntree argued that such representations indicated the 'lingering taboo' in talking about

---

[264] Lilian, bc3sw#24.   [265] For a typical example see O'Neil, *My East End*, 156.

[266] Leathard, *The Fight for Family Planning*, 17, 33.

[267] Clephane, *Towards Sex Freedom*, 231–2.

[268] Very few sex education books mentioned birth control, however. For an example of this, see Wile, *Sex Education*. An exception is March, *Sex Knowledge with a Special Chapter on Birth Control*. However, by 1945 the *Health Education Journal* reported on an educational scheme in operation at a northern direct-grant boys preparatory school where young men in their final year were taught 'family limitation, contraception' as part of a programme entitled 'On Being a Father': T. L. Green, 'Sex Education and Social Biology'.   [269] Stanley, *Sex Surveyed*, 74.

and revealing contraceptive practices.[270] It is likely that oral history interviewees responded in similar ways.[271] For example, I was strongly suspicious that Margaret, a costermonger's wife from Merthyr Tydfil, knew that slippery elm was an abortifacient despite her protestations of ignorance. When I first asked her about abortions she emphatically asserted that she didn't know anything and reiterated earlier statements about general sexual and contraceptive ignorance:

And was there anything that that girls who w- who got pregnant, but didn't want to carry on and have a baby, could do?

I dunno, love—dunno anything about that, don't know nothing about that. Real ignorant in them days, girl. Really ignorant.

So there weren't any abortions?

Yes, no, well could have been, could have been, I dunno. I just was naive.

When later I asked her about a specific abortifacient—slippery elm bark—(which when inserted into the vagina would expand, provoking a miscarriage), she appeared not to know whether or not it was a medicine. Such naivety was betrayed as disingenuous when, without mention of abortion or miscarriage, she declared she would not have used slippery elm if pregnant:

So did you ever hear of something called slippery elm?

(pause) Do I ever heard about slippery elm? Oh, is it a . . . medicine, or what?

No I think it's, like a piece of wood.

(whispers) Never. (normal volume) Oh, like a bark of—a bark of a tree, love?

Mm

(pause) Oh, I'd be too frightened, I would. Anyway, If I hadn't—if I hadn't had the baby I'd've had a baby after, so, didn't make much difference, did it?[272]

Indeed, in some instances professions of ignorance stretched credulity, and it is probable that many of the statements were not, in fact, literally true. A number of working-class women claimed to have been totally unaware of the process of birth. Dilys, born in 1906, whose husband was a postman in Swansea, for example, recalled:

I didn't know which way they were born. I always thought you had to cut and take out . . . I asked the nurse one day, and the answer I had was rude. She said 'same way it went in', that's what I had for my answer, and it's true isn't it?[273]

---

[270] Pierce and Rowntree, 'Birth Control in Britain, Part I', 7, and 'Birth Control in Britain, Part II', 123.

[271] It is important not to overstate the effect of embarrassment on testimony. Not only are most surveyors sensitive and alive to the importance of counteracting such a tendency, but also the desire of many surveyed to engage honestly with the questions asked was striking. On the validity of assuming testimony to be accurate, see Cook, *The Long Sexual Revolution*, 6.

[272] Margaret, bc3sw#13.   [273] Dilys, bc2#13.

This same story crops up again and again in the archival material.[274] That this collective anecdote was apocryphal is suggested by the ways in which the same terminology recurs in its exposition. A group interview repeated the punchline—'same way it went in'—and also described it as 'crude/rude':[275]

Half of us didn't know how it was going to come out.

That's true.

We used to wonder what was going to happen. (laughs)

Yes.

We were very dull when you think about it.

Oh yes.

Yeah.

You know, in comparison to the young ladies of today.

I did say to someone—er, well I was pregnant then—(whispers) 'where do babies come from?' you know—but I'm not crude: 'same way as it went in'.[276]

While it is clear that this story is unlikely to be 'literally' true, given that it is told by many in the same way, using identical or similar language, the fact that it appeared to be so relevant and important for so many is highly significant. These women in using false stories adopted an ignorant public persona. It is not the absolute 'truth' of such statements, but rather the degree to which the presentation of ignorance and naivety was part of these respondents' self-identity that is significant. As Luisa Passerini recognized, 'the raw material of oral history consists not just in factual statements, but is pre-eminently an expression and representation of culture'.[277] The performance of ignorance as a type of persona suggests that, regardless of the actual extent of knowledge, it was and is important for women to maintain their ignorance. The implication here is that, women genuinely believed in their ignorance, and acted accordingly. This might mean avoiding sexual discussions, resisting the temptation to decipher coded and euphemistic messages, keeping quiet about any information that was obtained, particularly if it had originated from unrespectable sources, and behaving as much as possible as if one did not know details of contraceptive methods. For example, Gertrude saw a French letter indecorously left in the wardrobe of a woman she cleaned for before she was married. Her knowledge of French letters which originated from this initial discovery was never revealed or acted upon, and she and her husband did not use

---

[274] See e.g. Leap and Hunter, *The Midwife's Tale*, 78–9; Kerr, *The People of Ship Street*, 82. Steve Humphries and Pamela Gordon's oral history of parenthood also reports the same phrase being used: 'many who asked where the baby would come from were told, "it comes out where it went in"': Humphries and Gordon, *A Labour of Love*, 6.

[275] A new line denotes another voice. I do not speak in this extract.

[276] Abertillery Group Interview, bc1#2.

[277] Passerini, 'Work Ideology and Consensus under Italian Fascism', 84.

French letters until they were later advised to:

> She asked me now to clean the bedroom out for her. So I go to clean the bedroom out now . . . she said . . . 'You can put, um, my clothes in the wardrobe' . . . So I goes in the wardrobe now, and there's a little pot—you know, like a round flower pot. I thought, what's this? And I could see a French letter in there. So I thought, oh, damny, I'm not gonna touch that. I thought, oh good God! I thought it was one—because of course you used to find out these things, you know, . . . And that was there. And I left it there, and I was . . . oh good God! What do you think of that? As if they couldn't 've got that away, and put it away, 'cos you were supposed to wash them and powder . . . put plenty of powder and things and put them in a little hanky in a box.[278]

Doctors frequently spoke directly to husbands, as they accepted that birth control was a male responsibility and also appreciated that a message relayed only to the wife might not be transferred to the relevant party. Indeed, when Harriet's doctor warned her not to get pregnant again, she revealed that she would not be able to tell her husband and asked her doctor to confront him himself: 'The doctor advised me not to have no more. Well I told him, I said "You won't tell my husband that". He says "I will", and he did.'[279] The example of Elizabeth will be presented at length. Born in 1918, in Tredegar, Elizabeth lost her virginity in a graveyard at the age of 16 to her unemployed miner boyfriend:

> You'll never believe where I was—Llandaff cathedral, in the graveyard, it was a tree with a seat all round it (laughs) that's where I lost my virginity (laughs)—sixteen years of age, Llandaff cathedral—so the times are no different to what they are today really, are they? (laughs) Yeah, never forget that.

Tell me how it happened

> Well, sitting on the seat and cuddling and all that and I went home, I said to my sister, I said 'Can you have a baby if you kiss anybody?'[280]—'cos we were that dull in them days, I really—but I wasn't pregnant anyway, but I was worried about it . . . she said 'Don't be so soft', you know—didn't tell me anything though, 'cos she wondered why I was pumping—she probably knew in her mind, I expect, but, err—I wasn't pregnant, I didn't get pregnant.

She got married soon after and used a wide variety of contraceptives: caps, pessaries, and condoms. When she later married the foreman of the clothing factory she worked in after her first husband's death, she did not reveal to her new husband her knowledge of these other methods.

---

[278] Gertrude, bc3sw#27.   [279] Harriet, bc3sw#15.

[280] It is clear from this quotation that Elizabeth knew there was more to conception than kissing, despite the wording of the anxieties she expressed to her sister. The notion that many girls worried that they might get pregnant as a result of merely kissing is another common self-representation of teenage girls and unmarried women in the twentieth century. The relationship between ignorance and pre-marital sexual behaviour is explored in Szreter and Fisher, 'Sexuality, Love and Marriage in England, 1918–1960'.

So why didn't you use contraceptives in your second marriage?
I don't know, he was—he knew when to draw back sort of thing. I never—I can honestly say I never used a thing all them fifteen years we were married before she came along . . .
And did you discuss with your second husband ever using any of the methods that you'd used with your first husband?
No, no we just left it to him.[281]

Ignorance was central to Elizabeth's persona. First, she used ignorance to excuse her pre-marital dalliances. Secondly, despite her knowledge of contraceptives she chose not to inform her less well informed second husband of alternative options, but rather to play ignorant and leave him to use the method he knew about.[282] The suspicion that oral testimony regarding ignorance is not always factually accurate leads to the more important realization that, in historical contexts, many women, like Elizabeth, will have *practised* ignorance and may have preferred not to reveal or act upon what they knew.

We need not take men's professions of awareness at face value either. Their assertions of wisdom may have hidden partial awareness of methods, acceptance of false information, or continued mystification by certain euphemisms. However, faced with the desire to limit family size, men knew that the onus was on them to appear knowledgeable and act as if they had researched the options and had made an informed choice.[283] Just as femininity was premised on innocence, so masculinity required the pretence of understanding and the behaviour to match. Indeed, in Elizabeth's narrative, at no point did her husband seek to discover whether or not she had any information that might help him choose a contraceptive. He silently, 'masterfully' took control of the situation and used the only method he was aware of.

CONCLUSION

It initially seems surprising that, despite the proliferation of contraceptive advice and the widespread use of family limitation in this period, individual voices from many sections of society professed their extreme ignorance of all sexual matters, including birth control methods. In order to understand the ways in which ignorance was maintained in the face of public discussion of the issue of birth control, we have to examine the ways in which people received information and how their

[281] Elizabeth, bc3sw#12.
[282] Furthermore, she may have sought to avoid embarrassing her husband by revealing that her knowledge was greater than his. In many relationships, men's supposedly greater knowledge of such matters meant that wives frequently adopted a 'Yes, dear' approach even when they had superior information.
[283] As Janet Holland, Caroline Ramazanoglu, Sue Sharp, and Rachel Thompson find in their contemporary studies of teenagers, 'young women appeared under pressure to safeguard their reputations, young men under pressure to demonstrate theirs': 'Reputations', 239.

prior experiences shaped the way in which that knowledge was understood and used. First, the information which individuals gained was often ambiguous and contradictory. Many therefore perceived themselves to be unsure of the 'facts' of birth control despite having some knowledge of the subject. What was learnt was gleaned from isolated incidents, accidental eavesdropping, and from dubious or euphemistic sources; as a result, awareness was only partial and information often distrusted. Secondly, we have to look at the social implications of acquiring birth control information. Many women had no interest in gaining birth control knowledge. In other cases where they did have some awareness, they remained silent and did not put the knowledge they had into practice. Women were not only more sheltered from the subcultures in which sexual information was spread but they also censored themselves, preferring to play an ignorant role. Men too spoke of a culture in which birth control information was often partial and distrusted. However, unlike women, they saw advantages in having knowledge of sexual matters and so were far more likely to go out of their way to rectify the gaps in their knowledge. Moreover, their reputations were not tarnished by the acquisition of knowledge and they had no reason deliberately to maintain their ignorance. Any knowledge acquired could be acted upon. It is therefore more important to examine the relationship between information and the ability to act upon it than to ascertain the precise extent of birth control awareness. In the following chapters the relationship between individuals' attitudes towards birth control knowledge and the practices they adopted will be developed. For women, an enduring sense of ignorance, coupled with an identity which prized the preservation of innocence, has important implications for our understanding of their attitudes towards methods and the discussion of family size ideals. For men, too, the awareness that they were likely to be better informed framed their approaches to contraceptive choices and the gender dynamics of family planning.

2

'It never does to plan anything'[1]

Deliberate Accidents and Casual Attempts to Avoid Pregnancy

Central to accounts of fertility decline is the notion that individuals started to plan their families. They discussed the issue and made calculated and firm decisions either to have a child or to avoid one. Indeed, new ideas about planning and communicating are characterized as having increasingly affected individuals' approach to life in various areas. What distinguishes 'traditional' societies from 'modern' ones is assumed to be the attempt to control, manipulate, or determine one's life. As Elizabeth Beck-Gernsheim has summarized: 'modernity has created its own model of behaviour for actively coping with the uncertainties of life under conditions of individualization. Its watchwords are: Plan! Bring the future under control! Protect yourself from accidents—steer and direct them!'[2] Demographic historians, in particular, have represented the increased used of birth control as part of a new 'modern' way of thinking and seen such a shift in mentality as a *necessary* condition for consistent and effective birth control use.[3] Ansley Coale's claim in 1974 that pregnancy and reproduction need to be perceived to be 'within the *calculus* of conscious choice' before successful and systematic family limitation can occur is virtually unchallenged.[4] He writes: 'Potential parents must consider it an acceptable mode of thought and form of behaviour to balance advantages and disadvantages before deciding to have another child.'[5] Similarly, the combined emphasis of the articles in the volume edited by Gillis, Tilly, and Levine 'is on the degree to which the European fertility decline was the product of conscious choice';[6] 'each decision to restrict fertility was an act of conscious calculation'.[7] It is assumed that couples

---

[1] Mass-Observation, TC Family Planning 1944–49, Neasden, TC3/1/B.

[2] Beck-Gernsheim, *Reinventing the Family*, 43.

[3] Ariès, 'On the Origins of Contraception in France'; id., 'An Interpretation'.

[4] The influence of these criteria is explored in Alter, 'Theories of Fertility Decline', 22–3. On the mismatch between Coale's necessary conditions and the individual representations of historical actors see Fisher, 'Uncertain Aims and Tacit Negotiation'.

[5] Coale, 'The Demographic Transition Reconsidered', 65.

[6] Gillis, Tilly, and Levine, introduction to *The European Experience*, 5.

[7] Levine, 'Moments in Time', 333.

engaged in detailed and explicit discussion of the matter. Parents are envisaged weighing up their reasons for wanting or not wanting a child and, accordingly, carrying out their decisions resolutely. In order to use birth control, it is thereby claimed, parents have to come to a *numerical* conceptualization of family size and perceive themselves capable of manipulating the timing of births.[8]

Yet we should not assume that discussing family limitation, planning births, and having a 'calculative' attitude towards family size were essential prerequisites of successful and systematic birth control practice. Although an 'ethos of planning' was emerging, such an approach appealed only to some in certain sections of society. A close look at available evidence on reproductive decision-making during the first half of the twentieth century suggests that a *calculative* attitude towards childbearing was not always central in deliberations about birth control, particularly in working-class communities.[9] Rather, those surveyed about attitudes towards family planning (from all regions and classes) placed considerable stress on the unpredictability of family size and pregnancy, emphasizing the casual, ill-informed, ill-thought-out way in which they approached family building. The majority denied that they were in a position to 'plan' their families; they used birth control while at the same time consciously preserving a fatalistic outlook. 'Family planning' was deemed necessary or appropriate only in particular circumstances. Apart from moments of crisis or dispute, which demanded explicit discussion of conception and childbearing, a number of alternative codes and beliefs combined to make the idea of planning one's family seem ridiculous, inappropriate, or unpalatable. Many believed that their limited knowledge of unreliable methods of birth control made planning an unrealistic aim. In addition, the attempt to control one's family was seen as cold-blooded and hubristic. Many also did not mind how many children they had, or when they had them; thus there was no need to 'plan' their families. Birth control was used on occasion with the intention that pregnancy would 'accidentally' occur from time to time. This was neither 'spacing' nor 'stopping'; the aim was to have a smallish family emerge 'naturally' without premeditation or design. Furthermore, some were uncomfortable debating sexual matters, and planning one's family was seen as too overt a negotiation of sexual practices. Many women left it to their husbands to decide the details of contraceptive acts and avoided discussion of the issue. Although the concepts of planning and control were not entirely absent from British society—ideas such as 'family planning' did make small inroads into some middle-class households in

---

[8] van de Walle, 'Fertility Transition, Conscious Choice, and Numeracy'.

[9] Gigi Santow argues that the 'resonances of the term "calculus"' in Coale's set of conditions should be avoided. She suggests reinterpreting the requirement more broadly, seeing only 'a general desire for some control over the timing of conception' as necessary for controlled marital fertility: Santow, 'Coitus Interruptus and the Control of Natural Fertility', 23; Wally Seccombe similarly recognizes 'the targeting conception is a modernist and middle-class projection on proletarian couples in the past' and argues for a reconfiguration of the 'decision-making problematic', although he nevertheless regards the fertility decline as representing a 'sea change' in the mind set of individuals: *Weathering the Storm*, 189.

the inter-war period—it is important to recognize that planning was not universally adopted, was widely denigrated, and was certainly not necessary to the successful, regular, and consistent use of contraception. Indeed those few who presented their contraceptive strategy as deliberate or premeditated often did so apologetically, and sought to defend themselves from a contemporary culture which perceived such calculations as cold, manipulative, and unnatural.

'SEE WHAT HAPPENS AS THE YEARS GO BY':[10] A CAVALIER APPROACH TO FAMILY PLANNING

Many of those surveyed by contemporary interview studies, as well as by recent oral historians, rejected the idea that their contraceptive behaviour represented a deliberate or decisive break with past sexual mores, and presented an approach to family building that was in sharp contrast to that envisaged by scholars of the demographic transition. Their narratives highlighted a casual, ill-informed, ill-thought-out approach to family planning. Stories did not revolve around ideas about family sizes, attempts to time births, or decisions to have no more. Rather, testimony directly and explicitly dismissed the idea that families could or should be planned. Respondents emphasized that they had no definite ideas about the size of family they wanted and made no clear resolutions whether or not to have a child at any particular point. Despite the acknowledged use of contraception, families were presented as emerging organically, pregnancies 'just happened' and children 'just came'.

Millie, an office cleaner from Oxford, for example, denied having a calculative attitude towards family size. She stressed that she did not have a fixed or clear idea about how many children she wanted and that she did not have any strong intentions with regard to spacing:

One didn't avoid—avoid it [conception]. I mean, I thought I would have, as I came from a big family—but we didn't any of us have a lot of children, you see.[11] The most was three. No, oh, one of my sisters did have five. Yes, that's right (continues talking about siblings' children)

So did you plan to have those big gaps?
No, no, it just happened. No, I mean—didn't do anything to prevent it or anything. Just the way it went.

Did you talk to your husband about when to have children and whether to have children?
No. No, we never bothered, either of us. 'Cos we were fond of children, always have been. So, it didn't worry us. I don't think I would have wanted a big family though, none the more for that. Because—had he had a better job I might have done, or, but, er, I found it enough to keep three children on what he was earning.

---

[10] Mass-Observation, TC Family Planning 1944–49, Marylebone, TC3/1/C.
[11] Note the fatalistic sense that fertility was not wholly controllable. This is explored below.

Hmm. So did you ever do anything to try to not get pregnant?
No (quizzically). Well, [he] took, er, yes, precautions—themselves, yes, but I didn't.[12]
What did he take?
Well, I suppose you—wearing something I suppose, more or less, yes, that was it. Yes, I suppose that's what it was.[13]

Yet such a mentality did not preclude the regular and effective use of birth control. Rather, such couples used contraception, but only with the general hope that family size would then be kept down, rather than to ensure a particular timing or spacing of births. Many insisted that 'planning' was not an appropriate term to describe their behaviour. Jack 'decided we'd like a family' but did not plan, 'not as the word mean, plan, no, I mean, we tried to have, er a child and then, well the family just happened, you know, just happened along.'[14] As Lella Secor Florence recognized, the use of birth control did not indicate that births were calculated: 'in numerous families no child is ever planned. The method adopted is known to be fallible, and as conception is almost certain to take place sooner or later . . . the parents prefer to wait "till it comes along".'[15] Slater and Woodside concluded that 'parents rarely carry out a consistent plan'.[16] Lewis-Faning similarly found that many did not plan how many children to have at marriage. Eighty-four per cent of the working class sample who married between 1910 and 1924 did not 'plan' their families. By the 1940s this had changed, but nevertheless 'even in the most recently married group, less than fifty per cent planned the size of their family'.[17] When, in March and April 1944, Mass-Observation asked its panellists to comment on contraceptives and family-planning decisions, many of these predominantly middle-class respondents talked about the impossibility or undesirability of planning one's family. A teacher from Essex, for example, 'did not plan our family beforehand, though we agreed that we could not manage more than three', and many of those interviewed for the *Britain and her Birth-Rate* survey also claimed to prefer to leave conception 'to chance'.[18] Brett Harvey's study of women in 1950s America was 'surprised by how many of the women I interviewed seem to 'drift' into motherhood, rather than *deciding* to get pregnant'.[19] Ralph LaRossa, in a 1977 study, was taken aback by the casual attitude to pregnancy presented by some of his respondents. He interviewed a couple expecting their first child who did not view the plan to have a child as a 'major decision in their lives'. The couple

went so far as to say that they felt they had put more thought into when to get their cat than they did into when to have a child. When I asked whether they had planned the pregnancy,

[12] The emphasis on male rather than female action is highly significant and is explored below.
[13] Millie, bc3ox#21. It must be stressed that she showed no obvious signs of embarrassment.
[14] Jack, bc3ox#13. [15] Florence, *Progress Report on Birth Control*, 131.
[16] Slater and Woodside, *Patterns of Marriage*, 180.
[17] Lewis-Faning, *Report on an Enquiry into Family Limitation*, 149. Among those who did not use birth control, a number were reported as having a 'fatalistic attitude to the arrival of children': ibid. 175.
[18] Mass-Observation, DR 3535, reply to March 1944 Directive; Mass-Observation, *Britain and her Birth-Rate*, 54–8. Mass-Observation, TC Family Planning 1944–49, TC3/1.
[19] Harvey, *The Fifties*, 89.

I was first given the impression that they had used something of a laissez-faire approach (if it happens, it happens).[20]

It is important to pay attention to such narratives. Frequently such claims are seen to be contradicted by evidence of birth control use. The idea that planning is a necessary concomitant of birth control practice is so entrenched that any evidence of such behaviour is seen as direct proof of deliberate 'planning'. The authors of Mass-Observation's *Britain and her Birth-Rate* were confused when they found that those who presented themselves as 'non-planners' and who claimed no knowledge of contraceptive techniques often had small families with large gaps between them. They interpreted the self-representation of 'leaving it to chance' as indicating that no attempt was made to limit family size (except perhaps limited adoption of abstinence). The small families achieved by such couples were eventually interpreted as evidence of low fecundity. It did not occur to the surveyors that such material might indicate that birth control could be used without 'planning', that birth control use might be compatible with 'leaving it to chance'.[21] Similarly, Elizabeth Roberts concluded that 'most, indeed almost all, couples planned their families' despite testimony asserting the opposite.[22] Yet assertions that families were not planned, despite the use of birth control, should not be discounted. Rather than assuming that any use of birth control indicates that births were in fact planned, close attention to these narratives uncovers the variety of decision-making processes that accompanied contraceptive behaviour and the range of birth control strategies employed. For many, an unplanned approach to family building was a conscious and positive strategy: couples did not always use contraception and distrusted the methods they had; moreover, couples also sought to avoid discussing sexual matters and wished to retain a belief that the future was uncontrollable and unpredictable. They did not want very many pregnancies, but wanted those they had to be surprising, unpremeditated, and spontaneous; they did not want designer babies.

'WE GOT WISER AS WE GOT OLDER':[23] MOTIVATION AND FAMILY-PLANNING PROCESSES

Instances of couples who discussed birth control and planned pregnancies (or their avoidance) were limited to particular circumstances—to times when the need to use birth control was unusually pressing, or occasions when couples disagreed fundamentally about their approach to the issue.

---

[20] LaRossa, *Conflict and Power in Marriage*, 33. Rather than exploring the interesting implications of this representation he focuses on how, after further probing, he managed to obtain information about the abandonment of previously used contraceptives, which he interprets as evidence of 'planning'.
[21] Mass-Observation, *Britain and her Birth-Rate*, 87–93.
[22] Roberts, *Women and Families*, 76–7.   [23] Iris, bc2#8.

The extent to which couples discussed or planned having a child or avoiding pregnancy varied considerably according to strength of feeling about the matter, as did the conscientiousness with which any birth control strategy was put into regular action. Historians and demographers have tended to assume that individuals were either completely indifferent to the possibility of pregnancy or desperate to avoid it. Models of fertility change which use the language of calculation and planning see a sharp divide between those who use birth control and those who do not. There is little recognition that the regularity of birth control use will vary alongside changing degrees of motivation.[24] In fact only those who had strong reasons for limiting their family size, especially those who were warned that a future pregnancy was medically perilous, presented themselves as having engaged in 'planning behaviour'. Only in such circumstances was the matter discussed and clear-cut resolutions to adopt birth control made.

Some discussed family limitation explicitly if their determination to use birth control increased, for example after an unexpected pregnancy or after a difficult or dangerous birth. Most commonly it was health reasons which prompted discussion of birth control, or the planning of future pregnancies. Fears of maternal debilitation, mortality, miscarriage, stillbirths, and infant deaths dominated the testimony of the few who made clear and determined decisions to use birth control, particularly those that were openly articulated between husband and wife. Before Elma's first child she and her husband had not discussed family-planning matters, but after the traumatic experience of birth they were not prepared to contemplate having another:

They damaged her face. Used forceps. They made a real mess of her . . . And I wouldn't've had another child if you'd've paid me millions of pounds, I wouldn't've had another one . . . I love children but I never had a chance. 'Cos Percy said 'That's it, no more children.' Me husband said 'no more', not after that.

Having stressed how her husband would not talk about sexual matters, the situation now changed, they talked extensively about avoiding pregnancy:

So did you talk with your husband about being careful?
Yes, we used to talk about it, yes. We, we never hid anything; we weren't frightened of discussing anything . . . we just said we won't have any more children, that that was—that was it. Make sure we don't have any more children.[25]

Similarly, Ann had a casual attitude towards family size at the beginning of her marriage:

You had a four-year gap before your son and the daughter . . . Did you plan that gap?
No, just happened . . . we didn't plan, we didn't plan anything, it just happened, sort of thing, people didn't them days, I don't think. If they got pregnant, they got pregnant.

---

[24] An exception is Sagi, Potter, and Westoff, 'Contraceptive Effectiveness as a Function of Desired Family Size'. This point is also recognized by Beckman, 'Measuring the Process of Fertility Decision-Making', 74–5.   [25] Elma, msf/jm/bl/#42.

When her daughter died soon after birth, however, her attitude changed: 'I wanted one to replace the one that we lost.' And after the next pregnancy she and her husband resolved not to have any more: 'Oh, I told him, I said "I'm not having no more", I'd had enough and I had a very bad time on the one.'[26]

A jeweller from Leicester, born in 1895, 'did not discuss or make any plans about having children in the early days of married life' until 'after the second boy arrived'.[27] For the first years of her marriage, Hilda and her husband, who at the time was a gardener in Wiltshire, used condoms 'sometimes, not very often', as they were not anxious to avoid pregnancy: 'we never decided on anything . . . never bothered about it. If we'd had more, we'd have had more'. After her second child was born, however, they switched to using withdrawal all the time. Her motivation to avoid pregnancy was significantly increased after her doctor told her 'it wasn't advisable to have another . . . 'cos if I had any more children I'd still have the same trouble, and, I mean, that's no joke'.[28]

The choice of method was also frequently changed in such circumstances. Higher motivation led respondents to consider the range of methods available rather than simply using the most familiar, easiest or best-known option, and a change in method was equally likely to be prompted by the increased discussion and planning brought about by a more pressing need to reduce family size. The desperation of those who wrote to Marie Stopes, many of whom had been warned not to risk another pregnancy, perhaps reveals this tendency to search for a new method of birth control if the stakes were raised.[29]

Angela and Hugh, who lived in Preston, had been using condoms and pessaries. They recognized that, with pessaries in particular, pregnancy might occur, but that that did not matter. Then after a difficult birth, the determination to avoid pregnancy increased; alarmed by irregular periods, they discussed the matter with a doctor who suggested using two methods simultaneously and fitted Angela with a cap:

Well then I had, err, a very difficult confinement, err, and so we—it was a bit tricky—risky having another child . . . and you could talk to your doctor and this is what he suggested: 'You can't just depend on one thing, you must use the two', so we went along with his advice which we did.
So then did he send you to a clinic or did he fit the cap?
(overlapping) No, he fitted it, yeah.[30]

A doctor's warning in particular was invariably taken seriously. Those who had distrusted medical methods of birth control might be persuaded by a doctor that new methods were better and more reliable. A doctor's warning also sometimes provided more information about methods and precise details about where modern appliances might be obtained, and perhaps a referral to a birth control

[26] Ann, bc2#24.   [27] Mass-Observation, DR 2708, reply to April 1944 Directive.
[28] She suffered from breast abscesses after both births. Hilda, bc3ox#31.
[29] See W. Seccombe, 'Starting to Stop', 171–2, on the fears, anguish, and worry about pregnancy expressed by those writing to Marie Stopes.   [30] Angela and Hugh, msf/kf/ht/#18.

clinic.[31] Doris was told to go to a family-planning clinic in Blackburn after her third child was born. She went and was given a cap which neither she nor her husband liked using. For a short while they persevered, using it in conjunction with their preferred method of condoms. The determination to avoid pregnancy meant that an unpopular method was conscientiously employed (for a short time at least):

Them tablets came out. I went up on the family planning when I had the third one, yes— because I mean I weren't so good after I'd 'ad the babies. So they asked me to go to the family planning, which I did . . .

Well, he didn't like really, ya know, but you 'ad it to do—you 'ad it to do anyway because . . . —we used to use both didn't we?— . . . we were that bothered really 'cos . . .

What you mean the condom as well?

Yeah . . . we were using them together.[32]

While health concerns dominated testimony on articulated birth control choices, other situations might also provoke a determined decision to avoid birth and a 'planned' approach to the timing, or spacing of pregnancy. Some presented themselves as initially having allowed their families to grow spontaneously, and depicted birth control use as a present but sporadic, casual, and unarticulated element of their sexual relations, a situation which changed once a number of children had been born and the desire to stop childbearing altogether was formed.[33] Such couples adopted a regime of both spacing and stopping, but the crucial difference was that spacing behaviour did not require marital discussion, whereas stopping was presented as a more deliberate, planned, and articulated strategy.

A further situation which might lead to the discussion of birth control practices was when couples had strongly conflicting ideas about the size or spacing of the family desired:

I remember one argument we had, went—went on a long time—it started before we got married. Sheila said it was her wish to have six children and I said (laugh) 'Not bloody likely!', and umm, 'Oh', she said, 'it's up to me, I, I'll be the one that has'—I said, 'Yes, I'll be the one that—who has to put up with them!' . . . I was very rude and said that if she wanted to do that sort of thing, to make her number up, she better see the milkman! (laughs) That was it. I wasn't gonna have a hand in it. (pause)[34]

Some had conflicting ideas about contraception, which were openly argued about.[35] What distinguishes Doris from the majority, who did not regularly or

---

[31] Stopes, *Mother England*, is dominated by complaints that doctors would not provide concrete contraceptive advice. See also L. Hall, ' "Somehow very distasteful" '.

[32] Jake and Doris, msf/srss/bl/#22.

[33] See also Potter, Sagi, and Westoff, 'Improvement of Contraception during the Course of Marriage'.   [34] Patrick, msf/kf/ht/#16.

[35] It is also possible that the expectation of conflict inhibited communication for some couples. One woman interviewed by Mass-Observation avoided 'questions that bring trouble between man

explicitly discuss family planning, was the fact that she and her husband had opposing desires:

So tell me about the discussions you would have with your husband about whether to have children and when to have children.
Oh dear, that caused animosity (laughs) . . . He wanted children, and I didn't. I had such a bad time on Frances—first one—that it put me off children altogether. You know, I had to have instruments and um—although I had a baby at home, the doctor—I had two doctors there and they put me under and delivered her, sort of thing, you know—I thought, after that, 'No thanks I'm not having more children' . . . we didn't argue, we just, um—he was very docile sort of man—quiet and, um—although he loved children, he respected my wishes, I suppose, and in the end I thought, 'Oh well it's not fair I'd better give in', kind of thing, so there we are.[36]

Unless couples had pressing and urgent reasons to avoid pregnancy, there was often little need to discuss the matter. Rather than necessarily being determined to avoid pregnancy or anxious to get pregnant, most had ambivalent attitudes towards the timing of pregnancy and the size of family. Contraceptive strategies emerged which accommodated such fluid aims and intentions towards family size. An interventionist and determined approach to contraception was likely to be adopted by those couples for whom another pregnancy was to be avoided at all costs, typically for health reasons, or for whom the topic was too fraught to be ignored. The silence on matters of family planning was frequently broken when motivation was high. 'Planned' birth control behaviour is best viewed, therefore, as the outcome of a period of crisis or dispute rather than as a prerequisite of birth control behaviour.

The majority rejected the notion that their family was planned as they were far more cavalier about the possibility of pregnancy, even while they were employing birth control methods. Slater and Woodside found that in practice 'Contraception is haphazard, as if the parents did not know clearly what they did want, or were too lazy, indifferent or incompetent to carry out their wishes effectively.'[37] Lella Secor Florence noted the existence of patients at birth control clinics who

---

and wife'. Mass-Observation, TC Family Planning 1944–49, TC3/1/F. Janet Askham argues that many couples avoid the discussion of subjects likely to cause arguments or conflict. Certainly the negotiation of contraception has the potential to be a fraught topic. Emotions, opinions, and tempers were likely to run high over aspects of sexual activity and pregnancy. See Askham, *Identity and Stability in Marriage*, 33–54. Martin Sussman maintains that conflict often impeded the use of contraception, arguing that 'sex relations' were often a form of 'crisis resolution'. Often when 'a couple who have employed a contraceptive device for a reasonable period of time . . . suddenly stop using it without any logical explanation and . . . virtually abandon a family planning program' it is because sexual activity is being used as a way to solve a marital crisis or dispute. See Sussman, 'Family Interaction and Fertility', 103. An example of this is the testimony of Edith, bc2#23: 'he purposely avoided having any children for the first couple of years, it was only because we'd had a row that we had the first one, in making up, that was the trouble. And I'm going to be quite honest, the second one was just the same.'

[36] Doris, bc3sw#6.   [37] Slater and Woodside, *Patterns of Marriage*, 180.

preferred to ' "drift with the tide"—to "take pot luck"—rather than to make the effort to exert some control over their own destinies'. These women who grew 'careless about taking precautions' were found to be 'rather pleased when the new baby arrives'.[38] A part-time porter did not 'really want any more. But if any came along I shouldn't grumble.'[39] An office worker 'intended to have children, but no special number in mind'. He and his wife were therefore happy to 'let nature take its course', while a mechanic 'was not averse to having children' but was using contraception. As a result, the conception of his children was best described as 'accidental'.[40] Another, a surveyor, who had been married for three years in 1944 had only a 'vague idea' about family size which was 'very unplanned at the moment' and a fitter from Coventry had not 'planned anything at all'. Children, 'just happen and then we say, "oh yes, we have always wanted one"!'[41] Louisa provided further evidence that birth control use did not always result from a firm decision to avoid having another child:

No, there wasn't a time I didn't want to be pregnant, not in my mind, I just—we were just careful and if there was anything to do with sex my—my husband used, as they called them then, a French letter—if we wanted sex, we were careful that way.[42]

Individuals had various reasons for using birth control, but often these were only loosely maintained. In a significant number of instances couples presented themselves as acting, 'unthinkingly', in accordance with common practice. Withdrawal, in particular, was so much an accepted, 'normal' form of sexual activity that it could be used without active or strong contraceptive aims. Indeed Lella Secor Florence concluded that it 'was so common that many women think of it not as a contraceptive but as a normal part of sexual intercourse'.[43] One couple was reported to have had 'trouble conceiving' as they had 'got coitus interruptus down to such a fine art that it is difficult for him to come in the vagina'.[44] Many other respondents had difficulty articulating the reasons behind their contraceptive behaviour. They predominantly represented their desires about family size as having had rather indeterminate and imperceptible influences. Some talked about poverty, aspirations for certain lifestyles, models of family life and marriage, and their ambitions concerning the raising of their children, but only in the abstract. A number mentioned a desire to avoid the large families they grew up in and others wanted to avoid the pain of labour. Such reasons were, however, presented by the majority as vague, post-hoc rationalizations, rather than as thoughts and deliberations that preceded determined decisions to avoid pregnancy. They influenced

[38] Florence, *Progress Report on Birth Control*, 62, 66.
[39] Mass-Observation, TC Family Planning 1944–49, TC3/1/F.
[40] Mass-Observation, DR 2111, reply to April 1944 Directive; DR 3182, reply to April 1944 Directive.
[41] Mass-Observation, DR 2808, reply to April 1944 Directive; DR 2818, reply to April 1944 Directive.   [42] Louisa, bc3ox#14.
[43] Florence, *Progress Report on Birth Control*, 211.
[44] Woman courting in the 1920s. Interview transcript, A&M: GC/105/23.

aims but were not sufficiently thought out or strong to turn such aims into resolutions or plans.

Those who did not have firm contraceptive strategies, and those who did not have a strong motivation to avoid pregnancy, did not necessarily use birth control with the degree of conscientiousness usually assumed by studies of fertility decline. Slater and Woodside's research in the mid-1940s presented contraception as 'carried out spasmodically and with a great deal of careless-ness'. Mass-Observation's *Britain and her Birth-Rate* concluded that, while as much as 90 per cent of parents might make some attempt to limit fertility, 'the proportion who use any method consistently is considerably smaller'.[45] Lewis-Faning found 145 respondents (12.5 per cent) who abandoned the use of birth control for no discernible reason, despite not wanting to get pregnant.[46] Many respondents acknowledged that the determination and consistency with which they used birth control was far from perfect. This irregular use clearly lay behind their presentation of a complaisant attitude towards the exact size and spacing of their family. Phyllis did not know why she had only two children and 'wouldn't've minded more'. She 'just had what came' and trusted her husband to 'not finish properly' and 'get away before the seed starts'. Yet that was not 'why I didn't have any more', since 'it wasn't . . . every time'.[47] Many used methods irregularly knowing that they were risking pregnancy, and indeed were happy with this regime, knowing it reduced the chance of pregnancy while not minding if con-ception were to occur. As a university staff tutor told Mass-Observation, 'we did not intend to have children . . . though we knew the risk we were taking at the time our son was conceived'.[48] Similarly, a housewife from York thought 'it was hardly the time to have a child [but] we didn't completely rule out the possibility and decided to trust to luck rather than use birth control'.[49] Hugh used a sponge for a short while despite thinking 'it was very risky', as he did not really mind if a pregnancy occurred: 'it was at the time when it wouldn't have mattered had it happened'.[50]

Thus, many did not have firm plans or desires with regard to family size. They did not have very strong opinions about the particular spacing of their families or clear intentions as to an ideal number to be born. Such couples used contracep-tion with varying degrees of consistency, in the knowledge that such behaviour would be likely to fulfil their modest and realistic desires with regard to family size. When pregnancy did occur it was not necessarily categorized as a 'contracep-tive failure': it wasn't an unwanted birth or an 'accident'. Rather, they expected, and did not object to, the occasional pregnancy. Their contraceptive behaviour illustrates the practice resulting from a vague goal to delay, or have fewer, or no

[45] Slater and Woodside, *Patterns of Marriage*, 204; Mass-Observation, *Britain and her Birth-Rate*, 54–5.   [46] Lewis-Faning, *Report of an Inquiry into Family Limitation*, 118.
[47] Phyllis, bc3ox#17.   [48] Mass-Observation, DR 2156, reply to April 1944 Directive.
[49] Mass-Observation, DR 1362, reply to March 1944 Directive.
[50] Angela and Hugh, msf/kf/ht/#18.

more, which might be the aim at any stage of a marriage, and which was not necessarily maintained.

'YOU CAN'T EVER KNOW WHAT'S IN STORE FOR YOU':[51] THE IMPOSSIBILITY OF FAMILY PLANNING

Using birth control without planning or discussion was a justified and accurate form of self-representation, analysis of which is informative about the nature of birth control decision-making and the details of behaviour. First, many felt unable to plan, given the unreliability of birth control methods and the uncertainties in their knowledge of fertility control. Secondly, birth control methods were associated with a 'modern' approach to life from which many wished to distance themselves. They sought to use birth control while at the same time maintaining an ethos which allowed 'nature' to determine the precise timing of pregnancy (at least early on in their marriages) and allowed family building to remain organic, spontaneous, and mysterious. Claims that families were not planned were not disingenuous; planning was not a necessary condition of birth control use, and indeed an unplanned approach to family building was a deliberate and conscious birth control strategy.

Many felt that 'planning' was inappropriate and impossible because confusion still dominated their perception of reproduction. Conception was frequently presented as a highly complicated and contingent process, far from fully understood. It was widely recognized that fertility varied among individuals, that while some were infertile or sub-fertile others were particularly prone to pregnancy.[52] Planning was impossible given that 'you don't always 'ave children do you when you, you 'ave intercourse?'[53] and given that some, like Lorna's cousin, only had one son for whom 'they tried and tried', whereas others 'never tried, no, it just happened'.[54] As one woman reported to Mass-Observation: 'I don't think they really can plan. I feel you can't always arrange these things; you can't always be too clever.'[55] Another claimed that 'it all depends on the person if they have a lot or not',[56] while another felt that she was 'not sufficiently fertile ever to be able to plan my family'.[57] Similarly, Dilys's perception of the sheer quantity of sperm and eggs led her to think that she could not control the size of her family:

And there's withdrawal like, and you never sure of that, because it only wants one egg to meet up with the other see and there are so many eggs there that it's only chance. Never tried to get pregnant, it was just ordinary like.[58]

[51] Mass-Observation, TC Family Planning 1944–49, Marylebone, TC31/C.
[52] See also Luker, *Taking Chances*, 88.   [53] Eleanor, msf/kf/bl/#11.
[54] Lorna, msf/kf/bl/#25.   [55] Mass-Observation, *Britain and her Birth-Rate*, 60.
[56] Mass-Observation, TC Family Planning 1944–49, Shoreditch, TC3/2/A.
[57] Mass-Observation, Dr 1346, reply to March 1944 Directive.   [58] Dilys, bc2#13.

Many, particularly among the working classes, saw fertility as having an inherited component.[59] Indeed, a number saw the high fertility of their relatives, and particularly their parents, as an indication that they too were likely to have a large family. While they might make attempts to limit their family size, ultimately there was an uncontrollable, hereditary element to conception which prevented them from 'planning' their families. As one part-time typist in Gloucester commented, 'it's not a matter is in your hands'.[60] Hilda, for example, had a husband who was careful, yet she remained surprised that this was so successful given that she and her husband both came from large families:

So how many children did you have?
Two.

So you had a much smaller family than the one you grew up in?[61]
Yeah, yes, surprised me really. 'Cos my husband, he come from a big family. Now he was the same, you see, he come from Blackfriars Road, and there was about eight of them.

So how did you only have two?
Just careful I suppose he was.

What does that mean?
Well, take the kettle off before it boiled, they used to say, you know.[62]

The frequent presentation of contraceptive behaviour as 'unplanned' and vague attempts to reduce family size also reflected the degree of confidence respondents had in their knowledge of methods and their reliability. Many stressed the limited contraceptive options available, and frequently juxtaposed this with statements about the much wider availability of effective contraception today.[63] There was among many a pervasive feeling that methods were not reliable enough to allow confident fertility control and certainly did not provide the luxury of being able to 'plan' one's family. Withdrawal was risky, condoms were rumoured to have holes, and caps and pessaries were thought to provide an incomplete barrier which might slip out of place. One panellist told Mass-Observation that planning was impossible: 'contraceptives were not reliable enough for that'.[64] Nancy claimed not to know about birth control methods: 'we didn't have them things in them days'; instead 'it was up to yourselves'. All you could do was 'just be careful'; 'he would have to get away from you pretty quick'. As a result, each month 'you'd say

---

[59] On the importance of ideas about heredity in contemporary culture see e.g. Richardson, *Love and Eugenics in the Late Nineteenth Century*.

[60] Mass-Observation, TC Family Planning 1944–49, Gloucester, TC3/1/F.

[61] She was one of ten children.   [62] Hilda, bc3ox#5.

[63] Lee Rainwater also found that 'lower class women very often assess their knowledge of contraception at marriage as low and they tend to feel that they are only modestly well-informed even at present'. As a result he concluded that 'couples at the lowest class level seem to show relatively little confidence that they will be able to make successful use of the methods known to them'. He groups his 409 interviewees into four classes, based on husband's occupation: upper-middle class, lower-middle class, upper-lower class and lower-lower class: Rainwater, *Family Design*, 290–1.

[64] Mass Observation, DR 2771, reply to April 1944 Directive.

"Thank God for that"' when a period arrived. 'You just had to sort of, trust to luck, really. You could have had a big family.'[65] Busfield and Paddon also acknowledged that people adopted birth control practices with varying degrees of faith. They argued that 'the difference in the degree of control which people feel they have over pregnancy and birth is at times revealed in the language that they use when talking about them.'[66] Respondents frequently spoke of 'falling' for a child rather than, for example, 'going in for one'.

Other factors and beliefs about the 'mystery' of conception (such as whether female orgasm was an essential component) further complicated the practice of birth control and reinforced the notion that pregnancy was unpredictable.[67] Agatha, who worked as a parlourmaid in Surrey, got married in 1940 aged 30, and soon fell pregnant despite having used birth control. She continued to use birth control for the rest of her married life and did not conceive again. Yet, she did not characterize herself as having successfully calculated her family size or as having had the means to control her fertility. Rather, she pointed out that contraception was not wholly reliable and feared that her own inability to avoid orgasm might increase her chances of falling pregnant. Like others she additionally believed that her mother's high fertility was a signal of her own:

I was never—I never 'ad faith in anything like that myself because I'd 'eard of others—girls getting into trouble yer see, having a baby and they'd been using condoms—so of course naturally you'd—it puts you off doesn't it, that kind of—to 'ave full faith in them . . . And I was always afraid that I would be the same [as my mother], thought if I'd one I'd 'ave another and another and another and that, and I think that spoilt my marriage a lot really, being scared . . . well I think you do get a nice feeling now and again but I didn't very often sort of thing, I think it was because I was tense all the time, scared I was gonna 'ave a baby . . .

Were you scared even when you were taking precautions or when your husband was being careful?
I'd still get scared yes. I was always glad for my monthly period to come along to put me at ease, yeah . . . To tell you the truth I don't know—I don't know how that come about, but I must have had a thrill when I 'ad Anthony, mustn't I, my son . . . Must 'ave done to 'ave joined up, mustn't you? Must join up together when you're making love, otherwise there wouldn't be a baby would there?

But if you didn't have the thrill did you then know that you couldn't get pregnant?
Oh, yes, yes.

So is that why you tried to avoid having the thrill?
Yeah, probably it was.[68]

---

[65] Nancy, bc3ox#22.   [66] Busfield and Paddon, *Thinking about Children*, 48.

[67] See also McLaren, *Reproductive Rituals*, 55, for a recognition that men and women did not have a rigid, mechanical view of reproduction. He argues that a number of factors were commonly thought to affect fertility, only some of them in the hands of the individual.

[68] Agatha, msf/kf/ht/#7.

Peter, a stripper and grinder in a Lancashire cotton mill, also stressed the unreliability of withdrawal, which, combined with the unpredictability of the female orgasm, further prevented the confident calculation of one's family size:

. . . you can jump too late can't you, and miss your footing! . . . What I was saying is this: like you can be having intercourse . . . you can pull off at Mill Hill but still the woman hadn't climaxed, right?[69] But he's just a fraction late, right? And then a bit after—after intercourse is finished, a woman can release, right? And she can be caught can't she?

How can she be caught?

Well, for the simple reason he—as I say, he hasn't got off quick enough and, er—train got into Blackburn quicker than what he thought (laughs)! And then after a while she—after they'd 'ad it and they're—she's getting dressed again we'll put—making it getting her clothes on, she could climax then couldn't she? But there's part of his sperm in her . . . and then she can, she can contract, couldn't she?

So does she have to climax in order to?

Oh, she'll 'ave to do.

To get the sperm?

If she doesn't climax there's no chance of any pregnancy, no, no they both 'ave to climax, you should know that.

So would you say that one way of avoiding pregnancy was avoiding her climaxing?

Pair of 'em avoiding it . . . But if, as I say, he's a bit late, and then she could come on after, like that sperm's in her and it could form the egg and start it off.[70]

'IT'S NOT VERY NICE TO HAVE IT ALL CUT AND DRIED':[71] THE ADVANTAGES OF FATALISM

The representation of fertility as beyond human control was not simply a negative response to 'primitive' contraceptive methods and particular constructions of

[69] Mill Hill was a suburban station in Blackburn. 'Getting off at Mill Hill', the stop prior to the Blackburn terminus, was a common euphemism for withdrawal. Santow charts the growth of transport metaphors with the Industrial Revolution: 'Coitus Interruptus and the Control of Natural Fertility', 37.

[70] Peter, msf/kf/bl/#26. Thomas Laqueur argues that a 'two-seed' model of generation, which sees female orgasm as vital to conception, remained common 'in the imaginations of many people' despite the rise of the 'two-sex model': *Making Sex*, 99. See also McLaren, *Reproductive Rituals*, 20–1; Cook, *The Long Sexual Revolution*, 127–8. Many editions of Aristotle's *Masterpiece*, a popular sexual advice book in circulation from the seventeenth century onwards, claimed that 'equal vigour' was required by both parties during coition in order for conception to occur. Victorian editions were less explicit on the matter but nevertheless argued that 'the greater the woman's desire for copulation is, the more likely she is to conceive': *Aristotle's Works*. A number of oral history respondents had read Aristotle's *Masterpiece*. On its impact in the twentieth century see also Porter and Hall, *The Facts of Life*, 205; Jonathan Rose, *The Intellectual Life of the British Working Classes*, 206–7.

[71] Mass-Observation, TC Family Planning 1944–49, Paddington, TC3/1/B.

biological processes. The claim that family size could not be planned among oral history respondents was also part of a more positive narrative, and part of an explicit critique of modern values. Not only were contemporary families seen as receiving detailed sex education and having access to new reproductive technology (notably the Pill), but, in addition, they were characterized as obsessively planning aspects of life which should not be calculated but rather should be left to nature. Many rejected what they saw as the overly deterministic approach to life adopted by modern society, and saw a calculative attitude towards such unpredictable variables as pregnancy and childbirth as detracting from the mystery and magic of reproduction. Such views are also apparent in archival material. As one of Mass-Observation's panellists commented: 'I do not believe that a force like human physical love can be controlled without losing some of its force and beauty.'[72] Technology had, in the view of many people, both encouraged a futile belief that the future was controllable that could only lead to disappointment, and introduced an assumption that aspects of life which should be surprising, spontaneous, and miraculous could be controlled and determined. An engineer told Mass-Observation that one should not 'plan in any exact way' as 'precision may lead to disappointment'. As a result, 'no number was ever mentioned by either of us as a "target"'. This couple chose instead to 'see how things worked out . . . if one came by accident neither would be unduly upset'.[73] Mass-Observation's *Britain and her Birth-Rate* revealed the dominance of this way of thinking in 1944. One 27-year-old woman from Paddington tried and failed to plan: 'no-one can be so clever, nature doesn't work on those lines'. Another woman, 26 years old, thought it 'hopeless to try and start planning because if you plan for two children, you might end up with none or twice as many. I've had the laugh over many smart people over that.'[74]

And did you decide to have four?
Well, you ought to take life as it comes, innit? Take life as they come. Yeah.

Do you know whether you wanted a big family or a small family?
No, no, I was easy, I was. See we had two boys and two girls and that was it.

And how about your wife. How did she feel about how many children she wanted?
Oh, she didn't say nothing. She didn't have any bother. So that was it. And never bothered since.

So you didn't plan your family?
No, no.

And did you limit the size of your family? (repeats)
No, didn't, no, like see, we left it as it come. Didn't bother about it.[75]

---

72 Mass-Observation, DR 1234, reply to April 1944 Directive.
73 Mass-Observation, DR 3359, reply to March 1944 Directive.
74 Mass-Observation, TC Family Planning 1944–49, Paddington, TC3/1/B.
75 Hugh, bc3sw#23.

The recognition that 'things never work out according to plan' was a positive stance: 'that's why it's a pity to plan too definitely'.[76] Thus, for many, a general preference for a 'smallish' family was combined with a sentimental rejection of a cold, calculating approach to childbearing. To 'control' births was frequently presented as inappropriately unemotional. Birth control preferences and practices were designed to allow a family to emerge naturally and spontaneously without direct intervention, calculation, or control. As one 29-year-old woman told Mass-Observation in 1944, in response to a question about family planning: 'I should like to still have some surprises in life.'[77] Another wanted to 'leave it to chance' as 'Married life is a gamble anyway'.[78] Oral history respondents voice similar sentiments:

No, no just took things, sort of naturally and let things 'appen if they wanted to, or if they didn't well that was it.[79]

What did you do to plan your family?
Oh, I don't know. We just—just life went on as it were. We didn't ever really stick to any hard and fast rules of any sort.[80]

We didn't decide anything, we just took what came. No more came . . . If they come they come, that was it. We weren't bothered . . . Never thought about it. Never thought about how many children, like that, if they came they came, you know, we didn't bother . . . we didn't talk about things like that, those days. (laughs) Not like nowadays is it? I don't think we ever wanted any more, if they'd've come along they d've come, otherwise we were quite content.[81]

'Not planning' was also linked to a definition of sexual intercourse as spontaneous, natural, uncontrived, and also, crucially, unplanned.[82] Such a construction meant that sexual intercourse without using contraception was important even for those who sought to avoid pregnancy. As Kristin Luker found, 'the degree of planning and foresight that contraception demands can make a desirably warm and intimate emotional experience appear impersonally "cold blooded" '.[83] One woman told Mass-Observation, 'its [*sic*] more chance than anything . . . you gets excited and forgets yourself', while a man similarly commented ' "sexcitement" does not beget cold-blooded care'.[84] Another woman failed to use her cap because 'We're very much in love, and everything else went out of my mind.'[85] Similarly a

---

[76] Mass-Observation, TC Family Planning 1944–49, Marylebone, TC3/1/C.
[77] Mass-Observation, TC Family Planning 1944–49, Hampstead, TC3/1/B.
[78] Mass-Observation, TC Family Planning 1944–49, Women at Osrams, TC3/1/G.
[79] Maud, msf/kf/bl/#18.   [80] Bryan, msf/kf/ht/#25.   [81] Vera, bc3ox#8.
[82] Caroline Bledsoe convincingly argued that such factors continue to dominate the discourse surrounding birth-control use in contemporary American society: Bledsoe, 'Contraception and "Natural" Fertility in America'.   [83] Luker, *Taking Chances*, 42.
[84] Mass-Observation, *Britain and her Birth-Rate*, 60; Mass-Observation, DR 3330, reply to April 1944 Directive.   [85] Florence, *Progress Report on Birth Control*, 191.

man interviewed by a Television History Workshop insisted that 'assiduous' use of French letters was impossible:

> sex . . . is a question of impulse, or the moment, and the impulse might come over you so strong when you're young that you're out of French letters . . . you intend to withdraw it. You may think you've done so and you haven't . . . Unless you're going to—um as in Orwell's book go round . . . with a belt of contraceptives on, it's bound to happen sometime even if you practice birth control.[86]

For Charlie, a boilerman in Penarth docks, the conception of his daughter was constructed as a particularly happy event precisely because she wasn't planned.[87] Rather, she was the product of an especially passionate and spontaneous night during which he and his wife 'forgot ourselves'.[88] Similarly, Christopher, a builder from Kirkhall, conceived his last child when they 'went for a walk . . . to the local golf . . . he was conceived in the bunker, in the sand (laughs)'. He hadn't used contraception or withdrawn because 'I wasn't, just, just spontaneous was that, spontaneous, spontaneous was that, yeah, it was.'[89] For many, too clear a contraceptive strategy, too openly planned, too assiduously adhered to, detracted from the natural approach to sexual frequency. Conception was a natural by-product of intercourse and was therefore seen as something that should not be too carefully or systematically controlled or artificially prevented. In this context withdrawal was frequently chosen because it did not completely eliminate the natural chance of conception, nor did it introduce an element of planning, preparation, or artifice into the dynamics of sexual intimacy. Lorna, despite the fear that she might get pregnant as she was never sure whether her husband had managed to withdraw, rejected all other forms of birth control, preferring a method which did not require discussion, did not turn sex into a 'science' and was both natural and spontaneous:

> you relied on your p-periods to say you were all right . . . I mean, we took it as it come, er, and, and, and, we didn't make a science out of it or er, or, er—we didn't make a meal of it . . . There's always that fear anyway unless you are using contraceptives . . . I didn't worry till after. Didn't worry till after. You didn't worry till after . . . it, it wasn't a—it wasn't a fetish with us, you know it were just spontaneous, though.[90]

That such couples used birth control with a degree of consistency challenges the prevalent argument that, for successful[91] fertility control, decisions must be conceived as having been 'overt', 'deliberate', and 'calculated', and based on clear numerical notions of an ideal family size. Historians have assumed that those exhibiting a 'depressive, fatalistic attitude towards having children', such as that of

[86] 'In the Club', A&M: GC/105/103.

[87] Kristin Luker reports similar stories of moments which were seen as too romantic to be sullied by the use of contraception: *Taking Chances*, 50.   [88] Charlie, bc2#25.

[89] Christopher, msf/kf/bl/#34.   [90] Lorna, msf/kf/bl/#25.

[91] Indeed, the very use of the word 'successful' is problematic, and dependent on assumed understandings of the aims and desires of historical actors.

an East End mother who told Mass-Observation 'it's no manner of use to decide at all, for your fate's your fate and you can't alter it', were incapable of controlling their families.[92] Etienne van de Walle argues that women displaying such attitudes 'lack the frame of mind and the clear numerical standard that would allow them to make sense of small families and the means to obtain them'.[93] Yet the types of narrative which are used to illustrate the 'unthinkability' of fertility control in some past and present cultures are also exhibited by individuals who used birth control.[94] Reenie, below, had six children while using withdrawal, and Florence, whose father was a publican, only had two:

Things just happen . . . What I say is: what's for you, you'll have. If I wasn't to have six, I wouldn't have had six.[95]

We never used to discuss it. My mother used to say what will be will be and you won't stop it. That was the way she advised us to look at life . . . I was never interested because I used to think, what's for you you will have and you have to make the best of your life. You used to—see years ago, five, six or seven was nothing in families.[96]

Such fatalism needs instead to be viewed as a 'positive' ideology, in which an acceptance of the unpredictability of the future and what comes 'naturally' were valued.[97] Many did not seek to cheat fate, they embraced the unpredictability of family size, were determined to accept any pregnancies that occurred, but hoped not to get pregnant too often.

So were you worried during that period that you might get pregnant?
Occasionally, occasionally, I were, yes, but I didn't let it worry me too much, I thought 'What has to be'll be'.[98]

---

[92] Mass-Observation, *Britain and her Birth-Rate*, 58. Similarly, Caroline Bledsoe has challenged the distinction between traditional and modern societies and revealed that despite the high fertility of Gambian populations, and the prevalence of such statements as 'All the children God gives me' in response to questions about the number of offspring desired or planned, women were well aware of contraceptive options and indeed used contraception according to their own specific needs: 'Contraception and "Natural" Fertility'.

[93] Van de Walle, 'Fertility Transition, Conscious Choice, and Numeracy', 496, 495. Few have challenged the idea that such a mentality was necessary to the successful use of birth control, though many have argued that such a mindset was in evidence in pre-industrial societies. See e.g. Biller, 'Birth Control in the West in the Thirteenth and Early Fourteenth Centuries'; the image of a woman in the past as a 'pathetic . . . victim of her own fecundity' is criticized in McLaren, *Reproductive Rituals*, 1.

[94] A similar argument is presented by Mary Jo Maynes, who criticizes Alwin Ger's characterization of mining families in Saxony in the 1860s as 'irrational'. She argues for the importance of a 'different rationality of limitation', such as those she came across in German autobiographies of families, which were only small but nevertheless felt that 'control over fertility was either unthinkable or unmanageable': Maynes, 'The Contours of Childhood', 115.

[95] Reenie, bc3sw#26. Although she had an unusually large family, her testimony was not unusual.

[96] Florence, bc1/pilot/#4. She felt 'birth control' was 'a weakness. You can control that yourself.' This was probably a reference to withdrawal, though she might have been referring to abstinence. This pilot interview was not included in the sample.

[97] See L. Edgell, 'Couples Whom Nothing Seems To Suit', 249, for a discussion of contemporary family planning services' response to such views.   [98] Eva, msf/kf/bl/#9.

The decline in fertility does not necessarily reflect the adoption of 'a more calculating attitude about childbearing', and the historian's task is not therefore the explanation of 'a cultural revolution that erodes . . . fatalist passivity . . . and brings the possibility of preventive action within the realm of conscious choice'.[99] Indeed, the use of such terms as 'calculated' and 'planned', to describe the decisions made to use birth control, is to proscribe certain sets of explanatory variables available to historians. A much vaguer, less calculated, more fatalistic and haphazard presentation of family-planning decisions dominates much of the first-hand testimony on family limitation.[100] Oral history interviewees acknowledged that their generation had smaller families than previous generations, but they did not see their actions as 'revolutionary'. Rather, they stressed the extent to which their family-planning methods were traditional, the extent to which their choices were not radically different to those of their parents, and that they were only doing what everyone 'knew about' and 'did'. In presenting such narratives, respondents self-consciously distanced their perceptions of their own approach to family building from that associated with the modern world. Their approach to fertility control was directly linked to the mores of the past, of their parents' generation, despite the fact that the contrast in size between those families interviewed and the families they were raised in was frequently noted. For a great many respondents, the use of contraception did not reflect the adoption of a firm and constant strategy for 'family planning'. This research has found that the majority of couples interviewed did not perceive themselves as having been in a position to 'plan' their families. They saw their contraceptive options as limited, their knowledge incomplete or unsatisfactory, and the methods available somewhat untrustworthy.

'HE DIDN'T DISCUSS ANYTHING THAT HE SHOULDN'T DISCUSS WITH A WOMAN':[101] GENDER AND TACIT DECISION-MAKING

Central to many understandings of contraceptive practice in the historiographical literature is the claim that effective birth control use requires 'sufficient communication' between spouses.[102] Parents are envisaged weighing up the contraceptive methods available, discussing the pros and cons of further childbearing, and deciding to act accordingly. The argument runs that consensus is thus only reached and acted upon after detailed, explicit and careful discussion about having children. Diana Gittins and Elizabeth Roberts concur that 'an important factor in limiting families' was 'the ability of husband and wife to discuss the

---

[99] W. Seccombe, *Weathering the Storm*, 192;. Tilly and Scott, *Women, Work and Family*, 172.

[100] On the 'language of fatalism' see also E. Ross, *Love and Toil*, 98.

[101] Elma, msf/jm/bl/#42.   [102] Coale, 'The Demographic Transition Reconsidered', 65.

question'.[103] J. Mayone Stycos, Kurt Back, and Reuben Hill concluded that 'communication between partners would seem necessary to ensure effective birth-control practice', despite citing evidence to the contrary.[104]

Many individuals, however, claimed that they did not talk about contraception to their partner. The claim that family size was not planned was backed up by assertions that birth control and family limitation were not discussed. A 30-year-old woman from Hampstead told Mass-Observation in 1944 that 'we both felt rather shy talking about these things', and 'thought most young couples do', and a 33-year-old from Marylebone 'wouldn't trouble to ask' her husband's views.[105] Busfield and Paddon also found that 'as many as 28% of couples claimed never to have talked about birth control when they first married and some 37% of couples said they now never talked about the subject'.[106]

Bertha felt that the suggestion she might have talked to her husband, an engineer, about family size or contraception was ridiculous. She and her husband used withdrawal:

And did you talk to your husband about how many children you wanted?
No, course not. They came—they came, or they didn't. So that was it.[107]

It might be tempting to discount assertions that birth control practices were never discussed and to interpret such claims as evidence either of the difficulties interviewees faced in accurately remembering or reconstructing complex decision-making processes in the past, or of the reluctance on the part of respondents to reveal the nature of their deliberations about this sensitive topic to an interviewer.[108] However, not only does testimony indicate little sign of embarrassment and much evidence of a frank attempt to describe past experiences accurately, but it also shows the ways in which tacit negotiation was conducted, or unspoken consensus reached. Discussion was not necessary for those couples who left the enactment of a birth control strategy to one partner, or for those who recognized they shared the same assumptions regarding family size.

A Harlesden woman married in 1933 thought that she and her husband 'share[d] the same opinion, although I haven't ever asked him'.[109] For some, contraceptive behaviour was not necessarily accompanied by explicit negotiation; it

---

[103] Roberts, *A Woman's Place*, 92; Gittins, *Fair Sex*, ch. 5.

[104] Stycos, Back, and Hill, 'Problems of Communication Between Husband and Wife', 213. One recent study has challenged the assumption that increased communication between spouses improves the chances that couples will agree to use birth control: Dodoo, Ezeh, and Owuor, 'Some Evidence against the Assumption that Approval of Family Planning is Associated with Frequency of Spouses' Discussion of the Subject'. Others have recognized that, in some cultures, 'family planning is so taboo that even husbands and wives do not discuss it': E. Rogers, *Communication Strategies*, 36–7.

[105] Mass-Observation, TC Family Planning 1944–49, Hampstead, TC3/1/B; Marylebone, TC3/1/C.   [106] Busfield and Paddon, *Thinking about Children*, 241.

[107] Bertha, bc3ox#41.

[108] On the difficulties of asking questions about marital communication see Askham, *Identity and Stability in Marriage*, 39.

[109] Mass-Observation, TC Family Planning 1944–49, Harlesden, TC3/1/B.

was simply the enactment of an expected form of marital behaviour, the expression of normal marital roles. Many couples began marriage jointly assuming that the husband would use a male method of contraception some of the time. Action might then be taken without any discussion of the matter. Annie's husband, a painter and decorator in Oxford, started using condoms from the beginning of their marriage in 1929 and did so consistently throughout. She and her husband quickly realized that 'they didn't want children'. The use of contraception was 'automatic'; they did not 'bother' to talk about it. Even when the method failed (they had two children), they did not discuss or reappraise their contraceptive behaviour. Annie had almost nothing to say each time I asked her about discussing family size or discussing contraception:

So tell me . . . did you talk to your husband, when you didn't want any children? Did you talk about having children with your husband?
Well, we didn't really. He just—I just—we just thought we didn't want any. That was all! Wasn't much . . .

So tell me about the discussions you had with your husband about not wanting to have children.
Well, I don't know anything. It just come automatic. I didn't want—he didn't want any, and that was it. We never bothered talking about it . . .

And you talked to your husband about using condoms? Can you remember?
No, he just used them and that was it. But, neither of us wanted any more children.[110]

For Hetty and her husband, a bus driver, an easily reached consensus, coupled with a casual attitude to the particular timing of births, meant that 'in-depth' discussion was unnecessary:

. . . we didn't have much of a discussion. We didn't want to start a family straight away . . . but, um, you'd have to know my husband to realize the attitude he would take—it was a case of, um—well I'd like to have a baby—we'll have a baby sometime and a, er, girl for me, a little boy for you and, er, there was no proper—no in-depth discussion about it—it was a case with him—well if it happened it would be jolly good, you know, I'll be very pleased, and if it didn't, well it didn't. And that was all.[111]

Some analyses of contraceptive behaviour have noted the tendency for such decisions to be implicit and rarely discussed. Frank and Scanzoni argued that in many households the decisions to use contraception were best described as the result of '*spontaneous consensus*, in which, as a result of shared preferences, parties concur on a set of actions, even though they have never verbalized them'.[112] Kristin Luker argues that contraceptive decision-making was often the result of tacit co-ordination in which couples 'trie[d] to anticipate one another's expectations but did not discuss them'.[113] This was also how Busfield and Paddon interpreted the information from the respondents in their survey who claimed they did

---

[110] Annie, bc3ox#27.   [111] Hetty, bc3ox#12.
[112] Frank and Scanzoni, 'Sexual Decision-Making', 55.
[113] Described in A. Carter, 'Agency and Fertility', 73.

not discuss contraception: 'not talking about a subject at a particular point in time may simply mean that ideas and information have already been shared, and agreement has been reached. It is also likely that the use of certain methods of contraception provokes more discussion than others, and that once the method has been selected there is little more said about its use'.[114] Indeed in 1933 Leonora Eyles recommended the cap for this very reason. She recognized that discussing birth control made sex either clinical and calculated or seedy and illicit. Such difficulties were avoided by female methods whose use did not need to be negotiated during the sex act and which allowed couples to agree once on their use and never mention it again: 'one discussion, preferably before marriage, on the whole subject should be enough, and the whole subject can be dismissed, with all its atmosphere of a doctor's consulting room or the less pleasant suggestion of the rubber shop and surreptitiousness'.[115]

For many couples a tacit understanding that birth control would be used at certain times during the marriage gradually evolved. It was understood that too large a family was undesirable and that certain steps would have to be taken. The simplistic assumption that using contraceptives requires the 'rational' evaluation of the costs of childrearing has led to the assumption that overt, consensual, and in-depth discussion of family planning is necessary for the 'successful' use of birth control. For many couples, family-planning decisions and contraceptive strategies evolved without explicit discussion or contrivance. Overt communication and conjugal debate were not necessary conditions of efficient, consensual contraceptive behaviour. Contraceptive behaviour did not always involve 'planning' or clear decisions made before the birth of each child. Birth control practice was much more likely to be the result of oblique and complex processes in which roles, responsibilities, expectations, and commitments emerged gradually, incrementally, and almost unnoticed. Indeed, such an approach to family planning was positively embraced; an ethos of family building which rejected family planning as cold and clinical valued an implicit decision-making process which did not suggest that the birth of children was premeditated or designed.

The assumption that the drive to use birth control was led, primarily, by women has also contributed to the argument that direct communication is essential to the successful use of birth control.[116] Models which envisage women

---

[114] Busfield and Paddon, *Thinking about Children*, 241; Wetlesen, *Fertility Choices and Constraints*, 63. Janet Finch and Jennifer Mason's analysis of familial roles with regard to family responsibility is helpful in understanding the dynamics of implicit decision-making. They explore a type of negotiation they term 'non-decisions', by which they mean 'the process of reaching an understanding about family responsibilities without *either* open discussion *or* any party having formed a clear intention as far as we can tell . . . it represents the spectrum where negotiations are most implicit . . . In very many cases when people talk about how they (or someone else) came to accept responsibility for helping a particular relative, they cannot reconstruct a consciously formulated strategy, or identify a point in time when there was an overt agreement. The arrangement just emerged.' The indication is that, for many, contraceptive responsibilities evolved in a similar way. Finch and Mason, *Negotiating Family Responsibilities*, 74.   [115] Eyles, *Commonsense about Sex*, 97.
[116] Caldwell, 'Direct Economic Costs and Benefits of Children', 470.

persuading husbands to practise contraception are also likely to stress the importance of discussion about contraceptive behaviour between couples. A substantial number of women, however, did not talk about birth control with their spouse because it was in fact their husbands who initiated and controlled fertility limitation strategies.

The absence of detailed discussion about family planning also reflected the reluctance of couples to discuss sexual matters. The relationship between husbands' and wives' sexual relationships and the practice of contraception remains unexplored, in particular the sexual dynamics of decision-making and the effects of attitudes towards sex and sexual roles on the decision-making process.[117] Even though Elizabeth Roberts found it difficult to talk to her respondents about birth control, 'bedevilled as it is by inhibitions, ignorance and reticence about sex and sexuality', she does not reflect on how these inhibitions might have complicated the negotiation of family limitation options between the couples she studied.[118] It is also widely recognized that such inhibitions frequently hinder contraceptive use among modern generations, yet such an understanding is rarely used to explore the dynamics of discussion and decision-making with regard to contraceptive use in the past.[119] J. Mayone Stycos, Kurt Back, and Reuben Hill's sociological studies of Puerto Rico in the 1950s are unusual in recognizing the relevance of discussions about sex and the articulation of family-planning desires: 'If husbands and wives are not accustomed to discussing sexual matters in general, it may be that they also hesitate to discuss family-size ideals.'[120] Many couples lacked the vocabulary to talk about sexual practices, and found the words they knew coarse and unsuitable for serious or respectable articulation between partners.[121]

A further advantage of an implicit decision-making process was that it avoided embarrassing discussion that skirted close to sexual issues. Many interviewees asserted that discussion of contraception was avoided because it meant talking about sex. Jack observed:

The, um, taking precautions was just left to me to do . . . I don't remember talking much about sex, not in a—not in a—might be a bit spicy way, but, no, don't remember talking

---

[117] As Ellen Ross argues, we cannot ignore the fact that 'reproductive behaviour is not a specific life compartment, but a part of sexual and social relationships between women and men and within communities': *Love and Toil*, 98.　　　　　　　　　　[118] Roberts, *A Woman's Place*, 85.

[119] For example, Holland, Scott, Sharpe, and Thomson, 'Don't Die of Ignorance', 117, on the difficulties many women have in imposing condom use on partners given the 'complexity and contradictions of the processes of negotiation over condoms, even despite the threat of Aids'; see also Lees, *Sugar and Spice*, on the conflict many teenage girls encounter between the need to use contraception and the construction of spontaneous sex as the only legitimate excuse for female teenage sexual activity.

[120] Stycos, Back, and Hill, 'Problems of Communication', 209.

[121] L. Hall, 'Impotent Ghosts', 67–8. Hall argues that Stopes and other writers 'managed to extend the boundaries of subjects upon which couples could talk', and provided 'concepts and vocabulary . . . distinct from . . . smutty male subcultural discourses'. See Watts on the need to 'see language as a social resource', the command of which 'allows the speaker access to . . . power and influence': Watts, *Power in Family Discourse*, 1.

much about it—didn't discuss it much I don't think we did, no. As I say it was left mostly to me to make the decisions on—in that situation.[122]

Millie stressed that she did not talk to her husband about sex and presented that fact as one reason why she and her husband never discussed using contraception:

I probably didn't talk about them [condoms], because anything like that was so private and, well, you didn't talk about things like that . . . Never! It's strange but it's silly—it sounds silly now, I suppose. But it's a known fact that you didn't talk about sex at all. It just happened and that was it, just when you felt like it. (laughs)[123]

Lella Secor Florence also found women unable to discuss the subject with their husbands. These wives could not ask 'if her husband would use a sheath, or if he minded having to withdraw . . . as she could not talk to him about such things'.[124] Women's sexual identities and the determination to preserve a passive naivety about sexual matters made it extremely difficult for them to make open contraceptive demands or initiate discussion about the issue.[125] Men's superior knowledge of contraception and a general reluctance on the part of both parties to discuss the matter meant that some men presented themselves as having been unilaterally in control of family-planning decisions.[126] One man wrote to Marie Stopes 'without her knowledge' for advice as his wife had told him 'not openly but indirectly' her fear that 'another baby would kill her' and he was unsure of his ability to reliably withdraw and his wife was 'dead against the so-called "preventatives" '.[127] Another also wrote to Marie Stopes for advice without telling his wife: 'I do not wish her to know it, as it would be a constant source of worry to her as it has been with me'.[128] One woman who subsequently attended a birth control clinic in Cambridge asked her doctor for advice after he warned her of the health risks of a further pregnancy: 'he told me that it was the business of my husband'.[129] As late as the 1970s, Geoffrey Gorer concluded that there was 'a widespread, if not very articulate, belief among the working classes that it is the husband's prerogative to determine whether any form of birth control should be used and that it is unseemly, almost unwomanly, for the wife to take the initiative'.[130]

---

[122] Jack, bc3ox#13.   [123] Millie, bc3ox#21.

[124] Florence, *Progress Report on Birth Control*, 134.

[125] This point was recognized by Frank and Scanzoni: 'if the woman does not define herself as sexually active, making contraceptive matters explicit may result in dissonance between her own self-image and the one implied by that sort of explicit discussion': 'Sexual Decision-Making', 61.

[126] See also the analysis of oral interviews conducted by Margaret Williamson where men were in charge of the decision to use birth control; even where the decision was portrayed as joint, testimony revealed that in almost all cases, 'women continued to take a passive role in birth control decisions': Williamson, ' "Getting Off at Loftus" ', 13.   [127] Stopes, *Mother England*, 42.

[128] Ibid. 46–7.   [129] Florence, *Birth Control on Trial*, 151.

[130] Gorer, *Sex and Marriage in England Today*, 133. Research in other countries has found similar instances of male knowledge and responsibility for contraception obviating the need for conjugal discussion. Research in Puerto Rico discovered a significant number of relationships in which many husbands believed that 'the sphere of family planning is their prerogative alone: For some men, the idea that the wife's view should be taken into consideration on the matter of family planning would seem

Women concurred and many praised their husbands for using birth control without embarrassing them by discussing sexual matters:

No, he wasn't a sexual man, he never discussed it . . . he wasn't that sort of man. He, he, he was, er, quiet and refined—refined sort of man he was, he didn't—he didn't discuss anything that he shouldn't discuss with a woman.[131]

First-hand testimony thus emphasized the husband's role. The most common representation of the decision-making process connected the lack of discussion with the expectation that some sort of action would be taken by the husband: 'we didn't do much talking . . . he used to get them and I used to rely on him that he got them'.[132] One woman told Mass-Observation, 'you know what men are when it comes to that. No use talking.'[133] One woman, courting in the 1920s 'wouldn't have dreamt of the woman taking contraceptive measures, not at all. I mean it was always the man who thought it was his responsibility, so that was how—we never discussed it. We just knew that would be it.'[134] In many households, the stress on the paucity of in-depth discussion with regard to birth control reflected the simple expectation that men would act:[135]

Well, I never really asked what he knew about it. As I say, we didn't discuss it really . . . You husband produces one when necessary. I didn't know such things existed . . . you know, it was a very secret thing. And nobody mentioned it. But now it's very open isn't it?[136]

So did you talk to your wife about using French letters and . . .

Oh no, no, no, it wasn't discussed as such it was just accepted, yeah . . . it was an unspoken thing, you see, you just accepted it, oh yes, yes, yes, no—and there was no secrets—as far as you could call them secrets—there were no secrets between man and wife, it was just the accepted thing.[137]

Abortion might prompt more open deliberation. In part, because the search for an abortifacient was coitus independent, there was less embarrassment associated with its articulation. In addition, the decision to use an abortifacient was more likely to be adopted at times of crisis and therefore provoke debate between husband and wife. However, men were sometimes kept in the dark about abortion attempts. Two respondents did not tell their husbands of the abortions they procured. In neither case did this reflect his likely opposition to the procedure; rather, it underscored the tendency of couples to maintain silence about contraceptive matters. Dolly did not think her husband, a miner, would want to know that she

radical. As expressed by one "lower-class" male: "I am the one who uses birth control. She doesn't know the secret. The woman gets pregnant when the man wants her to" ': Stycos, Back, and Hill, 'Problems of Communication', 208. Similar results are reported in Karra, Stark, and Wolf, 'Male Involvement in Family Planning'; M. Carter, ' "Because he loves me" '.

[131] Elma, msf/jm/bl/#42.   [132] Louisa, bc3ox#14.
[133] Mass-Observation, *Britain and her Birth-Rate*, 60.
[134] 'In the Club', A&M: GC/105/23.
[135] See also Fisher, ' "She was quite satisfied with the arrangements I made" '.
[136] Maria, msf/kf/bl/#8.   [137] Ernest, bc3sw#2.

was taking an abortifacient in the early 1950s. It had little to do with him and he did not need to be informed:

'Cos I didn't want to [tell him]. Didn't want to I thought no, I ain't.

Did you think he would've objected?
Well, I dunno, because he was never into anything like that. It was when he was football-mad. Yeah.[138]

The idea that contraceptive use required in-depth conjugal discussion is challenged by testimony which emphasized the incremental and implicit forms of negotiation through which desires with regard to family size and spacing were revealed. Moreover, male knowledge of birth control methods and many women's reluctance to talk about sexual issues meant many couples preferred to let the husband use birth control without openly planning their pregnancies or explicitly discussing family limitation.

'MAN MUST TAKE HOLD OF HIS DESTINY':[139] THE ETHOS OF PLANNING

A new mentality, which transformed individuals' approach to the future and valued planning and forethought, was not necessary to the successful use of birth control. Rather than being a necessary condition of birth control use, planning one's family, discussing its size and spacing, and consistently using contraception regularly at times when pregnancy was not desired reflected a particular approach to family life. This ethos which focused on planning, predicting, and controlling the future was rejected by many families as inappropriate and impossible. It was, however, embraced in a few middle-class homes. These individuals presented themselves as part of a self-conscious minority aware that their approach challenged the dominant culture. Some of these individuals argued that the attempt to plan for the future was sensible and prudent, and criticized those who did not as selfish, vulgar, or common, while others apologized for adopting what they realized was widely regarded as a cold-blooded and excessively rational approach to family building.

A positive reaction to using birth control to 'plan' one's family (rather than to limit its size) was rarely expressed except by a few middle-class individuals. In 1965 Elizabeth Draper characterized 'planning for betterment and entering into commitments on a progressive basis in furtherance of those plans' as predominantly 'a "middle-class" attitude or state'.[140] Lewis-Faning concluded that 'the greatest amount of planning has occurred consistently in the highest social class and . . . the least amount has occurred in the lowest class'.[141] Mass-Observation

---

[138] Dolly, bc3sw#17.   [139] Mass-Observation, DR 3438, reply to April 1944 Directive.
[140] Draper, *Birth Control in the Modern World*, 120.
[141] Lewis-Faning, *Report of an Inquiry into Family Limitation*, 149.

found a positive correlation between school-leaving age and the feeling that 'families should be planned'.[142] In June 1944 Mass-Observation produced a report based on the letters written by a sample of predominantly 'better educated' and 'more literate' people on the declining birth rate. 'Only two people out of a hundred writing admit[ted] that their familes arrived not by design but by chance'; a few others denied planning, but 7 per cent 'pitied and despised' large families.[143] Among the oral history sample a few of the middle-class respondents had clear ideas about the number of children they wanted, or thought they could afford, and were not prepared simply to accept what life dealt them. Such couples, despite finding it difficult to talk about sex, nevertheless clearly and openly debated family-planning issues. Edward, an engineer, and his wife, for example, were 'a sensible pair' who 'always talked everything over', and 'to bring them up properly' they 'decided that we'd stop' at two.[144]

Yet this testimony also bears witness to the dominance of the alternative approach, which denigrated premeditation or planning in contraceptive matters. Those who advocated planning one's family were defensive; these respondents felt the need to justify their actions against a charge that they had been cold-blooded, and retaliated by denigrating the unplanned family as old-fashioned. Such narratives positioned conscious planning as a modern approach which relatively few other people were thought to accept or adopt.[145]

Planning one's family might be presented as new, modern, and enlightened. One chemistry student regarded such an approach as ideal: "I firmly believe . . . man must take hold of his destiny and not be blindly led by uncontrolled natural forces. I believe in planning in all spheres.' Yet it was a goal that was in 1944 unattainable without 'wider dissemination of birth control information'.[146] Others who also enthusiastically embraced a new calculative approach to life in general and family size in particular sought to bolster their view by denigrating those who failed to plan as primitive and foolish. Some of those who had large families experienced such disapprobation: 'they feel sorry for you'; 'Yes, 3 or 4 children is considered vulgar and quite out of date.'[147] A husband commented on the 'misery' suffered by his wife 'by those nasty loud remarks, not to her, but at her, concerning rabbits and their habits'.[148] A family with four had been 'called lustful and irresponsible producers, when in actual fact we are two young people very much in love'.[149] A tax inspector from

[142] Of those surveyed who had a secondary education, 63% felt that families should be planned, whereas of those who had only an 'elementary education' 40% said 'leave it to chance'. Mass-Observation, *Britain and her Birth-Rate*, 57.

[143] Mass-Observation FR2111 'Population Problems' June 1944, 49, 38.

[144] Edward, bc3ox#15.

[145] Ellen Ross recognizes that birth-control campaigners' 'new vocabulary' of planning was not necessarily widely used or understood by many within the working classes in the late nineteenth and early twentieth centuries: *Love and Toil*, 97; see also Bland, *Banishing the Beast*, 190–1.

[146] Mass-Observation, DR 3438, reply to April 1944 Directive.

[147] Mass-Observation, FR 2111 'Population Problems' June 1944, 39.   [148] Ibid. 40.

[149] Ibid. 39.

Northern Ireland who wrote to Mass-Observation in 1944 criticized those, particularly in the 'lowest economic class', who have 'appallingly large families' and who 'can't be bothered' to use contraceptives.[150]

However, in labelling those who refused to 'take control of their lives' by planning their families as feckless, those who adopted the new ethos of planning also had to defend themselves against the charge that their attitude towards their families was ruthless and unfeeling. The tax inspector quoted above felt the need to weigh up her behaviour against the accusation that using family planning was cold-hearted:

There is something cold hearted about doing anything and I think that is why people get 'caught' as they put it. But I personally should lose a lot of self respect if I had a baby by accident'.[151]

Gerald and Esme, similarly, recognized that in carefully planning their family they were adopting a new approach to family building which challenged the common notion that one's family, even if limited in size, should nevertheless be allowed to grow 'naturally' without calculation or premeditation. They planned their family precisely, in order to take advantage of certain tax benefits, and were concerned to deny that this meant they were 'cold-blooded'. Esme explained:

the tax er, situation was that if you had a child before the end of the tax year . . . you got a whole year's er allowance . . . And so we worked out that—you see we were very organized—we worked out that if we could arrange to have our babies in March we'd get a year's tax rebate, or whatever. And we did that with the other two, didn't we? One was born on the thirteenth, one on the fifteenth of March. I know it sounds cold-blooded but we were hard up and, er, and in any case it didn't matter because as soon as we decided we wanted to have a baby I conceived and er, er, so you know there was no doubt about it. All this talk these days about people being infertile and so on, can't understand it at all.[152]

Such precise calculation also characterized the plans made by another Mass-Observation panellist who sought, however, to use her plans to enhance the romance of conception, thereby resisting any accusation of cold-heartedness. She described how 'everything went according to plan'. Her child was conceived while on holiday in Guernsey because she and her husband believed that 'conception should take place in beautiful surroundings . . . while we were both feeling happy and contented'. The holiday was carefully timed nine months before March as 'we had agreed beforehand that the Spring was an ideal time for a baby to be born'.[153] Similarly, Naomi Mitchison's comments on birth control betrayed an awareness that many people were 'thrilled' by 'happy or surprising accidents' and argued that it was 'braver and nobler and

---

[150] Mass-Observation, DR 1066, reply to April 1944 Directive.   [151] Ibid.
[152] Gerald and Esme, msf/kf/ht/#9.
[153] Mass-Observation, Dr 2916, reply to April 1944 Directive.

more civilized to have only intentional children'; 'there is a particular thrill in saying "now is the time, to-day or to-night, in such and such a city or forest, we will beget our child" '.[154]

That it was seen as a middle-class trait to try to control one's family by planning births is also revealed by a closer analysis of those few from within the working-class samples who also engaged in such calculations. Among the working classes it was those respondents who self-consciously wished to 'better themselves' and distance their own lives from their backgrounds, or from the working-class communities around them who represented themselves as having openly discussed contraceptive issues.

Sarah, for example, deliberately dissociated herself from her friends and neighbours. While they did not bother to plan for the future or care about how many children they had, she broke away from such ideas by marrying a man from 'outside the normal rut'. She characterized her new set of friends as planners who had 'started to think for themselves', and considered how to run their lives according to their aspirations and financial positions. Thus she and her husband discussed contraception and family size, after which time she then left the decisions to him, because he earned the money:

I didn't want a lot of children either (pause) and money was in short supply and we'd come to our—a lot of us young ones had come to our senses by then that we knew that having children kept you poor all the days of your life . . . And that's—that's when all this explosion started that people started thinking for themselves and uh, uh, we want more money, we want less hours (chuckle) . . . it was . . . like an explosion: 'We're not having, we're not, we're not having kids like our mothers have kids', you know, that was it. Because we sort of had the idea that the more children that you had, the poorer you were, but you see . . . I married, I married a boy out of the ordinary rut, I mean, there weren't many of us cyclists, you see, and we, we—us four—us cyclists, we're—we're a dotty lot, you know, they thought we were . . . dotty, they did really. And we'd a few, um, vegetarians amongst us and a few, um, intellectuals and uh, you got—you got mixing ideas and that's what it was, you know, and you—your thoughts went beyond just a mundane existence. (chuckle) You got me?[155]

Similarly, Gertrude, a miner's daughter who married an electrician, was determined to make her way up in the world and knew this meant planning her life in a way that her contemporaries did not, and that even her husband was not inclined to. In beginning a story about deciding to use birth control she immediately sidetracked into talking about general ambitions in life:

. . . and I mean I thought I couldn't afford it [more children], I thought that was enough, and I wanted to, you know, I was—I said to my husband when I got married: 'Now what's your ambition?' He made fun of me because I said that—I wanted to know, I wanted to do something.[156]

[154] Mitchison, *Comments on Birth Control*, 13.
[155] Sarah, msf/kf/bl/#30.   [156] Gertrude, bc3sw#27.

Eva also, in presenting herself as a planner, deliberately contrasted herself with her 'rougher' neighbours. She clearly sought to be 'better off' than her peers as illustrated by the reaction to the car she bought:

He said 'Well', he said, 'to bring them up proper as they ought to be', he said, 'we can't afford any more', I said 'I know that' . . . I told him I didn't want a big family, I told him right away, I says, 'Two's enough to bring up, for me', you know . . . they seemed to be a rougher type where there's a bigger family . . . I think they're a bit uncouth in their ways and their manners many a time . . . We did have a small car and we thought we were right well-off in them days, I mean, there were nobody else had them around us, and they used to think they were right well-off, Sandra and Stuart.[157]

It is ironic that demographers have focused on these isolated cases of middle-class or 'aspirational' working-class families as typical actors of fertility decline. At the very end of the process of decline, at the point at which in all communities fertility control was well established, such an approach was viewed as novel, pioneering, and unusual. A 1944 Mass-Observation panellist, married early in the 1920s, contrasted her views with those of 'younger friends' among whom she felt the vogue for planning was mistaken:

It doesn't appear to be in the nature of my husband or myself to make a plan about a family. We accepted the inevitable, we certainly never had a plan. I note this atmosphere of planning among younger friends, but I have taken it to be a catch word of the times and perfectly meaningless. It seems obvious there can only be a negative plan. One assumes that to plan means to act in a particular way against the natural trend of events or against the natural instincts of people.[158]

CONCLUSION

This chapter has revealed dynamics of decision-making about contraceptive use and highlighted the range of aims and aspirations that accompanied the choices made. Rather than representing a clear break from an earlier, fatalistic mentality which was careless as to the size or spacing of one's family, rather than always being the result of determined and discussed decisions to avoid pregnancy, birth control was frequently used sporadically, with the aim of reducing the general risk of pregnancy without preventing it altogether. While some had very strong reasons to avoid pregnancy (particularly later in a marriage) and might have adopted birth control conscientiously and resolutely, and while a few members of the middle classes sought to carefully control the growth of their families, many others represented birth control decisions as implicit, vague, casual, and amorphous.

Henry neatly summarized the rationale behind many couples' contraceptive behaviour. He claimed he wanted a small family, but that he 'never really planned'.

---

[157] Eva, msf/kf/bl/#9.   [158] Mass-Observation, Dr 2193, reply to March 1944 Directive.

He was prepared to accept 'whatever his family size turned out to be'. His use of condoms and withdrawal was merely to 'keep it in perspective':

No we just took things as we went, I think—both of us never really planned anything— whatever was to come, we accepted it . . . make your life around whatever your family turns out to be, that's the way Dee and I have taken it on . . .

But . . . you were using contraceptives

Oh, well, I suppose, yes, yes, you were, er, trying, like, not to . . . have as many as you can in that sense of it—you were trying to keep it in its right perspective like . . . [159]

This chapter has highlighted the tendency of individuals retrospectively to reject the idea that they had sought to engineer their family size or spacing and minimize the extent to which birth control practices were discussed, debated, or deliberated. Other surveys have found similar avowals. Yet the widespread use of contraception by such families has always been taken as evidence that family-planning ideas were in fact present and that open discussion must indeed have taken place. Accounts of the massive change in fertility behaviour during the early twentieth century should instead take into account the complex forms of behaviour and motivation presented here. If we simply see family-planning decisions as conscious calculations to be contrasted with a fatalistic passivity towards pregnancy exhibited by former generations we proscribe the types of explanation that are plausible. Clear social or economic reasons for limiting family were not always at the forefront of respondents' minds.[160] While birth control use was seen as economically expedient, a great deal of uncertainty surrounded respondents' family-size choices, as did a casual irresolution in their attitude towards childbearing. Nevertheless, in this vague and indecisive way contraception was used, and it was efficient enough to affect significantly the frequency with which pregnancy occurred.

Of course, we should not necessarily take retrospective evidence at face value, and should remember that such testimony is a carefully constructed representation rather than a precise recollection of past events. However, whatever amount of birth control use and planning took place, the fact that so many represented themselves as unable and unwilling to plan is not only significant but revealing of the dynamics of practice. By paying attention to such testimony, important aspects of behaviour are exposed. First, such testimony draws attention to the lack of confidence many had in birth control given both the perceived unreliability of methods and the biological unpredictability of fertility or conception. Secondly, these representations highlight the value placed on a natural approach to life which accepts what fate gives one. Thirdly, these narratives draw attention to the lack of conscientiousness with which birth control was used, and fourthly,

---

[159] Henry and Dee, bc2#27.

[160] For a review of studies which focus on parents consciously and explicitly weighing up the costs of childbearing see Blake, 'Are Babies Consumer Durables?'.

to the low motivation behind many attempts to restrict births. Fifthly, these narratives reveal the gendered dynamics of birth control choices; men's greater knowledge of methods and their wives' reluctance to discuss sexual matters placed responsibility upon husbands to silently employ family limitation measures. Finally, such narratives expose the role future planning played in the cosmology of individuals. To 'plan' one's family was not a simple matter of working out whether and when children were desired and acting accordingly. It reflected a forward-looking and optimistic approach to life. Such connotations meant that it was an ethic which appealed to the self-consciously modern. Those who aspired to self-betterment, who sought out and took advice, and who regarded the world as 'on their side' were those who embraced the ethos of planning. It was an attitude which was evident only in a few, mainly middle-class, households who regarded those who did not plan as primitive, ignorant, and feckless. Not 'planning' was thereby denigrated as a characteristic of the thoughtlessness of those living in poverty, who lacked the energy or drive to take the simple measures needed to provide themselves with a higher standard of living merely by having smaller families. Many of the working classes did indeed reject this cosmology (as indeed did many other middle class voices), and did not see the future as something one could or should control, calculate or plan for. Of course, they were not feckless, ignorant, or lazy. Rather, carefully planning one's family was viewed as misguided and even dangerous. It was nicer to be surprised when pregnancy occurred instead of coldly engineering births, while one could only be disappointed if one attempted to determine the size and spacing of one's family precisely. Those who rejected the mentality of planning and calculation were not incapable of restricting their family size, but they adopted an entirely different approach to the begetting of smaller families than has previously been envisaged by historians or demographers.

3

'The majority went back to withdrawal'[1]

The Survival of Traditional Methods of Birth Control

There has been considerable debate as to which methods of birth control were predominantly used during the first half of the twentieth century. It is generally argued that while traditional methods of birth control (withdrawal, abortion, and abstinence) dominated practice during the initial stages of the fertility decline (during the late nineteenth and early twentieth centuries), condoms, caps, and pessaries were increasingly chosen during the inter-war years.[2] Yet oral history evidence, the extant qualitative material, and a careful reading of sociological survey material all suggest that, far from being replaced by condoms or caps, withdrawal remained the mainstay of family limitation practices long into the twentieth century. Although many did try appliance methods, the extent to which they were disliked has been underestimated.[3] Far from rejecting traditional methods in favour of modern appliance forms of contraception, many used a range of methods.[4]

---

[1] Florence, *Progress Report on Birth Control*, 144.

[2] Langford, 'Birth Control Practice'; W. Seccombe, *Weathering the Storm*, 181; Mason, *The Making of Victorian Sexuality*, 59–60; Levine, *Reproducing Families*; J. Peel, 'The Manufacture and Retailing of Contraceptives'; Szreter, *Fertility, Class and Gender*, 559–60; Cook, *The Long Sexual Revolution*, 112–13. In the case of the United States, scholars have argued that the fertility decline occurred alongside a widespread uptake of new forms of reproductive technology. This contrasts with Britain, where the decline initially took place using older non-appliance methods. See e.g. Brodie, *Contraception and Abortion in Nineteenth Century America*.

[3] Hera Cook is unusual in emphasizing the extent to which appliance methods of contraception (especially condoms and caps) were 'difficult and frustrating' for users in the inter-war period: *The Long Sexual Revolution*, 122–42.

[4] This chapter concentrates on a particular set of methods—withdrawal, abstinence, female caps and pessaries, abortion, and condoms—which dominated both contemporary discussion of birth-control choices and oral history testimony. The extent to which non-reproductive sexual acts, such as anal or oral sex, were employed is extremely difficult to ascertain. Oral history respondents rarely mentioned such practices. One woman hinted at the use of mutual masturbation: 'you knew you couldn't get into any danger while his hand was there', and another woman and her husband 'would kiss each other's private parts' (Agatha, msf/kf/ht/#7; Catherine, msf/kf/ht/#1). See Szreter and Fisher, 'Sexuality, Love and Marriage in England, 1918–1960'. Moreover, there is extremely little material on such practices in contemporary sources or surveys. See Cook, *The Long Sexual Revolution*, 129–30. Extended lactation was not explored sufficiently in the oral history interviews (a regrettable oversight), nor was much mention made of the use of douches, which might have been more commonly used than is frequently recognized, since their employment was often combined with the use of other methods (such as a cap) and not necessarily mentioned as a separate element of the package. Hera Cook, however, indicates that survey material reveals very little evidence of douching or syringing among English women: *The Long Sexual Revolution*, 114.

Moreover, a significant number merely experimented with appliance methods before rejecting them and continuing to use traditional methods such as withdrawal, abstinence, and abortion.

'EVERYBODY HAD FRENCH LETTERS IN THEIR POCKET':[5] THE RISE OF APPLIANCE METHODS

Our knowledge of the use of different methods of birth control stems largely from a number of social surveys conducted in the first half of the twentieth century. In 1914 Ethel Elderton detailed the fertility patterns of communities 'north of the Humber', alongside the observations of local correspondents on the spread of birth control propaganda, the nature of contraceptive practices, and the prevalence of abortion.[6] In 1916 the National Birth-Rate Commission surveyed 791 college women (mostly from Oxford and Cambridge) and their female relatives.[7] In 1932 Enid Charles published the findings of a questionnaire survey set up by the Birth Control Investigation Committee: 432 responses from middle-class women married between 1880 and 1929 were analysed, along with 198 questionnaires received from those who had attended Nurse Daniels's birth control clinic and 244 who used the Birmingham Women's Welfare Clinic.[8] By far the largest and most influential enquiry was undertaken between 1946 and 1947 by E. Lewis-Faning for the Royal Commission on Population:[9] 11,078 women in hospital (not for gynaecological or maternity reasons) were interviewed and 3,281 of these were used to compile the final report.[10] Lewis-Faning's survey covered those married between 1900 and 1947. In 1959 the Population Investigation Committee (PIC) surveyed 2,350 men and women married since 1920.[11]

Qualitative material also provides information on methods used. Birth control pioneers received thousands of letters from members of the public asking for advice and information.[12] Various clinics reported on the success of their centres,

---

[5] Elizabeth, bc3sw#12.

[6] Elderton, *Report on the English Birth-Rate*. Whether the research for subsequent parts was ever conducted is unknown to the author; certainly, none was published.

[7] National Birth-Rate Commission, *The Declining Birth-Rate*.

[8] Charles, *The Practice of Birth Control*.

[9] Lewis-Faning, *Report on an Enquiry into Family Limitation*. The findings of twentieth century research into contraceptive practices are usefully summarized in Langford, 'Birth Control Practice'.

[10] Hospitals in London, Glasgow, Oxford, Hampshire, Leeds, Northampton, Liverpool, Norwich and Cambridge, Devonshire and Cornwall, and Aberdeen were surveyed.

[11] Pierce and Rowntree, 'Birth Control in Britain', Parts I and II. See also Langford, *Birth Control Practice and Marital Fertility*.

[12] See the letters written to Marie Stopes held at the British Library and in the Archives and Manuscripts Collection at the Wellcome Library for the History and Understanding of Medicine. These have been analysed in, for instance, W. Seccombe, *Weathering the Storm*; Davey, 'Birth Control in Britain during the Inter-War Years'; Faulkner, ' "Powerless to prevent him" '.

sometimes conducting small surveys of patient responses.[13] Mass-Observation panellists were asked in March 1944 to write describing the choices they had made or were making about having children, and in April 1944 were invited to comment on methods of contraception, their awareness of the different types, and opinions regarding their availability and reliability. Mass-Observation also carried out a 'sex survey' following the Kinsey Report in America, which included questions about birth control. A number of subsequent sex surveys also provide accounts of birth control practices, albeit for later cohorts, such as Slater and Woodside's *Patterns of Marriage*, Eustace Chesser's *The Sexual, Marital and Family Relationships of the English Woman*, and Geoffrey Gorer's *Sex and Marriage in England Today*.[14] Occasionally oral histories also obtain narratives of contraceptive behaviour, such as Elizabeth Roberts's research in Barrow, Lancaster and Preston, Diana Gittins's work on south Wales and Essex, Margaret Williamson's study of East Cleveland, and Natalie Higgins's investigation of Birmingham and Hull.[15]

This evidence is frequently used to establish that the use of two particular appliance methods—female caps and condoms—increasingly dominated contraceptive practice during the 1920s, 1930s, and 1940s. In all the surveys later cohorts revealed greater knowledge and use of technological methods. Yet it is a mistake to conclude that appliance methods replaced traditional methods such as withdrawal, abstinence, and abortion. Increased reporting of awareness and use of condoms and caps has frequently been presented in such a way that continued use of withdrawal is masked or ignored.

The idea that appliance methods replaced traditional ones stems, above all, from the findings of Lewis-Faning, whose official survey was both the largest and the most rigorously planned and executed. Placing all users into one of two categories—appliance users and those who used non-appliance methods *only* (withdrawal, abstinence, and rhythm)—he reported a significant increase in the appliance user category. Only 2 per cent of those married before 1910 used appliance methods of birth control. This rose steadily to 37 per cent of the cohort marrying between 1935 and 1939.[16] Other surveys have reinforced this finding and have identified condoms as the most dominant of available appliances. Forty-six per cent of those married between 1930 and 1939 surveyed by the 1959 PIC survey used condoms, a figure which rose to 51 per cent for those married between

---

[13] See e.g. Norman and Vera Himes, 'Birth Control for the British Working Classes'; Florence, *Birth Control on Trial*; SPBCC, *Birth Control and Public Health*; Florence, *Progress Report on Birth Control*.

[14] Stanley, *Sex Surveyed*. Slater and Woodside, *Patterns of Marriage: A Study of Marriage Relationships in the Urban Working Classes* (1951); Chesser, *The Sexual, Marital and Family Relationships of the English Woman* (1956); Gorer, *Sex and Marriage in England Today: A Study of the Views and Experiences of the Under-45s* (1971).

[15] Stanley, *Sex Surveyed*. See Roberts, *A Woman's Place*; Gittins, *Fair Sex*; Williamson, ' "Getting Off at Loftus" '; Higgins, 'Changing Expectations and Realities of Marriage'.

[16] Lewis-Faning, *Report of an Inquiry into Family Limitation*, 52.

1950 and 1960.[17] While the use of female caps was significantly lower than the use of condoms, they too were increasingly employed, particularly after the 1930s, when the number of clinics increased, as did the likelihood that practical birth control advice would be given by doctors or other health professionals.[18] Pierce and Rowntree reveal the slow growth in the popularity of caps, which were used by 9 per cent of those married between 1930 and 1939, 11 per cent of those married between 1940 and 1949, and 13 per cent of those married between 1950 and 1960.[19] They asked cap users where contraceptive advice had been obtained, and found that 153 had received information from a doctor and eighty-six had attended a birth control clinic.[20] The oral history material collected by this author is consistent with other evidence of an increase in appliance use. Although any observation is impressionistic and should not be seen as having any statistical significance or rigour, if the oral history sample is split into those born in or before 1914 and those born after 1914, the rise in popularity of condoms is striking. Only around 46 per cent of respondents in the earlier cohort tried condoms, as opposed to 58 per cent of those born after 1914. Indeed, of the fifteen respondents born before 1906, only five used condoms (33 per cent), a figure which rises to 46 per cent of those born between 1906 and 1910, and to 53 per cent of those born between 1911 and 1915. Of those born before 1914, only 9 per cent used caps, as opposed to 23 per cent of those born after 1914. Indeed, of the six people interviewed born after 1926, only one did not use a cap, while only one of the fifteen interviewees born between 1899 and 1905 tried this method.

Surveys have failed, however, to draw attention to the continued importance of traditional methods alongside the rise of appliance forms of birth control. Withdrawal remained the most frequently mentioned method of birth control in both qualitative testimony and survey data throughout the period. The sole use of non-appliance methods, deemed by Lewis-Faning to consist almost entirely of the use of withdrawal, continued to represent a significant level of reported birth control practice: 39 per cent of those married between 1926 and 1930, 33 per cent of the cohorts married between 1931–1935, and 29 per cent of the 1936–40 cohort were users solely of non-appliance methods.[21] Indeed, as Hera Cook has pointed out, while the proportion of birth control users relying on withdrawal decreased, actual numbers of people reporting reliance on withdrawal rose as the proportion of people reporting the use of birth control as a whole increased among the cohort married between 1910 and 1940.[22] Moreover, it is crucial to note that the design of Lewis-Faning's survey probably greatly underestimated the use of withdrawal: his appliance user category includes all those who also used

---

[17] Pierce and Rowntree, 'Birth Control in Britain, Part II', 127.

[18] Clinic attendance figures remained low before 1930: on average, most saw fewer than five women per week. See Bourke, *Working-Class Cultures*, 56.

[19] Pierce and Rowntree, 'Birth Control in Britain, Part II', 127.   [20] Ibid. 135–6.

[21] Lewis-Faning, *Report of an Inquiry into Family Limitation*; see also Langford, 'Birth Control Practice', 52.   [22] Cook, *The Long Sexual Revolution*, 122–4.

non-appliance methods, as long as they had used an appliance method at least once. Many of those who used withdrawal, but who also used condoms or other appliances, are therefore misleadingly hidden in an 'appliance user' category. The 1959 PIC survey also found significant levels of withdrawal use: 50 per cent of those married between 1930 and 1939, 42 per cent of those married between 1940 and 1949, and 40 per cent of those married between 1950 and 1960.[23] Moya Woodside and Eliot Slater's work concluded that withdrawal was 'the generally accepted and most widely used method'.[24] Clinic data revealed the same: their workers concurred that 'before coming to the clinic . . . by far the commonest [method] is *coitus interruptus*'.[25] The popularity of withdrawal was also a key feature of oral history testimony, with 71 per cent of those born between 1899 and 1914, and 61 per cent of those born between 1915 and 1930 using this method. Despite the increase in use of appliance methods, for the period before the Pill, withdrawal remained the dominant method of birth control.

Abortion was also a significant traditional method of birth control, use of which may have increased during the inter-war period.[26] The main source on the prevalence of abortion in the early stages of the fertility decline is Ethel Elderton's 1914 report on the north of England. The material from 'local correspondents' is dominated by descriptions of abortifacients, and comparatively little is said about available contraceptives. Two 'respectable' women in York exclaimed that 'probably eight in ten' 'working women take drugs' and frequently 'perform illegal operations on themselves in the crudest and most appalling fashions'.[27] Anxiety about the extent of abortion rose significantly during the inter-war period when it was seen as a major contributor to the rise in maternal mortality, particularly in deprived areas.[28] In 1933 the British Medical Association set up a special committee to 'consider and report on the medical aspects of abortion'.[29] By 1938, abortion was the subject of a government inquiry to investigate 'the prevalence of abortion . . . and to consider what steps can be taken . . . to secure the reduction of maternal mortality and morbidity arising from this cause'.[30] A number of

---

[23] Pierce and Rowntree, 'Birth Control in Britain, Part II', 127. A useful summary of findings is in Langford, 'Birth Control Practice'.

[24] Slater and Woodside, *Patterns of Marriage*, 199. Even later surveys, such as a subsequent project conducted by the PIC in 1967–8, found high levels of withdrawal use: 47.4% of those married between 1941 and 1950, and 46.6 % of those married between 1951 and 1961, used this method: Langford, *Birth Control Practice and Marital Fertility*, 27. See also Cartwright, *Parents and Family Planning Services*, and *How Many Children?*, 12.   [25] SPBCC, *Birth Control and Public Health*, 20.

[26] McLaren, *Birth Control in Nineteenth-Century England*, esp. ch. 13; Gittins, *Fair Sex*; Knight, 'Women and Abortion in Victorian and Edwardian England', esp. 57.

[27] Elderton, *Report on the English Birth-Rate*, 137.

[28] See especially Ministry of Health, *Interim Report of the Departmental Committee on Maternal Morbidity* (1930) and *Final Report of Departmental Committee in Maternal Mortality and Morbidity* (1932); Campbell, Cameron, and Jones, 'High Maternal Mortality'; Ministry of Health, *Report on Maternal Mortality in Wales*, p. xi. See also Marks, *Metropolitan Maternity*; Loudon, *Death in Childbirth*; McIntosh, ' "An Abortionist City" '.

[29] British Medical Association, *Report of Committee on Medical Aspects of Abortion*, 4.

[30] Ministry of Health, *Report of the Inter-Departmental Committee on Abortion*, p. vi.

smaller investigations into the practice were also conducted, some of which sought to quantify the scale of the problem, the majority simply asserting its prevalence and recommending various forms of action. Doctors suspected that a great many reported miscarriages had been deliberately induced, while the British Medical Association voiced alarm at the open sale of abortifacients in such forms as 'female pills' and the ease with which substances such as slippery elm bark could be obtained from pharmacists. Marie Stopes claimed abortion rates had reached 'epidemic' proportions, and in birth control clinic literature the frequency with which pregnant women arrived asking for assistance was regularly highlighted.[31] The professor of midwifery at the University of Birmingham concluded that among 3,000 women she surveyed in the early 1930s, 35 per cent had 'aborted at some time or other during their sexual life', indignantly noting that women had no qualms about terminating an unwanted pregnancy.[32] Lewis-Faning found that 12 per cent of the 7,287 pregnancies reported were terminated before term and that 14 per cent of these (122) were acknowledged to be criminal interventions. These, he concluded, were 'very low estimates'.[33]

Among the oral history sample, twenty-five respondents (13 per cent) (five from south Wales, five from Oxford, ten from Hertfordshire, and five from Blackburn) reported personal experience of abortion. One woman from the Hertfordshire sample performed an abortion on a friend, as did another Welsh woman, and two instances of medically performed therapeutic abortions were reported.[34] Sixteen presented their attempts to abort as successful, although some wondered whether they had even been pregnant in the first place. The remaining nine accounts were about attempts made to abort a child that was subsequently born. There was no particular pattern in abortion attempts recounted. The method most frequently referred to, both by those who attempted abortion and by those who recalled others' abortions, was drinking gin, usually while in a scorching hot bath. Various concoctions obtained at the chemist were also frequently mentioned, with 'penny royal' being the herb most often cited. Slippery elm bark played a prominent role in horror stories among those respondents interviewed in south Wales, but no one claimed to have used it themselves. Only two women sought the assistance of an illegal abortionist, and only one went through with the attempt, yet 'back-street' abortionists played a prominent role in third-person accounts. There was no particular stage in marriage at which abortion attempts were likely to occur, and in at least seven cases abortion was not a single attempt

---

[31] See e.g. Stopes, *Preliminary Notes on Various Technical Aspects of the Control of Conception*, 8–12.
[32] Beckwith Whitehouse, 'A Paper on the Indications for the Induction of Abortion', *BMJ* (20 Aug 1932), 337.   [33] Lewis-Faning, *Report of an Inquiry into Family Limitation*, 165–73.
[34] The *British Medical Journal* reported in 1932 that the number of therapeutic abortions was on the increase with more doctors carrying out terminations for a greater variety of reasons: *BMJ*, 255/2 (1932), 337–41. That doctors were performing therapeutic abortions, which many feared were technically illegal, was deliberately brought to public attention by Aleck Bourne, who allowed himself to be prosecuted after having induced an abortion for a 14-year-old victim of gang rape. See also 'When is Abortion Lawful?' *BMJ* (20 Feb. 1937), 393–4.

but rather a regularly adopted practice to ensure the monthly appearance of a period.[35] All but one involved a marital pregnancy, in contrast to third-person stories which much more frequently concerned illegitimate conceptions, and one was the product of an affair.[36] There is no indication that abortion was in decline as appliance methods became increasingly used.

Most historians have assumed that abstinence declined with rise of appliance methods, but they have little evidence to establish this.[37] Although there is little direct evidence attesting to the use of abstinence, complex narratives of restraint and continence throughout the period from a variety of sources mean it cannot be dismissed as a likely contraceptive strategy.[38] Some survey evidence suggests that it was rarely used. Enid Charles found that only sixteen individuals (of 432) reported its use; Lewis-Faning claimed levels of abstinence were negligible, and the PIC survey of 1959 found low rates of abstinence.[39] Ethel Elderton argued that in some working-class families it was not acceptable: 'Self-restraint? . . . Not much! If my husband started on self-restraint, I should jolly well know there was another woman in the case! Nay.'[40] Yet there is some limited statistical support for the use of abstinence. The National Birth-Rate Commission's 1916 inquiry found that 188 said they did not limit their family and 289 admitted using some form of birth control. Of these 105 claimed to use 'continence'.[41] McCance's study, conducted between 1929 and 1930, asked women to keep diaries in which they noted their sexual frequency. It found women aged between 23 and 45 reporting a median sexual frequency of 3.7 times per menstrual cycle.[42] The report on the health clinic set up in Peckham in the 1930s observed a 'high percentage' of cases in which 'rarity of connection' contributed to the deliberate avoidance of

[35] Ada, bc3ox#28, Margaret, bc3ox#18, Dilys bc2#13, Thomas, bc3sw#11, Christopher, msf/kf/bl/#34, Catherine, msf/kf/ht/#1, Roger, msf/kf/ht/#10.

[36] On the prevalence of the abortion of legitimate, as opposed to illegitimate, foetuses, see Knight, 'Women and Abortion in Victorian and Edwardian England', 59.

[37] Simon Szreter suggests that the use of abstinence declined during the inter-war period, although he maintains it continued to be practised by a significant minority even into the 1960s. Hera Cook, by contrast, places the decline in abstinence much later, with the development of reproductive technologies such as the 'cheap, thin and pre-lubricated' condom of the late 1950s and the Pill in the 1960s: Szreter, *Fertility, Class and Gender*, 406, 559–60; Cook, *The Long Sexual Revolution*, esp. 155–62.

[38] Historians' discussions of these narratives usually focus on the late nineteenth century: see Bland, *Banishing the Beast*, 283–6; Cominos, 'Late Victorian Sexual Respectability and the Social System', Parts 1 and 2. On the twentieth century, see e.g. National Birth-Rate Commission, *Problems of Population and Parenthood*, which declared it an 'imperative to maintain the idea of sexual self-control in marriage as well as before it' (p. xlvii).

[39] Lewis-Faning, *Report of an Inquiry into Family Limitation*, 8; Charles, *The Practice of Birth Control*, 29; Pierce and Rowntree, 'Birth Control in Britain, Part II', 127.

[40] Elderton, *Report on the English Birth-Rate*, 137.

[41] National Birth-Rate Commission, *The Declining Birth-Rate*, 323. A further 167 respondents did not answer questions on birth control.

[42] McCance, Luff, and Widdowson, 'Physical and Emotional Periodicity in Women', esp. 608. There was very considerable variation around this average, however.

childbearing.[43] Lella Secor Florence describes men as 'moderate and self controlled': many 'habitually leave intervals of two, four or six weeks . . . many others practise abstinence over long periods, six months or a year after the birth of a child'.[44] Oral history also gives us some evidence of abstinence: eleven respondents explicitly mentioned employing abstinence. Eva was told to avoid a further pregnancy, so she and her husband, a cobbler, 'lived very carefully and more or less, you know, did without sex'.[45] Paul Thompson reported similar cases, such as the couple who 'decided we'd be strong-willed and sleep in separate beds'.[46] In addition, thirteen respondents either put their low fertility down to low sexual frequency or deliberately reduced their coital frequency at a specific point during marriage. Ada remembered the first three years of her marriage as a time when they had sex 'probably three times a week', but after 'having the children . . . you don't bother so much'. After her fourth child was born it was 'very rarely . . . probably once a month'.[47] When Bryan and his wife decided to stop having children they 'avoided showing the same interest' in each other as before: 'we weren't having sex —only about once a fortnight, or once every three weeks'.[48] Frank was anxious, given that his wife had been warned not to risk another pregnancy. However, he recalled that since they were not the sort of couple who were 'twice every night and three times on Sundays' the injunction to avoid childbearing did not have too 'noticeable' an effect on their relationship.[49] Such evidence is suggestive of the importance well into the twentieth century of reduced coital frequency in maintaining small family size.

'YOU WOULDN'T EXPECT ME TO TELL YOU, WOULD YOU?':[50] THE UNDER-REPRESENTATION OF CONTRACEPTIVE PRACTICES

Not only is there direct evidence to suggest that traditional methods remained significant despite the increased use of new appliances, but it is plausible to suggest that the way in which much of this evidence was collected served to underestimate the true extent to which these traditional practices were used. Those carrying out surveys experienced considerable problems obtaining representative samples, framing questions to include all methods, and interpreting euphemistic, ambiguous, or inconsistent data. These difficulties were especially likely to lead to an underestimation of the extent of traditional method use: such methods were

---

[43] I. H. Pearse and L. H. Crocker, *The Peckham Experiment: A Study in the Living Structure of Society* (1943), 258, quoted in Cook, *The Long Sexual Revolution*, 158. Enid Charles also thought it likely that the frequency of sexual intercourse declined at the end of the nineteenth century: *The Practice of Birth Control*, 102–3.   [44] Florence, *Birth Control on Trial*, 119.

[45] Eva, msf/kf/bl/#9.   [46] Humphries and Gordon, *A Labour of Love*, 21.

[47] Ada, bc3ox#28.   [48] Bryan, msf/kf/ht/#25.   [49] Frank, msf/srss/bl/#16.

[50] Merlin, msf/kf/bl/#35.

predominantly used by those communities under-represented in surveys, and were frequently categorized or described in terms that were misunderstood by surveyors.

All those conducting surveys suspected that many would not reveal all the details of their contraceptive practice. Indeed, Mass-Observation's *Britain and her Birth-Rate* deemed information on actual birth control practices to be too unreliable to be worth collecting and sought instead opinions from individuals about the declining birth rate and how to encourage couples to have more children.[51] Concern with the honesty of replies has been heightened by the attempt to match reports of birth control use with fertility data and the dates of pregnancies. Lewis-Faning concluded that, in a considerable number of families, the number and spacing of children did not tally with the claim that birth control had not been used.[52] In his survey, for example, only '15 per cent of the women questioned from the 1900–9 marriage cohort acknowledged regulating their fertility', and only '40 per cent of the marriage cohort of 1910–19'. Langford concurs: 'it is inconceivable . . . that women married in the period 1910–19 in Great Britain had had only 2.8 children on average by the time of the Family Census in 1946 but that 60 per cent of them had never used any form of birth control'.[53] Considerable debate surrounds these 'missing birth controllers'.[54] The methods which were left unmentioned, but which were most likely to have been used, were abortion, abstinence, and withdrawal, since the questions asked and those who were asked them served to limit the admission of traditional method use: the illegality of abortion deterred many from saying they had tried it; narrow definitions of contraception militated against the admission of the use of abstinence and withdrawal; and the focus on interviewing women affected the extent to which the use of male methods, especially withdrawal, was declared.

Many women were inclined to keep secret any experience they had had of abortion, and unless something went wrong illegal abortions were unlikely to come to the attention of the authorities. Lewis-Faning was well aware that the information he received on abortion significantly underestimated the extent of the practice, and the Birkett Report into abortion concluded in 1939 that it was 'manifestly impossible . . . to reckon . . . the prevalence of abortion'.[55] Statistical analysis of the material collected by the Joint Council of Midwifery's survey of 3,300 women in municipal hospitals following a miscarriage was abandoned because of the impossibility of using the data to come to any reliable understanding of the ratio of spontaneous to induced abortions.[56] Pierce and Rowntree decided to omit all

[51] Mass-Observation, *Britain and her Birth-Rate*, 55.
[52] Lewis-Faning, *Report of an Inquiry into Family Limitation*, 60.
[53] Langford, 'Birth Control Practice', 61.
[54] See e.g. Cook, *The Long Sexual Revolution*, 108–10.
[55] Lewis-Faning, *Report of an Inquiry into Family Limitation*, 165–73; Ministry of Health, *Interdepartmental Committee on Abortion*, 5.
[56] This survey has been studied in Thomas and Williams, 'Women and Abortion in 1930s Britain'.

questions about induced abortion from their survey on the grounds that accurate information was impossible to obtain.[57]

Oral testimony also suggests that not all respondents were prepared to reveal details of attempts at abortion. June, who had begun to train as a nurse, for example, openly debated the wisdom of revealing that she had considered aborting her first child in the mid-1930s:

> I was very disappointed and probably upset, as you might say, that I was pregnant early on like that . . . And, er, in fact, to be perfectly honest, between you and me . . . I'm not going to say it now . . . but er, I did, I did consider having an abortion.[58]

Four women explicitly denied having had an abortion before revealing the action they did, in fact, take:

> *When did you first hear about abortion?*
> ESME   Oh well, gosh, I mean, I suppose, er, er, one must've read about it . . . illegal abortions, which did happen and women frequently died of course . . .
> GERALD   My earliest memories of that conjures up some old female manipulating knitting needles of all things . . .
> *And did you ever know anyone who had an illegal abortion?*
> ESME   An illegal one? No, no I didn't. I know—I didn't know anyone who got pregnant without being married when I was young. That's true.
> *And did you ever hear of people bringing on periods?*
> ESME   No, y-you mean thinking they were pregnant and, and, er, and trying to, er, um, well—I did it once myself, didn't I? After Susan was born. With tablets.[59]

Here Gerald and Esme revealed a common distinction drawn between abortions and bringing on a period, which only emerged through careful questioning. Similarly, while Christopher did not deliberately cover up his wife's attempts at abortion, information about this did have to be teased out:

> Oh yes, well, you get them scares now and again . . . with her periods.
> *And what would she do at that time?*
> Well, she didn't bother, no, she didn't bother . . .
> *Didn't bother what?*
> Taking, taking, any . . . She used to take gin you see. I know she used to take gin . . . She'd just—just have a—just have a drink of gin . . .
> *Were there any other things that you could do at that . . . when your, when your period was late?*
> No, no . . . She'd take these pills you know, take these pills, Penny Royals. She used to know what to get from the chemist, 'cos she was working in the chemist shop.[60]

Diana Gittins also suspects that many of her respondents 'may well have had abortions themselves' without revealing the fact. None admitted personal involvement,

---

[57] Pierce and Rowntree, 'Birth Control in Britain, Part I', 9.   [58] June, msf/kf/ht/#27.
[59] Gerald and Esme, msf/kf/ht/#9.   [60] Christopher, msf/kf/bl/#34.

but she points to 'the detail of some of the accounts, the fact that many knew of abortionists, their names and addresses—as well as the knowledge of certain home-made abortifacients'.[61] Similarly, Eleanor knew that the chemist in Daisy Street in Blackburn sold penny royal which 'you brewed . . . in a pot', while Doris knew the address in Oxford of a chemist who 'didn't actually do an abortion, but he would give you the pill if you went soon enough'.[62]

That the survey data underestimates the extent of abortion is also suggested by the testimony of health professionals, politicians, and moral campaigners, all of whom presented abortion as a national scourge. Yet the claims of birth control clinic campaigners that a significant proportion of those attending were seeking an abortion should be interpreted as part of their own attempt to establish themselves as a respectable alternative to abortion and to persuade donors and the government that by supporting birth control clinics they might help reduce the number of illegal abortions, or even ameliorate maternal mortality and morbidity. Such assertions of the prevalence of abortion both reflected and fuelled anxiety about the problem.[63] By the beginning of the twentieth century abortion had replaced infanticide in the public imagination as a subject for concern.[64] However, the moralistic tone, decrying poisonous potions, sordid operations, and veiled advertisements, detracts from the authority of claims about its prevalence, making it extremely difficult to assess the true scale of abortion or the role it played in controlling family size.[65]

The ways in which surveyors phrased questions about birth control served to increase the likelihood that instances of the use of withdrawal and abstinence would remain unreported. Many suspected that respondents misinterpreted questions, and that they assumed that only instances of appliance method use were being charted and failed to mention practices that did not require a contraceptive device.[66] Attempts were made by most of those conducting such surveys to ask questions in such a way as to preclude any omissions, such as presenting cards listing a variety of possible methods, using popular euphemisms when asking questions, or asking further specific questions about the use of birth control even after a

---

[61] Gittins, *Fair Sex*, 150; see also Leap and Hunter, *The Midwife's Tale*, 94–6.

[62] Eleanor, msf/kf/bl/#11; Doris bc3ox#20.

[63] See e.g. Elderton, *Report on the English Birth-Rate*; Himes, *Practical Birth-Control Methods*, 38 and 148–50; Campbell, Cameron, and Jones, 'High Maternal Mortality'; Ministry of Health, *Report on Maternal Mortality in Wales*; Parish, 'A Thousand Cases of Abortion', 1107–21. See also McIntosh, ' "An Abortionist City" ', 77–84.

[64] See Sauer, 'Infanticide and Abortion', 91; Tony Ward charts the changing legal approach to infanticide in the twentieth century in 'Legislating For Human Nature': see esp. 257 and 263–5.

[65] See Brooke, ' "A New World For Women"?', 8.

[66] Mass-Observation's 'Little Kinsey' concluded that one in twelve did not know what the term 'birth control' meant, and one person in twenty-five was 'wrong': Stanley, *Sex Surveyed*, 95. See also Westoff, Potter, and Sagi, 'Some Estimates of the Reliability of Survey Data on Family Planning', 57.

denial. However, most concurred that their procedures remained unsatisfactory.[67] Lewis-Faning's interviewers' attempts to be comprehensive probably confused their interviewees: they told their respondents that 'contraception' meant 'the use by either sex of any means whatsoever whereby coitus (the act of union between man and woman) may be experienced, while at the same time the fusion of the ovum with the spermatozoon may be averted so that conception does not take place'. If a negative response was given, interviewers were told to ask specifically 'whether her husband had been "Careful" '.[68] Pierce and Rowntree found that 18 per cent of all informants initially denied the use of birth control, only to acknowledge later the use of a non-appliance method when specifically asked if they had used the 'safe period', withdrawal, douche, breast-feeding, or abstinence.[69] Slater and Woodside also felt withdrawal was under-represented given that 'many do not perceive *coitus interruptus* (withdrawal) to be a form of contraception, regarding "birth control" as something chemical or mechanical'.[70]

Working-class oral history respondents similarly did not associate withdrawal with the language of 'birth control' and reference to it was not necessarily viewed as an appropriate response to a question about family limitation. Gladys, for example, did not use birth control, but admitted 'being careful':

We never heard about anything. No mention of birth control at all. If you didn't want more children, then you had to be careful didn't you? Or get your husband to be careful (laughs). But, it's not easy is it? No, no it isn't (laughs).[71]

Similarly Fred explained when asked about his family size that 'we took the necessary precautions—condoms mostly'. He had to be prompted to remember that withdrawal was also commonly used: 'Oh yes, yes, aye, we used to do that, yeah.'[72] Those who used appliance methods in conjunction with traditional methods were probably significantly under-represented, as in many surveys a positive response to a question about appliance methods often meant that follow-up questions about the use of non-appliance means were not necessarily asked, and certainly the point was not likely to be pressed. Pierce and Rowntree wondered whether many, 'weary' in a long interview, did not 'trouble to outline their whole contraceptive history'.[73]

---

[67] See Langford, 'Birth Control Practice', on the different ways in which questions about birth-control methods were phrased to try to ensure full and detailed results without omissions, and the problems with such attempts. See also Westoff, Potter and Sagi, 'Some Estimates'; Busfield and Paddon, *Thinking about Children*, 236.

[68] Lewis-Faning, *Report of an Inquiry into Family Limitation*, 49.

[69] Pierce and Rowntree, 'Birth Control in Britain, Part I', 30–1. It should be noted, of course, that the absence of appliance methods in this list means that such interviewees were not given the opportunity belatedly to 'report the use of condoms' or other appliance methods. See Langford, *Birth Control Practice and Marital Fertility*, 57.

[70] Slater and Woodside, *Patterns of Marriage*, 194. See also Florence, *Birth Control on Trial*, 20.

[71] Gladys, bc1/pilot/#3. This pilot interview was not included in the sample.

[72] Fred, bc2#14.   [73] Pierce and Rowntree, 'Birth Control in Britain, Part I', 124.

The questions asked about abstinence were especially likely to exclude its practitioners. A number of surveys defined abstinence narrowly as the complete avoidance of sexual intercourse for a substantial period of time.[74] Both Lewis-Faning's survey and the 1959 PIC investigation counted only 'no intercourse for six months or more' as significant.[75] Lewis-Faning also discounted 'abstinence of periods of less than six months' when claiming that abstinence was negligible. Enid Charles's survey almost completely disregarded abstinence, claiming it was not a method of birth control.[76] Moreover, the tendency on the part of surveyors to ignore partial abstinence is consistent with assumptions that birth control generally was used in a planned and constant way. If, as was argued in Chapter 2, family limitation strategies were frequently seen as intermittent attempts to moderate the chance of falling pregnant rather than concerted efforts to avoid conception, then we should expect that occasional or inconsistent use of abstinence will not have been characterized as a method of birth control by users responding to surveys about contraception.

While we might concur that defining abstinence as total continence for a period of more than six months is an overly strict definition, obtaining material to assess the relationship between fertility levels and coital frequency presents significant problems. Coital frequency data is rarely collected and justifiably scorned.[77] Enid Charles, for example, worried that enquiry into 'the frequency of sexual intercourse' would 'limit the number of replies which can be obtained' and so no such data was sought.[78] Although oral history provides plenty of detail about coital frequency, it is evidently unlikely to provide accurate information, and such material is frequently contradictory. In some instances, qualitative data on the regularity of sexual intercourse is likely to overestimate the practice, while other material probably underestimates it.

Many might have claimed to have been 'relatively' abstinent in the mistaken assumption that others had sex more frequently. Women in particular presented themselves as having been 'undersexed' or sexually modest; yet this should be linked to the tendency of women to present themselves as sexually passive, rather than seen as clear evidence for abstinence. Male identity too, while not concerned with sexual passivity, nevertheless prized sexual consideration and moderation. Statements about the absence of sexual obsession, and claims that couples were 'normal' rather than 'over-sexed', were common. Interviewees' self-representation

---

[74] Sloan argues that such questions excluded most cases of attempted abstinence or reduced coital frequency: 'The Extent of Contraceptive Use'; see also Cook, *The Long Sexual Revolution*, 109.

[75] Pierce and Rowntree, 'Birth Control in Britain, Part II', 123; Lewis-Faning, *Report of an Inquiry into Family Limitation*, 49; Peel and Carr, *Contraception and Family Design*, 74.

[76] Charles, *The Practice of Birth Control*, 31.

[77] There is considerable debate on how best to obtain accurate information on coital frequency. See e.g. Udry, 'Coitus as Demographic Behaviour'; Clark and Wallin, 'The Accuracy of Husbands' and Wives' Reports of the Frequency of Marital Coitus'. See also Call, Sprecher, and Schwartz, 'The Incidence and Frequency of Marital Sex', esp. 648.   [78] Charles, *The Practice of Birth Control*, 16.

as 'moderate' and having a low sexual frequency was also influenced by a desire to distance themselves from the mores of today's society, which they regarded as too 'highly sexed'; thus, regardless of their actual coital frequency, respondents were engaged in a deliberate attempt to contrast their behaviour with perceived modern excesses. Penny 'didn't make love quite so often . . . you know it—it happened, you know, quite normally . . . I mean, it was sort of couple—three times a week or something like that. I mean . . . it was all quite natural . . . you know lots of kissing and—er slobbering and no toe sucking and there was nothing like that.'[79] Instances of abstinence might remain unreported, especially if abstinence was not viewed as a contraceptive method or strategy but rather a response to circumstance. Norman, who was working in a distillery, did not see himself as having used abstinence as a form of contraception but remembered that for about a year following a stillbirth in 1944 his wife, who was desperate not to fall pregnant again, avoided sex altogether.[80] Reg's wife found it difficult to have sex in case she woke her small child: 'she was always tense, sort of listening, waiting, you know, for the child to wake'.[81] Instances of abstinence are also potentially hidden behind euphemistic descriptions such as 'being careful', 'not going too far' and 'not bothering' which are usually taken to refer to the use of withdrawal.[82] Yet it is not entirely clear that 'being careful' invariably referred to coitus interruptus. Self-control was used in reference to both abstinence and withdrawal. In her evidence to the National Birth-Rate Commission, Marie Stopes recognized that, whereas ' "self-control" is used by some as synonymous with complete abstinence . . . the laity . . . [use it] to indicate the evil practice of *coitus interruptus*, as well as various other practices'.[83]

That surveys concentrated on interviewing women reduced the frequency with which male methods, especially withdrawal, were reported. Enid Charles, for example, was aware that this was a problem; on finding that 'it is probable that in the majority of unions involving contraceptive measures at the present time, the male partner is the active agent', she regretted that 'attention [is] focused somewhat exclusively on feminine reactions to contraception' and 'hoped that a later study will be made of the contraceptive experiences of a number of men'.[84] Such a study did not materialize. A number of female oral history respondents in this project denied the use of any form of birth control. Only after further questioning did it become clear that they were specifically denying 'personal' use and failing to mention the actions their husband took (which most frequently meant withdrawal).

---

[79] Penny, msf/srss/ht/#20.   [80] Norman, msf/kf/ht/#17.   [81] Reg, msf/kf/ht/#36.

[82] The variety of local euphemisms for withdrawal is interesting and important. In the Netherlands, for example, withdrawal is referred to as 'Voor het zingen de kerk uit', which translates as 'leaving the church before the singing starts' (singing in church is associated with the finale of the service). I am grateful to Rogier de Kok for this observation. On the variety of global euphemisms, see Santow, 'Coitus Interruptus and the Control of Natural Fertility', 35–8.

[83] National Birth-Rate Commission, *Problems of Population and Parenthood*, 245. These issues will be developed in Szreter and Fisher, 'Sexuality, Love and Marriage in England, 1918–1960'

[84] Charles, *The Practice of Birth Control*, 16.

It is highly likely that a number of female respondents to fertility surveys similarly failed to mention male methods, regarding them as nothing to do with them. One survey, which included men, found them far more likely than women to report the use of withdrawal, and women far more likely to deny the use of birth control, especially male methods. They concluded that 'women . . . may have deliberately interpreted the questions on methods in rather literal terms and denied that they personally ever took any contraceptive measures'.[85] A few women professed themselves unaware of the contraceptive purpose behind withdrawal, or were unsure of whether or not withdrawal had taken place. One 'family planning educator', recalling her first relationship in the late 1950s, thought 'he may have withdrawn . . . I wouldn't have really been aware of that, because—it was all terribly vague. It was about love and passion and—and not about sex, if that makes any sort of sense'.[86]

The class and regional focus of much work on birth control has also been likely to under-represent the degree to which traditional methods survived alongside the rise of new appliances. Historians have long noticed important class differences in fertility rates and assumed too that traditional methods remained far more commonly used in working-class households than in more affluent homes.[87] Less frequently pointed out are the regional patterns of method use and the resilience of traditional practices in parts of the country. The urban focus of most surveys conceals the greater dominance of traditional methods in rural areas. The significant growth in the adoption of appliance methods—caps and condoms—was primarily restricted to southern suburban middle-class communities, despite the rise of clinics in working-class areas. Lara Marks, for example, claimed that evidence from birth control clinics revealed an increase in middle-class use of the female appliance methods rising from 9 per cent to 40 per cent between 1910 and 1930 while the use by the working classes only rose from 1 per cent to 28 per cent.[88] Yet the evidence we have has encouraged historians to underestimate the continued use of traditional methods, especially abortion, in middle-class circles.

All appliance methods are seen as having been used earlier and to a much greater extent in the middle classes than the working classes. Lewis-Faning, using the five Social Class groups used by the Registrar-General, found that in the cohort married before 1910, although appliance use was small, 9 per cent of Social Class I reported some use of appliance methods, as opposed to 1 per cent of Social Class II and 2 percent of Social Class III. For the cohort married between 1935 and 1939, 53 per cent of Social Class I were using appliance methods, 34 per cent of

[85] Pierce and Rowntree, 'Birth Control in Britain, Part I', 16; see also 'Birth Control in Britain, Part II', 124–7.

[86] 'In the club', A&M: GC/105/22. See also the story by Mary McCarthy, *The Group*, in which the husband announces to his unsuspecting and anxious wife that there was no danger of conception: ' "My dear girl," he said, "we just employed the most ancient form of birth control. Coitus interruptus, the old Romans called it".' Quoted in Devlin, *Motherhood*, 46.

[87] See e.g. McKibbin, *Classes and Cultures*, 304–8.   [88] Marks, *Sexual Chemistry*, 188–9.

Social Class II, and 25 per cent of Social Class III.[89] Enid Charles also argued that sheaths and newer clinical methods were predominantly used by the middle classes while coitus interruptus was far more common in lower social groups. Abstinence was only mentioned by those from Social Classes I and II.[90] Pierce and Rowntree concluded that, particularly among later cohorts, there was a significant decline in the use of withdrawal and an increase in the use of the cap by non-manual (professional, managerial, and white-collar) classes.[91] In all their cohorts, caps and condoms were more frequently used in the non-manual classes than in the working classes, who revealed much higher use of withdrawal and other 'minor methods'.[92]

Middle-class appliance use reflected their greater access to sympathetic doctors and greater readiness to seek medical advice on the matter.[93] As the Society for the Provision of Birth Control Clinics commented, 'the well-to-do can and do get advice on contraception', but such knowledge is still withheld from the 'poor and helpless'.[94] Suspicion has remained that the middle classes were over-represented in clinics, even those designed to help the working classes. In the absence of case notes or information on the occupations of mothers or their husbands it is very difficult to ascertain the status of patients attending clinics. On the one hand, the large number of sponges provided at some of Marie Stopes's clinics—this being the method reserved for the 'ignorant' and 'unintelligent' (i.e. very poor)—suggests a large contingent of working-class patients, as does the large proportion for whom fees were waived by local authority clinics. The Rhondda clinic had no consultation fee, and of the 183 women who attended in 1936 only twenty were required to pay for their appliances.[95] Norman Himes claimed in 1932 that 90 per cent of attendees at British birth control clinics were from the working classes, with one-third unskilled.[96] However, Nurse Ellen Williams complained in 1928, when Marie Stopes's caravan clinic was stationed in Leeds, that all fittings were of

---

[89] The Registrar-General assigned class on the basis of the husband's occupation. Lewis-Faning, *Report of an Inquiry into Family Limitation*, 52 and 30, describes the classification as follows: Class I: Professional etc.; Class II: Intermediate between I and III; Class III: Skilled Workers; Class IV: Intermediate between III and V; Class V: Unskilled Workers, not gainfully occupied and information not given. On the limitations of these categorizations see Szreter, 'The Genesis of the Registrar-General's Social Classification of Occupations'; id., 'The Official Representation of Social Classes'.

[90] Charles, *The Practice of Birth Control*, 67.

[91] Pierce and Rowntree, 'Birth Control in Britain, Part II', 142.   [92] Ibid.

[93] However, during the 1930s the Birth Control Advisory Bureau aimed to assist middle-class women as there are 'very few general practitioners who are experienced in birth control methods and the fitting of a cap pessary': Nurse M. R. Hooper, *The Voice of Experience* (London: Birth Control Advisory Bureau, 1938), 9, copy in TC Mass-Observation, Family Planning 1944–49, Birth Control Leaflets and Booklets, TC3/2/E.   [94] SPBCC, *Birth Control and Public Health*, p. viii.

[95] Rhondda Urban District Council, *Report of the Medical Officer of Health and School Medical Officer, for the Year 1936*.

[96] Himes, 'Birth Control in Historical and Clinical Perspective', 9. The clinics surveyed were voluntary ones in north Kensington, Manchester, Wolverhampton, Cambridge, Liverpool, Birmingham, Glasgow, Aberdeen, and Cannock.

'Good class mothers—none of the poor mothers who really need our help.'[97] The Birmingham Women's Welfare Centre's survey of 1932 found the majority of women who visited—65 per cent of the total—were wives of 'skilled and semi-skilled workers'. A significant minority of clients were from middle-class occupations, considerably in excess of their representation in Birmingham as a whole.[98] North Kensington Women's Welfare Clinic also concluded that attendance was dominated by 'the more prudent, far sighted, and intelligent elements of the working classes'.[99] In the 1920s, the Cambridge clinic had 'an excess' of patients from Social Classes I and II compared with the population at large.[100] Not only did many middle-class people attend clinics designed for the very poor, but the lower classes were found to be much less likely to use the method provided regularly or properly. Those of the 'lower social grade' were found by North Kensington Women's Welfare Clinic in 1934 to have 'less inclination to persevere with the method'.[101] Middle-class testimony was much less likely to be hostile to the cap, such as the housewife and statistician living in Welwyn Garden City in 1944, who told Mass-Observation she had 'used a Dutch cap . . . and so have numbers of my friends, with complete success'.[102]

Despite the rise of appliance method use in middle-class homes, traditional methods nevertheless continued to be used, even abortion. The practice of illegal and self-induced abortions among the middle classes has been ignored.[103] Such abortions are generally presented as an urban working-class fertility strategy: as the president of the British Medical Association concluded, it was 'usually committed by ignorant women under dirty conditions'.[104] The middle classes are assumed to have had the social power to obtain 'therapeutic' abortions, or to have had better access to effective and reliable birth control methods. One such woman acknowledged that 'in my circle, if you were desperate you would go to a doctor and he would refer you to a psychiatrist . . . and they would abort'.[105] The Birkett Report also noted the existence of 'the qualified medical practitioner who practices criminal abortion, and may receive high fees for his services'.[106] Since the evidence available to historians about abortions is largely the product of middle-class anxiety about the practice among working-class communities, enquiries into the practice deliberately concentrated on deprived areas, and weeded out any more

[97] Nurse Ellen Williams to Mrs Bootle, 24 June 1928, BL Add. MSS 58621.

[98] Charles, *The Practice of Birth Control*, 126.

[99] North Kensington Women's Welfare, 'Research and Miscellaneous Statistics, 1927–1950, Analysis of 1000 cases in 1934', A&M: SA/FPA/NK/93.

[100] Charles, *The Practice of Birth Control*, 154.

[101] North Kensington Women's Welfare, Research and Miscellaneous Statistics, 1927–1950, Analysis of 1,000 cases in 1934, A&M: SA/FPA/NK/93.

[102] Mass-Observation, DR 1346, reply to April 1944 Directive.

[103] McKibbin argues that resort to illegal abortion was rarely chosen by the middle classes: *Classes and Cultures*, 307.

[104] 'Doctors and Criminal Abortion', *BMJ* (6 Nov. 1937), cutting in A&M/SA/BMA/C.483.

[105] 'In the Club', A&M: GC/105/23.

[106] Ministry of Health, *Report of the Interdepartmental Committee on Abortion*, 43.

affluent members of society from the investigations.[107] Historians may consequently have underestimated the use of illegal, clandestine, and self-induced methods of abortion by middle-class individuals. Lewis-Faning also found 'little difference between social classes' in the extent of abortion reported, and even suggested that 'incidence of attempted abortion increased with social status'.[108] Patricia Knight has noted the existence of relatively expensive abortion remedies, presumably marketed at, and discreetly bought by, middle-class customers.[109] Nor were middle-class methods notably different from those of their working-class counterparts. Hubert, who was employed as a journalist before the Second World War, initially asked his doctor for advice, but after he was 'advised against it' his wife 'tried to get rid of the child herself' using such tactics as 'bumping down stairs'.[110]

The conclusion that the rise in appliance method use was much more a feature of middle-class than working-class behaviour must also be mediated by an understanding of regional differences in contraceptive behaviour. In the north of England, in rural districts, and in Wales, evidence suggests that appliance methods were not as widely adopted as in southern suburban communities, even amongst the middle class. Recently historians have begun to argue that local culture was a prime determinant of fertility patterns and exerted more influence over behaviour than class identity, and that 'people would tend to behave like their neighbours: the dominant social group having the greatest influence over locally accepted norms of behaviour'.[111] Elidh Garrett and colleagues argue that, although 'professionals of Class I were the earliest group to achieve large numbers of small families', their behaviour was regionally specific, with 'professional and white-collar couples living in predominantly working-class areas rather slower to move towards the small family norm'. Concomitantly, members of the working classes 'living in middle-class neighbourhoods . . . appear to have begun to limit their fertility earlier . . . with greater success, than their peers elsewhere'.[112]

In rural areas in particular, but also in much of the north of England and Wales, there is much less evidence of an increased use of appliance methods and much more evidence of the resilience of traditional forms of birth control. Our evidence for rural areas is limited, but all that there is suggests very low use of appliance methods and a dominance of traditional means of fertility regulation. Almost all surveys are weighted towards urban respondents. For example, 85 per cent of Lewis-Faning's material 'referred to marriages spent mainly in urban areas', the vast majority from London and Glasgow.[113] In the countryside, appliance methods remained much less easy to obtain and were seldom used. Ethel Elderton

[107] Brooke, ' "A New World for Women"?', 51.
[108] Lewis-Faning, *Report of an Inquiry into Family Limitation*, 167–71.
[109] Knight, 'Women and Abortion in Victorian and Edwardian England', 58.
[110] Hubert, msf/kf/ht/#32.
[111] Garrett, Reid, Schürer, and Szreter, *Changing Family Size in England and Wales*, 244.
[112] Ibid. 321.   [113] Lewis-Faning, *Report of an Inquiry into Family Limitation*, 35.

concluded that 'in rural areas knowledge is not so widely spread and opportunities for purchase are fewer'.[114] There was found to be little 'Malthusian propagandism' and no large factories where employees could share knowledge and experience. Abortion, also, was found to be far less common in rural areas, a discovery she put down to the difficulty in finding out about and obtaining suitable potions, instruments, or assistance.[115] Few clinics were set up in country areas. One woman, living in 'the old barn' in rural Gloucestershire, complained in 1944 to Mass-Observation that her nearest 'clinics are Bristol and Oxford—much too far away for most people to attend'.[116] Sometimes urban clinics were visited by women from outlying rural areas. Such instances were usually worthy of particular notice. In Cambridge, the 'number of patients who come from the surrounding villages, many wives of agricultural labourers', was surprising.[117]

The variation in rural economies and fertility has also been stressed by historians, yet very little is known about the different contraceptive choices made by various kinds of rural dwellers. It is argued that farmers reduced their fertility before agricultural labourers, and that average family size in rural areas dominated by small villages and market towns fell more rapidly than in isolated hill-farming areas.[118] Ethel Elderton noted considerable variation in rural fertility levels: where mines had recently been sunk fertility was especially high, while in rural districts close to large urban areas there was more use of birth control. For example, in Hunslet rural district, despite the dominance of both mining and agriculture, the easy 'intercommunication by tram and train with Leeds' where 'neo-Malthusian literature and appliances abound' resulted in a significant 'reduction of the birth-rate in the neighbourhood'.[119] Here, the evidence of country dwellers travelling to nearby urban clinics is illustrative: the Exeter clinic found a large proportion of 'patients come from the surrounding villages',[120] and the Aberdeen clinic was attended by numbers of farmers' wives, often 'just crofters', giving 'every appearance of being poor'.[121] Even the North Kensington Clinic found that women attended 'from the country districts outside a 20 mile radius of London'.[122]

Only in suburban areas of southern Britain is the evidence for a shift towards appliance methods and away from traditional ones significant; elsewhere withdrawal remained dominant. Oral history suggests that it was primarily among those interviewed in the southern regions of Oxford and Hertfordshire that condoms and caps were adopted in significant numbers. Only in Hertfordshire was the dominance of withdrawal challenged, where only 42 per cent reported its

---

[114] Elderton, *Report on the English Birth-Rate*, 35.   [115] Ibid.

[116] Mass-Observation, DR 3423, reply to April 1944 Directive.

[117] SPBCC, *Birth Control and Public Health*, 12.

[118] See Reay, *Rural England's Labouring Lives*, 98–102; Garrett, Schürer, and Szreter, *Changing Family Size*.   [119] Elderton, *Report on the English Birth-Rate*, 107.

[120] SPBCC, *Birth Control and Public Health*, 16.

[121] Margaret Rae to Marie Stopes, 26 Oct. 1934, BL Add. MSS 58630.

[122] North Kensington Women's Welfare, Research and Miscellaneous Statistics, 1927–1950, Analysis of 1,000 cases in 1934, A&M: SA/FPA/NK/93.

practice. Here condom use was particularly important, along with relatively high levels of female methods, abortion, and abstinence. In the suburban south of England, the use of condoms and other appliance methods was a characteristic of working-class as well as middle-class practice. Unlike working-class respondents in Oxford, Blackburn, and south Wales, in Hertfordshire a low use of withdrawal was a feature of all respondents regardless of class background. The method use reported by the working-class respondents in Hertfordshire was thus representative of their locale rather than of their class.[123] In all areas bar the home county of Hertfordshire withdrawal was the most common method reported. However, these regional and class variations look slightly different if material on the patterns of method use, experimentation, and rejection are incorporated. Such a focus further reinforces the finding that withdrawal remained a popular method despite the increasing availability of appliance methods. While a regional divide in methods used is noticeable, with urban, industrial, working-class areas revealing much higher dominance of withdrawal use than middle-class suburban regions, the fact that the latter types of area showed greater experimentation and use of appliance methods should not cloud the continued importance of withdrawal. In Hertfordshire, the finding that only sixteen respondents (40 per cent) used withdrawal whereas twenty-six (68 per cent) used condoms is slightly modified by the finding that, of the nine respondents who used both condoms and withdrawal, only one preferred condoms, one used both equally, while the remaining

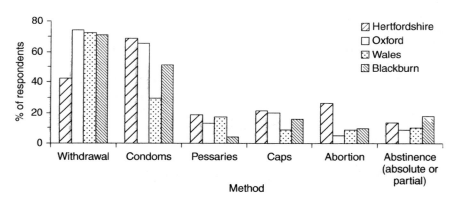

Figure 1. Birth-control methods reported by oral history respondents

[123] By contrast, the middle classes in Blackburn were representative of their class rather than their region. Of the thirteen respondents of social class I interviewed in Blackburn, only five used withdrawal and eight used condoms. In fact, if the middle-class respondents are removed from the Blackburn sample, then it becomes much more similar to other working-class areas, such as south Wales: 82% of the remaining Blackburn respondents reported using withdrawal, and 47% reported the use of condoms.

seven presented themselves as having merely flirted with condoms, adopting them rarely or rejecting them immediately.

The dominance of withdrawal and lack of uptake of condoms or other appliance methods was especially striking in the mining area of south Wales. Of those interviewed in south Wales, 73 per cent reported having used withdrawal, while very low condom use was revealed, with only 29 per cent using them. Enid Charles also concluded that coitus interruptus was the only method used by miners.[124] The isolation of the Welsh mining valleys perhaps affected the easy availability of condoms, or the ease with which men might obtain them, particularly if they sought to get them somewhere they would not be recognized.[125] Moreover, that mining was a reserved occupation during both world wars may also have had an impact. Those serving in the army were introduced to condoms (particularly in the Second World War), an experience which many miners did not have. In the textile town of Blackburn, the oral history material shows no evidence of a turn to appliance methods, despite the lower fertility rates of that region than other working-class districts and the assumption that in such areas female economic power translated into greater contraceptive use.[126] The low use of pessaries is significant here given that they were probably the most easily available female method. It might be argued that condoms, caps, and pessaries were less easily available outside of the south of England.

The rise of appliance methods is only therefore in evidence in southern suburban areas. Traditional method use is underestimated by the available data, both qualitative and quantitative, in part because interviews tend to have been with women, many of whom did not regard it as appropriate or relevant to mention traditional methods such as coitus interruptus, abstinence, or abortion, and in part because insufficient attention has been paid to regional as well as class variations in method awareness and use.

'IF YOU DIDN'T HAVE ANY FRENCH LETTERS . . . YOU LEFT HER BEFORE YOU FINISHED':[127] PATTERNS OF METHOD SELECTION

The continued importance of traditional methods of birth control alongside the rise of appliance methods is particularly apparent when one examines the context of method selection and patterns of use. Rather than replacing traditional methods,

---

[124] Charles, *The Practice of Birth Control*, 67. Only seven respondents came from mining occupations, however.

[125] By the 1930s and 1940s the majority of sheaths sold in the UK were produced in the south of England, notably by the London Rubber Company: J. Peel, 'The Manufacture and Retailing of Contraceptives', 122.　　[126] See e.g. Gittins, 'Women's Work and Family Size Between the Wars'.

[127] Norman, msf/kf/ht/#17.

new appliance forms of birth control frequently simply added diversity to contraceptive practices. Indeed, in a number of cases new methods were merely experimented with, before being rejected in favour of withdrawal, abstinence, and abortion.

The fact that people frequently use a range of forms of contraception at different times and in different contexts has been and continues to be largely neglected by surveys.[128] The assumption is that people were looking for one method and looking to choose the 'best' method they knew about. Questions focus on obtaining information about the number of methods *ever* used and not on preferences, choices, or patterns of adoption.[129] Douglas G. Sloan criticizes social demographers for treating 'the proportion of respondents who have ever used contraception' as the 'prime statistic . . . Couples need only use contraception once in their lives to be included in it.'[130] Some surveys only ask for the 'main method' to be outlined, whereas some ask respondents to list methods 'ever used' without attempting to discern the relative importance of the methods tried; others fail to distinguish between past and present use, and some lump methods together, not distinguishing between withdrawal and abstinence, or between types of appliance methods.

The acknowledgement that appliance methods might have been used alongside traditional methods is rarely seen as significant.[131] A central flaw in some surveys is the failure to recognize that the use of an appliance method did not generally mean that traditional methods were phased out. This problem is particularly acute in the case of Lewis-Faning's report, which categorized the material in such a way that a considerable proportion of the practice of withdrawal (and the use of other traditional methods) was overlooked (see above). Throughout his survey a great distinction is drawn between 'appliance users' and those who use 'non-appliance methods *only*' without acknowledgement that 'appliance users' might also have used traditional methods. His material has consistently been misinterpreted to reveal a decline in the use of traditional methods, especially

---

[128] See Santow, 'Coitus Interruptus in the Twentieth Century', 772.

[129] This is criticized in Tsui, 'The Dynamics of Contraceptive Use'.

[130] Sloan, 'The Extent of Contraceptive Use', 383. Sloan points in particular to the tendency of those who take part in fertility surveys to conceal certain elements of their contraceptive behaviour. I agree with Sloan that we need to study the different ways in which people respond to questions about birth control, particularly the implications of denials followed by admissions of contraceptive practice. However, I do not concur that such obfuscations reveal the limited use of birth control or that we should give greater emphasis to biological factors to explain fertility decline.

[131] Enid Charles's questionnaire was the exception in asking what methods were used, when, how frequently, and whether methods were used in conjunction with each other. She found 'the majority' using 'a number of different methods . . . successively': Charles, *The Practice of Birth Control*, 25, and especially the chart at pp. 28–9, which illustrates the complexity of common contraceptive method combinations. An American survey in 1940 also recognized the extent to which, among appliance users, coitus interruptus served as an 'alternate or secondary method', although their questionnaire was not sophisticated enough to measure this: Riley and White, 'The Use of Various Methods of Contraception', 903.

withdrawal. Lewis-Faning himself concludes that, since 1920–4, 'the use of non-appliance methods . . . has steadily declined'.[132] In fact, his material cannot be used to establish such a decline; it only reveals that appliance methods were increasingly tried. It does not tell us whether such users also used traditional methods or, crucially, whether appliance methods were preferred.[133]

A closer look at the available data suggests that the increased use of appliances was not at the expense of traditional methods. Rather, the picture is one of multiple method use. The combined use of withdrawal and condoms was the most popular fertility-reducing strategy reported by oral history respondents, but condoms were not replacing withdrawal. Of the fifty-one respondents who used both condoms and withdrawal, only two (4 per cent) abandoned withdrawal in favour of a regime dominated by condoms. Thirteen respondents (26 per cent) combined both methods, using whichever was convenient at the time, while sixteen (31 per cent) simply experimented with condoms only to reject them in favour of withdrawal. Of the remaining twenty who continued to use both methods, thirteen (26 per cent) presented withdrawal as their main method and condom use as occasional, while seven (14 per cent) presented condoms as their main method, sometimes supplemented with withdrawal. The 1959 PIC data also revealed the dominance of condoms and withdrawal; among multiple method users 83 per cent had condoms in their repertoire and 63 per cent resorted to withdrawal.[134]

Indeed, many of those who experimented with appliance forms of birth control, particularly caps, did so for short periods of time before abandoning them.[135] Of the thirty cap users, only eight presented themselves as satisfied with the method, and of these, two nevertheless stopped using it.[136] The majority of cap users disliked the method and most abandoned them. Four continued to use the cap, despite disliking it, either because their husbands refused to use anything else, or because a doctor ordered its use. It is very difficult to assess the extent to which those who attended clinics used the appliance methods provided. As Helena Wright commented, many 'patients . . . do not appear after being taught the method'.[137] Sometimes those who did not return were visited, although this was

---

[132] Lewis Faning, *Report of an Inquiry into Family Limitation*, 59.

[133] Ibid. 54. Lewis-Faning also found complex patterns of method use with 'combinations of two or more types of method common', as well as frequent changes of method. These were not analysed or described in any detail, however. In fact such combinations are presented as methodologically irritating in the attempt to analyse the effectiveness of birth control by method used (ibid. 134).

[134] Pierce and Rowntree, 'Birth Control in Britain, Part II', 139.

[135] Modern family-planning programs also often conclude that methods are frequently abandoned within twelve months: Ross and Frankenberg, *Findings from Two Decades of Family Planning Research*, 48–54.

[136] There were fewer than thirty instances of cap use: if the method was mentioned by both parties of a couple, both reports are counted.

[137] Helena Wright, 'Birth Control. Course Notes', 22 June 1939, *British Postgraduate Medical School*, A&M: PP/HRW/B15/2.

expensive and ran the risk of infringing the confidentiality of the client.[138] Four hundred of Birmingham's 'patients' were 'visited by the clinic nurse', and six months after the caravan had toured south Wales its clients were paid a visit at home.[139] In the early 1930s Nurse Daniels surveyed many of those who had attended her clinic and been fitted with Dutch caps, though she surmised that far more satisfied customers bothered to respond.[140] The most extensive follow-up survey was conducted in the early 1950s, when over 900 interviews were conducted with women who had attended the Birmingham clinic in 1948, but had since stopped attending.[141] Such surveys were limited in their success. When in the early 1950s the Kensington Women's Welfare Clinic sought to canvass the views of 600 women who had attended twice but since lapsed, less than 25 per cent replied.[142]

Long-term success is even harder to ascertain. These follow up reports generally occurred relatively soon after an initial consultation. Nurse Daniels, for example, classed any use of her method for longer than a year as a success; in Birmingham 400 women were visited after 'about three years' use of contraceptive methods.[143] The few clinic records on the success with which caps were used present a mixed picture. On the one hand, much grateful correspondence was received from women who claimed to have benefited considerably from using the cap and were glad to be able to reject previous methods. Not only were pregnancies reported to have been successfully prevented, but the general marital happiness and health of both husband and wife were claimed to have vastly improved. However, there was also a significant number of dissatisfied customers, and an even greater proportion who were less than enthusiastic about the method. Lella Secor Florence 'honestly admit[ted] that there are very few indeed among patients at the Clinic who *like* the pessary as a method of contraception'.[144] Many of those who went to clinics rejected clinic methods in favour of withdrawal, such as the woman who went to the North Kensington Women's Welfare Clinic in 1937 but did not return since her 'husband did not "like the idea of the cap"'. She did not like the sheath, so they 'continued C.I. [coitus interruptus] and appear quite satisfied'.[145] The Society for the Provision of Birth Control Clinics found that the abandonment, either 'temporarily or permanently', of clinic methods was 'not infrequent'.[146] When the Birmingham Women's Welfare Centre visited 216

---

[138] See SPBCC, *Birth Control and Public Health*, 7.   [139] Ibid. 15.

[140] Nurse Daniels's survey forms part of Enid Charles's analysis: Charles, *The Practice of Birth Control*, 113.

[141] On the Birmingham follow-up survey, see the account in Florence, *Progress Report on Birth Control*.

[142] North Kensington Women's Welfare Follow-Up Survey, 1952–1956, A&M: SA/FPA/NK/201.   [143] Charles, *The Practice of Birth Control*, 114, 125.

[144] Florence, *Birth Control on Trial*, 68. She is referring to the type of cervical cap predominantly recommended at the Cambridge clinic in the 1920s.

[145] North Kensington Women's Welfare Patient Follow-Up Reports, 1936–7, A&M: SA/FPA/NK/93.   [146] SPBCC, *Birth Control and Public Health*, 24.

women who had been given Dutch caps in 1932, they reported that thirty-five had abandoned the method, four had 'partially abandoned' it, and forty-five had never used their cap. A further fourteen failed to use the method successfully.[147] The later Birmingham report found that, of 914 women interviewed (all of whom had stopped attending the clinic), only seventy-seven were using the cap prescribed.[148] Ninety per cent of those found to have rejected the cap had turned to an alternative method of birth control—predominantly withdrawal, especially among those whose husbands had 'manual' jobs.[149] Withdrawal was rarely totally abandoned in favour of a new method. A new method tended either to supplement a regime that continued to be dominated by withdrawal, or to be rejected in favour of coitus interruptus.

Examining the use of contraception throughout a couple's marriage reveals that appliance methods were frequently used for short periods of time when motivation to avoid pregnancy was particularly strong. It was also at such moments that couples were likely to come into contact with health professionals who frequently advocated female caps or condoms. However, it is a mistake to assume that couples using contraception were highly motivated or that they were seeking to use the most reliable method they could. Despite the availability of more reliable methods of birth control, many lacked sufficient motivation to put them into practice over the long term and instead turned to traditional methods which were familiar and perceived as easier to use.

For many periods of married life, although contraception was regularly employed, the desire to avoid pregnancy was limited in strength. In these circumstances, withdrawal was often chosen as the easiest method: it was already known about and did not require preparation. There were, for many, long periods in which contraception was used merely to reduce the chance of pregnancy, rather than to eliminate the possibility altogether. Indeed, many began married life without determining when they wished to start a family or how many children they would have. A great many respondents, as outlined in the previous chapter, did not 'plan' their families or start marriage with a clear idea of how many children they wanted or when they wanted them. In such circumstances birth control was a low priority and might be used only some of the time. Determination or resolve was also likely to fade, and contraceptive use might succumb to what Lella Secor Florence termed 'old inertia', or a tendency to get 'out of the habit'.[150] Long periods of successful contraceptive use frequently induced 'carelessness' or a re-evaluation of the risks of pregnancy. Many concluded that one could use contraception with less regularity, or abandon appliance methods altogether, without significantly increasing one's chances of getting pregnant. Angela and Hugh's resolve to avoid having a child faded: 'I had a very difficult confinement, and so we—it

[147] Charles, *The Practice of Birth Control*, 130–1.
[148] Florence, *Progress Report on Birth Control*, 103.   [149] Ibid. 109–10.
[150] Ibid. 51, 192.

was a bit tricky—risky having another child, but then you forget over the years.' After the doctor told them to avoid pregnancy at all costs they used both a cap and condom every time they had sex: 'you were scared of becoming pregnant again . . . you wouldn't rely on one of them'. However, such resolve did not last. They did not use the cap 'for a long time' and it was abandoned.[151] One of Busfield and Paddon's respondents initially used a sheath 'pretty regularly'. A long period without pregnancy led to the assumption that conception was unlikely: 'we thought I was past it'; 'we took chances . . . we sort of got a bit cocksure'.[152] A 36-year-old Mass-Observation panellist admitted in 1944 that he and his wife had 'drifted out of the habit of contraception'.[153] Many others chose traditional methods of birth control until later in marriage at which point higher motivation to avoid pregnancy resulted in a change of strategy.[154] Roger, for example, remembered how initially his wife 'wasn't worried at all, she said, "que sera, sera!", what will be, will be, but, when she had the boy, she said, "We'd better be a bit careful because," she said, "I'm—I can ovulate very quickly now".'[155]

A pressing need to avoid pregnancy increased the chance that one traditional method would be used—abstinence. In oral history testimony all clear cases of abstinence were represented as short-term reactions to contraceptive crises. Terence, a self-employed decorator, had heard that women were particularly at risk of pregnancy during the menopause, and during that period, 'fear of, er, making her pregnant again stopped you'.[156] Doris, a typist, 'had to have this op and I couldn't do it if I was pregnant' and since 'he wasn't prepared to use anything . . . I said the only thing is to sleep separately . . . we did that for, I suppose it was about three months', but 'that couldn't' last' and 'before they sent for me for the op . . . he came back to sleep with me and I used pessaries'.[157] One of the few abstainers in Enid Charles's survey practised it after both the safe period and coitus interruptus had failed, because not 'even the smallest risk could be faced'.[158]

Many of those combining methods used whichever was perceived as the most convenient at that particular moment. Many found traditional methods simpler than appliance methods. One woman stated that she and her husband used 'French letters' unless 'it was spontaneous. . . then we would use coitus interruptus'.[159] Another used the sponge provided by Stopes's Cardiff clinic some of the time, but 'her husband withdraws when she is "too tired to bother with [her] sponge"'.[160] Agatha used withdrawal more than condoms, because 'perhaps he'd

[151] Angela and Hugh, msf/kf/ht/#18.
[152] Busfield and Paddon, *Thinking about Children*, 238.
[153] Mass-Observation, DR 2683, reply to April 1944 Directive.
[154] See also Potter,. Sagi, and Westoff, 'Improvement of Contraception during the Course of Marriage'.   [155] Roger, msf/kf/ht/#10.
[156] Terence, msf/srss/bl/#15.   [157] Doris, bc3ox#20.
[158] Charles, *The Practice of Birth Control*, 56.   [159] 'In the Club' A&M: GC/105/23.
[160] Nurse Florence Gordon to Marie Stopes, 21 July 1939, BL Add. MSS 58625.

run out of having the French letters'.[161] Pru, whose husband was stationed in Scotland with the navy during the war, similarly found withdrawal more convenient: 'for instance, it depends what time—if he was away up in the north of Scotland and it took hours to come down and he hadn't got one, then we'd withdraw'.[162] June's 'mood' determined whether withdrawal or a condom was used. She preferred sex using withdrawal, so 'if I was feeling a bit more amorous than he was, he would, er—we would get as far as doing it without and then he would withdraw'. Her husband preferred condoms, so if 'he was feeling more that way and I wasn't, I would suggest he used a—used a French Letter so he would get his climax and I wasn't bothered, you see'.[163] Gill used condoms, caps, and withdrawal, but chose withdrawal on the occasions described as spontaneous and abandoned: if 'you were doing it somewhere where the cap wasn't around, you know. Like on the carpet in the sitting room or something.'[164] One couple who attended a clinic in Cambridge used the sheath in winter and a cervical cap in the summer.[165] The circumstantial nature of contraceptive decisions is also evident in clinic data which revealed that those using caps often did so sporadically, according to whim. North Kensington Women's Welfare Clinic noted that patients often turned to withdrawal when on holiday or away from home, as many neglected to take their cap with them.[166]

CONCLUSION

The assumption that appliance methods of contraception increasingly replaced the resort to traditional means, especially withdrawal, abortion, and abstinence, reflects a misinterpretation of flawed survey data. The design and analysis of surveys have served to underestimate the endurance of such methods. Important regional and class differences also draw attention to the limited impact appliance methods had in some communities. Most importantly, analysis of contraceptive practice has failed to look at patterns of method choice. Assuming that appliance methods were self-evidently better than their old-fashioned alternatives, the use of an appliance method has itself been seen as indicative of a decrease in the popularity of traditional means of birth control. Whether or not appliance methods were accepted or rejected, whether or not traditional and new appliance methods coexisted, and the circumstances in which one method was chosen over another have

[161] Agatha, msf/kf/ht/#7.   [162] Pru, msf/kf/ht/#12.   [163] June, msf/kf/ht/#27.
[164] Gill, msf/kf/bl/#48.   [165] Florence, *Birth Control on Trial*, 81.
[166] North Kensington Women's Welfare, Research and Miscelleaneous Statistics, 1927–1950. Failures 1 Apr. 1935–31 Mar. 1936, A&M: SA/FPA/NK/93; see also Florence, *Progress Report on Birth Control*, 51, 191.

all been neglected. In fact, evidence suggests that withdrawal, abortion, and possibly abstinence remained crucial elements in flexible and contingent fertility strategies. Some did not like the new methods they tried and reverted to familiar ones, while many others used a range of types of birth control, including traditional ones.

4

'We did try one of them rubber things once, but we didn't like 'em'[1]

The Advantages of Traditional Methods of Birth Control

Despite the increased availability and use of appliance methods, traditional forms of birth control, especially withdrawal, remained significant throughout the first half of the twentieth century. Condoms were increasingly used, but female appliance methods such as caps and pessaries were much more rarely employed and frequently rejected if tried. Despite important class and regional differences, the dominant picture is of male method use, particularly withdrawal, and a continued reliance on traditional methods, including abortion and abstinence. The continued prevalence of traditional types of birth control challenges our understanding of the criteria behind method choices. It has been seen as self-evident that 'traditional' methods were regarded as unreliable and unpalatable and thus were employed only as a last resort. It is assumed that the increasing availability of 'modern', 'better', and 'more reliable' methods of contraception during the course of the twentieth century can only have led to more satisfactory and more frequent use of birth control. In fact, withdrawal, abstinence, and abortion had considerable advantages. For many, the desire for natural, private, and spontaneous sexual relations made non-appliance methods preferable; concerns about the safety and reliability of appliance forms of birth control undermined the appeal of new contraceptive technologies; and the idea that contraception was a man's role fostered the use of male methods such as withdrawal.[2]

The early twentieth century saw considerable developments in reproductive technology: the invention of caps and diaphragms and their dispersal in a growing number of birth control clinics from the 1920s; the manufacture of spermicidal pessaries; the commercialization of sheaths; and, in the early 1930s, the production of the latex condom.[3] Despite this, the use of non-technological methods persisted. Experts wondered why, 'in spite of such obvious disadvantages, is . . . [withdrawal]

---

[1] Lucy, msf/kf/bl/#10.

[2] Many of the themes explored in this chapter (albeit in a much-condensed form, using material from the Blackburn working-class sample) can be found in Fisher and Szreter, ' "They Prefer Withdrawal" '.

[3] See J. Peel, 'The Manufacture and Retailing of Contraceptives', esp. 119–20.

practised by millions of people'.[4] Surely, they argued, withdrawal was ineffective and unpleasant, abortion potentially lethal and morally abhorrent, and abstinence unsustainable?[5] They concluded that traditional methods continued to be used only because barriers still stood in the way of appliance methods: continued ignorance, financial prohibition, embarrassment, or moral disapproval.[6] Eustace Chesser, for instance, claimed that withdrawal was practised 'because the couple concerned know no other contraceptive technique'.[7] Clinic workers highlighted the 'vigorous local opposition' which prevented clinics being set up and discouraged potential patients from attending:[8] Lella Secor Florence remembered that clinics were set up in 'an atmosphere of controversy' and 'encountered much odium and obstruction'.[9]

To a certain degree such negative considerations did affect the extent to which appliance methods were used. Some did have moral objections to using any artificial method of family limitation. Some were too shy to attend a clinic or to buy a condom from the chemist. Some were unaware of appliance methods or how to get hold of them. Others found them too expensive. Many, however, had positive reasons for adopting abstinence, withdrawal, and even abortion.[10] Withdrawal in particular had real advantages in the context of marital relations in the inter-war period: it provided a simple, easily understood, convenient, male-dominated, 'natural' method of family planning which did not require overt, regular discussion between spouses. Even its unreliability was not seen as a disadvantage; many wished to reduce the probability that pregnancy would occur rather than eliminate the chance of conception altogether.

'WE DIDN'T KNOW ANYTHING ABOUT CONTRACEPTIVES THEN':[11] IGNORANCE AND METHOD CHOICES

In part, the lack of uptake of appliance methods of birth control can be ascribed to ignorance. Lewis-Faning's survey found that 27 per cent of those who did not use

[4] Chesser, *Love without Fear*, 153.

[5] The continued reliance on traditional or indigenous methods of contraception or abortion in many developing countries has similarly exasperated contemporary family-planning providers. See Newman (ed.), *Women's Medicine*.

[6] Historians have accepted and reiterated these conclusions: see e.g. McKibbin, *Classes and Cultures*, 305; W. Seccombe, *Weathering the Storm*, 187.   [7] Chesser, *Love without Fear*, 153.

[8] See e.g. the 'vigorous local opposition' which hampered the running of the clinic in Oxford (SPBCC, *Birth Control and Public Health*, 14), or the Abertillery clinic which was allegedly 'killed by gossip' (*Western Mail* (1937), cutting in A&M: SA/FPA/A13/46.1; Douglas, 'Women, God and Birth Control').

[9] Florence, *Progress Report on Birth Control*, 20–1. She also noted that the 'attempted obstruction' was to many clinics' advantage: it had 'scarcely any effect other than to advertise the clinics'.

[10] Geoffrey Gorer concluded in the 1970s that 'the prejudice against *coitus interruptus* does not seem to be rationally founded' after having discovered that 'this method was preferred by some of the respondents who [were] among the happiest of all the married people I was analysing': Gorer, *Sex and Marriage in England Today*, 136.   [11] Sally, msf/kf/bl/#31.

appliance methods of contraception pleaded a 'lack of knowledge'.[12] As explored in Chapter 1, a general sense of bewilderment about sex and contraceptive techniques abounded, and knowledge of various methods of birth control was frequently only obliquely understood. The least popular methods were the least well known and the most difficult to get hold of. Eva stated that, early in her marriage, in the early 1930s, 'we heard about the birth control issue but we didn't know the practicalities . . . I would have gone [to a clinic] otherwise'.[13] Not all chemists sold contraceptive appliances; Boots, for example, refused to sell condoms.[14] Of all appliance methods, condoms were by far the most popular: this was directly linked to their visibility and availability, since they were advertised in barbers' windows, newspapers, and magazines, and distributed by the army.

There is also evidence to suggest that exposure to information about newer forms of contraception sometimes contributed to the decision to use a traditional method. Paradoxically, information about new appliances sometimes reinforced the idea of family limitation in general without fostering the use of a different type of birth control, even if the literature itself explicitly condemned traditional choices.[15] A number of respondents claimed to have used coitus interruptus after having read birth control advice literature. Oxford couple Joe and Delia, for example, claimed to have used withdrawal as a result of reading the advice given in a Marie Stopes book in the early 1940s, despite the fact that Marie Stopes felt that 'in any normal marriage its use is to be condemned' as 'this method has without doubt done an incredible amount of harm' to the 'nervous systems of both man and woman'.[16] That Marie Stopes mentioned condoms was also remembered, but not that she found them 'inadvisable for regular use' and the cause of 'much harm':[17]

But I did buy this book, a lady doctor who wrote it. It was well known then and we read it, and it gave a good advice in it.

So what sort of advice does it give?

I can't remember now. I think it was mostly talking about using condoms, such as there was then, and the man wasn't allowed to let his sperm go into the woman. That was the main thing.[18]

Harriet, who married a steel worker in 1935, revealed the subtle effect books had on local communities: shared between friends, and read quickly, often in secret, the details of the message might be lost, and only the general gist absorbed. Harriet could only vaguely remember Marie Stopes. She was shown one of Stopes's books but did not have time to read it properly. Such knowledge was of no

[12] Lewis-Faning, *Report of an Inquiry into Family Limitation*, 183.   [13] Eva, bc1#1.

[14] S. Anderson, ' "The most important place in the history of British birth control" ', 25.

[15] Roy Porter and Lesley Hall also recognized that 'reading may confirm habits rather than change them': *The Facts of Life*, 6.   [16] Stopes, *Contraception*, 69.

[17] Ibid. 156, 158. For a summary of Stopes's attitude to a range of contraceptive technologies see Neushul, 'Marie C. Stopes and the Popularization of Birth Control Technology'.

[18] Joe and Delia, bc3ox#29.

use to her when she found her drunken and Catholic husband did not mind how many children she had and did not believe in using birth control. The only method she could remember Stopes mentioning was the Catholic-approved safe method. Despite Stopes's denigration of this strategy, in her reading of Marie Stopes Harriet only absorbed information about the method she already knew about courtesy of the Catholic Church:

Had you heard of a woman called Marie Stopes?
Well, there was a book about her, wasn't—? Well, I dunno . . . wasn't she on about birth control and all that? Yeah . . . . some women told me about it one day, and they showed me her book, you know that's how I knew about her.
And did you read the book?
Well, I read some—it . . . I didn't read it all, mind, much as I can remember of it, was 'ow to control, the b—you know . . . it told you what to do . . . certain days you'd—I, I, forget now. It was about, sex, you know, certain times of the month, where you had to be careful and all that, but that's all I can remember about it, 'cos I didn't read all the book.[19]

Information about new methods was therefore not necessarily perceived as a challenge to existing beliefs or understanding; indeed, there was a tendency to misinterpret the advice of clinics and of sex and birth control manuals such as those produced by Marie Stopes, in an attempt to accommodate such advice alongside existing views about contraception. Many used withdrawal because it was the method they had heard most about. It was familiar, socially acceptable, and easy to understand. For some, then, their choice of contraception simply reflected the decision to use a familiar method that required no extra research. Thirty-seven per cent of those surveyed by Lewis-Faning who did not use an appliance method claimed to have 'disliked the idea of experimenting'.[20] Lella Secor Florence noted that, for older women in particular, 'to embark on a birth control method which entails a complete change in habits of thought and practice embedded in a lifetime' was extremely difficult.[21]

The paucity of clear, good-quality, non-euphemistic, and trustworthy information about appliance methods of contraception may have played a role in restricting the uptake of new methods, but we need to seek additional factors to explain the continuing popularity of traditional forms of birth control. Several contemporary birth control advocates were surprised to find that, even after exposure to scientific alternatives, many patients preferred using withdrawal, and that even those who followed clinic advice nevertheless continued to 'rely mostly' on coitus interruptus.[22]

---

[19] Harriet, bc3sw#15.   [20] Lewis-Faning, *Report of an Inquiry into Family Limitation*, 182.
[21] Florence, *Progress Report on Birth Control*, 51.
[22] See Florence, *Birth Control on Trial*, e.g. 97, 143, 157; see also ead., *Progress Report on Birth Control*, 83.

'I CAME OUT WITH A LOT OF TEETH CLEANER':[23]
EXPENSE, EFFORT, AND EMBARRASSMENT

Difficulties in obtaining appliance methods also undoubtedly contributed to their unpopularity. Those promoting appliance methods of birth control frequently worried that their cost was off-putting. Withdrawal and abstinence were free, and although abortion could be expensive, it did not usually require a regular, predictable expenditure. Enid Charles estimated in 1932 that some reusable sheaths, which 'can be used with complete safety for two or three months', were cheaply available at between 9*d.* and 1*s.* 6*d.* Disposable versions and some 'expensive brands' were, however, 'very costly'.[24] Pessaries at 2*s.* per dozen were deemed out of reach for the 'very poor', among whom nightly intercourse was 'not uncommon'.[25] Most clinics charged a registration fee and often cost price for appliances, though payment could be waived, and most stressed that those who could not pay did not have to. The Llantrissant council discussed the possibility of reimbursing bus fares, and the clinic in Caerphilly in 1937 cancelled the registration fee, wiped out all back debts, and 'decided to give appliances free in cases where the patient was below a certain scale'.[26] The Society for the Provision of Birth Control Clinics charged 1*s.* for a consultation, claimed to request only a small sum for appliances, and allowed the poor to pay in instalments.[27] Yet in their various clinics, payment demands were reported to be inconsistent: 'for example, in Exeter you might pay six pence while in North Kensington you might pay two pounds'.[28] Many campaigners felt that free services should not be provided indiscriminately and that 'self-respecting people would prefer to pay something'.[29] Margaret Rae, nurse at Stopes's Aberdeen clinic, was convinced that those who were given complimentary appliances 'are the ones that . . . let us down' and who failed to return or renew the cap, whereas the 'poor mothers who . . . pay their share [are] reliable and appreciate their method'.[30] Marie Stopes

[23] Joe, bc3ox#29.

[24] Charles, *The Practice of Birth Control*, 166; Dr Killick Millard informed the medical committee of the National Birth-Rate Commission in 1927 that condoms cost 'ninepence or one shilling each': National Council of Public Morals, *Medical Aspects of Contraception*, 115.

[25] Charles, *The Practice of Birth Control*, 166. Rendall's pessaries were sold at 2*s.* 6*d.* per dozen in 1927: Medical Trading Company, *Supplement to Books on Birth Control*, 1927, BL Add. MSS 58640.

[26] A&M: SA/FPA/A11/9.   [27] SPBCC, *Birth Control and Public Health*, 8.

[28] Freda Parker, social worker at North Kensington Clinic in the 1930s, 'In the Club', A&M: GC/105/30. For a comparison of the charges made by a range of clinics in 1929, see BL Add. MSS 58600.

[29] Marie Stopes to Florence Gordon, 10 Jan. 1938, BL Add. MSS, 58625. Similar beliefs are common among modern-day population planners. In Haiti, clinic doctors 'insist that when clients are asked to pay for a method they consider it more valuable', although it is estimated that when all costs are taken into account the average cost to the patient of attending a clinic is $50. See Maternowska, 'A Clinic in Conflict', 112.

[30] Margaret Rae to Marie Stopes, 28 July 1941, BL Add. MSS 58613. See also Deborah Cohen, 'Private Lives in Public Spaces', 107–8, on the desire on the part of clinic staff to help the 'respectable working class' and not the 'undeserving poor'.

found it necessary to reprimand the nurse at the Cardiff clinic for allowing patients to leave and return when they had saved up enough money: 'This is not to happen again please . . . You must never allow anyone who comes to the clinic wanting to be fitted to go away because they cannot pay, unless you have absolute proof that they are trying to swindle you and are really well off.'[31] Yet Stopes's staff frequently wrote asking for clarification of this issue and sought guidance in distinguishing the truly deserving from freeloaders.[32] Often acutely aware of the financial problems of their clinics, many chose to err on the side of caution rather than generosity.

There is some indication that a perception of the expense of contraceptive appliances deterred some from trying condoms or pessaries, or attending clinics.[33] A factory worker told Mass-Observation that she went 'to a birth control clinic but I couldn't afford the material (10/-)'.[34] Lella Secor Florence thought women preferred male methods for financial reasons: using a female method (such as a cap) was a drain on their housekeeping money, whereas the cost of a male method would be borne by the husband's wallet.[35] Some respondents such as Sarah, who married an upholsterer in 1939, commented that the Rendall's pessaries she obtained 'were expensive, we being tight with money'.[36] Terence, a decorator from Blackburn, used withdrawal more than condoms since he found them 'very expensive': 'sometimes you couldn't afford them'.[37] Nancy's husband, a pipe fitter from Oxford, 'never used to like' condoms and commented on 'what a waste of money it was'.[38] Jake an engineer, was proud to obtain his condoms, 100 at a time, direct from the wholesalers in the 1940s: 'I saw it advertised in paper, you could get 'em wholesale price . . . I used to get a box-full . . . I could get about a hundred packets for a pound . . . and it were a lot cheaper.'[39] John also used withdrawal rather than paying for condoms. Like cigarettes, he could have afforded them but preferred to save his money:

. . . we wouldn't have the blinking money [for condoms] would we? I say I never smoked for the simple reason when I started work I couldn't afford them and they were only five for tuppence then like, couldn't afford them. Well, say I could afford them but I'd have to do without other things that I fancied, like.[40]

The effect of the cost of appliances on method choices should not be overstated, however. Lewis-Faning found only 1.4 per cent of the non-appliance

[31] Marie Stopes to Florence Gordon, 10 Jan. 1938, BL Add. MSS 58625.

[32] Marie Stopes responded: 'where you are satisfied that to pay they would have to curtail necessary food, give it free. Where, however, they are able or spending on going to the cinema, buying beer or artificial silk stockings, then make them pay.' Marie Stopes to Nurse Florence Gordon, 7 Nov. 1937, BL Add. MSS 58624.

[33] See J. Peel, 'The Manufacture and Retailing of Contraceptives', 116; Brookes, 'Women and Reproduction 1860–1939', 159.

[34] Mass-Observation, TC Family Planning 1944–49, Women at Osrams, TC3/1/G.

[35] Florence, *Progress Report on Birth Control*, 210–11.   [36] Sarah, msf/kf/bl/#30.

[37] Terence, msf/srss/bl/#15.   [38] Nancy, bc3ox#22.

[39] Jake and Doris, msf/srss/bl/#22.   [40] John, bc2#26.

method users referring to the cost of appliances.[41] Most comments about the expense of appliances were made in the abstract, and were rarely personalized accounts or detailed recollections of actual choices made. Rather, reference to expense proved an easy way to dismiss the possibility that one might have considered using them, or to justify the contraceptive choices made:

Had you heard of French letters?
Yes, but would never, I've never ever had anything to do with them. Yes I have heard of that, yes, but I've never had anything to do with them. In fact, to be honest, we never had any money for anything extra, it was only the bas—bare necessities.[42]

Like Rhonda, above, many reports of the expense of condoms took the form of clichéd references to the general poverty of working-class life, which, while not irrelevant, served a particular purpose during the interview. Referring to the cost of condoms was for Rhonda an effective way of avoiding any suggestion that she might have had anything to do with condoms. Deflecting the conversation into a generalized discussion of the experience of poverty was, for working-class respondents, an effective means of moving the interview away from embarrassing topics, rather than a convincing indication that condoms were rejected for financial reasons, as the following two examples indicate:

So did you know about French letters in those days?
Oh yeah, there was (laughs), but the money wasn't, well you could hardly afford things like that, anyway, I mean the money wasn't coming up to it. I used to sit and turn coats, and things like that for the little girl when she was small, you know, couldn't afford to go down the shops and buy all the time.[43]

No pill about in them days.

Was there anything else about?
Nothing, nothing, no. You didn't have the money to buy 'em if they did.[44]

More specific and compelling were concerns about the embarrassment involved in obtaining contraceptive appliances and complaints about the effort required to use them. Those promoting appliance methods frequently addressed such concerns and claimed they were easy to use. At the annual meting of the Society for Constructive Birth Control in 1928, the pro-race cap was defended: the claim 'that it is difficult to insert . . . and that there are an enormous number of failures . . . is not substantiated by the facts'.[45] In practice, however, training patients to use cervical caps, diaphragms, and sponges correctly proved a major difficulty.[46]

[41] Lewis-Faning, *Report of an Inquiry into Family Limitation*, 182.   [42] Rhonda, bc3ox#24.
[43] Beatrice, bc3sw#5.   [44] Margaret, bc3sw#13.
[45] Annual Meeting of the CBC held at the Essex Hall, Essex Street, Strand, 22 Nov. 1928, BL Add. MSS 58589; Norman Haire also reported that 'women find this quite easy. I have only found four women who could not, or would not, learn to use it': National Council of Public Morals, *Medical Aspects of Contraception*, 154.
[46] Clephane, *Towards Sex Freedom*, 209–10; Florence, *Birth Control on Trial*, 26; D. Cohen, 'Private Lives in Public Spaces', 105.

In Aberdeen the 'country women' required 'a good deal of teaching'.[47] Marie Stopes rather uncharitably noted that 'there is always a percentage of extremely stupid and unreliable women whom it is difficult to instruct', and a follow-up report on the Manchester Clinic commented that women whose houses were found to have 'several layers of dirty dishes' had failed to employ the method while at a 'spotless doorstep would be found a success'.[48] Similarly when an Aberdeen patient 'handed her cap back', unprepared to continue persevering, the exasperated nurse complained: 'That is the unemployed for you—they often don't appreciate all the kindness done of them.'[49] Enid Charles rather more sympathetically concluded that difficulties did not necessarily reveal the 'stupidity and fecklessness' of some patients, finding similar problems expressed by 'the more intelligent women'.[50] Sylvia Dawkins, a family-planning doctor interviewed by Television History Workshop, explained the complex examination procedures and difficulties experienced in determining which method was suitable and finding the right size:

If you gave a barrier method you had to instruct the people how to use it. You fitted them with, say a diaphragm, instructed them, asked them to go home and practise putting it in and out, come with it in, so that we could be sure they got it right, you see, and knew what they were doing. Then we gave them the cap, and we didn't on the first occasion because you couldn't fit them properly the first occasion, they were tense. When they'd come back with the cap in they were relaxed and you found the size wasn't anywhere near right.[51]

Stopes's preferred method of birth control—the small cervical cap—was the most complex available, required the most elaborate fitting procedure, and moreover was, by the clinics' own reckoning, unsuitable for many. A woman who attended the Aberdeen clinic in 1935 reported her difficulties:

I have done my best to try it out but it seems hopeless to me the sponge seems too big. I get it in as far as possible but there is always one side seems to come out . . . it seems to press against where I was torn and it pains me.[52]

Those who had been physically affected by frequent pregnancy or poor gynaecological care often could not use the cap. Nurse Williams wrote to Marie Stopes from Swansea in May 1929 that 'the uterine conditions of the mothers on the

---

[47] Margaret Rae to Marie Stopes, n.d. [1935], BL Add. MSS 58603.

[48] Marie Stopes to Victor Roberts, 12 Dec. 1924, A&M: PP/MCS/C.15; Charles, *The Practice of Birth Control*, 158.

[49] Margaret Rae to Marie Stopes, 28 Mar. 1939, BL Add. MSS 56811. On the tendency of many in recent family-planning services to alienate clients by imposing their own ethos on those attending clinics and demanding that users conform to their own notions of responsibility, see Joffe, *The Regulation of Sexuality*.

[50] Charles, *The Practice of Birth Control*, 15.

[51] *In the Club? Birth Control This Century*, programme on Channel 4 (Television History Workshop), 1988. See also the descriptions of procedure in clinic reports e.g. SPBCC, *Birth Control and Public Health*, 21. On the need to rehearse the use of caps before using them as a contraceptive, see Florence, *Progress Report on Birth Control*, 90–1.

[52] Nurse Rae to Marie Stopes, May 1935, BL Add. MSS 58603 (the letter is not punctuated; punctuation has been added for clarification).

whole is not good. The sponge and the sheath being practically the only suitable methods'.[53] Many others were nonetheless given caps. Gertrude, for example, who married an electrician in 1925 and attended a birth control clinic in Aberdare, was given a cervical cap, which appears to have been unsuitable despite the clinic's determination to fit it:

. . . couldn't wear what the woman did, I couldn't hold it. I went—I don't know how many times they tried to fit me, and you had to go on the table and be examined and all that, see, before they would. But I couldn't, I wasn't, I should have been stitched and I wasn't, so I couldn't hold it.[54]

Similarly, one woman who attended the caravan clinic when it was stationed in south Wales 'was too tender to use a sponge' as she had been 'badly lacerated after severe labour', and another was 'very stout and found it awkward to place' her appliance.[55] In Aberdeen, the nurse had difficulty teaching a blind woman: 'she does not see how to put the method in'.[56] Sometimes those who had problems inserting caps and sponges were given other methods, such as the sheath.[57] However, patients were expected to keep trying.[58] Many were sent away, sometimes with written instructions, and told to practise before coming back for further teaching. It is hardly surprising that some lost patience. Dorothy was given a cap at a clinic in Oxford during the war after her doctor insisted it was not safe for her to risk another pregnancy. She 'found it awkward to fix' and went 'back to the clinic' a few times until she 'got fed up trying to fix it properly'. When the clinic proved unsympathetic, Dorothy abandoned the method: 'I said, "I'm sorry, I can't get on with that." "Well", she said, "it's up to you if you have kids." '[59] By 1956 Margery Spring-Rice wondered whether 'complacent' distribution of the cap 'to all and sundry' ought to be revised. She concluded that only a small proportion of patients used it efficiently, whereas for those of 'sub-normal intelligence' or 'living under impossible conditions it is useless to prescribe the cap'.[60]

Despite greater experimentation with female methods of contraception such as the cap amongst middle-class women, similar dislikes were expressed. Enid Charles's survey of contraceptive practice among primarily middle-class women found that the 'most frequent source of dissatisfaction' with the cap 'is fitting and adjusting'.[61] Moreover, female caps usually had to be used in conjunction with a

---

[53] Nurse Williams to Marie Stopes, 6 May 1929, BL Add. MSS 58621; see also Cook, *The Long Sexual Revolution*, 134.   [54] Gertrude, bc3sw#27.

[55] Nurse Charlotte Fowles to Marie Stopes, 22 Mar. 1930, Jan. 1930, BL Add. MSS 58622.

[56] Margaret Rae to Marie Stopes, 24 Feb. 1935, BL Add. MSS 58603.

[57] On the rare circumstances in which the sheath was advised in Stopes's clinics, see 'Spacing for Health: The Use of Condoms', *Birth Control News*, 17/3 (Feb. 1939), 35.

[58] See Maternowska, 'A Clinic in Conflict', on the tendency of family planning providers to insist that clients have the method clinics deem to be the most suitable, whatever the views or objections expressed by the user.   [59] Dorothy, bc3ox#30.

[60] Margery Spring Rice to Dr. Edwards, 2 Feb. 1956, A&M: SA/FPA/NK/154.

[61] Charles, *The Practice of Birth Control*, 53.

spermicide: either contraceptive jelly had to be smeared around the cap before insertion or a spermicidal pessary was inserted after the cap. Some clinics and health professionals additionally recommended douching with a solution of soapy or vinegary water after sex.[62]

It also proved difficult to persuade many women that they needed continuing medical supervision of their contraceptive practices. Patients were usually required to return for regular check-ups. The Society for the Provision of Birth Control Clinics recommended a 'medical examination and renewal of pessary . . . every six months at least'.[63] In the North Kensington clinic it was found that 'hundreds of them were never heard from after their first or second visits'.[64] While many may have continued using the methods provided, others, such as Margaret, a hotel manager, found the requirement to keep attending the clinic a disincentive to continued use:

Oh yes . . . she was a private one . . . and I was fitted with a cap.

And what was that like?

Well, it was a bit uncomfortable, you know, I'd to keep going back and having it checked.[65]

One woman found it impossible to return to North Kensington Women's Welfare Clinic as she was working, while many others 'found it difficult with . . . small children'.[66] Another wrote asking for appliances to be sent to her instead of having to revisit since, living in Pinner, she found it 'so difficult to get to town between feeds'. She asked that if this was not possible, male methods be sent instead.[67] In Birmingham 'no new cap is supplied unless the patient is re-examined by the doctor', but in practice caps might be sent through the post, particularly to those who lived far away from the clinic, with the instruction that a local doctor should be consulted to 'check the size and fit'.[68] Margaret Rae found that mothers unable to get to clinics 'send little girls or boys 10 to 12 yrs with a note'. She regarded such behaviour 'unsympathetically' as a sign that the mothers were 'lazy' and refused to 'supply children'.[69] Even conscientious and content users found it difficult to keep attending. At first, Eva, who started going to Marie Stopes's clinic in Cardiff soon after it opened in 1937, would revisit regularly: 'every now and again I would say, "Well I've had this *x* amount of time: do you think it's time I had a new one?"' However, she did not maintain this level of devotion to the regime and eventually stopped using the method in favour of another: 'after a while we stopped going [to the clinic] so often. I stopped using it after the war.'[70] In 1950 the Family

---

[62] Himes, *Practical Birth-Control Methods*, 71–6.

[63] SPBCC, *Birth Control and Public Health*, 21.

[64] Norman and Vera Himes, *Birth Control for the British Working-Classes*, 610.

[65] Margaret, bc3ox#18.

[66] SA/FPA/NK/93. See also the difficulties women had in finding time or opportunity to revisit clinics: Florence, *Progress Report on Birth Control*, 112–13, 207–8.

[67] Mass-Observation, TC Family Planning 1944–49, Letters to Birth Control Clinic (Marie Stopes), 1944, TC3/2/D.   [68] Florence, *Progress Report on Birth Control*, 94.

[69] Margaret Rae to Marie Stopes, 6 Mar. 1942, BL Add. MSS 58614.   [70] Eva, bc1#1.

Planning Association sought to investigate the extent to which patients continued to use clinics over a period of years. They found that, in twenty-three clinics, 47 per cent of those who attended in 1947 returned in 1948, and 34 per cent in 1949. In Darlington, however, only 16 per cent returned in 1949. By 1951, in the fifteen clinics that returned figures, only 19 per cent of those first seen in 1947 were still attending.[71]

There were also objections to the effort required in using and caring for contraceptive appliances. Hugh, a miner with four children, found French letters involved 'too much potch-billy . . . you gotta wash 'em, and powder 'em after, like, innit?'[72] Many men chose withdrawal, according to London gynaecologist R. A. Gibbons, because they found it 'easier . . . to prevent conception' than using 'any other' method.[73]

The embarrassment caused by trying to get hold of contraceptive appliances also worried those promoting such methods. Indeed users, from all classes, frequently reported that this made them reluctant to use technological methods of contraception. Leslie, a miner from Pontypridd, never used condoms because:

We didn't like to go into the chemist shop, 'cos there was nothing in the toilets at the time to put the money in the machines, there was nothing in toilets then. You had to go ask some—, and always three parts of time there was all women behind the counter, and [I] was too shy to ask for them.[74]

Some respondents avoided such problems by obtaining condoms or pessaries by mail order. Others went to suppliers in neighbouring towns, while others asked braver friends to obtain them on their behalf. Fred 'would always go somewhere where they didn't know me' and Betty's husband Harry got condoms for his neighbour when he made a trip away from home to Newport: 'Harry went into a chemist down there, where nobody knew him . . . he goes into this chemist and he got some for him—give it [to] him.'[75]

Many women were reluctant to attend birth control clinics for this reason, as Ida, who attended the Rhondda Birth Control Clinic in the early 1930s, admitted: 'When you were outside you did feel a bit self-conscious—going in without a baby—it was obvious what you were there for.'[76] Gertrude made a quick exit when she glimpsed an acquaintance already inside the Aberdare clinic.[77]

[71] North Kensington Women's Welfare. Perseverance Ratio Sub-Committee, 1952, A&M: SA/FPA/NK/197. Some family-planning programmes in developing countries have realized the effort and commitment required to continue using prescribed methods of contraception: 'Consider the amount of sustained practice required for the typical pill adopter in a less developed country. If the woman is about thirty years of age when she adopts, she is expected to take 3,000 pills during the next fifteen years, attend the clinic 185 times, and pay the equivalent of four months' family income. No wonder there is a high degree of discontinuance.' E. Rogers, *Communication Strategies*, 38.

[72] Hugh, bc3sw#23.

[73] National Council of Public Morals, *Medical Aspects of Contraception*, 166.

[74] Leslie, bc3sw#1.   [75] Fred, bc2#14; Betty, bc3sw#19.

[76] Ida, bc1/pilot/#1. This pilot interview was not included in the sample.

[77] Gertrude, bc3sw#27.

Birth control clinics adopted various strategies to attract those too shy to be seen seeking birth control assistance. Marie Stopes's clinic in Cardiff had no markings and was situated in a residential street and had net curtains in the window.[78] It was noticed that women were much less embarrassed attending gynaecological clinics than sessions where birth control advice alone was provided. The clinic in Penarth became known as the Mothers' Consultant Clinic and other clinics held sessions in the premises of maternity and child welfare centres. Nurse Williams reported having been 'besieged . . . by husbands' wanting information for their wives who 'didn't want to be seen coming to the caravan', especially during daylight hours. She inflexibly asserted that she could only help wives, and during clinic hours.[79] Freda Parker, a social worker at the North Kensington clinic in the 1930s, also identified embarrassment as a major hurdle to the use of female appliances: the women 'had no words' for the sexual areas of their body and were reluctant because, by coming to a clinic, 'you were admitting that you were having inter-course'. She recalled additional reasons for their discomfort: 'very poor women still have their dignity . . . and a lot of them hadn't got nice underclothes and were afraid to come with ragged knickers and perhaps a dirty petticoat'.[80] One family-planning doctor was horrified by the lack of sensitivity shown to the women wait-ing to be examined: 'a nurse would come streaking along, saying, you know, "Knickers off girls, stockings down", and I found it really quite upsetting'.[81]

'Traditional' methods were preferred, particularly among the working classes, because they were not a cause of potential social shame. Withdrawal had the dis-tinct advantage of requiring no direct interaction with any supplier. Eleanor, a Lancashire weaver, and her mechanic husband, 'did that what they—you know, what everybody were doing'. They chose withdrawal after experimenting with a condom which 'were no good', in part because her husband found them 'such a struggle to put on', and in part because he refused to go and get them: 'He would-n't go in . . . men don't. Eh! They go into—chemist now and instead of buying condoms they'll buy a toothbrush or something.'[82] As a chemist also remembered: 'When a solitary man came in, asked loudly for a tube of toothpaste, and then lin-gered anxiously while the girl assistants discreetly disappeared, you knew what he really wanted.'[83] A further advantage of withdrawal was its simplicity. It required no prior research, preparation, cost, or effort. As Lella Secor Florence found, hus-bands 'do not seem to mind withdrawal—they prefer this method, with its free-dom from preparation'.[84] Twelve per cent of non-appliance users interviewed by Lewis-Faning 'could not be bothered' to try appliances, and Norman and Vera

[78] 'Behind the Scenes. The Year's Work: An Address to Members at the Annual Meeting by Dr. Marie Stopes', *Birth Control News*, 16/5 (Dec. 1937), 54.
[79] Nurse Williams to Marie Stopes, 6 May 1929, BL Add. MSS 58621.
[80] 'In the Club', A&M: GC/105/30.   [81] Faith Spicer, 'In the Club', A&M: GC/105/17.
[82] Eleanor, msf/kf/bl/#11.
[83] S. Anderson, ' "The most important place in the history of British birth control" ', 24–5.
[84] Florence, *Birth Control on Trial*, 102.

Himes also found that patients at a birth control clinic 'hated to "mess around" or they "couldn't be bothered" '.[85] Procuring an abortion also appears to have been much less embarrassing. Unlike contraception, which was associated directly with the sexual act, abortion was connected primarily with the business of having children. Nurse Rae could not understand the reluctance of women to attend a clinic, given their willingness to obtain abortifacients:

It makes me wild . . . mothers with pram full of children *always* complaining—yet they say—Oh I don't want to come. Oh I wouldn't like to use this or that, Oh I couldn't touch myself, *No*—but they will touch themselves plenty if to procure aborsion [*sic*] and spend money and take all sorts of things.[86]

Thus many preferred an uncomplicated method of birth control that was easy to use, did not require regular attendance at a clinic or visits to the chemist, and did not need elaborate after-care and post-coital tidying up.

'IT IS DIFFICULT TO SEE WHERE MORALITY ENTERS INTO THE MATTER AT ALL':[87] RELIGION, ETHICS, AND THE CHOICE OF BIRTH CONTROL

The slow uptake of appliance methods of birth control and the use of traditional methods (especially abstinence) was also frequently attributed to the persistence of moral and religious objections to the principle of conception control.[88] Indeed, some of those who used appliance methods presented themselves as self-consciously challenging Christian ideals in their approach to fertility limitation. Eva's testimony revealed her own personal pride at having been one of the first to attend a birth control clinic in opposition to prevailing moral and religious attitudes: 'Well, as you can imagine, when I was young family planning was just not thought of. It was almost indecent to talk about it.' She saw herself following a new path in opposition to a culture where 'for generation after generation women accepted that they were there to bear children. And if they had more children than they wanted, then it was God's will. That type of thing you see. Well, you were flying in the face of God when you decided you weren't going to have children.'[89]

However, most respondents made no explicit connection between their birth control practices and their religious beliefs, in part because messages emanating from churches during the first half of the twentieth century were mixed and

---

[85] Lewis-Faning, *Report of an Inquiry into Family Limitation*, 182; Norman and Vera Himes, *Birth Control for the British Working-Classes*, 611.

[86] Margaret Rae to Marie Stopes, 10 Oct. 1939, BL Add. MSS 58612 (the letter is not punctuated; punctuation has been added for clarification).   [87] Eyles, *Commonsense about Sex*, 64.

[88] See Szreter, *Fertility, Class and Gender*, 410–11; Seccombe, *Weathering the Storm*, 167; Mass-Observation, *Britain and her Birth Rate*, 184–6; Stanley, *Sex Surveyed*, 73, 102–3.

[89] Eva, bcl#1.

indirect. At a grassroots level few churchmen chose openly to discuss the matter with their flock. Only Catholics were unanimously and vociferously opposed. However, this is not to argue that moral beliefs, some of which were circulated in religious settings, did not have a strong impact on birth control practices and the choice of method. Rather than dissuading people from limiting their families, however, religious discourses framed the topic as a personal matter, unsuitable for open discussion. Christian moral beliefs emphasized the private nature of sexual relations, and deemed all public articulation of sexual issues indecent. In this context, many couples did not see the restriction of pregnancy as prohibited or morally dubious, but valued methods which did not infringe the privacy of the relationship between husband and wife.

Many interviewees, in all regions, saw no connection between their contraceptive activities and their religious beliefs. This was most striking in the case of abortion, where some appeared completely unaware of moral objections to the practice. Except in the case of Catholic respondents, it was striking how little religion was mentioned in the context of the discussion of personal birth control use. Eliot Slater and Moya Woodside also found that religious beliefs 'had remarkably little influence on the men and women of our sample' with regard to family size and contraception, as did Mass-Observation's report on 'population problems'.[90] Only 8 per cent of the interviewees who reported to Lewis-Faning that they did not use any form of birth control had religious objections to the practice, a figure which was consistent throughout all cohorts by marriage date.[91] Catholics were the exception, though some were confused as to whether or not withdrawal was sanctioned, and some defiantly used artificial methods. Felicity's husband 'wouldn't use the artificial means . . . he was very devout in his religion'.[92] Daphne used the 'rhythm system' because 'the church approved of that scheme to a certain extent'.[93] Walter 'broke all faith' in 'deciding to use condoms'.[94]

Churches were divided on the issue of birth control during the first half of the twentieth century.[95] The evidence they gave to the National Birth-Rate Commission's investigation of the declining birth rate in 1916 was mixed, with the majority of Anglican clergy 'almost unanimously' opposed to the use 'of mechanical and chemical devices' while many 'conscientious and high-minded laymen . . . openly justify the use of preventives'. Catholic and Jewish representatives were against the use of birth control, while the Free Churches delegation,

---

[90] Slater and Woodside, *Patterns of Marriage*, 188–9; Mass-Observation, FR 2111 'Population Problems', June 1944, 50.

[91] Lewis-Faning, *Report of an Inquiry into Family Limitation*, 174, 183.

[92] Felicity, msf/kf/bl#37.   [93] Daphne, msf/jm/bl/#38.

[94] Walter, bc3sw#9.

[95] See Soloway, *Birth Control and the Population Question*, 233–55; McKibbin, *Classes and Cultures*, 308–11. In the nineteenth century there were no reported attacks on the Malthusian League by church bodies or by Victorian clergymen: D'Arcy, 'The Malthusian League', 435.

caught between the inclination to 'condemn the use of all mechanical or chemical means of prevention' and respect for the 'moral independence' of Nonconformists, maintained silence on the matter.[96] The Lambeth Conference of 1930 cautiously sanctioned the use of birth control within marriage, but there remained opposition behind the scenes. Nor was the Catholic Church united in its condemnation of birth control. Despite Pius XI's issuing *Casti Connubi* in 1930, prohibiting married couples from engaging in any act which would hinder the 'natural power of procreating life', it was only in 1968 that Pope Paul VI's unexpected encyclical *Humanae Vitae* ended decades of confusion on the matter by outlawing all forms of 'artificial' contraception, including the Pill (which had initially been developed with Catholic objections to other methods in mind).[97]

It is likely that these divided views were reflected in local communities. Some clergy from all denominations used the pulpit to rail against 'immoral' practices (as the stereotype of the Nonconformist minister in isolated chapel communities would have it); others simply ignored the issue, while some, albeit euphemistically or obliquely, advocated sensible use of birth control.[98] Indeed, when Angela and Hugh got married, in 1947, they went to see the Methodist minister for a 'chat': 'He made a remark: "We've had our children when we wanted them". That's indicating birth control. So Gail came along more or less when we wanted her.'[99] Similarly, in the 1920s, Ernest experienced his church's growing interest in sexual matters:[100]

See, our vicar was that type of man, and in-inculcated the basics of discipline . . . he educated us in everything appertaining to sex, even talking about the diseases involved, that's what he was warning us about, which we would never have learnt had he not taught us, so he prepared us for life in that respect, and of course, as I said, we had Marie Stopes's book after we were married, which again educated us in the way of life, you see.[101]

Inside most churches, however, birth control was rarely mentioned. Sid, a Catholic respondent, used the language of Christian morality in response to all questions about family size and family limitation. While not specifically linking contraceptive practices to religion he betrayed a general belief that fertility should not be interfered with. Rather, he wanted 'nature' to dictate the shape of his life, to

---

[96] National Birth-Rate Commission, *The Declining Birth-Rate*, 66–7.

[97] See e.g. Noonan, *Contraception*, 387–475.

[98] For an excellent study of the various responses to the issue of birth control adopted by members of the Catholic clergy in Quebec, see Gervais and Gauvreau, 'Women, Priests, and Physicians'; Margaret Douglas connects the closure of a birth-control clinic in Abertillery in 1926 with Nonconformist opposition, and those involved in the birth-control clinic campaign in Wales frequently argued that Nonconformist influence was a factor behind disappointing attendance figures, 'Women, God and Birth Control', 110–122. Rosser and Harris found, however, that active Welsh Nonconformists tended to have the smallest families: see *The Family and Social Change*, 180.

[99] Angela and Hugh, msf/kf/ht/#18, married 1947, two children.

[100] A number of sex and marriage manuals were written from a specifically Christian perspective by members of the clergy. See e.g. H. Gray, *Sex Teaching*; Weatherhead, *The Mastery of Sex*. See also L. Hall, *Sex, Gender and Social Change*, 121–2.   [101] Ernest, bc3sw#2.

avoid 'messing about', and to accept what God ordained:

So what could you do—to not have too big a family?
Never done nothing!
Nothing at all?
No, just nature. Yeah. God decided that two was enough for us, and that was it. We had 'em . . . I got no words to express it. I mean, peoples say they're don't gonna have a large family . . . What God sends you'll have, and that's it! . . .
So tell me what you used to think about birth control? (repeats)
Never entered me head, love . . . As I told you, what nature send—that was it. If my wife had had another child, we should've had a child and that would have been it! I don't believe in all this bloody messing about, and mucking about . . . .Well, we wasn't sent on the world for that. We were sent here on the world—born to have a family and bring 'em up and look after 'em, and see that they're all happy . . .
When you were in church, would people say that things like birth control were wrong?
Well, you never heard anybody talk about that sort of stuff them days. No, by golly, no . . . you got your bible and your prayer book, and we were more interested in the sermon than what was chattering about one another. Yeah.[102]

When Sid was specifically asked about the extent to which the Church had warned against the use of birth control, it did not occur to him that contraception might have been mentioned in Church at all, unless it was the personal chatter of a fellow member of the congregation. Thus, despite the fact that it was his religious outlook which primarily framed his determination to let his family grow naturally, such beliefs were not consciously linked to specific Church teaching. That the Church did not mention the issue was also asserted by Vera, an Irish Catholic who married a non-Catholic dental mechanic in Hertfordshire, and who used the rhythm method and condoms early in her marriage. She explained that any mention of the issue was prohibited: 'they don't talk about it in church . . . [yet] everybody that goes to church knows . . . you're not supposed to use contraceptives'.[103]

The very fact that the Church was silent on sexual or contraceptive issues imparted a specific message: all information or articulation of such topics was disreputable and morally tainted. As Ross McKibbin argues: 'The Anglican and Catholic Churches not so much dissuaded people from practising contraception as surrounded its use with guilt and tension.'[104] Sally did not know what the Church taught about birth control or abortion, giving such talk 'a wide berth . . . because we felt it was right that we should keep ourselves to ourselves, and we did'.[105] The central moral message here, reflected by a very large number of respondents, was that one's sexual life was secret, and should be conducted in

---

[102] Sid, bc3ox#34.   [103] Vera, msf/kf/ht/#34.
[104] McKibbin, *Classes and Cultures*, 311.   [105] Sally, msf/kf/bl/#31.

private. Most felt that any steps taken to avoid pregnancy should be kept between partners and not open to public discussion. This was highlighted by the indignation and shock expressed by Felicity when Jesuit priests sought to instruct her in contraceptive issues as part of her pre-marital conversion course in the early 1950s. Rather than appreciating spiritual advice in such matters, she was offended that the Church would dare to pry into her private life or insult her by explicit discussion of matters which should have remained personal:

The flipping Jesuits told me about this. Just imagine . . . in fact it got on my nerves so much I said, er, to Julian, 'I'm not going to change' . . .

They told you about the way they thought we should live. And the things we hadn't to do. It was all this not eating meat in those days at certain days, you know, well, it's not like that now. And, er, contraception was a big thing . . . I mean, honestly the way they talked, they always used to tell you to withdraw and things like that

. . .

I mean we weren't married and—talking about withdrawal and I didn't know what it were all about properly. Huh . . . .he said 'We don't believe in contraception except this counting the days . . . between your periods'. That was it . . . . Oh yes, that priest was very, very explicit. I don't know how he knew all that but he did . . .'e told us what to expect. Which I didn't like very much . . . I thought it was too intimate.[106]

Such comments reveal the subtle influence of 'Christian' ethical beliefs on the practice of birth control. Some respondents, albeit in coded and imprecise terms, expressed a link between family limitation and a desire not to tamper with nature or God's will. In addition, a minority of respondents saw the preservation of the secrecy of conjugal relations as a moral imperative. Such beliefs fostered the use of withdrawal and abstinence and the rejection of appliance methods. Traditional methods were morally more acceptable. They did not infringe the privacy of sexual activity and could be construed as 'natural', whereas appliance methods raised thorny questions about the extent to which family limitation interfered with God's plan, fate, or the natural order of the world and might be associated with illicit or immoral behaviour such as pre-marital sexual activity or promiscuity. A missionary's wife told Enid Charles that she had chosen abstinence because it was 'nature's own method'.[107]

Most believed that all sexual matters should be private, hence all discourses which broke public silence were disreputable. In working-class communities especially, to be 'decent', one was expected to refrain from discussing contraception, to avoid sexual conversations, and to maintain a respectable level of ignorance. Thus Bertha would not have anything to do with French letters, describing them as a 'terrible thing' and herself as 'a bit of a prude'. Her main objection to condoms was the way in which people had crudely talked about them in the Lancashire factory

---

[106] Felicity, msf/jm/bl/#37.   [107] Charles, *The Practice of Birth Control*, 56.

in which she had worked. Thereafter, she associated them with indecent behaviour. She consequently refused to use them in her marriage:

'Mongst all those girls, 'cos some of them used to—some of them used to be really crude, you know, I used to think, oo how dreadful, used to make me shudder

. . .

Well I didn't want them! I mean I didn't want—no—that sort of thing (pause).[108]

Sally was not at all curious to see the French letter that had been abandoned outside the shop in Blackburn where she worked:

. . . 'Have you ever seen a French letter?' I said 'No.' She says 'D'you want to?' I said 'No.' She said 'Well, do come and have a look.' I said 'No.' I said 'you won't get me near enough, I don't want . . . dirty things' . . . It was—somebody had been in the back during the night and left it there. But I couldn't tell you what it were like . . . .I thought 'ignorance is bliss'. It was. I didn't want to know these dirty sex habits.[109]

For some, then, any information at all about birth control methods was morally tainted: 'Anybody who discussed it was accused of being dirty and filthy and, you know, crazed, that sort of thing, you know.'[110] For some, simply obtaining a contraceptive appliance was too public, and a betrayal of the privacy of marital sexual relations. Lorna and her husband were too embarrassed to get a condom because 'we never discussed, what went on in your bedroom was in your bedroom'. Nor could she ask other mothers' advice: 'Not on that subject, no, no, no as I say 'cos was, it was private, private to me and their life was private to them.'[111] Moreover, many of the contexts in which birth control information was obtained were directly linked to 'seedy' worlds of illicit sexual behaviour. Many men came into contact with condoms when they were provided by the military for use with prostitutes, and some associated advice literature, such as Marie Stopes's books, with pornographic works, and her clinics with back-street abortionists:

There was one or two books went the rounds of the fellas. What we used to call 'dirty books' but um . . . Marie, Marie . . . the sort of things you you didn't let anybody see when you were reading them.[112]

The association of birth control appliances with illicit sexual behaviour is illustrated by Thomas who used condoms only when stationed in London during the war, when he was afraid of venereal disease, and not during his married life:

Five to twelve, like, I met her—park closed at midnight—I embraced her twice in five minutes, once without an overcoat and once with a bloody overcoat.

What does that mean?

A preventative on, right? I never used to bother with them, but up there you had to, like . . . you would hear talk of all this disease man . . . I said 'You can't leave nothing around'.[113]

---

[108] Bertha, bc3ox#41.   [109] Sally, msf/kf/bl/#31.   [110] Norman, msf/kf/ht/#17.
[111] Lorna, msf/kf/bl/#25.   [112] Sam, msf/srss/ht#28.   [113] Thomas, bc2#18.

The incorporation of appliance methods into the 'respectable' practice of family limitation within marriage could be seen as difficult or impossible. One man wrote to Marie Stopes complaining that the sheath 'renders the "sex act" sordid and destroys the aesthetic side entirely'.[114] Another insisted that he was not 'a man of Immoral Habits' but had been advised 'to use . . . French letters'. He sought advice because his 'wife said they were repulsive and not natural'.[115] Similarly Peter could not 'insult' his wife by using condoms, which he associated with wartime prostitution:

When we set sail for France, they called our platoon, Ten platoon, up on top deck, and an officer, he's a bit of a package in his hand and he's going round, coming down t'front line, he's giving everybody six French letters and he comes t'middle line and I'm set next t'this lad and he's laughing, he says, 'Jenkins, what the hell are yer laughing at?' He says, 'I thought you said we were goin' fighting them'!

And did you never use French letters?

No, no, I think it's an insult to a woman . . . I've always thought that. They used to give 'em us in t'army, well, I never used them . . . I think it's degrading to a woman . . . It's degrading to a woman if you're living with 'em, er, I wouldn't dream of using 'em, no.[116]

Gladys saw Marie Stopes's failure to respect the public silence on sexual matters as the cause of her unpopularity. She chose withdrawal because it was a private method which did not require any 'dirty speak':

We don't speak dirty, you know, not us old ones. No, 'twas, it was a matter of self-control for a man, wasn't it? (pause)

Had you ever heard of a woman called Marie Stopes?

Oh I heard about her, she was this c—birth control woman, wasn't she? She was very unpopular. Ah, I remember her, but er it was terrible thing what she was doing then. We were narrow-minded, you didn't discuss sex with anybody, you didn't even talk about periods, nothing like that, you never talked about it . . . People didn't believe in it then, no they believed in natural families. She was very unpopular.[117]

In choosing methods, individuals had to negotiate various moral associations. For some, condoms, pessaries, and female caps suggested either that one had come into contact with disreputable sources of information or even that one had engaged in seedy sexual encounters. Withdrawal was the method least associated with illicit sexual behaviour. Some descriptions of contraceptive methods drew out the contrasting moral meanings of different practices. Some of the terms frequently used to describe condoms—preventatives, sheaths, or protection—suggested that the type of sex one had when using them was dangerous. Pregnancy was one such hazard but other risks, such as disease, dirt, and immorality, were also implied. Common terms for withdrawal (and abstinence)—'being careful', 'using common sense', 'being restrained'—focused less on the dangers of sexual

---

[114] Quoted in L. Hall, 'Marie Stopes and her Correspondents', 31–2.
[115] Stopes, *Mother England*, 58.   [116] Peter, msf/kf/bl/#26.   [117] Gladys, bc3sw#28.

intercourse and more on the moral qualities of the user. The withdrawer was considerate, decent, moral, and controlled. In this sense, the man who used the condom could be perceived as seeking self-interestedly to protect himself, while the withdrawer was engaging in an act of selfless courtesy.

In summary, during the first half of the twentieth century the message emanating from the various churches on the question of contraception was far from clear. Only the Catholic Church specifically rejected contraception, and even here many Church members were confused as to whether withdrawal as well as the rhythm method was sanctioned or not. The recommendation to exercise self-control was ambiguously interpreted, and might be thought to indicate either abstinence, rhythm, or withdrawal. Many in the churches accepted that birth control was likely to be adopted by most couples, felt it ought to be permitted within marriage, and even encouraged its use. However, birth control did touch on a number of moral questions such as the relationship between reproduction and nature or God's will, the importance of the privacy of sexual relations within marriage, and aspects of sexual behaviour considered to be immoral or outside the sanction of the Church such as extra-marital relations, pre-marital relations, and prostitution.

The majority of respondents outlined their contraceptive behaviour without making reference to either ethical or religious issues. While moral tenets were important to a considerable number of respondents, they tended to be extremely general and non-specific. They guided, rather than determined, contraceptive behaviour. However, the idea that one needed to keep one's sexual relationships private in order to be 'moral' had a strong influence on some people's birth control choices. These respondents would avoid anything which made their sex lives a public matter: they thus refrained from seeking spiritual advice about methods or investigating the Church's attitude towards birth control. Instead, they sought out methods which did not challenge the private nature of the sexual act, did not require open discussion of sexual issues, and did not necessitate any revelation of one's intention to limit one's family size. Thus methods such as withdrawal and abstinence were preferred, as privacy was maintained and the 'sanctity' of the relationship upheld.

'In the early stages it was a game':[118] Moral Debates and the Practice of Abortion

Even a traditional method such as abortion did not raise ethical concerns to the extent to which new appliance methods did. Abortion has often been assumed to break clear ethical codes and has been thought to represent an unpalatable and dangerous family-planning option, both by historical actors and modern commentators. That it was resorted to by many women is thus seen as testament to

---

[118] 'In the Club', A&M: GC/105/22.

their desperation and to the lack of alternative reproductive choices.[119] In fact, abortion was often used despite knowledge of the dangers it posed and of possible alternative methods. Such women were not always helpless or desperate; as Leslie Regan argues, 'the widespread acceptance of abortion, expressed in word and deed during the era of its illegality, suggests the persistence of a popular ethic that differed from that of the law and the official views of medicine and religion'.[120] Abortion was not generally placed in an entirely different moral category from contraception. Many were ignorant of, or at least indifferent to, the arguments which stressed the rights of the unborn foetus and the sanctity of embryonic life.[121]

Many interviewees, from middle-class as well as working-class communities, as the two examples below illustrate, were not aware of the existence of arguments condemning abortion on the grounds that a foetus has a right to life, and most did not feel the need to defend their or anyone else's actions against such 'moral' objections:

Do you know the funny thing is that the emotion of it didn't—wasn't ever mentioned. What a dreadful thing you'd done or don't you feel you've killed a baby—that never came in, no. Nobody ever thought of that and it was never mentioned or discussed.

Did you think of that?

I didn't no, I, I must admit I don't think I thought of it . . . more from the girl's point of view you know, she's got herself out of a mess sort of thing. Terrible but—but this isn't how, how, how we thought in those days.[122]

One thing that strikes me is that nowadays when people talk about abortion, some people say that it's very, very wrong to do that, that it's like murder.

Oh, I'd, no, never believed in that.

When you were considering taking those pills?

Oh no! I mean, I did—I didn't want it, that was it. Full stop.[123]

Very few oral history respondents (around five per cent) unequivocally suggested that they felt that abortion was 'morally' wrong:[124]

The only thing I'm dead nuts against is abortion . . . 'cos I know quite a lot of my friends had abortions and it—that's really—I mean, that's taking a life, isn't it?[125]

Oh I think it's dreadful. I think it's a sin. Because you're taking a—even when, even when you've just caught—you're taking another life away, aren't you?[126]

---

[119] See e.g. Cook, *The Long Sexual Revolution*, 116; McIntosh, ' "An Abortionist City" ', 95.

[120] Regan, *When Abortion Was a Crime*, 21. See also McLaren, 'Women's Work and Regulation of Family Size', 75.

[121] An extended analysis of the points made here can be found in Fisher, ' "Didn't stop to think, I just didn't want another one" '; ead., 'Women's Experiences of Abortion before the 1967 Act'.

[122] Judith, msf/kf/ht/#33.   [123] Margaret, bc3ox#18.

[124] By 'moral', I refer exclusively to arguments that assert a foetus's 'right to life' and condemn abortion as a form of murder.   [125] Aileen bc3sw#14.

[126] Marilyn, msf/kf/bl/#7. It is worth noting, also, that both these quotations ended with a question. In contrast to the assertively voiced views of those who did not see any moral problem with the practice of abortion, these respondents sought the interviewers support and agreement for their views.

Sally suspected that God or nature might punish those who attempted abortions:

I always had the feeling that if you took anything to stop nature it served you right what it did to the baby . . . not, not bad things, but it made them—so I believe—very bad tempered, very short tempered, naughty babies. Unruly.[127]

Similarly a woman interviewed by Mass-Observation worried that her daughter was 'plain' because 'I didn't want her' and 'took gin and pills and everything'.[128] One interviewee made an attempt to induce an abortion despite being 'against it really'.[129] Those middle-class respondents who did have moral concerns about abortion tended to qualify their objections.[130] Thus, Reg was 'not against it, umm, but I'd hate—I'd really hate to be those persons that had to make that decision . . . because they know that they're killing something'. He 'believed in it' in cases of disability and also approved if a 'woman had had an abortion because, umm, she had so many children she couldn't support them'.[131] Similarly Phyllis, despite being Catholic, reasoned that her own abortion was justified on the grounds that 'God wouldn't want me to leave my two children without a mother'.[132]

The distinction between the present-day dominance of moral arguments and their absence in working-class communities before the debate surrounding the aftermath of the legalization of abortion in 1967 was revealed by Maria, who latter regretted her own 'back-street' abortion:

Well, it was arranged that she came to the house—I lived with Graham's mother then, but his mother and him were both out. And she brought with her some carbolic soap and she used hot water and she just more or less syringed you out with it. And then about three days after it all started coming away from you. But it were—it were awful really and it's a thing I'm very, very sorry about. . . . now's I've got old and they start talking about it being murder, you know it makes you think really.[133]

Birth control clinics were horrified at the extent to which working-class patients simply accepted abortion as a valid method of limiting family size. They found that many potential patients refused to draw a moral distinction between controlling their fertility after rather than before conception. They found themselves inundated with demands for abortions:

We have had two requests for abortion this week and both seemed to think that the clinic existed for the purpose. The unlawful side of it had not struck them at all. The other said,

---

[127] Sally, msf/kf/bl/#31. All of the above quotes come from active Anglicans (one of whom was raised as a Catholic).

[128] Mass-Observation, TC Family Planning 1944–49, Hampstead, TC3/2/A.

[129] June, msf/kf/ht/#27.

[130] Angus McLaren contrasts the middle-class concept of the 'sanctity of embryonic life' with the 'working-class . . . notion that life was not present until forty to eighty days had passed': 'Women's Work and Regulation of Family Size', 75.   [131] Reg, msf/kf/ht/#36.

[132] Phyllis, msf/kf/bl/#5.

[133] Maria, msf/kf/bl/#8. Esther, bc3ox#13, also regretted her attempted abortion on moral grounds, this feeling of remorse only emerging long afterwards.

'surely you are going to do something for me.' I had to explain to her very plainly that we did not teach how to destroy life.[134]

Many patients did not 'look upon bringing on a period as wrong'.[135] Nor did they necessarily prefer contraceptive methods or find them 'morally' more satisfactory. One woman at Stopes's Cardiff clinic thought the cervical cap she was given was 'disgusting': she had 'got rid of things regularly for years' which was 'much easier'.[136] Indeed, some found abortion much more acceptable than using other methods of fertility control. Madeline Kerr was amazed at the views of a Catholic woman she encountered in her 1958 study of Liverpool. This woman had refused to use contraception, stating, 'It is definitely a sin.' However, she found abortion permissible: 'I mean to say I don't say I've never taken anything. We all do at times don't we? You just say to yourself it's late.'[137]

Many women did not consider themselves to be 'destroying life' as they took abortifacients before they were certain they were pregnant; these were sometimes taken as early as the expected period itself in order to ensure that it came on. For some, taking pills was a regular practice associated more with menstruation than with pregnancy. Esme, a bank clerk, for example, 'missed a couple of periods and I thought I was pregnant . . . you went to a chemist's and you got some tablets and I took them and I did in fact get a period but whether I was pregnant or not, I don't know, of course'.[138] One of the abortionists imprisoned in Holloway and interviewed by Moya Woodside claimed that 'sixty percent of married women' make sure 'they bring the period on' each month.[139] The thought process behind the practice sometimes avoided facing up to the implication that a child might have been conceived.[140] Many women did not necessarily confront the possibility that they might be pregnant, still less its further implications.[141]

The distinction drawn between abortions and 'bringing on periods' (a practice completed before one was certain that one was pregnant) was clearly revealed by

---

[134] Florence Gordon to Marie Stopes, 10 Dec. 1937, BL Add. MSS. 58624.

[135] Mrs Underwood to Marie Stopes, 20 Nov. 1935, Bl Add. MSS 58629.

[136] Florence Gordon to Marie Stopes, 21 July 1939, BL Add. MSS 58625. L. A. Parry's investigation of criminal abortion also concluded that many women demanded abortions 'without being conscious of any moral or legal offence': *Criminal Abortion*, 155.

[137] Kerr, *The People of Ship Street*, 83.   [138] Gerald and Esme, msf/kf/ht/#9.

[139] Woodside, 'Attitudes of Women Abortionists', 33. Woodside also found that few abortionists worried about the moral consequences of their actions: 'I knew it was against the law, but I didn't feel it was wrong': 'The Woman Abortionist', 37.

[140] See also North Kensington Women's Welfare Centre, Notes Regarding Abortions, Research and Miscellaneous Statistics, 1927–1950, A&M: SA/FPA/NK/93; E. Ross, *Love and Toil*, 104.

[141] We should not see this as a 'denial of reality'. As Newman argues, it is only 'according to the definitions of modern society' that 'a woman is either pregnant or not pregnant'. In fact, 'conception involves a continuum of events'; by the time the first period is missed not all stages of conception from 'penetration of an ovum, cell division, formation of an embryo, implantation in the endometrium and nourishment from the maternal placental system' have taken place. See Newman (ed.), *Women's Medicine*, 16.

Catherine, who married a watchmaker in 1941. She declared that she 'didn't know anyone who had an abortion', and that 'bringing on a period' was different:

There were times when you thought you might—and of course you didn't have your periods, you know—was going 'Oh Lord!' And you didn't really want it to happen . . . I suppose I thought well, I'd better take something . . . I suppose I took this ginger, or (chuckles) gin or something . . . you thought 'Oh, well we'll try that and see if that starts your period off'.[142]

In cases where women were sure that they were pregnant nevertheless early attempts to abort might be viewe differently from terminations attempted at a later stage in pregnancy. Some other women who knew they were pregnant nevertheless drew distinctions between early and late abortions:

Under a certain date yes, under a certain date it's only a bit a jelly . . . just a bit a jelly . . . over a certain date—no, it's a little—a little boy, but under a ce—say it's two month end, and your doctor says you are pregnant—I should imagine that'd be right . . . but say four month—it's a baby, it's a baby.[143]

Similarly, Betty took abortifacient pills, but saw this as quite different from having an abortion:

I wouldn't have an abortion . . . you could take a pill and that pill could work straight away and you could—well they'd only just be a little seed there wouldn't there? Well, if you have abortions—I mean that baby's formed.[144]

Traditionally, in working-class communities, 'quickening' appears to have been a widely accepted indication that foetal life was present and should not be interfered with.[145] However, it was not only with very early abortions that terminations were attempted without much deliberation about the moral acceptability of the practice. Nor were the women who spoke about 'bringing on a period' totally unaware of what they were doing. They did not always resort to euphemisms to shield themselves from their actions, and often referred to aborted foetuses as 'babies'. Abortion was not necessarily chosen only as a last resort, nor when the negative consequences of having a child were particularly high and motivation reached extreme or desperate levels. An examination of abortion admissions to Camberwell Hospital between 1930 and 1934 noted what were termed the 'trivial' reasons for resorting to abortion provided by some women.[146] Nor was abortion always attempted reluctantly, in the absence of contraceptive alternatives.

---

[142] Catherine, msf/kf/ht/#1.   [143] Eleanor, msf/kf/bl/#11.   [144] Betty, bc3sw#19.
[145] McLaren, *Birth Control in Nineteenth-Century England*, 246; id., *Reproductive Rituals*, 102–12.
[146] Parish, 'A Thousand Cases of Abortion', 1110. Modern studies have also noted the variety of reasons women sought illegal abortions: see e.g. Luker, *Taking Chances*, 13; N. Lee, *The Search for an Abortionist*, 26–57.

Pregnant women could take abortion-inducing steps in a very light-hearted manner, even presenting it as a joke between friends:[147]

There were uh, all sorts of things, you used to take . . . Penny Royal and . . . Holland's Gin (chuckle). Things like that, uh, (pause). Yes, it (giggle), it used to be a joke—it was jokey talk, you know (chuckle), and you'd have—you'd have a laugh and there'd be quite a few of us around you know (chuckle), and having a laugh about it and—but . . . it was all part of life then—they'd either go and have an abortion straightway (chuckle), or they'd let the baby go on.[148]

I can tell you a funny bit. Um, my neighbour next but one, she had three children I think, and she went in for a fourth, and she'd read somewhere that there were these tablets, two and six each, which was a fortune then, half a crown like, so she said 'Do you want one Iris?' I said, 'No,' I said 'I don't think I'll bother,' 'cos we were pregnant at the same time. 'Oh, I'm going to have one.' They were great, big, dark green jellies, like a jelly sweet like, oval sweet. So, anyway, she took it. Done nothing for her. She was still pregnant. We used to laugh and do things like that. Then she'd take blue, she took a square of blue in a glass. Stupid things she used to do, you know, because she didn't want any more children like. But, er, it's funny looking back at it, but she could have killed herself couldn't she? (laughs)[149]

It was a game. It was very unreal, and although you'd wait every month for your period . . . it was bravado and there wasn't real fear . . . if your period was a little late, and that was real fear and—twitch twitch—and I did in fact drink a whole bottle of gin on one occasion out of fear. Um, but in the early stages it was a game.[150]

This testimony suggests that, for most ordinary women during the first half of the twentieth century, the 'abortion debate' as articulated in contemporary Western culture was not a factor in practical decision-making.[151] Such moral ambivalence highlights the inadequacies of assuming that appliance forms of birth control were automatically preferable to traditional practices. Moral questions were seldom crucial in determining contraceptive strategies. Indeed, in the inter-war period, there was little ethical objection to the use of abortion as a form of family limitation. Moral objections were associated rather with new appliance methods, which might be seen as unnatural, connected with illicit sexual activity, or injurious to the privacy that it was felt should surround marital sexual relations.

[147] Mary Zimmerman also argues that abortion was not always characterized by conflict or trauma: 'Experiencing Abortion as a Crisis', 134. See also R. Woolf, 'Changes', 70, who argues that 'the guilt that women are supposed to feel after an abortion is exaggerated; what guilt there is is imposed on them by conventional attitudes, and the conditions of the abortion'.
[148] Sarah, msf/kf/bl/#30.   [149] Iris, bc2#8.   [150] 'In the Club', A&M: GC/105/22.
[151] American research into a number of women who had illegal abortions in the 1950s and 1960s revealed similar attitudes (although the researchers did not acknowledge this): 'I felt nothing. I didn't feel anxious. I think I was stupid. No, I was not stupid . . . I just went to take care of business . . . I just got on the train. Not only did I not think about the moral or ethical implications, I didn't think about the physical possibilities.' Messer and May, *Back Rooms*, 21.

'TOLD CAP WOULD CAUSE CANCER':[152] HEALTH
CONCERNS AND METHOD CHOICE

Health concerns were also an important criterion in evaluating contraceptive choices. All methods were perceived to have health risks; some forms of abortion were seen as particularly risky, whilst rumours that withdrawal and abstinence were psychologically or physically damaging were common. Yet this does not mean that appliance methods were any more trusted; indeed, they were often seen as even more damaging than traditional forms of birth control.

In the case of abortion, fears of physical damage to either the mother or the foetus were far more distressing than moral concerns. Abortions were widely felt to be dangerous, and stories emphasized the gruesome details:

They knew ways and means of getting rid of them which I would never do.

Why was that?

Oh God, too dangerous. A friend of mine, across the road there, she did all sorts of things to get rid of it, it was a wonder she didn't kill herself. I remember once she was walking around, blood pouring from her. How the heck she survived I don't know.[153]

Women were being aborted by the most incredible means, you know, and they were very crude. Err, some people were saying that you jam a bar of caustic soap up—up the woman, you know, and that would bring everything down, which it did and it caused terrible pain . . . there was these back-street women that professed to do abortions . . . and invariably the person that would have been aborted would finish up in hospital, you know 'cause infections and all sorts of things popped in.[154]

Fear of hurting oneself, or of giving birth to a damaged child, dominated the recollections of those who attempted abortions. Hubert worried when his wife, a nurse, threw herself down the stairs that 'the results would be pretty horrendous for her and for the child as well.'[155] June, the daughter of a bank manager, was talked out of having an abortion by her mother who warned her that she might ruin her chances of having a child in the future:

She just said 'Oh don't do anything like that, it's—it's er—not the right thing to do and you never know it . . . you might not be able to have any more children' and all that sort of thing. She was against it and I took her advice.[156]

Esther, wife of a painter and decorator, was desperately worried when her daughter was born that her attempts to abort had caused lasting damage: 'I just thank God that she was all right when she was born, because she was absolutely black, and they had to pump this stuff out of her, I think it's what I'd taken.'[157] Similarly,

---

[152] North Kensington Women's Welfare, Research and Miscellaneous Statistics, 1927–1950, Failures, 1 Apr. 1935–31 Mar. 1936, A&M: SA/FPA/NK/93.   [153] Doris, bc3sw#6.
[154] Reg, msf/kf/ht/#36.   [155] Hubert, msf/kf/ht/#32.   [156] June, msf/kf/ht/#27.
[157] Esther, bc3ox#13.

a midwife who gave evidence among that presented by the Midwives Institute to the Birkett Committee felt that 'the reason women so frequently asked if the baby was "all right" at birth was because they had so often taken abortifacient drugs'.[158]

The perceived degree of danger was also the main criterion used to distinguish between the different methods for terminating a pregnancy. Dilys tried to discriminate between methods she would take and those she would not. Salts were fine but quinine and gin were both too dangerous (although she admitted using quinine):

Oh, they used to have a bottle of gin . . . I never took gin or anything like that, couple of doses of salts, nothing shifted, leave it alone . . . no gin, no, nothing like that . . . if you took quinine . . . it could bring on blindness in the child . . . oh, horrible, bitter, I did take that . . . Didn't do no good, not a bit of good . . . Very strong, but I wouldn't do anything like that, in case it harmed the child.[159]

Going to an abortionist, rather than using drugs or instruments to induce an abortion oneself, was viewed as the most risky means of bringing on a miscarriage. This was at least in part due to greater public awareness of tragedies resulting from visits to abortionists, as such incidents were more likely to result in a prosecution and newspaper coverage.[160] Edith was persuaded by her husband to go to an abortionist when pregnant with her second child in 1939, but in the end could not go through with it for fear she might die:

Well, he had two sisters himself and they were very much against having children, 'cos I know when I was going to have my daughter, they persuaded him, for me to have an abortion, which those days, wasn't a legal thing, it was done illegal by an old woman. It was done illegal . . . they persuaded him and he did ask me to get rid of her. Well, funny enough, he made this appointment, through his sister, and it was a lady out in Canton that I was to go this day, to this house, to get rid of her. . . . I went, and I got as far as the lady's door, and d'you think I could knock that door? I couldn't knock the door. I just couldn't go through with it myself, you know . . . I just couldn't go, couldn't go . . . . it wasn't so much the child I was thinking about, it was thinking about my own health, I thought I was going to die if she cut me open, I thought she'd be cutting me open, like, you know, to get this baby out, and I was so afraid of it myself that really I was afraid to go, although I went, I still couldn't make it, no.[161]

Esme, a bank clerk, saw abortion as 'absolutely horrifying and illegal' and thought any such attempt would put one 'very much at risk', but she had no such concerns

---

[158] Potts, Diggory, and Peel, *Abortion*, 258.   [159] Dilys, bc2#13.

[160] Without accurate information on the extent of attempted abortions or the number of injuries or deaths resulting from abortion attempts, it is very difficult to estimate how dangerous abortions were. Barbara Brookes argues that 'women knew from experience that, despite the protestations of the medical profession, abortion was relatively safe', especially within a context in which maternal mortality was not insignificant. It is likely that the dangers of abortion were exaggerated by respondents just as much as by commentators at the time. Brookes, *Abortion in England, 1900–1967*, 42; see also McLaren, 'Abortion in England, 1890–1914', 390–1.   [161] Edith, bc2#23.

when taking abortifacient pills, which she, 'actually, didn't really' consider were dangerous. 'I didn't know what they'd do, but I hoped that they would just bring on my period.'[162]

It has been assumed by historians that the denigration of traditional methods of birth control, particularly withdrawal, on health grounds, concerned users and encouraged the use of new technologies. Withdrawal was widely portrayed as having severe psychological and physical drawbacks. Those providing contraceptive services championed the safety of their methods and thought that providing an alternative to dangerous traditional methods (particularly abortion) was a key part of their likely appeal. Marie Stopes's avowed aim was to 'lift sex matters out of the gutter' and 'Charing Cross Road rubber' shops by providing 'occlusive caps and diaphragms' in place of the 'resort to the abortionist'.[163] Thus clinics allied themselves with a modern medical approach and with official health-care services, and sought to distance themselves from other outlets of birth control information, which they saw as disreputable, unqualified, and dangerous.[164] However, we cannot assume that people saw modern methods as necessarily better for their health. Many were suspicious of modern medicine and, as clinic workers soon realized, the 'scientific' approach was not always reassuring. As one clinic reported, 'the working woman has a deep-rooted resistance against seeing the doctor on any account, and she is dismayed at the prospect of an examination'.[165] Many providers were aware that the 'medical aura' of birth control clinics was off-putting and did what they could to create a domestic ambience in their centres.[166] Marie Stopes instructed her nurses to 'rub in the homely atmosphere' when informing others of the clinics,[167] and in Leicester the medical staff 'didn't wear a uniform' in order to create a 'friendly non-medical approach to the whole thing'.[168] However, the medical associations of birth control clinics were unavoidable. Indeed, for many women, it was medical need that prompted attendance. Local-authority-run clinics were supposed to provide birth control advice only for those who had medical reasons for avoiding pregnancy. The central aim of appearing clinical, safe, and clean was clearly at odds with the desire to seem motherly. This tension was played out in clinic spaces in which rooms, decorated in a style aping a contemporary domestic sitting room (with flowery or pastel wallpaper) were filled with tables full of gleaming medical equipment. Photographs of babies (reminiscent

---

[162] Esme, msf/kf/ht/#9.

[163] Marie Stopes to C. H. Birkitt, Chief Supplies Division, Rubber Control, Ministry of Supply, 26 May 1944, BL Add. MSS 58639.   [164] See also Himes, *Practical Birth-Control Methods*.

[165] Florence, *Birth Control on Trial*, 26.

[166] On the rift between middle-class birth controllers' insistence on 'scientific' birth control, which required the examination of all women, and the views on and approaches towards contraception and abortion of the working-class people they targeted, see McLaren, *A History of Contraception*, 227.   [167] D. Cohen, 'Private Lives in Public Spaces', 113 n. 8.

[168] Arcott, *Mothercraft and Maternity*, 63. See also Fuller, *On the Management of a Birth Control Centre*; Haire, *How I Run My Birth Control Clinic*.

of family portraits) hung next to framed copies of the medical qualifications of the staff.

Rumours that scientific methods of birth control had dangerous side-effects were absorbed by many from all classes.[169] Lewis-Faning reported that 8 per cent of women who did not use appliance methods worried that they were harmful.[170] Evelyn Fisher, who worked at a Marie Stopes clinic in London, failed to establish a clinic in south Wales in the late 1920s because she found 'the women were afraid to use' caps.[171] Nurse Gordon noticed that 'the prejudice against the use of Caps seems great' when trying to set up a clinic in Swansea in the early 1940s: 'at every meeting the same questions are asked and repeated, the chief one is, don't caps cause cancer!'[172] Lella Secor Florence also found that 'even after instruction at the Clinic, a patient will write in great anxiety to know whether it is possible for the pessary to get lost inside, or whether this or that story she has been told about the ill-effect of contraceptives is true'.[173] In 1956 these concerns had not abated: 'patients . . . want reassurance that contraceptives do not cause cancer, tuberculosis or disease of the genital organs; that they will not interfere with normal menstrual periods, or cause sterility'.[174] Indeed, Florence identified 'a general tendency to blame the cap for any symptoms of ill health'.[175] Similar dislikes and suspicions of unfamiliar new appliances were mentioned by interviewees. Leslie's fear or cancer lay behind his wife's refusal to go to the clinic in Pontypridd that his sisters had attended in the 1930s:

'Ooh, my wife never went any—like that. Oh no, no, no. But she didn't believe in anything like that.'

Why was that?

Oh well, she don't know, she didn't believe in it. Perhaps, I was so much of a dead nut against it, causing cancer, things like that.'[176]

Vera, an Irish Catholic who moved to Hertfordshire as a teenager, remembered Marie Stopes as 'the organizer of French letters', a method 'she wouldn't have anything to do with', in part, because 'they can cause damage'.[177] Judith too

---

[169] Some authors of a National Birth-Rate Commission report declared 'all unnatural modifications of marital association, and all artificial contraceptive methods by mechanical or chemical contrivances . . . are harmful'. Other contributors, despite agreeing that 'most artificial contraceptive methods at present employed are harmful', condoned the 'use of the best contraceptive methods' as 'less detrimental' than bearing a large family: National Birth-Rate Commission, *Problems of Population and Parenthood*, p. clxiii. See also W. Seccombe, *Weathering the Storm*, 162. On the debates in medical journals about the physiological safety of birth-control methods see Geppert, 'Divine Sex, Happy Marriage, Regenerated Nation', 411–14.

[170] Lewis-Faning, *Report of an Inquiry into Family Limitation*, 175, 182.

[171] Parkes and King, 'The Mothers' Clinic', 168.

[172] Florence Gordon to Marie Stopes [?1943], BL Add. MSS 58632.

[173] Florence, *Birth Control on Trial*, 144.   [174] Florence, *Progress Report on Birth Control*, 71.

[175] Ibid. 197.   [176] Leslie, bc3sw#1.   [177] Vera, msf/kf/ht/#34.

was suspicious about the coil when she first came into contact with it in the late 1940s:

Then there was something called the coil and I'd heard that hadn't worked for some people so I was very much against that . . . I didn't like the idea because that was metal and I thought with my nursing training I don't think this is a good idea, you could get cancer of the cervix and er, I was thinking on those lines, so I—I never took the coil.[178]

Such fears were not always alleviated by clinic campaigners. Marie Stopes also declared that caps caused cancer, excepting her own 'pro-race' version, and frequently denigrated the appliance methods chosen by rival clinics as less efficacious or as positively harmful.[179] Doubts about the safety of new methods were not confined to the suspicions of clinic clients. Dr Mizzen, who worked at the Maternity and Welfare Clinic in Swansea, resisted the establishment of a birth control clinic on the grounds that she did not 'believe caps are safe or reliable' or that 'women should be taught to fit caps themselves'.[180]

The worry that appliance methods of contraception might not be hygienic also worried many users. Fears of germs, dirt, and infection were conjured up by the elaborate cleaning required in caring for an appliance, the mess and debris occasioned by its use, and the internal touching needed to put it in place. Indeed, many women recoiled at the idea that they would have to touch their sexual organs when inserting a female method of contraception.[181] Lewis-Faning found that 'too messy' was an oft-mentioned reason behind the abandonment of a birth control method. A. Susan Williams interviewed a woman in the Rhondda Valley who described using the cap given to her at a birth control clinic as 'a mucky process', and middle-class interviewees told Enid Charles that quinine pessaries were greasy and odorous and soiled the bedlinen.[182] She found that caps and diaphragms were frequently distrusted because of the 'necessary cleaning' and 'attention to hygiene'.[183] One man complained to Marie Stopes that the 'lubrication supplied . . . detracts from the physical contacts' and that 'the odour and

---

[178] Judith, msf/kf/ht/#33.

[179] See R. Hall, *Marie Stopes: A Biography*, 260; Stopes, *Contraception*, 168–206. Stopes denigrated the Dutch cap in an exchange with Norman Haire in *The Lancet* in 1922: see issues for July (pp. 195–6), 19 August (p. 419); 9 September (p. 588), cited in Geppert, 'Divine Sex, Happy Marriage, Regenerated Nation', 413. On the relationship between birth-control methods and cancer, see also Drysdale, *The Small Family System*, ch. 5, 'Do Preventive Methods Cause Cancer?' (pp. 72–82); O. C. Beale, *Racial Decay*, 212–15. The health problems of artificial contraceptives were discussed in National Birth-Rate Commission, *The Declining Birth-Rate*, 136–41, 246–58.

[180] Joyce Daniel report to Margaret Pyke, 1934, A&M: SA/FPA/A11/76.

[181] See Cook, *The Long Sexual Revolution*, 151.

[182] Lewis-Faning, *Report of an Inquiry into Family Limitation*, 50; Williams, *Women and Childbirth in the Twentieth Century*, 108; Charles, *The Practice of Birth Control*, 55. Natalie Higgins also argues that the perception of female appliances as dirty lay behind her respondents' sense of repulsion regarding such methods: 'Changing Expectations and Realities of Marriage', 229.

[183] Charles, *The Practice of Birth Control*, 54. See also Pohlman, *The Psychology of Birth Planning*, 386.

discharge' upon removal was 'very distasteful . . . perhaps the biggest drawback of all'.[184] Not only were such procedures tiresome, but they also posed practical problems in many working-class homes which even by the 1950s had 'no opportunity for privacy. The housewife may have no bathroom, no running hot water, and only an outside lavatory shared, in some cases, with other families . . . she often feels acute embarrassment when she has to wash her cap at the kitchen sink.'[185] Jane, a civil servant, disliked the cap as it was messy and unhygienic, requiring treatment with disinfectant powder. Similarly, she disliked French letters, which had to be used in conjunction with a messy cream:

And you say you didn't like the diaphragm they gave you.

No, I didn't . . . I used to have to keep it um, in—had a special little box to keep it in . . . this powder, was it Fuller's Earth or something? Something like that . . . I didn't like using it, it just wasn't comfortable. Er—just stopped, just stopped using it then, didn't I? . . . I never used—I never liked using contraceptives because it always so, I don't know, it always seemed so messy.[186]

Similar comments were made by other interviewees:

It was a little tablet . . . a jelly, sticky thing . . . it used to be awfully messy, awfully messy. We used to have, have a towel under me. You can tell it wasn't sort of a—you know you sort of had to prepare for it.[187]

She described them as 'messy', because once I'd discharged . . . her mess was still there to clear up. So I don't think she was—she weren't that keen on it.[188]

It is in this context that the supposed health risks of non-appliance methods need to be understood. The ill effects of withdrawal were less off-putting than those associated with new reproductive technologies. Many, especially among the middle classes, had heard, like Stanley, that withdrawal was

not good for your health . . . when you're at the peak, and you know you have to withdraw quick. And they reckon that's bad. Bad for the nervous system. I never did fathom—er, they say it could send you blind . . . That was a common thought amongst the young men of my generation. You could go blind. I don't know why though.[189]

One woman attributed her husband's indigestion to his use of withdrawal over a six-year period.[190] Bernard, a journalist, rejected withdrawal, as 'I was always told that if you do too much of that'll endanger your health, you're interfering with the natural flow.' However, he also feared that caps and 'those sorts of things—it can endanger your health'. He therefore chose condoms.[191] Nellie also thought

[184] W. E. Owens to Marie Stopes, 30 Mar. 1939, BL Add. MSS 58642.
[185] Florence, *Progress Report on Birth Control*, 207. See also Cook, *The Long Sexual Revolution*, 154.
[186] Jane, msf/kf/bl/#32.
[187] Margaret, bc3ox#18.   [188] Alfie, bc3ox#35.   [189] Stanley, bc3ox#38.
[190] Stopes, *Mother England*, 3.   [191] Bernard and Diana, msf/jm/bl/#45.

withdrawal was bad for her husband, a train driver, yet they continued using it because of the disadvantages of other methods:

Um, well, as I said, my husband was very good. He used to withdraw. That symptom. Mind, he used to worry a lot, but it wasn't really good really—not for him, as the books tell me. Well, as he told me himself, because he had to . . . all he kept thinking about was being careful and that was no good really, but, er, that's the only way . . . I mean, the only way—not like what they've got now. I mean, he did try, what was called French letters in them days, but I didn't like them, because they made me sore. 'Oh,' he said, 'I won't use it then. I use the withdrawal symptom. Just have to be careful. That's all.'[192]

Despite the fact that Marilyn's husband, a hairdresser, was unhappy with withdrawal and concerned about the health risks of the practice, she insisted they continue with it. She particularly feared that the insertion of a foreign material, in the form of a cap, into the delicate organs of a woman's body created considerable risk of physical injury or infection, and reasoned that a 'natural' method such as withdrawal could not actually be dangerous:

Tell me about about the discussions that you and your husband had about using contraception.

Well, he said he had a friend and his wife, er, had got a cap. And he said, 'Do you want go?' I said 'No, I'm not going nowhere' I said, 'No' I said, 'I'm perfectly happy wi' what we're doing and I'm not prepared to—I'm not prepared to risk me health.'

So what did you think was unhealthy about caps?

Well um this friend of mine she used to keep it in a jam jar wi' disinfectant but it made me feel sick, um.

Where did she get it?

I think she went to t'clinic somewhere . . . I don't think it's wise meself to use—um, if you're married—because your inside—in a woman—she's—her inside is very open. Now a man isn't, he's enclosed, everything's closed in. So there's only one like—only—where he can get any germs—er, anything, but a woman is open, in't she? Now when you start putting something that's not—that's foreign, that doesn't belong to your body you're asking for trouble . . .

And then when he were ill with his er—he said I'd done it with making him, er, with making him use contraception—I'd—I'd made him have this illness. I made him ill, he said. He, er, didn't blame it on drink and smoking. Er, do you know, I put a cigarette out as he were dying? . . . He said I'd caused his illness through—through making him withdraw.

So what did he think was dangerous about withdrawal?

Well, it weren't natural. But what were difference wi' stuff going on in the bed or going in you, what the difference? So I couldn't've made him ill. It were in his mind, that.[193]

For many of those interviewed withdrawal was less connected with disease and dirt than other methods. Rather, especially among working-class respondents, it was constructed as a 'natural', non-interventionist solution to the problem of

[192] Nellie, bc3ox#19.   [193] Marilyn, msf/kf/bl/#7.

family limitation which did not involve any artificial (and possibly germ-laden) form of mess. Alfie, for example, tried pessaries and condoms but rejected them because 'it seemed foreign', and he could practise 'withdrawal at any time, and that's how I used to be'. It was 'definitely' his preferred method: 'It seemed more natural somehow.'[194] Similarly, Elizabeth did not like condoms and preferred withdrawal because she did not 'like anything artificial like that'.[195] Health concerns dominated the evaluation of all methods. However, it was technological innovations, such as female caps, which raised the biggest fears of serious disease or infection.

'IT'S PROBABLY BETTER WITHOUT':[196] SEXUAL PLEASURE AND METHOD CHOICE

The argument that modern methods of contraception were self-evidently preferable to traditional ones is often premised on the understanding that withdrawal and abstinence spoilt the sex act. Ross McKibbin's comments are typical: 'As a technique, withdrawal . . . required the kind of continuous self-discipline that frequently had deleterious effects on the sexual lives of both men and women and on their relationships with each other. Neither husband nor wife, but particularly not the wife, was likely to find much satisfaction in intercourse when the merest "slip" could end in disaster.'[197] It was certainly the case that methods of birth control might be abandoned if they were seen as interfering with, or diminishing the enjoyment of, sexual intercourse. However, contemporary constructions of what constituted sexual pleasure led many to choose traditional methods. The disadvantages of non-appliance methods, and in particular the deprivations caused by withdrawal, were seen as less severe than the drawbacks of technological methods. While new appliance methods might require elaborate preparation and detract from the spontaneity of the sex act, withdrawal was favoured as it required no forethought. Indeed, some men did not view withdrawal as a lessening of their sexual pleasure, but rather valued the skill required to practise it effectively and saw its successful use as a mark of their sexual prowess.

Many believed that good sex should be uncontrived, spontaneous, and 'natural'. Sex was to be engaged in when the mood emerged, in the right circumstances, and as the result of ordinary desires. It should not be routine, planned, or predictable:

And how important would you say sex was to your marriage?

Well, it is—it's one way of showing love one to another because that's what it's all about. But not, not greedy. Not um, not—not a man, as I say, demanding his rights—you know

---

[194] Alfie, bc3ox#35.

[195] Elizabeth, bc3sw#12. At the end of the nineteenth century the very terminology used to describe methods used for family limitation—'artificial checks'—constructed these activities as 'unnatural'. The term 'birth control' was not in circulation before 1914: Bland, *Banishing the Beast*, 191.   [196] Catherine, msf/kf/ht/#1.

[197] McKibbin, *Classes and Cultures*, 304–5.

coming together spontaneously, you know—come here and have a cuddle you know—and then one things gets one to another, you know. Oh it's, it's very, very important in the right atmosphere, the right frame of mind.[198]

Appliance methods were seen to undermine the spontaneity which was necessary for sexual pleasure. Esther and Jack concluded that some methods 'take a bit of understanding and preparation . . . which . . . takes the edge off of things'.[199] Women who abandoned the caps provided by birth control clinics, predominantly in favour of withdrawal, commented that the 'preliminaries spoilt the romance' and that 'arranging beforehand to wear a cap made intercourse for that particular night a duty'.[200] Others found the calculating, clinical attitude which attended appliance method use off-putting.[201] A clerk from Macclesfield, born in 1907, told Mass-Observation that the 'greatest distraction' of 'modern contraceptives' was their tendency to 'direct a natural urge into a clinical experiment'.[202] Similarly, a man complained in 1939 to Marie Stopes that spontaneous 'cohabitation' was 'completely spoiled' by the wait for the spermicide to melt: 'This "calculating" atmosphere . . . ruins the psychological environment necessary.'[203] Dilys had little patience for her husband's carefully tended condom: 'He used to have such a nice tin, and talcum powder and keep it tidy. I said "By the time you get it on all desire's gone".'[204] Similarly, Emily would not consider using the pessaries her neighbour kept in a box beside her bed because 'I don't really think it should interfere with sex.'[205] Claris could not understand 'what they see in' condoms: 'I should imagine if it was a man he'd get tired by the time he (laughs), he fiddled with them things.'[206] Larry and Doreen disliked condoms because he 'wouldn't like to keep putting something on and having to pull it off and all that'. Moreover, 'he kept losing them. He wasn't putting them on properly and then I had to fish, diving inside myself to find where it had gone, so he said "Bugger that".'[207]

Many respondents chose traditional methods such as withdrawal as they were perceived as the most natural, basic, and uncomplicated methods available, and required the least interference with the spontaneity of the sexual act, needing no planning or organization.[208] Nor was this view confined to working-class respondents.

---

[198] Lorna msf/kf/bl/#25.   [199] Esther and Jack, bc3ox#13.

[200] Florence, *Progress Report on Birth Control*, 115.

[201] Kristin Luker argued that for couples in California in the 1970s the 'degree of planning and foresight that contraception demands can make a desirably warm and intimate emotional experience appear impersonally "cold blooded" ': Luker, *Taking Chances*, 42.

[202] Mass-Observation, DR 2512, reply to April 1944 Directive.

[203] W. E. Owens to Marie Stopes, 30 Mar. 1939, BL Add. MSS 58642.   [204] Dilys, bc2#13.

[205] Emily, msf/kf/bl/#13.   [206] Claris, bc3sw#10.

[207] Larry and Doreen, msf/kf/bl/#20.

[208] Many of those who adopted partial abstinence and deliberately reduced their coital frequency valued it as a method that allowed occasional, spontaneous sex when couples could not help

Committed Quakers Mark and Joanna, who were both civil servants, for example, preferred withdrawal because it allowed Mark to be 'lazier'. He commented: 'I mean you can't—you can't be spontaneous with a condom, that's the point.'[209] One guide to contraception was unusual in recognizing the suitability of withdrawal in this regard: 'the advantage of this method is that it can be employed by a couple who, instinctively giving way to sexual excitement, have not any preventive at hand'.[210] For those who valued spontaneous and uncontrived sexual experiences, withdrawal had a clear advantage over other methods. Not only was no technology involved, but it was felt to be a method which required no prior knowledge, experience, or education. Pleasurable love-making was deemed to be artless, ingenuous, and simple. Withdrawal did not conflict with the attempt to create sexual experiences which were natural, unplanned, and instinctive.

Even though it allowed spontaneity, withdrawal was nevertheless viewed as having disrupted some of the erotic pleasures of sexual intercourse:

How did you feel about withdrawal? . . .

Well, it weren't a lot of that—it—to me it was wrong, like, you were just climaxing to pleasure and everything stops don't it?

Hmm.

And it's just—it's not right . . .[211]

I—you could never properly judge the moment to withdraw. At the moment when you were virtually going 'hummm!', you know, into heaven—you can't do a specifically controlled thing like that, it's ridiculous to expect to.[212]

Cecil 'decided that, you know, that this withdrawal business was a waste of time . . . It was just a sheer lack of satisfaction.'[213] Moreover, it was not simply men who talked about the disadvantages of withdrawal. Some respondents thought that withdrawal was more detrimental to women's enjoyment of intercourse. Doreen, for instance, commented that while her husband could be brought to orgasm outside of intercourse, she had to accept 'half measures':

Was using withdrawal in any way a sacrifice for him or you?

Er, well I've forgotten now because we got used to it. He didn't—he didn't finish . . . he could have help. It's the woman that can't have help . . . accept what you get—half measures. Half a cup of tea instead of a full 'un.[214]

---

themselves. Modern culture similarly sees the possibility of spontaneous sex as a major advantage of the Pill, and the lack of spontaneity as a reason why many fail to use condoms despite risks of a sexually transmitted disease or HIV infection. See e.g. Sobo, *Choosing Unsafe Sex*; Moore and Rosenthal, 'Contemporary Youths' Negotiations of Romance'; Lees, *Sugar and Spice*; Holland, Scott, Sharpe, and Thomson, ' "Don't die of ignorance" '; Holland, Ramazanoglu, Sharpe, and Thomson, *The Male in the Head*, 40–5.

[209] Mark and Joanna, msf/kf/ht/#22.   [210] G. Hardy, *How to Prevent Pregnancy*, 43.
[211] Peter, msf/kf/bl/#26.   [212] Gerald and Esme, msf/kf/ht/#9.
[213] Cecil and Wyn, bc3ox#40.   [214] Doreen and Larry, msf/kf/bl/#20.

Violet voiced a similar complaint:

So what do you do, being careful?

Well, they used to say, go all the way, but you didn't have to go all the way, if you didn't want to be pregnant (laughs).

So how far would you go?

Just half way.

What does that mean?

Well, satisfy the man and not the woman.[215]

A number of men were sensitive to such problems: 'If it was interrupted, uh, she could perhaps finish me off easily enough, I couldn't easily always, easily finish her off.'[216] One man wrote to Marie Stopes for an alternative to 'coitus interruptus which is most unsatisfactory from my wife's point of view and therefore from mine because my climax is reached as a rule just as the pleasure for her is about to begin'.[217]

Despite the drawbacks of withdrawal, it was often seen as interfering least with the spontaneity of sexual intercourse, and its sensory disadvantages regarded by some as less severe than those associated with alternative appliance methods. Condoms, in particular, especially among working-class respondents, were seen as numbing the pleasures of intercourse, as indicated by the common euphemisms used to describe them: 'washing your feet with socks on'[218] and 'like having a toffee wrapper on'.[219] Frank did not like withdrawal, but found it preferable to French letters, which 'dulled the sensation'.[220] Thomas, who disliked using condoms because 'you wanted the real thing didn't you? The raw material, not half and half', did not feel similarly short-changed when practising withdrawal: 'Oh, no: it's better to do it that way.'[221]

Finally, for a few respondents, withdrawal was seen as positively enhancing the sensory pleasures of sexual intercourse. Such narratives stressed the degree to which withdrawal was a sexual skill which, once mastered, created a positively exciting, and mutually enjoyable, sexual dynamic. Colin, who began his working life as a farm hand, avoided using French letters, as his friends told him they reduced sexual pleasure, and instead used withdrawal. He found it to be an especially pleasurable form of sex. Avoidance of ejaculation was presented as enabling prolonged and more enjoyable sexual experiences without fear of pregnancy. Through regular withdrawals, Colin could make sex 'last longer' which made him

---

[215] Violet, bc2#15.   [216] Norman, msf/kf/ht/#17.

[217] Quoted in L. Hall, 'Marie Stopes and her Correspondents', 31.

[218] Terence, msf/ssrs/bl/#15.   [219] Marilyn, msf/kf/bl/#7.

[220] Frank, msf/ssrs/bl/#16.

[221] Thomas, bc2#11. Hera Cook has revealed that male authors of sex and marriage manuals were far less enthusiastic about the advantages of condoms than were female writers: *The Long Sexual Revolution*, 139.

'happy'. Moreover, by withdrawing Colin felt he significantly enhanced his wife's experiences. She 'enjoyed it better' because the confidence she felt that pregnancy would be avoided enabled her to 'let herself go':

... when she knew I was withdrawing she was enjoying it better, see ... she thought, well, everything's safe—above board—so she'll let herself go ... Now, I could get in bed and if I got an erection I could make it last a long while. But I'm afraid that if I had sex I were a wash out, it didn't last so long. It only lasted—sex only lasted as long as I ejcalated [*sic*] and then it were finished ... I had to, what's they call it? I had to have sex and yes, I had to have a lot of withdrawals to let the steam get down and then I could have sex again. But once I shot me ejcalation it'd gone. You'd have to wait another two hours before I'd get a hard on. But if I kept withdrawing without having an ejcalation I could make it last longer like you know ... (laughs) Eeh, dear me. But if the woman's happy and you're happy and she's satisfied who cares how long it lasts or how big it is, how little it is, if they're enjoying theirself. That's it.[222]

Men valued their ability to control themselves during intercourse; brand names for condoms such as Hercules sought to appeal to men's desire to increase their 'staying power' (as well as connoting the indestructibility of the condom).[223] The ability to withdraw effectively was seen as an element of this sexual skill. Reg, who joined the Royal Marines immediately after he left school, proudly described building up his withdrawal muscles by the 'delightful game' of masturbating and then holding back.[224] He used the rhetoric of virility, power, and self-control to describe his mastery of withdrawal. He described how, having practised his technique while serving in the army in the jungle, he came home to his wife with something 'extra' to offer:

And how did you feel about withdrawal?

Well I didn't know any other way. (laughs) ... I suppose when you went into abuse, which you found was very, very delightful, the whole game—the name of the game was that you should bring yourself up as far as you dare and get all that lovely whatsaname and then stop, hoping that it would be there—because if you ejected then, of course, you lost all the steam and everything else, you'd have to wait. So, if you played it you could—you could carry on like that and masturbating ... you just hold back 'cause you've got nobody there, you were miles—or in the middle of the jungle or anywhere else and nobody could see you. And then you'd do it again and bring yourself up and you'd play on that maybe half an hour or an hour in those times so you were really tightening up all the muscles that you could, so I suppose that when you got back home and you came to the ejaculation, then, of course, you could hang on because your muscles and everything else had been developed, but you

---

[222] Colin, msf/kf/bl/#36.   [223] See also the American 'Trojan' brand.

[224] This was an interesting view in the light of admonitions, common in the late nineteenth and early twentieth centuries, that frequent masturbation was physically debilitating and that sexual as well as moral strength was heightened by the self-control required to avoid it. Edward Kirk, in *Talk with Boys about Themselves*, in 1905, warned that 'self-abuse' would 'stunt your growth', 'wreck your health', and turn you in to 'an enfeebled unmanned man': quoted in Hunt, 'The Great Masturbation Panic', 595–6.

had that little extra (laugh), you know. Or we were taught that—alternatively to that you could go to that sort of place, right on the very edge and withdraw, and then stop for a few minutes and then go back in again, erm, which would extend your lovemaking, of course, you could do that for quite a period with strength and, you know, strong will and all the rest of it. But of course, it was about practice.[225]

Henry, who began work as a dumper driver on construction sites, similarly displayed pride in his ability to withdraw, linking it to his strength of 'will power': 'Use your power, your will power to—if it's the withdrawal system like, it's a lot of will power, I was able to do it, there you are, that was it.'[226] Rather than seeing withdrawal as restricting on his sexual pleasure, Edward, an engineer, stressed repeatedly his proficiency at the technique—his 'strength'.[227] His masculinity was enhanced by the ability to practise it:[228]

So when you were married, what did you use at the times when you didn't want your wife to get pregnant?

Self-control. I never used a condom. Never. I was always a very strong man, very very strong, and between the two of us we, you know, could both get satisfaction. Mind you, it took a while to sort of get to that stage, but I think if you really try hard enough, you can do these things . . .

And you never wanted to use a French letter?

Well, I, I, I—no, I don't think I would, really. I heard, erm, one or two people say it's like ea-eating a toffee with the paper on, and such things as that, like, you know, but er, no, as long as I was capable of controlling myself—and there, and erm, I did . . . I was strong enough to be able to hold—so that she could have her (pause), whatever they call it, you know, explosion, and that, and I could just withdraw, o-on there. And um, no it, it took a little while to get into this, y-you know—'cause I, I'm sure she was frustrated a few times, like you know, in our first periods of married life, on there, but we got over that, and, er, it worked out very well.[229]

While traditional methods presented some difficulties or frustrations, newer appliance methods presented equal, if not greater, barriers to sexual enjoyment. Reactions to forms of birth control are not universal and cannot be predicted: one woman who married during the 1920s 'never felt I was missing out' by using

---

[225] Reg, msf/kf/ht/#36.   [226] Henry, bc2#27.

[227] Withdrawal was linked to a rhetoric of masculinity much articulated during the late nineteenth and early twentieth centuries which focused on strength, muscular power, and self-control. The League of Health and Strength was founded in 1906, while 'Uncle Bob's' booklets helped boys 'Gain Five Inches Chest Expansion', or 'Develop Powerful Arms': see Bourke, *Working-Class Cultures*, 43–5. On this topic in an American context, see also Rotundo, *American Manhood*, 221–46. Sex education literature also increasingly encouraged boys to delay gratifying their sexual urges, and 'emphasized the joys of building manliness though exercise and self discipline': see Campbell, *Sex Education Books*, 35, and also Mort, *Dangerous Sexualities*, 193–6. Admonitions against masturbation similarly contributed to this theme: see L.. Hall, 'Forbidden by God, Despised by Men'.

[228] An Italian study also found that the ability to master withdrawal was a source of pride for many men: Jane and Peter Schneider, 'Demographic Transitions in a Sicilian Rural Town', 259.

[229] Edward, bc3ox#15.

withdrawal, although 'it's in disrepute . . . I've heard people say, "Oh that's awful", but, um, we didn't find it so'. For her it was the sheath's interference with the spontaneity of sexual intercourse that was unpleasant: 'you see with the sheath you get nicely carried away and going up to heaven quietly and next thing is he stops, walks over to put the sheath on, well I mean that's the most unromantic thing in the whole world'.[230] Non-technological methods were frequently preferred because they fitted better into contemporary ideas about the place of sex within marriage; in particular, a method such as withdrawal enabled spontaneous encounters which were not calculated or contrived, and in some cases allowed men to demonstrate the extent of their sexual skills.

'HE HAD ALL THE STUFF, I DIDN'T':[231] GENDER AND METHOD CHOICE

That the most commonly used methods of contraception (withdrawal and condoms) were seen as male methods is of crucial importance in explaining their popularity. Women frequently sought to remain naively removed from sexual matters, including the negotiation of contraceptive practice or management of a contraceptive strategy. This meant that female methods such as the cap, which required women to attend a clinic or consult a clinician, were either employed reluctantly or rejected altogether. By contrast, men saw it as their role to take the initiative: hence methods that men were expected to learn about, obtain, or take responsibility for were preferred.[232]

Methods such as caps and pessaries were disliked and their use avoided in part because women were expected to acquire them. In the inter-war period, a clearly gendered system existed in which men were responsible for obtaining 'male' forms of contraception and women were expected to obtain 'female' methods. It was women alone who were expected to attend clinics where caps would be obtained. The emphasis in all clinics was to give women the responsibility and power to control contraceptive use.[233] As one clinic worker remembered:

. . . we were very much orientated towards the female method and in those days, the days that you're speaking of, the twenties and thirties . . . I think—that we thought the female method was (a) safer and (b) in the hands of the female who after all was going to have the baby and therefore had a more inbuilt er, need for constant use of it.[234]

---

[230] 'In the Club', A&M: GC/105/23.   [231] Doris, bc3sw#6.

[232] This does not tally with one analysis of letters written to Marie Stopes, which concludes that 'male methods of birth control were disliked and not to be tolerated if an effective female method could be found': Davey, 'Birth Control in Britain during the Inter-War Years', 338.

[233] Norman Haire did, however, provide lectures on birth-control methods for 'poor men' in the early 1920s: *How I Run My Birth Control Clinic*, 5.

[234] Freda Parker, who was a social worker at the North Kensington Clinic in the 1930s: 'In the Club', A&M: GC/105/30.

The Society for Constructive Birth Control was forthright in expressing this philosophy:

The fundamental teaching of our President and the Mothers' clinics has been that contraceptives used by the male are less physiologically right than the best type used by women . . . where possible the wife should be properly fitted at a Clinic with the contraceptive best for her own use.[235]

However, most women were reluctant to take birth control into their own hands. Rather, their beliefs about sex and gender roles, their approach to sexual knowledge, and the dynamics of sexual relationships meant that women did not want responsibility for contraception. Many women were therefore horrified at the thought of having to obtain contraceptive appliances themselves, and refused to acquire 'female' methods of contraception by attending clinics or buying pessaries. Many women were deeply embarrassed at the prospect of attending a clinic: whatever 'the social and economic backgrounds of the patients . . . nearly all approach the Family Planning Clinic in a state of nervous apprehension'. 'It takes courage to come to a place like this', commented one. 'You don't know anything about birth control . . . and you don't like to talk about such things.'[236] One woman who later became an adviser at a family-planning clinic remembered the mortifying shame and discomfort she felt in the Kensington clinic in the 1930s:

. . . it was somehow quite sort of painful to have it sort of well, 'Come along dear' and you know, 'This is the cap and this is the way you use it, and squat down on your haunches' and—I—I was frightfully embarrassed about the whole thing, it really sort of had a—had a terrible effect on me. I don't know how I ever managed to use the cap at all.[237]

In contrast to the expectations of clinic campaigners, couples almost universally asserted that it was and should have been the husband's responsibility, alone, to use contraception. Phyllis, wife of a Bristol docker, did not explain how she managed to limit her family; it was 'just up to my husband then, wasn't it? That's all.'[238] Millie, the wife of an upholsterer in Oxford, similarly 'thought it was his place, anyway. I didn't think it was mine'.[239] Ross McKibbin is unusual in noticing that 'responsibility for contraception was traditionally the man's sphere' which women could not risk invading.[240] 'Taking the initiative' was central to prevailing male sexual identities and anathema to those of women; hence methods which the man might be expected both to obtain and to take responsibility for at the point of sex were favoured.

---

[235] 'Spacing Babies for Health: The Use of Condoms', *Birth Control News*, 17 (3 Feb. 1939), 35. See also Himes, *Practical Birth-Control Methods*, 57, 67.

[236] Florence, *Progress Report on Birth Control*, 42–3.   [237] 'In the Club', A&M: GC/105/43.

[238] Phyllis and John, bc2#26.   [239] Millie, bc3ox#21.

[240] McKibbin, *Classes and Cultures*, 306. For a French parallel see Accampo, 'The Gendered Nature of Contraception in France', 257–8. She argues that female methods were rejected by French women because 'most women did not know or feel comfortable with their bodies, and many women felt an aversion to anything related to sex'.

Although husbands might be responsible for marital contraceptive strategy, this gendered system, in which men were primarily expected to obtain and use male methods, meant it was difficult for them to obtain female forms of birth control.[241] Despite the determination of birth control clinic campaigners to construct family limitation as a women's issue, they noticed that many husbands attempted to take responsibility even for female methods. Nurse Cook told Marie Stopes that in Leeds 'we get more men here than we have ever had before, asking for advice for their wives, who are too nervous to come'.[242] Remembering her experiences at a birth control clinic, E. S. Daniels[243] wrote in *The New Generation* (the journal of the Malthusian League, a prominent society for the promotion of birth control) 'it is often the husband who persuades the wife to visit, and it is he who usually does the correspondence . . . Only five women have been to me without the knowledge of their husbands'.[244] Nearly half of Marie Stopes's correspondents were men.[245] Yet, despite husbands' interest in female methods such as caps, their requests for help were often rebuffed by workers who claimed that they could advise only the men's wives. One Aberdeen husband sought to obtain birth control advice, thinking his wife 'would be difficult' to persuade to attend. The nurse insisted that an appointment was made for her. When she came, she proved too embarrassed and inhibited to instruct: 'she could not manage the Racial Cap' and 'would not try an alternative'.[246] A man arrived in Cardiff wondering 'if he could be seen by a man Dr.', and another 'very nice man' from Aberdeen came in 'having read a leaflet'.[247] Both were told to persuade their wives to attend. Indeed, a Family Planning Association leaflet would not even sanction the use of a sheath without consulting the wife: 'It is necessary for the wife to see the Clinic doctor once before she chooses this method, so to make sure that the couple know how to use a sheath properly.'[248]

[241] Conversely, it was considered inappropriate for a woman to attempt to obtain a male method of birth control. 'It was almost impossible for a woman to purchase a condom' (Sutton, '*We Didn't Know Aught*', 88). Indeed the selling of condoms in all-male environments, such as the barbers, underscored their status as a method which women were not expected to obtain. Maggie, a brick-layer's wife from Penarth, born in 1913, was horrified at the thought of getting a condom herself: 'Oh, I never went (shrieks and giggles) ohhhhhhh, no, no! I'd never go and get them.' Similarly, Leslie, a miner from Pontypridd, was appalled at the suggestion that his wife might have gone to get French letters: 'Oh no, my wife wouldn't think like that, oh no, she was too much of a lady, and she was a lady, I got to be fair, she was a lady.' That was 'up to the man it was, always up to the man, not to the woman, the woman never bothered, a man, always'. Maggie bc2#21; Leslie bc3sw#1.

[242] Nurse Cook to Marie Stopes, 14 Sept. 1928, BL Add. MSS 58621.

[243] Nurse Daniels gained notoriety when she was dismissed in 1922 for telling women who came to the Edmonton Maternity and Child Welfare Clinic where they could receive birth-control advice.

[244] 'Experiences of a Birth Control Nurse', *The New Generation*, 3/10 (Oct. 1924), 111. On men's interest in birth-control clinics see also Jones, 'Marie Stopes in Ireland', 269.

[245] L. Hall, *Hidden Anxieties*, 10.

[246] Margaret Rae to Marie Stopes, 10 June 1935, BL Add. MSS 58604.

[247] Nurse Florence Gordon to Marie Stopes, 29 Oct. 1937, BL Add. MSS 58624; Margaret Rae to Marie Stopes, 13 May 1938, BL Add. MSS 58604.

[248] Family Planning Association, *What Birth Control Is* (Jan. 1944); copy in Mass-Observation, TC Family Planning 1944–49, Birth Control Leaflets and Booklets, TC3/2/E.

This anti-male stance jarred with many couples' desire for a male-centred approach to family limitation. It was seen as a male duty to know about, obtain, and use contraception regularly, yet birth control clinics discouraged male interest in their premises and would only advise women. Since many men could not persuade their wives to attend clinics, male methods were much more likely to be used than female ones.[249] Given that it was thought to be the husband's role to acquire contraception, and that many men could not obtain female methods of birth control or persuade their wives to make an appointment at a family-planning clinic, it is not surprising that men restricted themselves to acquiring 'male' methods of contraception such as condoms, or relying on withdrawal.

Female methods of birth control, such as pessaries and the new caps, were also unpopular because of the effect they had on the gender dynamics of sexual intercourse. The practicalities of using a female method of birth control meant that women had to anticipate or prepare for sex. One family-planning doctor recalled the reluctance of women to 'take some sort of initiative in sex' by using 'female' methods: 'they'd say to me, "Well, when do I put it in because if I put it in and he doesn't want sex I'll feel such a fool".'[250] Lella Secor Florence found that many women were resistant to using caps because they were 'an unwomanly invitation to pleasures which are supposed to have been designed for her husband alone'.[251] Rather, women preferred methods which left all preparations 'in the control of the husband as most women regard initiative in sex matters as something exclusively the province of the husband'.[252] Gwen, born in 1914, was given a cap at a clinic in Pontypool after a difficult birth, and was clearly very unhappy with playing such a proactive role in sex:

It wasn't very, you know (half-laugh) I don't like talking about it really, but you had to put it in so long, you know, you didn't have intercourse until you put it in—so long—and then take it out and all that business. It was horrible really.

Withdrawal was much more satisfactory because she simply 'trusted him', and could thus be relieved of the role of preparing for sex.[253] Similarly, Doris, a bricklayer's wife from Pontypridd, preferred condoms to pessaries because he 'had all the stuff then, I didn't'.[254] Nellie liked neither the cap she was given at a clinic nor the role it required her to play before sex:

I didn't like that cap . . . and I didn't like the other [pessary] 'cos it was too messy, I just didn't like it, and I just said that he'd have to do something. It's easier for him. Like, wearing a French letter or doing what he did [withdraw].

So why was it easier for him?

Well, don't take long for a man to put a French letter on, does it? I mean, without me having to be messed about with. I'd rather it that way, you see.[255]

---

[249] Slater and Woodside, *Patterns of Marriage*, 201.   [250] 'In the Club', A&M: GC/105/17.
[251] Florence, *Birth Control on Trial*, 68.   [252] Ibid. 108.
[253] Gwen, bc3sw#18, divorced.   [254] Doris, bc3sw#6.
[255] Nellie, bc3ox#19. Note also her objection to the 'mess' involved in using 'female' methods. This is discussed earlier in this chapter.

Withdrawal supported rather than challenged gendered sexual roles. As a 'male' method it fitted into a dynamic in which men took the central role in initiating and driving sexual activity.[256] Many women sought to take as inactive a sexual role as possible. Withdrawal was the method of contraception which least impeded women's attempts to maintain a passive sexual identity.[257] 'Female' methods, by contrast, presented women with considerable problems. As Kristin Luker observed in a more recent context, it is not surprising that women often prefer to avoid contraception since in 'using a contraceptive, society proclaims the user to be a sexually active woman, a "cold-blooded" planner, a hard-eyed realist with no romance in her soul, and a woman who is perhaps too sexually active to be a "lady".'[258]

'THERE'S NO METHOD SAFE':[259] RELIABILITY AND METHOD CHOICE

That traditional methods were primitive and unreliable would appear to be irrefutable. One of the key reasons why barrier methods of birth control are assumed to be preferable to traditional methods, such as abortion, withdrawal, and abstinence, is their greater efficiency in limiting family size.[260] It is often claimed that traditional methods were self-evidently high-risk family-planning strategies: abstinence was difficult to maintain, withdrawal demanded an unrealistic level of continuous self-discipline on the part of the male, and abortions frequently failed. Yet the reactions of many individuals did not conform to these assumptions. Only a small minority who were especially determined to avoid a pregnancy, often on the advice of a doctor, would chose 'modern methods' on the basis of their officially proclaimed reliability. Most saw all methods, both traditional and new appliances, as uncertain. More importantly, many did not desire a risk-free, absolutely reliable form of contraception; rather, they accepted that contraception would regularly fail and that they would on occasion become pregnant. Birth control was merely used to reduce the frequency with which that happened.

The understanding that withdrawal was prone to failure was widespread. Iris used it despite thinking it was 'a chancy thing', and Jack saw it as 'hit-and-miss'.[261] However, this knowledge did not always lead respondents to turn to other methods, as these too were often distrusted. Sarah 'hadn't any faith' that the spermicide

[256] Pollack, 'Sex and the Contraceptive Act', esp. 73.

[257] Pohlman, *The Psychology of Birth Planning*, 328; Rainwater, *Family Design*, 237. Elinor Accampo's study of early twentieth-century France comes to a similar conclusion, arguing that women's sexual identities made them extremely reluctant to use female methods of birth control. They preferred methods which their husbands controlled: Accampo, 'The Gendered Nature of Contraception in France', 257–60. [258] Luker, *Taking Chances*, 51.

[259] Tim, msf/srss/bl/#19. [260] See e.g. McKibbin, *Classes and Cultures*, 305.

[261] Iris, bc2#8; Jack, bc3ox#13.

in pessaries would 'melt and . . . destroy the sperm' and Fred agreed 'there was always an uncertainty' in using a 'nurse's friend' (pessary) because, despite the presence of spermicide, he nevertheless 'ejaculated into the girl'.[262] French letters were much more widely trusted, but some still had doubts, particularly about the newer latex disposable condoms. Charlie liked the old sort which were 'very tough rubber . . . you get the same feeling . . . but you're safe, there's no damage at all'. Disposable ones by contrast 'could rip . . . and the damage is done'.[263] Peter also did not think French letters were reliable: 'when you come to think on it, it's like, it's only a thin fine sheet of rubber in't it?'[264] Others found the difficulties of using condoms created further risks:

That [condom] wasn't very successful. It was too thick, hard, and one night there was a calamity because the top disappeared, (laughs), the end of it disappeared and the rest of the night was spent searching for it (laughs)—there was no sex! Oh dear, panic stations![265]

Caps were also widely distrusted, especially among the working classes. Enid Charles found caps were frequently abandoned because users felt 'insecure', and the North Kensington clinic observed that many had 'no confidence in [the cap] method'.[266] Clinic workers found a number of patients were 'too nervous to trust sponge', or 'not sure of fit of cap'.[267] Such anxieties were, surely, stoked by the nurse in Aberdeen who told 'them about the sperm being alive for seventeen days' and sternly reminded women that the cap had to be used in conjunction with 'solubles' (spermidical pessaries).[268]

Caps were not easy to fit and patients legitimately feared they were not inserting them correctly. At the North Kensington Women's Welfare Clinic, one attendee had 'lax vaginal walls', in which the 'cap [was] not [a] good fit'; another found her cap had fallen out and another put her cap in upside-down.[269] Similarly, the nurse in Aberdeen had to warn patients 'about their long nails in fingers, as they may tear the caps'.[270] A woman who attended the North Kensington Women's Welfare Clinic in 1936 had 'broken rims of two practice caps', and worried that 'she would "never do it right"'.[271] Each week there were 'a few returning . . . with damaged

---

[262] Sarah, msf/kf/bl/#30; Fred bc2#25.   [263] Charlie, bc3sw#3.

[264] Peter, msf/kf/bl/#26.

[265] Helena, bc1/pilot/#2. This pilot interview was not included in the sample.

[266] Charles, *The Practice of Birth Control*, 53, 54; North Kensington Women's Welfare. Follow-Up Survey, 1952–1956, A&M: SA/FPA/NK/201.

[267] Fowles to Stopes, 22 Mar. 1930, BL Add. MSS 58622; North Kensington Women's Welfare. Failures, 1 Apr. 1935–31 Mar. 1936, A&M: SA/FPA/NK/93.

[268] Margaret Rae to Marie Stopes, 12 Oct. 1934, BL Add. MSS 58603.

[269] North Kensington Women's Welfare, Patient Follow-Up Reports, 1936–7, A&M: SA/FPA/NK/93.

[270] Margaret Rae to Marie Stopes, 30 Jan. 1942, BL Add. MSS 58614. She was reluctant to replace one torn cap on the grounds that 'case may have done it herself'.

[271] North Kensington Women's Welfare. Patient Follow-Up Reports, 1936–7, A&M: SA/FPA/NK/93.

caps'.[272] The manufacturers of the Haire pessary noted that if the user was constipated it would 'no longer be a protection against pregnancy'.[273]

Rumours abounded that government concerns about population growth prevented the distribution of safe appliances. A Mass-Observation panellist was told by a widow aged 60 that 'they're forced by law to put some that don't work in each packet. I know Rendell's [*sic*] do.'[274] Whether or not such rumours were believed, they betrayed the anxieties caused by appliances which required the user to trust technology rather than human effort. Moreover, there were some legitimate fears about the quality of birth control appliances. There was no British standard for condoms until 1964 and manufacturers' own tests of reliability were used to market appliances; less dependable ones were more economically priced.[275] Marie Stopes complained about the standard of some of the caps provided in 1941, after two of them were returned with the rubber and rim 'extremely bad and all bubbly and cockly' and a visible hole.[276] Problems had not been solved by 1944, when Margaret Rae reported that the faulty springs were causing 'no end of complaints' and 'making new cases nervous'.[277]

It is important to recognize that barrier methods of contraception were not self-evidently safe. Pessaries, caps, and diaphragms were novel, tricky to learn how to use, and worked according to sophisticated principles. The use of appliance methods required an understanding of their physiological effects: it was not obvious that a melting spermicide would provide a sufficient barrier, that an internal, unseen, and unfelt cap would prevent conception, or that thin rubber would not leak. One woman could not understand the mechanics of the cap and 'thought she put the Cap opening facing outward and that the husband put the Penis into Cap'.[278] By contrast, withdrawal worked according to a simpler principle, and was intuitively safe: 'like a motor car he won't go without petrol, will he?'[279] Enid Charles found a 'widespread belief that it [withdrawal] was a reliable method'.[280] Elizabeth distrusted the efficacy of caps and felt much more secure using withdrawal:

Which do you prefer of those [methods tried]?

Withdraw, oh yes, you knew you were safe then, you know.[281] 'Cos it was a worrying time though they got protection.

---

272 North Kensington Women's Welfare, Volpar-Acceptability Trials, A&M: SA/FPA/NK/97.
273 Directions for using Haire's Pessary, BL Add. MSS 58638.
274 Mass-Observation, DR 3453 (catalogued also as 1022), reply to April 1944 Directive.
275 Cook, *The Long Sexual Revolution*, 123.
276 Marie Stopes to G Watkins, Lamberts, 19 Feb. 1941, BL Add. MSS 58639.
277 Margaret Rae to Marie Stopes, 26 May 1944, BL Add. MSS 58614.
278 Margaret Rae to Marie Stopes, 12 Apr. 1937, BL Add. MSS 58604.
279 Les, bc3sw#4.   280 Charles, *The Practice of Birth Control*, 39.
281 Gigi Santow has also argued that the safety of withdrawal is generally underestimated: 'Coitus Interruptus in the Twentieth Century', 770–2. Lewis-Faning was 'surprised' to find no difference in the number born 'to those who used appliance methods and to those who relied on non-appliance methods': *Report of an Inquiry into Family Limitation*, 70.

So would you trust withdrawal more than caps?

Definitely, oh yes. Yeah.

Why was that?

I don't know, you felt safer, you know, not so messy, no.[282]

In addition, awareness of the fallibility of withdrawal rarely led to the abandonment of the practice. This was, first, because any pregnancy resulting despite the attempt to practise withdrawal was not entirely unexpected and, secondly, because such failures were frequently categorized as the result of human error rather than an indication that the method itself was unreliable. When respondents talked about the fallibility of withdrawal it was always in terms of user error. The method itself was not perceived as risking pregnancy. Rather, it was the likelihood that one might fail to practise the method properly which was recognized. By contrast, births that occurred despite the use of other methods of contraception were more likely to be seen as the fault of the appliance. Since such a failure would probably not have been manifest at the time of intercourse, a resultant conception would have been all the more surprising and unexpected.

Lella Secor Florence realized that the unreliability of withdrawal provided little disincentive to its continued use: 'despite all these disadvantages, and despite recurring pregnancies, couples surprisingly enough revert to this method over and over again'. Yet such couples might reject appliance methods on the grounds of reliability:

One woman who came to the [Birmingham] Clinic had borne seven children, although her husband had practised withdrawal . . . she was fitted with a cap and used it successfully until she heard that a neighbour had become pregnant while using the cap . . . she immediately lost faith in the cap and they resumed coitus interruptus despite their history of failure.[283]

When pregnancy occurred despite the use of withdrawal, such instances were predictable or expected 'slip-ups'. Depictions of its failures tended to be forgiving of the method, but reproachful of its users: 'it's not a safe thing . . . sometimes it overcame you'.[284] For another man, withdrawal was safer than other methods precisely because he felt confident in his ability to prevent mistakes: 'I thought [it] a safer way . . . You could slip up once and you'd be in bother but . . . you wouldn't let it get to that stage. [I had] two lads, and I were satisfied with them.'[285]

It is a mistake to assume that those who use birth control are primarily looking for a thoroughly reliable method of contraception. As Enid Charles recognized, 'the woman who begins to practise birth control . . . who wishes to have a family of a size appropriate to her income, or who merely wishes to ensure a reasonable

---

[282] Elizabeth, bc3sw#12. Note here the statement that caps were messier than withdrawal, and the effects of this comparison on her attitudes and the couple's behaviour.

[283] Florence, *Progress Report on Birth Control*, 83–4.   [284] Lorna, msf/kf/bl/#9.

[285] Larry and Doreen, msf/kf/bl/#20.

interval between births, may be satisfied with less reliability, if other advantages can be obtained'.[286] Lella Secor Florence also realized that women who did not 'worry unduly about subsequent pregnancies' were happy to 'rely on coitus interruptus in the intervals between births'.[287] Many respondents practised withdrawal (some of the time) because they were aiming to limit family size, rather than to prevent pregnancy. Such an approach to birth control did not require the use of the most reliable method available, nor even the consistent use of birth control. Oral testimony suggests that many wished to restrict the overall eventual size of their family but were prepared to adopt a method of birth control which was likely to result in the occasional pregnancy. Like Marian, they used birth control to prevent having a houseful of children rather than to space or plan their families: 'Well he were always careful, you have to be careful unless you were—you see—unless you want a house full of children, you've got to be careful.'[288]

Women in particular sometimes commented that they did not wish to eliminate the chance of pregnancy. Historians' assumption that women's motivation to avoid conception was likely to be high, and that their pleasure was contingent on their ability to separate sex from reproduction, needs to be balanced by the understanding that having children was central to some women's identity. We should not assume that the 'labour' of childbearing necessarily had a negative effect on women's perceptions of the risks of pregnancy, nor that the fear of pregnancy was always detrimental to women's ability to enjoy sex.[289] For a few women, pleasure and sex were intimately bound up with the risks of pregnancy. As one woman who wrote to Enid Charles revealed, 'part of the erotic component . . . is desire for a child . . . she is excited by the idea of being given a child, even though in crude fact she does not wish to become pregnant'. This woman regarded caps as unsuitable because they did not allow her to maintain 'this illusion' of potential pregnancy, and preferred condoms. An 'unconscious desire' meant the woman was happy to be somewhat 'careless'.[290] Similarly, a machinist's wife, born in the mid-1940s, rejected the Pill on the grounds that 'it takes the element of risk out of sex . . . it has made me less able to enjoy sex'.[291]

---

[286] Charles, *The Practice of Birth Control*, 14.

[287] Florence, *Progress Report on Birth Control*, 196.   [288] Marian, msf/kf/bl/#28.

[289] Hera Cook argues that we need to see women's childbearing roles as a burdensome form of 'labour' to understand their determination to avoid pregnancy: *The Long Sexual Revolution*, 11–12, 30–9. Ellen Ross draws our attention to the frequent fears and anxieties that accompanied childbirth during the Edwardian period: *Love and Toil*, 123–5.

[290] Charles, *The Practice of Birth Control*, 33.

[291] Gorer, *Sex and Marriage in England Today*, 141. Such voices, however, represent a positive attitude towards pregnancy that was intimately linked to the regular use of contraception. Such women could embrace the possibility of contraceptive failure and the arrival of another child precisely because they were confident that they would not have too many such accidents. These attitudes were not prevalent among mothers of a generation earlier. On the contrasting views of pregnancy in the Edwardian period between mothers who had already had a number of children, and those who had not, see E. Ross, *Love and Toil*, 125–7. Lara Marks also found some Pill users found the absence of risk had a detrimental effect on their enjoyment of sexual intercourse, Marks, *Sexual Chemistry*, 194.

Using a risky method was particularly appealing to those individuals who wished to get pregnant. For those couples who differed over family planning aims, the use of withdrawal could provide a compromise, as it reduced the chance of pregnancy while not eliminating it altogether. Larry did not want any more children after the birth of two boys, but his wife Doreen was keen to get pregnant. Withdrawal was a suitable and acceptable method for both because Larry felt it would prevent pregnancy while Doreen hoped it might fail:

He didn't want a big family, no. He said two was enough for anybody. I pleaded for another . . . I pleaded and begged but the answer was no, no, no, two was enough . . . I said 'Well, I want a girl'. He said, 'Well, that makes it worse because if you want a girl and you get another boy you'll want another'. He said 'I don't want a football team'. That was his answer, so he—he made the decisions really . . . He relied on hisself—he wouldn't wear any. So it was up him and I didn't mind because I wanted another you see, so it didn't worry me.

Had she been absolutely determined to avoid pregnancy, she might have insisted on the use of a more reliable method:

If I'd've got a girl then it might have been a different thing, I might have . . . suggested something else, protection or something like that. But . . . I did want a girl . . . He said 'I'll rely on meself', he just said 'I'll rely on meself'. So that was me left to wonder every month would I be all right? Would I be wrong? But it didn't worry me because . . . I really did want a girl.

Thus, for Doreen, the advantage of withdrawal was that it provided the opportunity for failure that she could encourage and try to provoke, albeit with little success:

And was he in control of the birth control practices so that he could decide whether to make you pregnant or not?

That was up to him. I never stopped him making a mistake, no.

Did you ever try to encourage him to make a mistake?

Tormented him but didn't win.

How did you torment him?

He, er, making him wait a bit long—well, I don't know keep tempt— . . . but he wouldn't give in, no. And he didn't drink so you couldn't get him drunk. You can never make Larry change his mind can we now?[292]

Similarly, Colin 'secretly' wanted a further child; he thus refused to use condoms, but was happy to employ withdrawal, knowing it was a method he could legitimately 'fail' at and thereby increase the chances of pregnancy:

I wanted to get her pregnant for a little lad earlier on . . . that's one of the reasons I never used thing [condom] you see . . . she used to take in that I'd withdrawn and I used to kid

---

[292] Doreen and Larry, msf/kf/bl/#20.

her, you know. Because she didn't want any more but secretly I wanted a little lad, I did want a little boy like, you know. . . . If it'd been another girl I'd've just give up like, you know. But I told her I wanted a little lad you know, but, er, she said, 'I don't want any more' . . . so, I kidded her like, you know, I said I'd withdrawn, you know, but I hadn't. Told lies—naughty boy. (laughs).[293]

Lella Secor Florence thought that 'the amazing thing about *coitus interruptus* is the reliance which couples continue to place on it even after they have had a number of failures'.[294] Such comments, echoed by other early providers of birth control advice, indicate the enduring misconception of its role in fertility reduction strategies. Withdrawal was popular because it worked according to easily understandable principles, and any accidents which occurred when using it were seen as expected rather than problematic: its unreliability thus did not lessen its appeal. Most importantly, it fitted into contemporary notions of family planning, which did not desire risk-free contraception but rather embraced the possibility of pregnancy alongside the adoption of birth control. For those couples who had not decided whether or not they wanted another child, or who disagreed on the issue, withdrawal provided a way of keeping family size under control while allowing occasional welcome 'failures'.

CONCLUSION

Withdrawal and other traditional methods of birth control had advantages that have generally been ignored. The continued dominance of withdrawal (as late even as the 1970s) has puzzled sociologists, historians, and clinicians who are united in the denigration of the practice. Throughout the twentieth century withdrawal was perceived as an unpleasant, unreliable, and unhealthy option. Gladys Cox, for example, reminded her readers that it was both the most 'primitive' and the 'most unreliable method in use' and highlighted four causes of failure: 'premature emission'; 'presence of spermatozoa in the pre-ejaculatory secretion'; 're-entry after ejaculation . . . without effective cleansing'; and 'motile sperms . . . which succeed in traversing the vagina and reaching the os'.[295] A leaflet on methods, first published in 1938, confirmed it was 'definitely unsafe', 'a great strain on the nerves', and likely in the long term to 'cause severe mental illness'.[296] Modern advice and family-planning literature has continued in this vein, actively promoting 'modern' methods alone, despite the fact that some recent studies have

[293] Colin, msf/kf/bl/#36.   [294] Florence, *Birth Control on Trial*, 100.
[295] Cox, *Clinical Contraception*, 121.
[296] Hooper, *The Voice of Experience*, 3, copy in Mass-Observation, TC Family Planning 1944–49, Birth Control Leaflets and Booklets, TC3/2/E.

revealed the failure rate of coitus interruptus as similar to that of the diaphragm and the rhythm method.[297]

During the first half of the twentieth century, withdrawal was further castigated as having severe psychological and physical ill effects. Leonora Eyles's popular *Commonsense about Sex*, first published in 1933, viewed withdrawal as psychologically 'disastrous'.[298] In the 1943 edition she was still of the opinion that 'To take the man's side of it . . . he cannot think of anything but getting himself away in time . . . he never really enjoys intercourse . . . so he begins to blame his wife for this . . . With the wife the case is even worse . . . Just as the woman may be reaching the climax it is all over.'[299] Gladys Cox summarized the deleterious effects upon which she thought the scientific community were agreed: for men withdrawal had the potential to cause 'hyperaemia in the lumbar and sex organs . . . leading to . . . changes in the prostate . . . hyper-irritability, exhaustion of the nerve centres . . . with consequent . . . impotence'. It might also provoke a range of 'psycho-neurotic manifestations . . . due to the tension of watchfulness . . . . at a time when there should be complete abandon'. For women, the effects were apparently equally dangerous. They were likely to suffer 'chronic congestion of the pelvic organs' resulting in 'back-ache, menorraghia and painful ovary'. 'Anxiety for fear of failure to time withdrawal' would lead to sexual inhibition and in some cases 'complete frigidity', while repeated frustration might cause psychic trauma in the shape of 'insomnia, irritability or emotional instability'.[300] R. A. Gibbons, a gynaecologist at the Grosvenor Hospital for Women, thought the wife suffered in particular: 'Under my own care I have had now many neurasthenic cases which I have entirely attributed to coitus interruptus.'[301] Marie Stopes further argued that women were especially 'deprived . . . of the beneficial absorption from the seminal and prostatic fluids'.[302]

Most literature of this period saw substantial reduction in sexual pleasure as the principal drawback of withdrawal. For Eustace Chesser in his *Love Without Fear*, since 'withdrawal involves the surrender of a certain measure of gratification, it must inevitably fail to yield the intense concentrated pleasure of uninterrupted

[297] Figures are as follows: withdrawal 19%, rhythm 20%, diaphragm 18%, condoms 12%, contraceptive pills 8%: Kowal 'Coitus Interruptus (Withdrawal)'. The failure rates for withdrawal are sometimes highlighted in such literature, which insists that, by contrast, 'for consistent and correct users, barrier method effectiveness is quite high'. It is rarely suggested that withdrawal might also be effective for careful users; rather, the ability of users to be skilled or controlled is doubted: Waldron, 'Cervical Cap'. In part this has been fuelled by the need to promote methods which also provide protection from sexually transmitted diseases, particularly in the post-AIDS era. Betsy Hartmann has criticized both family-planning providers' obsession with the Pill and their refusal to see other methods as advantageous for some women: see *Reproductive Rights and Wrongs*.

[298] Eyles, *Commonsense about Sex*, 90. The 1933 edition went through ten impressions before it was rewritten for the 1943 edition.   [299] 1943 edn., 62.

[300] Cox, *Clinical Contraception*, 122.

[301] National Council of Public Morals, *Medical Aspects of Contraception*, 166.

[302] Stopes, *Contraception*, 77. On the sceptical medical reaction to this book see Geppert, 'Divine Sex, Happy Marriage, Regenerated Nation', 424–30.

coitus'.[303] For van de Velde the 'most immediate effect' of coitus interruptus was 'an inhibition of erotic pleasure'. In place of 'relaxation, release, refreshment, triumphant yet tender satisfaction' users experienced 'acute tension and diffuse irritation . . . depression and exasperation'.[304] It was argued that women were equally affected. Eustace Chesser found that 'many women never feel satisfied unless there has been a rush of semen into the upper vagina'.[305] For Courtenay Beale, withdrawal meant a sexual act cut short before a wife could obtain any emotional or nervous reaction, leaving her in a 'condition of acute unsatisfaction'.[306]

Historians and sociologists investigating the fertility decline have largely accepted the assumptions embedded in such literature.[307] An influential recent historical study of Britain's fertility decline has concluded that no amount of determination or spousal co-operation could have made 'withdrawal and abstinence secure methods; "moments of weakness" and "slips" were commonplace'.[308] For Wally Seccombe, the low birth rates witnessed during the 1920s ands 1930s indicate that 'it has been necessary for the great majority of reproductive couples to replace "natural" methods with the regular use of contraceptives'.[309] Michael Mason reasons that barrier methods must have been preferred as they became available because of their 'banal' and 'obvious' advantages over withdrawal. 'To put the matter crudely, individuals seek pleasure in sex, and the new methods generally gave a better chance of more pleasure to both parties than extra-vaginal ejaculation.'[310] The assumption here is that withdrawal was so intrinsically unsatisfactory that it should inevitably have fallen into disuse once more efficient and pleasurable methods became available.

Yet such explanations have failed to account for the continued popularity of withdrawal, or to address the advantages that were evident to earlier generations. It was the most familiar and well-known method, and its use required no preparatory effort or expense. It did not challenge public morality nor, in particular, the need to maintain privacy in marital sexual relations. It fitted in with contemporary ideals that valued spontaneous and uncontrived love-making. It suited a culture in which men were expected to take responsibility for family-planning issues and for enacting them. Individuals concurred with contemporary birth control

---

[303] Chesser, *Love without Fear*, 153.
[304] Van de Velde, *Fertility and Sterility in Marriage*, 93–4.
[305] Chesser, *Love without Fear*, 153. [306] G. C. Beale, *Wise Wedlock*, 120.
[307] The failure to contextualize contraceptive choices and the mistaken view of contraceptive 'acceptability as something static and intrinsic to a method' is criticized by some modern family-planning providers. See Heise, 'Beyond Acceptability', 6.
[308] W. Seccombe, *Weathering the Storm*, 181. For an alternative viewpoint, though not focusing exclusively on Britain, see Gigi Santow. She has reinterpreted data on withdrawal use and the fertility decline, in the light of the scientific evidence suggesting that withdrawal, while not as effective as the Pill or IUD, is more reliable than either rhythm or the diaphragm and on a par with the condom. Santow, 'Coitus Interruptus in the Twentieth Century', 770–2. See also, on an entirely different culture, Peter and Jane Schneider, 'Coitus Interruptus and Family Respectability in Catholic Europe', 177–94. [309] W. Seccombe, *Weathering the Storm*, 181.
[310] Mason, *The Making of Victorian Sexuality*, 59–60.

campaigners that it had some disadvantages: it was thought to have deleterious effects on health, to interfere with the erotic pleasures of sexual intercourse, and to be unreliable. However, their respective understandings of these problems differed. First, many individuals felt *all* methods of birth control, including modern appliances, shared these shortcomings, and thus they did not view withdrawal's unreliability as a particular barrier to its use. Secondly, most were not looking for risk-free contraception and many actively embraced its unreliability in their family-planning strategies. Withdrawal ensured adequately enough that a family's size would be kept down; welcome 'slip-ups' would mean that a family would be slowly, if haphazardly, built, but in a way that did not appear too calculating or challenging to fate or God. For previous historians, assumptions about the 'obvious' or 'natural' problems of withdrawal have meant its use has been seen to highlight the limited availability of alternative reproductive technology, or related issues such as embarrassment in obtaining them, poor publicity, or expense.[311] This chapter has shown that, in addition, people had positive reasons for adopting the practice. Withdrawal was not a default choice, used only when there was no alternative, but one which fitted into the particular constructions of sexuality: private, male-controlled, convenient, easy, spontaneous, and natural.

[311] S. Anderson, ' "The most important place in the history of British birth control" ', 24–5.

5

'She was pleased to leave it to me'[1]

Gender Relations and Birth Control Practices

Previous chapters have revealed the central role played by men in contraceptive choices and behaviour. Men's knowledge of birth control was more extensive than women's, and men's networks of information about contraception were much more developed and varied. These differences in knowledge set the tone for behaviour. The dynamics of relationships in which men were meant to be informed and women ignorant fostered patterns of contraceptive activity which privileged male action and prized female passivity. Moreover, vague family-planning aims supported and even kindled the system of male responsibility for contraception: there was a general acknowledgement that a large family would be avoided and a tacit understanding that the husband would take contraceptive action some or most of the time. Implicit negotiation allowed women to maintain their practice of ignorance and sexual quiescence. Silent arrangements emerged in which men were frequently left to decide the specifics of birth control use. As a result, male methods of birth control (withdrawal and condoms) were much more frequently used than female methods (pessaries, caps, and abortion), as they facilitated male initiative, and such a male-dominated system was central to both husbands' and wives' sexual identities.

This chapter examines the implications of this finding for our understanding of gender relations in marriage. Previous analyses of the increased use of birth control have had at their centre the assumption that women were more concerned to reduce their family size than their husbands. As a result, women are placed at the forefront of explanatory narratives of demographic change, and are seen, in Wally Seccombe's phrase, as 'the driving force behind family limitation'.[2] John Caldwell, for example, argues that common to 'all fertility transitions' is 'women's increased

---

[1] Norman, msf/kf/ht/#17.

[2] Seccombe, 'Starting to Stop', 173. The claim that women were the 'driving force' behind family limitation is open to a number of meanings. There are three main areas in which responsibility for the use of birth control might be thought to be exercised in a family: level of motivation; access to birth-control information and appliances; influence in decision-making. I claim that in all three of these areas historical material has concentrated on women and has largely ignored evidence on men's roles.

ability to determine their own fertility'.[3] This interpretation, in its various forms, has invariably linked increased use of birth control with a rise in female power in marriage; either women took the initiative in implementing a birth control strategy or they had the power to persuade their husbands to act according to their desires.[4] The argument is summed up by Wally Seccombe: 'whatever strengthens women's capacity for self-assertion and undermines men's traditional conjugal rights will tend to hasten and deepen the fertility decline.'[5] Male perspectives on birth control use have not been presented as pivotal to the timing, causes, and nature of changes in contraceptive behaviour during the twentieth century.[6]

Some historians have recognized that male methods were predominantly used.[7] They have nonetheless remained wedded to the assumption that women were the driving force behind changing contraceptive behaviour, and have argued that men were merely reacting to female demands.[8] They view husbands' preparedness to use birth control as indicative of a change in men's attitudes, and a new responsiveness to their wives' needs and opinions.[9] They argue that the use of male methods of birth control is indicative of an attenuation of patriarchal power within marriage and the increased ability of women to influence decision-making.[10]

---

[3] Caldwell, 'Direct Economic Costs and Benefits of Children', 470.

[4] Shorter, 'Female Emancipation'; Gittins, *Fair Sex*; Ittman, *Work, Gender and Family in Victorian England*; Smith, 'Family Limitation'; Folbre, 'Of Patriarchy Born'. Development demographers, while increasingly aware of the importance of men in fertility declines, remain convinced that the use of family limitation practices reflects improvements in the status of women, their autonomy and control of decision-making. The Cairo International Conference on Population and Development, for example, resolved to design population programmes that worked to improve the status of women and enhance their decision-making capacity. United Nations, *Report of the International Conference on Population and Development, 5–13 September, 1994, Cairo, Egypt* (New York: United Nations, 1994), quoted in Amin and Lloyd, 'Women's Lives and Rapid Fertility Decline', 276.

[5] Seccombe, *Weathering the Storm*, 193.

[6] An exception is Banks, *Prosperity and Parenthood*.

[7] Others have emphasized the apparent rise in the level of abortion at the end of the nineteenth century which, it is claimed, continued in the years up to the Second World War. It is argued that 'autonomous', 'new-style' women, who 'saw themselves increasingly independent of parental and husbandly authority, masters of their own emotions, and, ultimately, of their own fertility', resorted to abortion in large numbers because they remained 'locked into old-style marriages' and were 'unable to inhibit conception because of the indifference or hostility of their husbands': Shorter, 'Female Emancipation', 612, 631.

[8] Helen Mayer Hacker argued in 1957 that 'changes in masculine roles' tended to be 'treated largely as a reaction and adjustment to the new status of women' and called for scrutiny of masculine social roles: Hacker, 'The New Burdens of Masculinity', 227.

[9] See e.g. Ellen Ross, who contrasts nineteenth-century husbands who would not 'consider sex or conception as a joint responsibility', with the 'small and quiet minority' which increased during the twentieth century who 'cooperated in limiting the woman's fertility': *Love and Toil*, 98–103.

[10] A number of historians draw attention to the existence of sensitive, warm, and generous husbands in both working-class and middle-class homes. See e.g. Bourke, *Working-Class Cultures*, 81–9; McKibbin, *Classes and Cultures*, 81–90, 164–76; Lummis, 'The Historical Dimensions of Fatherhood'; Mort, 'Social and Symbolic Fathers and Sons', 362. Other historians have seen such men as crucial to understanding contraceptive practice, presenting *only* those women blessed with companionate husbands as achieving the smaller families they desired. See Cook, *The Long Sexual Revolution*, 119; Gittins, *Fair Sex*, 146–56; Wells, 'Family History and Demographic Transition'.

According to this argument, male power gave way to the sensitive husband ready to modify his sexual behaviour in response to his wife's desire for a smaller family. Thus Robert Woods and Wally Seccombe are united in seeing the task for the historian as 'an appreciation of how women came to educate their husbands and to assert their influence in these matters'.[11] Yet the oral narratives of men and women in the final stages of the fertility decline did not primarily frame male behaviour as a response to women's demands; rather, contraception was viewed by both men and women as part of a male world: whether birth control was used, to what extent, and when, was left in the hands of the husband. This gave men a large degree of power over family size; when men and women disagreed it was generally the husband's view that prevailed. Male prerogatives in birth control decisions were usually respected and unchallenged. Rather than complaining about being excluded from this arena, many women professed themselves 'pleased' with this arrangement. First, they were by no means powerless: they had their own subtle ways of influencing matters. Secondly, they saw clear advantages in being absolved of the responsibility for contraception, seeing it as a burden rather than a power. Their own sexual identities, in which passivity and the appearance of naivety were highly valued, made them extremely reluctant to engage directly with the process of birth control decision-making or method employment. Men, on the other hand, saw taking responsibility for contraception as a key part of their identity and prided themselves on undertaking to use birth control regularly. Thus, to understand the regular and systematic use of birth control, we have to examine the cultures of both masculinity and femininity which underpinned it, which simultaneously convinced men that it was their role to make decisions about contraceptive use while encouraging women to withdraw from the process.

For young men in all classes during the 1930s and 1940s, birth control was seen as an essential element of a husband's duty. Male cultures encouraged men to see themselves as responsible for birth control. Some models of masculinity focused on birth control as supportive and considerate towards the wife. Yet this does not reveal that birth control was allied to the development of 'companionate marriages' in which wives' desires for smaller families were listened to by new, sensitized husbands.[12] Men who developed alternative models of acceptable masculine

---

[11] Woods, 'Debate: Working-Class Fertility Decline in Britain', 211, published in reply to W. Seccombe, 'Starting to Stop'. On the link between women's domestic power and increased fertility control see also Weller, 'The Employment of Wives, Dominance, and Fertility'. Some point, in working-class homes, to women's employment; others to the power exerted by the working-class 'Mam', and others (the majority) to a radical shift in marital relations away from the (Victorian) 'patriarchal' model to a 'companionate' one based on joint decision-making and egalitarian principles. This companionate model is seen to have been central to Victorian debates about the middle-class family and to have found a working-class version only after the First World War and initially only in certain areas of the country, such as those dominated by new industries or in districts where inter-war housing estates created new social networks. See e.g. McKibbin, *Classes and Cultures*, 70–90, 164–76.

[12] The companionate marriage was widely discussed and promoted from the beginning of the twentieth century. The general claim that at some point during the twentieth century marriages were restyled as partnerships of equality and comradeship is broadly accepted in contemporary

behaviour, including those who maintained a belief in the appropriateness of male authority within marriage, also regarded regular use of contraception as a husband's duty. The practice of birth control was seen as a duty to be performed by all men, from those seeking to be seen as domesticated through to those wishing to assert authoritarian control over the family unit.

'IT ALWAYS WAS A MAN'S WORLD':[13] MALE POWER AND CONTRACEPTIVE PRACTICES

Men's primary role in determining and implementing contraceptive strategy has rarely been acknowledged by historians. In part, this reflects an emphasis in much of the archival evidence on men who refused to use birth control. The image of unco-operative husbands, particularly in working-class homes, unwilling to restrain their sexual expression dominates much material of the period, such as the literature promoting birth control clinics. The husband of one clinic patient 'refused to take precautions saying he "wouldn't be muzzled up for anyone"!' while another, a 'beast of a man' married to a deaf and epileptic woman, 'would have relations with her when she was unconscious after the fits'.[14] Direct testimony provided first-hand evidence for the suffering experienced by women whose partners would not use birth control: 'My husband is so selfish he doesn't care so long as he gets what he wants what you suffer makes no differences to him in Fack he is

twentieth-century historiography. Two important texts were Lindsey and Evans, *The Companionate Marriage*, and Burgess and Locke, *The Family from Institution to Companionship*. Post-war sociologists and historians charted the empirical evidence for companionate unions in a wide range of communities. See e.g. Zweig, *The Worker in an Affluent Society*; Bott, *Family and Social Network*; Mogey, *Family and Neighbourhood*; Young and Willmott, *Family and Kinship in East London*; Klein, *Samples from English Cultures*, vols. i and ii; Goldthorpe, Lockwood, Bechofer, and Platt, *The Affluent Worker*; Young and Willmott, *The Symmetrical Family*. Some sociologists have emphasized the limited spread of companionate marriages during the first two-thirds of the twentieth century and stressed the communities in which marriages remained 'patriarchal'. Traditional industrial economies (especially mining districts) were seen as less likely to embrace companionate ideals. See e.g. Dennis, Henriques, and Slaughter, *Coal Is Our Life*; R. Hoggart, *The Uses of Literacy*, 41. Elizabeth Roberts argues that few marriages in Barrow, Lancaster, and Preston could be described as achieving a form of 'companionship': *Women and Families*, 95–105. See also E. Roberts, *A Woman's Place*, 202, 223–4; Laing, *Representations of Working-Class Life*, 37; Clark and Haldan, *Wedlocked*, 27; H. Hartmann, 'The Family as the Locus of Gender, Class, and Political Struggle'; Bell and Newby, 'Husbands and Wives'. Others have concentrated on the empirical difficulties faced in trying to define, identify, or measure companionate marriages, and the tensions inherent in its concepualization: C. Harris, *The Family and Industrial Society*, ch. 12; Platt, 'Some Problems in Measuring the Jointness of Conjugal Role-Relationships'; Atkinson, 'Gender Roles in Marriage and the Family'; S. Edgell, *Middle-Class Couples*; Leonard, *Sex and Generation*; Tolson, *The Limits of Masculinity*; Turner, 'Conjugal Roles and Social Networks'. For a detailed history of the development of the idea of the companionate marriage, see Lewis, *The End of Marriage?*, 45–71; Finch and Summerfield, 'Social Reconstruction and the Emergence of Companionate Marriage'.

[13] Edith, bc2#23.
[14] Nurse Florence Gordon to Marie Stopes, 15 Sept. 1939, BL Add. MSS 58625; Nurse Angeleri to Marie Stopes, 28 July 1944, BL Add. MSS 58626.

a Rotter.'[15] Clinics were presented as sanctuaries where working-class women whose husbands regarded them as 'coital chopping-blocks or child-bearing chattels' could find refuge.[16] Methods such as the cap were promoted precisely because they could be used without the knowledge of the 'indifferent' or 'uncaring' husband.[17] Sociological works have similarly highlighted the 'callous' husband who in working-class districts in the late nineteenth century frequently 'forc[ed] a trial of unwanted pregnancies upon his unwilling mate'.[18]

However, it is important to understand that such cases were often emphasized precisely because they were unacceptable or against the norm.[19] Nurse Rae at Aberdeen, despite complaining that 'men are so selfish on many occasions', upon hearing of a patient whose 'husband objected to the cap' admitted that such cases 'are very rare' and most are 'happy husbands and wives'. Indeed, she conceded that women had a greater tendency to 'confess' to having been too 'lazy to put the method in'.[20] Vera Houghton recognized that most women did not need to go to clinics because their husbands took responsibility for birth control: 'most of the women were there because their husbands had been supposed to be looking after them but hadn't'.[21] E. S. Daniels saw the widespread employment of male methods of birth control as 'testimony to these qualities in our men'.[22] One respondent to Mass-Observation saw her husband's disinterest in birth control as an example of his 'lack of training in husbandly duties and responsibilities'.[23] Lesley Hall has criticized the 'unflattering picture of the average male' presented by much of the material in the historiographical literature and much of the contemporary sexual advice books and surveys.[24] She adds:

The problem of birth control is and was often seen as something concerning women alone. The notion that men were reluctant to use birth control or even opposed to its use as diminishing their control over their wives has often been advanced. The idea of men as indifferent, if not wholly hostile, to the use of reliable methods of birth control . . . cannot be substantiated.[25]

[15] Quoted in L. Hall, 'Marie Stopes and her Correspondents', 34.

[16] Parkes and King, 'The Mothers' Clinic', 165.

[17] Although in many working-class homes this must have been impossible, the ability of women to insist upon birth-control use increased if female methods were adopted.

[18] Young and Willmot, *Family and Kinship in East London*, 4. See also e.g. R. Hoggart, *The Uses of Literacy*, 30; Klein, *Samples from English Cultures*, 439.

[19] More generally, Margaret Loane argued that the working-class father was not 'as black as he is painted' and that philanthropic 'prejudice against him is so strong that all evidence in his favour is unread or misread': Loane, *From their Point of View*, 144.

[20] Margaret Rae to Marie Stopes, 30 Mar. 1938, BL Add. MSS 58604.

[21] Lord and Lady Houghton, 'In the Club', A&M: GC/105, 39.

[22] Daniels, *The Children of Desire*, 36.

[23] Mass-Observation, DR 2903, reply to March 1944 Directive.

[24] Shani D'Cruze also acknowledges the importance of seeing the evidence of 'violent' men within the wider context of expectations and norms of 'good' husbands: D'Cruze, 'Women and the Family', 62. See also Anna Clark, 'Domesticity and the Problem of Wifebeating', esp. 29; Jacky Burnett, 'Exposing "the Inner Life"', 143–6; E. Ross, *Love and Toil*, 84–6; Collins, *Modern Love*, 106.

[25] L. Hall, *Hidden Anxieties*, 91.

Documentary material provides plenty of evidence of men who willingly used contraception, and oral history testimony consistently testifies to men's positive attitude towards the use of birth control:

Percy did it all . . . he was good, very, very good. He always backed me up. He was—he was the sort of man that you could talk common sense to. If we discussed something he always came up with the answer. He said we won't have any more bairns . . . I didn't know what he meant really until I thought about it. And I thought about it, well I thought it's—it's a sensible way, it's a very sensible way and that was it.[26]

A man's use of birth control was often framed as indicating consideration of his wife: it revealed his commitment to his role as her provider and protector. A number of women, like Elma above, were grateful to their husband for taking control of contraception. They felt lucky, looked after, and cared for. Men were seen to indicate the extent to which they cared for the relationship and their spouse by protecting her from pregnancy and providing the means by which this was achieved. However, as the above quotation reveals, women presented male consideration as paternalistic. The very fact that men took control of contraception and were expected to do so placed them in a position of power. This is most clearly revealed by those instances in which husbands were determined not to restrict family size or whose family-planning aims differed from those of their spouses. In cases where husband and wife disagreed about family-planning aims or hopes, the male view was frequently likely to prevail. Husbands had a considerable degree of 'power', in that they could refuse to adopt any form of birth control. In such circumstances women might try to change their situation, but they perceived their options as unsatisfactory: either they attempted to enforce a spell of abstinence, which was usually unsuccessful, or they had to resort to female methods, methods they often disliked.

Men were frequently given ultimate power to determine whether or not birth control would be used, what method was chosen, and the regularity with which it would be employed. The Population Investigation Committee concluded in 1959 that in Britain 'contraception is still part of the husband's prerogative'.[27] Many women saw themselves as reliant on their husband and acknowledged that in some circumstances there was little they could do should he prove reluctant. Some clinics saw men's opposition as reflecting their determination to remain in control of their wives' sexuality and fertility: 'resistance came from very poor and ignorant men—you know, what will she get up to . . . it threatened somehow their domination of their wives.'[28] Other clinic workers recognized the preparedness of men to use contraception, but nonetheless acknowledged the power this gave them. Lella Secor Florence realized that whether birth control was used or

---

[26] Elma, msf/jm/bl/#42.   [27] Pierce and Rowntree, 'Birth Control in Britain, Part II', 128.
[28] Interview with a social worker at the North Kensington Clinic in the 1930s, 'In the Club', A&M: GC/105/30.

not largely depended upon 'what the husband "will do" or "won't do" . . . Even when a wife is quite happy to use a cap, some husbands forbid her for no better reason than they "don't like the idea", or do not think the woman should take precautions'.[29] Even cases of cap use sometimes reflected men's power to determine contraceptive practices; men on occasion pressurized their wives into attending clinics. One man told Marie Stopes: 'I took my wife to you in order to be fitted for an occlusive cap (very much against her will) as I considered it would be a more efficient and beneficial method of birth control'.[30] Nurse Fowles found clinic patients who had been 'too nervous' to use a cap were often persuaded to try again, 'as the husband wishes her to do so'.[31] In cases of conflict, when one partner wanted more children and the other did not, the husband was in a much stronger position. Thus, Doreen presented herself as powerless to alter her husband Larry's determination to use withdrawal when she wanted another child. This was in part because it 'wasn't worth rows . . . if he doesn't want more'. However, as he acknowledged, it was also due to the fact that he was in control of the method used ('I put a stop to it'):

LARRY	We never discussed it.
DOREEN	What?
LARRY	This business of, er, family breeding.
DOREEN	I asked you 'Please could I have, try for another child?' You know that. You kept saying 'No, I don't want a football team.'
LARRY	I said I didn't want a big family.
DOREEN	Well, I didn't get one. You said 'We're just right, we've a two-bedroomed house and we've two boys, it means moving, no.' That's what you said.
LARRY	Well, I thought you were in the same mind.
DOREEN	No, I wanted to try for a girl and you wouldn't say yes.
LARRY	Well, I though it might've been a boy.
DOREEN	Well, if it had've been I'd've tried again for a girl.
LARRY	Well, that's why I'd'a—stop . . . that's why I put a stop to it.
DOREEN	Huh! Yeah, he's the bo— . . . he was the boss.
LARRY	Well, I was the boss then.[32]

Colin's narrative provided the clearest example of the ways in which the emphasis on male authority in conjugal relationships provided him with the power to decide on the number, spacing, and timing of pregnancies. His wife did not want any more children after the birth of two daughters. Colin, however, contrived to make his wife pregnant again while pretending to her that he was withdrawing during intercourse. Her ignorance, her placid acceptance that birth control was

---

[29] Florence, *Progress Report on Birth Control*, 134.

[30] Quoted in L. Hall, 'Marie Stopes and her Correspondents', 35.

[31] Nurse Fowles's follow-up visits: Caravan Clinic, 1930, BL Add. MSS 58622. On men's interest in birth-control clinics see also Jones, 'Marie Stopes in Ireland'.

[32] Doreen and Larry, msf/kf/bl#20. Larry also refused to let Doreen work, seeing this as a challenge to his position as provider: 'I felt as though I could keep her'.

the husband's responsibility, and her desire to keep him happy were used to explain why she did not explicitly object to this subterfuge:

I wanted to get her pregnant for a little lad earlier on.

Oh yeah.

And I think that's one of the reasons I never used [any]thing, you see. You know, I mean . . .

And what did she say?

Well, she was as dumb as me because I used—I used to tell her I used withdrawal. And, er, now—now woman knows whether you've—whether it's come or not, don't they like, you know, but she said—she used to take in that I'd withdrawn and I used to kid her, you know. Because she didn't want any more but secretly I wanted a little lad, I did want a little boy like, you know. . . .

As I've told you about me—and my wife we're quite placid and I'm saying to you my wife didn't know that I was ejaculating. But I don't know—my wife might've have done and to keep me happy she wouldn't say anything. And that's how we had our married life, see. But she never shouted at anybody, she'd take it in and you know . . . but anyway she—she was happen the old school type when they used to have nine and ten kids and one thing an' another and they'd, er, as Churchill said, 'lay back and enjoy it and shout happy England.' (laughs)[33]

However, Colin's case was further complicated by the fact that he was roundly criticized by the woman who lived next door for his callous disregard of his responsibilities towards contraception.[34] On the one hand, this revealed the ways in which male behaviour in working-class streets was subject to community control and female castigation. At the same time, he betrayed only a slight shame at his refusal to use birth control. His dominant feelings were of pride and relish in his power to determine whether or not pregnancy would occur, regardless of the opinions of others, and joy at the conception of the son he wanted:[35]

Woman next door t'us: 'Come here you'. Said 'What's to do?' 'You ought to be ashamed of yourself, you. Putting your wife in family way'. Said 'Oh?' 'Yes', she said, 'have you no more sense? Forty years of age and you're come with another'. You know. Oh she caught me, eh. (laughs) I were chuffed.[36]

Male power to determine contraceptive practice was further reinforced by the dominance of male methods. Whatever family-planning aims a couple may have

---

[33] Colin, msf/kf/bl/#36. Margaret Williamson's oral testimony reveals similar examples of the power that control of method gave men to determine fertility decisions in times of conflict: 'She wouldn't give in, so I did it purposely. I slipped up on purpose', ' "Getting Off at Loftus" ', 13.

[34] On 'gossip networks' which served to regulate public behaviour see Tebbutt, *Women's Talk?*; E. Ross, *Love and Toil*, 59.

[35] It is interesting to compare alternative evidence from earlier periods, in which women complained about their husband's refusal to use contraception because men 'regarded a large family as a public display of their manhood'. Chinn, *They Worked All Their Lives*, 141. See also *New Left View* debate, discussed in Laing, *Representations of Working-Class Life*, 51; Dennis, Henriques and Slaughter, *Coal Is Our Life*; Sigal, *Weekend in Dinlock*.   [36] Colin, msf/kf/bl/#36.

had, it was up to the husband to regularly put them into action. A decision to use condoms required the husband to obtain regular supplies:

After all said and done, as I say, if we'd've, you know, come to agreement it were up to me to to supply 'em, but I never did. I—I don't know, it must've, er, it must've, er—well I must've thought like there we no need really.[37]

A contraceptive strategy that relied upon male-driven methods also placed men in a pivotal position to decide whether or not to employ birth control at the necessary moment. Bryan kept his condoms in his own private drawer and decided each time whether to get one out or not:

I just took charge of it I s'pose . . . Oh, I used to have a special drawer upstairs, yeah, in the bedroom . . . . that was my little drawer (laughs) . . . I used to decide. I used to put one on and that was it.[38]

Alfie pointed out that during each sexual act he made the final decision, at the point of ejaculation, whether or not to withdraw: 'You can feel it coming, and you've got to make up your mind whether you withdraw or let it go.'[39] As Ellen Ross observes, 'sexual intercourse was, in the pre-war generations, actually a fairly difficult point at which a woman could try to prevent conception'.[40] One woman interviewed as part of an oral history of fertility and motherhood among Italian New Yorkers also revealed the difficulty of communication at the point of sex and the resulting male control of such 'decisions': 'A wife couldn't say to her husband "you have to pull back". He has to do it. You can't say that.'[41] For most women, influencing decision-making during sex usually involved passive reminders or exhortations:

Well, if I was having it off with my missus she used to say to me, 'Don't you dare' and I knew what she meant: 'Don't you dare leave it there'. 'Course I didn't. Well, a lot of times I did mind, well, as you know, I've had seven kids.[42]

A system which prized male control of contraception placed women in a position of vulnerability. In extreme cases, where a husband saw the use of contraception as an unwelcome restraint of his sexual power or a challenge to his virility, a wife had limited power to alter his decision.[43] In instances where a husband refused to use birth control, the wife might turn to female methods, enforce a period of abstinence or, in cases of unwanted pregnancy, attempt an abortion. All

---

[37] Frank, msf/srss/bl/#16.   [38] Bryan, msf/kf/ht/#25.   [39] Alfie, bc3ox#35.

[40] See E. Ross, *Love and Toil*, 98, although she argues that contraception was considered neither a male nor a joint responsibility.

[41] Ann Rosen Spector, Susan Cotts Watkins and Alice Goldstein, 'Demographic Patterns and Fertility Behaviour among Jewish and Italian Women in the United States, 1900–1940' unpublished paper presented at the Social Science History Association meetings, New Orleans, 1991, quoted in Santow, 'Coitus Interruptus in the Twentieth Century', 782.   [42] Walter bc2#20.

[43] As Eliot Slater and Moya Woodside concluded, 'women's contraceptive dependence' meant 'withdrawal becomes a weapon' in the hands of a husband able to determine whether and when a pregnancy occurs: *Patterns of Marriage*, 200–1. For additional evidence see the oral history material collected in Higgins, 'Changing Expectations and Realities of Marriage', 233–4.

such options were, however, regarded as unsatisfactory or unworkable. Abortion was perceived as dangerous, abstinence was difficult to achieve for any significant period of time, and female methods of birth control were unpopular. Women had very little power to alter the situation if faced with a husband who rejected the idea that it was his responsibility to employ birth control regularly.

Abstinence, for example, was extremely difficult to enforce. After the birth of her fifth child, Doris finally tried to impose a spell of abstinence on her milkman husband, who had for years refused to use birth control. This strategy lasted three months and was not attempted again:

There were sheaths for men or device for women. And I couldn't use the device for women because of the retroversion and my husband flatly refused to use anything . . . well, the fact was we enjoyed sex and he wouldn't withdraw. In fact, he probably couldn't. And I didn't want him to anyway . . .

So why didn't your husband want to withdraw or use a sheath?
Well, he just said it wasn't the same, you know. And he didn't want to be bothered. Why should he be bothered? We didn't mind have the baby now and again. We didn't really expect five . . . I must say that I used to get scared when he came near me. In fact, after the fifth one we slept separately for about two or three months, I suppose. But that couldn't last anyway.

Female methods were also difficult to use. Doris also tried pessaries and, after an operation on her retroverted womb, caps. Although she succeeded eventually in employing a cap, her husband's objections remained, making the strategy difficult to maintain despite her determination:

There was a family planning clinic you see that I went to and—but there were pessaries that you could use. But then he wouldn't wait for me to do that . . . it was no good me waiting when we felt like to say, 'hold on a minute'—because I think that spoils the spontaneity anyway . . . Then I had the operation. Repair job. And they put the womb right and then after that I could use birth-control devices, you see . . . although he didn't like me wearing it . . . he said he could feel it. But—very sensitive! But I still used it anyway . . . I mean, if he didn't like it that was too bad. I was a bit adamant about that. I was the one having the babies, wasn't I?[44]

This power and the belief on the part of men that it was their right and prerogative to decide whether or not to employ birth control was revealed in middle-class households as well. Antonia was also unable to contest her chartered accountant husband's refusal to use birth control. Like Doris, she was forced to use a cap, which she hated:

He knew I hated what I had and so we did talk about it, but he always refused to use anything himself.

Did you try them?
No.

What about withdrawal? Did you hear about that?
We knew about that but, er, we didn't do it. I mean, as far as he was concerned that wasn't—that wasn't, er, a proper result (pause). And he was supposed to know more about it

[44] Doris, bc3ox#20.

than me and as time went on I became aware that I knew a lot more about a lot of things than he did, but I could never have convinced him.[45]

Using female methods secretly was extremely hard. Helena Wright received a letter from an irate man whose wife had failed to prevent him finding out she had a cap:

you are surely separating a man & wife & robbing two fine little boys of the sight of their father they adore me & I am sure it will harm them when I am gone because they adore me far better than they do their mother. For a Lady to tell any Wife that she can do such a thing . . . that the husband has no choice in the matter at all I never thought that there was a Christian alive like it . . . my wife will never see you again I feel sure.[46]

Abortion was one method which women had the power to attempt, regardless of their husbands' views.[47] Testimony revealed occasions when women from all classes successfully sought an abortion despite their husbands' objections. One man wrote to Marie Stopes asking for advice, as his wife was continuing to attempt to abort, despite the fact that he had, 'pointed out to her the Danger of it all, and forbid her to take any of those Drugs for her own sake'.[48] Ed, a carpenter, 'played hell with' his wife for seeking to abort a pregnancy but she 'didn't want another child' and defiantly took some 'stuff' which 'started her periods off again'.[49] Hubert's wife asked him to obtain an abortifacient for her. When he refused, she took unilateral action, despite his opposition:

Well, my wife urged me to do something about it when the third child was coming. I made enquiries, though I didn't like to. I was advised strongly against it . . . . She was upset— didn't say very much. Tried to get rid of the child by herself.[50]

Other men chose not to voice their hostility, and kept their objections to abortion to themselves. Like many women, some husbands sought to keep the peace when faced with a desperate wife. June's husband, who owned a chain of grocery stores, 'didn't want me to' take an abortifacient but 'wouldn't've gone against it' as 'he wasn't that sort of a man . . . whatever I wished to do'.[51] Esther's husband, an unemployed painter and decorator,

grumbled about me having it . . . he said, 'you shouldn't take it', but I did, I was determined not to have it . . . No, I don't think he was very happy about it, but um we never had words about it . . . you see I think I was so annoyed with him, I blamed him you see, and I think he thought, well, oh let her have her way, you know.

---

[45] Antonia, msf/kf/ht/#35.

[46] Letter to Helena Wright, 24 July 1930, A&M: PP/HRW/B2. Helena Wright was a gynaecologist who specialized in family planning and sex therapy, author of the 1931 *Sex Factor in Marriage* and Chief Medical Officer of the North Kensington Women's Welfare Centre.

[47] Tania McIntosh sees the use of abortion as illustrative of male opposition to contraception, ' "An Abortionist City" ', 94.   [48] Stopes, *Mother England*, 75.

[49] Ed, msf/srss/bl/#23.   [50] Hubert, msf/kf/ht/#32.   [51] June, msf/kf/ht/#27.

Her husband agreed with this portrayal of events: 'You wasn't in a very good humour at the time, so I thought well it suits you . . . that wasn't one of the happiest times in our life, was it?'[52]

However, abortion was widely perceived to be dangerous and was not always successful. Moreover, the general acceptance of male power over contraceptive decision-making was revealed by the number of men who used their dominance to force an abortion on unwilling wives. Dougie suspected that a pregnancy was the product of an affair, and used his control of finances to insist his wife seek an abortion:

And then, a month or two later she said 'I'm pregnant', I said 'Well, it ain't my bugger', just like that (chuckle). I said 'You'd better get rid of it', I said, 'because I'm not keeping any other bugger's child' . . . 'Cos she knew I worn't give her money to keep it. That's one thing I wouldn't do.[53]

Another man, who was at the time unemployed, conducted the operation himself: 'I assumed all responsibility for it . . . I was intelligent enough to know that absolute cleanliness was necessary and I even wore a handkerchief around my mouth . . . immediately afterwards when my wife started to haemorrhage, went round to the local doctor.'[54]

Gender differences in sexual attitudes, roles, and knowledge put the onus on men to take responsibility for contraceptive practice. Most men presented the employment of a regular and effective contraceptive strategy as their duty within marriage. Although frequently this was viewed as the role of a good and sensitive husband, in nearly all cases of conflict between spouses the relationship meant that men could decide which form of birth control was to be used and when. Women had limited abilities to challenge this position, and found their own options for independent action were limited. Abortion, female methods, and abstinence were dangerous, distasteful, or difficult. While many men and women viewed male control of contraception as welcome, we should nevertheless recognize that such responsibility also placed men in a position of dominance, giving them a power that they recognized and sometimes openly enforced.

'I PREFER THE MAN TO HELP':[55] WOMEN'S PREFERENCES AND MALE-DOMINATED BIRTH CONTROL PRACTICES

Women generally accepted and valued male control of contraception. Despite the fact that women were ultimately reliant on husbands to implement any

---

[52] Esther and Jack, bc3ox#13.   [53] Dougie, msf/kf/ht/#5.

[54] Interview with a man courting in the 1920s, 'In the Club', A&M: GC/105/03. On men forcing their partners to try to abort a pregnancy in an earlier period, see Barret-Ducrocq, *Love in the Time of Victoria*, 129–31.   [55] Louisa, bc3ox#14.

contraceptive strategy and severely disadvantaged if their own reproductive aims diverged significantly from those of their spouse, most women were enthusiastic supporters of the gendered division of birth control responsibilities in this period. First, women's acquiescence in the face of male power over contraceptive strategy reflected an acceptance of male authority in marriage generally. Contemporary mores deemed it appropriate for the husband to have the final say in many family decisions. Many women from a variety of social backgrounds frequently placidly sought to avoid conflict and accepted this dominance, seeing it as an unchallengeable element of the husband's role as provider, breadwinner, and head of the household. Secondly, many women viewed male control of contraceptive practice as to their advantage. Many historians have assumed that women welcomed the opportunity to take control of their own fertility. Focusing on the 'sexual and reproductive suffering' of women during the first half of the twentieth century, they have argued that women would have had a strong desire to take responsibility for contraceptive strategy, in order both to control their family size, and to increase their sexual pleasure, now freed from the fear of unwanted pregnancies.[56] Observers at the time similarly regarded contraception as a form of sexual freedom for women whose 'justified dread of unwanted motherhood . . . has held [them] in servitude through the centuries'.[57] Such a conclusion ignores the costs involved for women in challenging male control of contraception. This is because it mistakenly views birth control as a domestic and female concern, associated with women's sphere of influence—the family—and ignores the sexual connotations of the subject.[58] Most women in this period, except in very highly educated, intellectual, or bohemian circles, adopted a sexual identity which prized sexual innocence and passivity. They were therefore reluctant to impose a female-led strategy which would have meant openly addressing sexual issues and would have appeared to them as sexually demeaning and immodest. Any active role in birth control contravened women's attempts to appear naive. Open discussion of the issue embarrassed them, and any direct role in implementing methods challenged their sexual passivity. However, women were not powerless to influence contraceptive strategy. Using subtle, indirect, and euphemistic tactics, many were able to state their views, put pressure on their husbands to act, and achieve their

---

[56] E. Ross, *Love and Toil*, 101; Holtzman, 'The Pursuit of Married Love'; Brooke, 'Gender and Working Class Identity', 782–3; Degler, *At Odds*. On the other hand, Angus McLaren argues that 'increased sophistication of contraceptives' in fact increased the 'fear of unwanted pregnancy' as the belief in the possibility of the 'perfect regulation of reproduction' made an 'unexpected pregnancy' 'all the more frightening': *A History of Contraception*, 244. Enid Charles even suggests that men had a greater desire to avoid pregnancy than their wives; whereas maternity brought women certain compensations, children burdened men with 'economic responsibilities': *The Practice of Birth Control*, 175.

[57] Clephane, *Towards Sex Freedom*, 220; see also Florence, *Birth Control on Trial*, 51, 104.

[58] See Gittins, *Fair Sex*, 161. Similarly, David Levine sees contraception as a 'woman's responsibility because 'she was responsible for most aspects of domestic life': *Reproducing Families*, 208.

reproductive aims effectively. Moreover, women saw little need to oppose male contraceptive practice. By the 1920s, most women could confidently anticipate that their husbands would implement birth control much of the time. Rather than seeing themselves as disadvantaged, many women saw their husbands' assumption of a dominant role as to their personal benefit.

'You just went along with it'[59]

Male authority over contraception reflected women's wider toleration of male power within marriage during this period. In all classes the question of marital power was contested and fraught. In some working-class homes the wife was given considerable influence in most 'domestic' decisions. Elizabeth Roberts makes this case particularly forcefully, arguing that in some families women were 'financial, household and family managers'.[60] In others, couples claimed to make 'joint decisions', while in others the man was positioned as an unchallengeable authority. Underlying all these different patterns of marital relationships, however, was an acceptance of the husband as provider and as head of the household. In this context, many women, in a variety of households in rural, urban, and suburban settings, saw their husbands' role in managing a contraceptive strategy as appropriate and reasonable. Despite this widespread acceptance of male dominance, during the 1930s some women were contesting existing gender roles and were reconsidering the allocation of responsibilities in some specific areas of domestic life. Yet it is important to recognize that women sought to adjust the gendered power dynamics of marriage in only minor ways, often desiring limited assistance with household chores, family leisure activities, and childcare. Significantly, women did not contest the man's role as prime decision-maker. Far from resenting their marriages as unequal, restricting, or subordinating, woman believed in a degree of male authority and willingly maintained it in their own personal relationships.[61]

Male control of decision-making was widely accepted: Maggie 'always relied on him for giving me the go on'; Emily 'was soft' and allowed her husband to 'tread on' her—'e decided everything'; and Sally's 'wasn't a pansy' and 'wouldn't be ordered about'.[62] In middle-class households too, male power was seen as both justified and acceptable and as one of the benefits of being the breadwinner: 'He was very much the boss. I like being told what to do—and he was the breadwinner.'[63]

---

[59] Sarah, msf/kf/bl/#30.

[60] Roberts, *Women and Families*, 83. Similarly, Carl Chinn claims that 'a hidden matriarchy dominated the way of life of the urban poor of England': *They Worked All Their Lives*, 23.

[61] See Bell and Newby, 'Husbands and Wives', on the internalization and acceptance by both men and women of unequal power relations and gendered roles, the legitimization of power through consent, and the description of 'institutionalised male supremacy' in Gillespie, 'Who Has the Power?', 457–8. See also the acceptance of male authority revealed in Ayres and Lambertz, 'Marriage Relations, Money and Domestic Violence'.

[62] Maggie, bc2#22; Emily, msf/kf/bl/#13; Sally, msf/kf/bl/#31.   [63] Gill, msf/kf/bl/#48.

Even those who initially presented their marital decision-making as joint and consensual concurred with this view. Many husbands presented themselves as listening to their wives' opinions, but only when it suited them. Ultimately, they assumed the right to accept or reject their spouses' point of view. Lorna initially described her marriage as one in which 'everything' was discussed:

My marriage were a happy one . . . we'd pull together and work together . . . You've to trust one another—work together, give and take—no use always taking . . . we discussed everything . . . er, er, any money matters . . . everything were discussed.

However, Lorna subsequently revealed that her husband was not to be 'tied down'. She complained that he did not 'realize what his wife wants' and expected to have his own way:

He couldn't . . . I don't believe in tying a man down—'you can't do this' and 'you can't do that'—but you'd—on the other hand, a chap has to, er, er, realize what his wife wants—that wants some thought—and don't be greedy and have it all your way—just—just work together and it does work. I did all the housework, he never . . . he tried to, he'd do the housework and he said to me 'Do you know—you know cock, it never looks like it's been done like you do it when I do it'.[64]

Although Thomas championed his own and his wife's ability to come to a compromise solution, his depiction of such disputes revealed his assumption that he had the final say: 'we didn't always agree on things, we always used to come to a compromise'. This meant 'if she thought I was in the wrong, she'd tell me'. Yet if Thomas 'thought she was in the wrong I'd bloody tell her . . . "Now shut up, don't want to hear no more about it—that, right?" And that was that.'[65]

Despite the general acceptance of male control over decision-making, many women were unhappy with some specific aspects of the male role and wished to modify their husbands' behaviour. Their dissatisfaction focused on the division of domestic labour, where women sought a little more consideration of the burdens of running a household. Lilian's husband was an accountant:

He wouldn't do much in the house and I used to say to him, 'I'm not your skivvy mind. I'm your wife!' That sort of thing, you know. And he began to realize, well, course when he was away—he was an officer in the Forces—'course he had somebody to wait on him. He had nothing to do! He had somebody to wait on him. Well, when he came home I suppose he thought it was going to be the same thing and he thought I was going to do it, see. He didn't, he had the wrong one! (laughs) I said 'No, I'm not your skivvy.' I said 'If you want it, you get it. I'm not your skivvy.' I said 'I'm your wife', (laughs) always remember that. But he realized after and he used to apologize sometime and he used to say, 'Oh well, course I forget'. He said 'I'm used to being waited on, and I've forgotten.' And I said 'You gotta come down to earth now!' (laughs)[66]

---

[64] Lorna, msf/kf/bl/#25.   [65] Thomas, bc3sw#11.

[66] Lilian, bc3sw#24. The experiences of the Second World War had a profound effect on many individuals' marriage relationships and attitudes towards sexual issues. For a full analysis of these in relation to the oral history material see Szreter and Fisher, 'Sexuality, Love and Marriage in England, 1918–1960'.

Yet such attempts were often limited in their success. Women frequently reported that men were only prepared to modify their behaviour in response to these demands to a very limited degree. Pam, who had been a parlour maid before she was married, was frustrated at her husband's refusal to help in the home and his regular attendance at the pub:

I used to say, oh, why don't you stop at home sometimes? . . . I used to think, yeah, you're enjoying yourself, I'm not, sitting here on my own . . . . I said once about washing-up, I said, 'Oh, you can wipe up', he said 'That's a woman's job.' (laughs) No he wouldn't help me.[67]

In a context of declining middle-class use of domestic staff such tensions were equally apparent in middle-class marriages. Esme also found attempts to 'domes-ticate' her husband, who was a board manager, were futile and might backfire:

ESME   I went out once on my own a year and that was to do the Christmas shopping. Now that I did resent. I really wanted to go out more on my own but you see, er, Gerald wasn't—his generation didn't believe that it was necessary for him to look after the children—so that I would have some freedom—at all. And on the one occasion when I did go out one year, when I came back it was absolute mayhem. They'd enjoyed it all right but, you know, there were nappies every-where that—you know, it was as though a typhoon struck the place. So I was doubly punished as it were, not that he intended to punish me . . . You put up with it, you struggled on regardless, you know. The idea was that the man had to go to work, he had to support you and therefore you had got to do your bit, you'd got to keep the home together, you'd got to cook the meals and do the shopping and do the—all the chores and look after the children and er, er, and um, his reac—his um, responsibilities ended there.

GERALD   You see in the background the ordinary chap about the house didn't have any-thing to do with domestic science . . . the unfairness of the situation might have been noted but it didn't get home to the point of me doing something about it—knowing I had to ought to—because it was quite foreign to my background.[68]

In addition, some women felt that asking their husbands to do too much was emasculating and demeaning. Catherine, despite wishing that her husband, a watchmaker, was 'a bit more domesticated', hating the fact that 'he was the boss' who 'expected you to be in the kitchen' and getting 'real mad if he was sitting, watching the television and there were jobs to do', nevertheless did not try and get him to do more. She was determined not to be like her neighbour, who treated her husband 'like dirt, belittling him and nagging him and all that sort of thing'.[69] Elma 'never asked' her husband, a policeman, to do more, as she did not 'believe in a man being a slave in the house, no'.[70] Men might equally be embarrassed to be

---

[67] Pam, msf/kf/ht/#19.   [68] Gerald and Esme, msf/kf/ht/#9.
[69] Catherine, msf/kf/ht/#1.   [70] Elma, msf/jm/bl/#42.

seen engaged in domestic work. Even in cases where men were domesticated, their reluctance to admit to this was testament to a culture in which it was seen as inappropriate for men to be engaged in household chores. Grace's husband sought to hide the fact that he sometimes dried the dishes from his overly domesticated brother, with whom he worked in the family engineering business:

Colin would dry the dishes and he used to say, 'Look sharp' if our Chris knocks at door, he said, 'I don't want him watch—catching me drying the dishes'. And his brother were making bread and doing everything, but Colin wasn't a bit domesticated . . . he liked a pint.[71]

There was a limit to the extent to which women wanted to modify male behaviour. Indeed, many wives prided themselves on their ability to cook and clean for their husbands unaided, and did not want their husbands to take on more domestic tasks. Martha 'liked 'im to get out for a night on his own . . . you don't expect them to do a lot when they come home, well I don't think so anyway, always 'ad a meal ready when they came 'ome at night'. Nor was labourer Frank's wife likely to have been unaware of or unaffected by his praise of her housekeeping skills: 'She were really good to the extent that believe me er I never lifted a spoon . . . if I put that kettle on in there I'd set fire to it, that's how much I know about cooking, she cooked everything.'[72] For some women, their pride in keeping the house was often measured by the extent to which their skills precluded the need for their husbands to be involved in the domestic sphere at all. Moreover, being the only one capable of running the home gave them a sense of power. Roger, a chartered surveyor, presented his wife as instigator of a clear division of labour within the home:

So what were your different duties around the house?
I never had any. She wouldn't give me any. She—I said 'Shall I do this?' 'No', she said, 'you go out working', she said, 'I'll do the house'.[73]

Women's attitudes towards this division between the husband's and wife's roles were shaped by conflicting desires.[74] While many sought assistance in the home, at the same time they did not admire excessively domesticated men and saw the exercise of male dominance as legitimate, reasonable, and even admirable. These opposing desires were most clearly revealed by Maria, who married a painter and decorator in Blackburn in 1940. She recognized that she had married an

---

[71] Grace, msf/srss/ht/#38. This attitude may explain the tension, described by Joanna Bourke, between the evidence for men's regular involvement in household chores and the dominant assertion that housework was women's work, conducted only by 'meek' and effeminate men: Bourke, *Working-Class Cultures*, 83. Ellen Ross recognizes that many men hide their involvement in domestic activities such as cleaning, childcare, laundry, and even sewing, darning, or knitting: Ross, *Love and Toil*, 69. Lella Secor Florence also observed men knitting in pubs in the 1950s: *Our Private Lives*, 39.

[72] Frank, msf/srss/bl/#16. [73] Roger, msf/kf/ht/#10.

[74] On the inherent conflict between contested models of marriage during the nineteenth and twentieth centuries see Hammerton, *Cruelty and Companionship*, 75.

undomesticated man because she wanted a 'hard', 'manly', 'gangster type'. She scorned 'feminine' men, like her sister's husband, who would allow themselves to be bossed around by a woman and were prepared to do anything in the house. At the same time, she wished her husband was more domesticated and less obstinate:

What sort of father was your husband?
Well, he wasn't one who would push a pram type, you know, he wouldn't. As she got older he would take her up on the fair and things like that. But um—like today married life seems to be with couples that they all share it. But them days it was like the women that did everything . . . Well, I used to think really that you should share and share alike but that never happened here. As I say, he would just bring his wage home and thought he'd done his bit then, you know.

Did you ever try to get him to do more?
Oh I tried but I never succeeded.

What was it about gangster types that you liked?
Well, they weren't like soft men really, you know, it's—as I say my sister—her husband did everything for her, but he'd been in the um Navy and he could wash, iron, cook, sew, do anything and Graham could do nothing, only paint.

Why did you like that?
Well, er, sometimes I used to wish I had a bit of help, you know, you got a bid fed up sometimes. But he never changed.

Did you try to get him to change?
Well, I used to try, yes, but it made no difference. In fact, one year, what had happened— he'd left some clothes hanging about and I threw them all down the stairs and do you know, we walked over them for a week and in the end I had to give in and pick them up, he wouldn't. Just being obstinate really.

. . .

But she used to give him orders, me sister, you know 'Do this, do that.'—weren't my cup of tea . . . I wouldn't like a man like me sister had, because I mean he would do everything for you.[75]

Many women accepted a man's refusal to co-operate with requests for domestic help as justified. Eileen, while clearly resenting the fact that her husband refused to let her go to work, never complained that he would not help around the house: 'He kept me at 'ome, I 'adn't to go to work, so I thought it was my job, get on with it, why should I grumble, it's my job.'[76] Eva, who married a Lancashire mechanic in 1934, also thought that it was unreasonable to want more help in the house:

Did you ever wish your husband did more domestically?
Eh, not really I, no 'ow could I? Because 'e, 'e did everything like as—I 'ad no bills to pay, 'e could do everything really, no, but sometimes eh—men in them days they didn't, eh, do much in the houses—domestic way, no, but they provided, 'e were a good provider.[77]

---

[75] Maria, msf/kf/bl/#8.   [76] Eileen, msf/kf/bl/#12.   [77] Eva, msf/kf/bl/#11.

Some women did wish that their men had taken a more 'joint' approach to aspects of marital life. However, they frequently presented this desire as an unworkable fantasy which might in fact be detrimental to a happy union. Agatha, who worked as a parlour maid throughout her marriage, wished she had a husband like those in romance novels who, 'did everything for them and shared everything and did everything to make them happy', but portrayed this as an unrealistic whimsy: 'that's the trouble with love stories, it puts you off a bit . . . they make them so . . . you think, oh dear, if only my hubby had been like that, sort of thing'.[78]

Male power in marriage was, therefore, sometimes contested. In particular, women wished for more domestic assistance, but imposed their own limits on the extent to which they expected men to co-operate and experienced considerable difficulties in persuading them to help at all. Most continued to accept the man's role as prime decision-maker. Even marriages which valued 'joint' decision-making gave the final word to the husband.[79] Despite recognizing the ways in which their own views were marginalized by existing gender roles, women did not seek a radical redistribution of gender divisions in household responsibilities or a reassignment of marital authority. Their acceptance of male control of contraception needs to be viewed in this context: many women revealed a reluctance to challenge the contraceptive strategy adopted by their husbands, even if they disagreed with it. Elizabeth Draper argued that women in 1965 were unable 'to raise the subject of contraception' as this was 'to invade the area in which he is dominant'; 'while refusing to take any steps themselves [they] will accept any method which is used by their husband as part of his dominant role in which he makes the decisions and takes the initiative', because they felt 'inferior to men and they admire "maleness" '.[80] His position as head of household was used to indicate that they should not defy him, and many placidly sought to avoid marital conflict. Sarah revealed that her husband, an upholsterer, had 'more say' in the question of family planning and the choice of method used, 'because he didn't want a lot of children'

---

[78] Agatha, msf/kf/ht/#7.

[79] Meg Luxton found that men in Manitoba in the 1970s and 1980s did not expect to help with domestic labour and could not be persuaded since such action was outside the bounds of acceptable behaviour: 'Two Hands for the Clock', 405, 412.

[80] Draper, *Birth Control in the Modern World*, 123. Some male respondents, such as Tim, msf/srss/bl/#19, professed to be unaware of their spouses' views on their contraceptive behaviour, only commenting that 'there were never any grumbles'. Studies in other countries provide interesting comparative material: Lee Rainwater's work in the United States also portrayed working-class women as fully accepting their husband's dominance as they were keen to avoid disputes or even discussions. This reflected, he concluded, their inability to 'assert' themselves: 'The middle ground of negotiation, give and take, and mutual understanding requires both too much faith in the basic goodness of men and too much assertiveness on the woman's part to be readily considered': Rainwater, *And the Poor Get Children*, 73. Recent research in India has also revealed that 'traditional beliefs' and the assumption that 'husbands should provide guidance to their wives' translated into an acceptance of male dominance in family-planning decisions: see Karra, Stark, and Wolf, 'Male Involvement in Family Planning', 30–2.

and 'he was the one who was bringing the money in . . . It were Jeffrey's choice. [pause] . . . you just went along with it.'[81] Iris said 'I'd like another one.' Her husband, a railway porter, refused, saying 'You've got enough', a conclusion she accepted since 'that's how we got on, I never fell out with 'im about anything'.[82] A teacher, married in 1911, wondered 'Was I consulted?' about the decision to use birth control after the birth of a son. She concluded: 'It is hard to say. It was so much taken for granted that I should acquiesce in such matters that decisions were announced as if we had both made them.'[83] Similarly, Felicity, who worked as a school secretary once her children started school, did not wish to challenge her Catholic husband's refusal to use contraceptive devices: 'he was so good in other ways that I went along with it'.[84] Antonia, daughter of a solicitor, viewed her husband as intellectually superior and assumed that he knew more about birth control than she did. She felt unable to confront his refusal to use contraception and his insistence that she continue using the cap that she hated:

I think you didn't talk about that [sex] because the man was supposed to know all about it and to do, you know, what was supposed to be done and therefore you didn't argue with him you assumed he was right. Which was the case in quite a lot of things. I remember him saying to me once quite seriously that women had smaller brains than men. And, at the time, I hate to tell you, I believed it. But later on I learnt better (laughs) . . . it was me that took the steps. I mean I used to have this Dutch cap which I hated . . . because condoms . . . lessened your pleasure and were much more of a nuisance . . . and he simply wouldn't have used them.[85]

In many households male use of birth control was presented as part of male marital dominance more generally. Edith summed this up: she was grateful that her husband, a shop assistant, took control of contraceptive decisions, but nevertheless recognized that this was a reflection of his dominance in the home. She expressed some resentment at his lack of domestication, but the use of birth control was a more welcome aspect of his authority:

No, he wasn't a bit domesticated, um, one thing I used to hate and that was washing up, and that's about all he would do. Men years ago did not take part in the home. They didn't, I mean when I see now all the young men out with the children in their pushchairs and you can see they know how to do the washing, they know how to make a meal—but our husbands never—never took on . . . You had to wait on your men and that was how it was those days. A man was a man and a woman had to do her job, like you know. Yeah . . .

The responsibility for limiting children seems to have been placed . . .

On the man, yes, it was. Yes it was it was placed on the man. But today you see the girls take over, don't they? It always was a man's world, a woman always had to do what she was told or be used when she was wanted. You didn't ask for it like, you know, oh you didn't say, oh I'd like to go to bed, I mean that's a thing you didn't do, because the first thing they'd

[81] Sarah, msf/kf/bl/#30.   [82] Iris, msf/kf/bl/#2; see also E. Ross, *Love and Toil*, 70.
[83] Mass-Observation, DR 1075, reply to March 1944 Directive.
[84] Felicity, msf/kf/bl/#37.   [85] Antonia, msf/kf/ht/#35.

think—I think—because they did—you wouldn't dare look at anybody else like or go about with anybody else like or make arrangements to meet anybody else like because they'd kill you. There was fear, you didn't take advantage, because they would have it out on you like.

But it was your husband who decided that you should only have, not very many children?
Yes, he decided yeah.[86]

'I'm not going to behave like a loose woman'[87]

Women's determination to leave contraceptive decision-making to their husbands does not simply reflect their acceptance of male authority in marriage. Birth control was an area where many women explicitly rejected the need for more female influence or responsibility. Whereas in some areas of domestic life women challenged male roles, albeit in limited and minor ways, they did not seek to question male control of contraception.

Historians view it as self-evident that women would not have viewed male control of contraception as in their interests. First, they see it as obvious that women would have wanted to take responsibility for their own fertility and family size, as they carried the heaviest burden of childrearing. Secondly, they argue that women would have wanted more fulfilling sex lives: this would have required female control of contraception as male dominance of both strategy and method left women constantly fearful of pregnancy and unable to take pleasure from the experience.[88]

Most women did not share either of these two assumptions. Although women usually took greater responsibility for children, most did not see birth control as a domestic matter, associated with family size or childrearing, but rather a sexual one. Many women during this period shied away from the open articulation of sexual matters. Whereas women might have been prepared to challenge men about some domestic issues, organizing birth control, unlike washing up, changing nappies, or cooking, meant taking on too explicit a sexual persona. As Busfield and Paddon argued, 'We had the impression that for the wife to be held to have the main responsibility for birth control the issue has to be defined more as one of having children, than of sex.'[89] Women's sexual reticence meant that they were

---

[86] Edith, bc2#23.   [87] Hubert, msf/kf/ht/#32.
[88] See e.g. R. Hall (ed.), *Dear Dr. Stopes*; Davey, 'Birth Control in Britain during the Inter-War Years'; Faulkner, ' "Powerless to prevent him" '. Histories of sexuality are dominated by images of unfulfilling marital sex: Ellen Ross highlights 'female sexual and reproductive suffering' (*Love and Toil*, 101); Ross McKibbin argues that men 'rarely expected a sexual response from their wives and some thought it unnatural when it occurred' (*Classes and Cultures*, 298); Elizabeth Roberts's oral history found that 'no hint was ever made that women might have enjoyed sex' (*A Woman's Place*, 84). However she does quote one example which hints that a slightly different interpretation might be afforded her respondents: 'He didn't do it so often but when he did he made a good job of it' (ibid. 96).
[89] Busfield and Paddon, *Thinking about Children*, 248. They maintain that women were involved in decisions about family size and spacing, if not about the negotiation of the specifics of sex and

keen to delegate direct and overt determination of contraceptive strategy to someone else.

Furthermore, most women did not see the control of contraception as sexually empowering or liberating, as historians have suggested. Certainly some did acknowledge the disadvantages of letting men take control of contraception; their reliance on their spouse, combined with the perceived unreliability of the methods he might use, fostered anxieties which often marred the experience of sexual intercourse. Fearful of pregnancy, many women reported an inhibitory inability to 'relax' and enjoy the experience. However, historians have often ignored the fact that despite these disadvantages women did not view taking control of contraception as a positive step: although trusting to men had its costs, taking responsibility would have been even costlier. For women, taking control of contraception meant talking about sex, preparing for sex, and adopting a sexual persona, steps which most women in this period would not countenance. Their sexual identity was bound up with passively receiving the sexual attentions of men. They hoped, upon marriage, to find a skilled lover, but did not complain or feel unlucky if they did not. Only rarely would they try to improve relations. With regard to birth control, seeking openly to improve one's sex life by opting to take control of contraception directly contravened this passive identity and was unthinkable for many. Thus most women preferred to accept the status quo—which meant the possibility of unsatisfactory sex—rather than take the lead and take responsibility for birth control.

This is not to argue that most sexual relationships were passionless or unfulfilling. In fact, women could accept their passive role, refusing to initiate contraceptive practice or openly seeking sexual pleasure, precisely because husbands saw the enhancement of the erotic possibilities of marriage as their job. Many men were extremely keen on arousing female pleasure, and professed to measure their masculinity through the discovery of sexual techniques they perceived as good for their partner. It was usually men who claimed disappointment if the match was sexually unhappy.[90] Moreover, husbands sometimes used birth control precisely because they thought it would remove their wives' fears of pregnancy and thus enhance her pleasure. Thus, far from viewing control of contraception as in their interests, women actively preserved a system of male control and interpreted the expectation that men would take responsibility for contraception as to their advantage.

contraception. See also David Sills, who criticized reports of family-planning officials and researchers who present 'sexual intercourse [as] comparable in emotional significance to cooking or washing clothes': 'Discussion', *Public Opinion Quarterly*, 28 (1964), 389–92, quoted in E. Rogers, *Communication Strategies*, 36.

[90] Lesley Hall argues that an emphasis on mutual sexual pleasure and on the effort needed to attain it was a new development of the inter-war period, and that many men 'appreciated the message': 'Impotent Ghosts', 62. Helen Hacker observed that in the 1950s in America virility was increasingly measured 'in terms of the ability to evoke a full sexual response on the part of the female': 'The New Burdens of Masculinity', 231.

Historians assume that birth control was seen as a domestic issue, linked to childbearing and childrearing. In so doing they categorize birth control as a female topic, associated with the woman's area of concern: the family. Thus they define the limitation of family size as central to the wife's role within the family unit. Most women, by contrast, defined birth control as a sexual matter rather than a domestic one. Stella divorced herself from all aspects of birth control decision-making and management. She regarded such issues as part of a different 'department' of life than having children: 'I loved having my children, I simply adore them, but with regards that department I'm not very interested, I don't know why, but I'm not.'[91]

The sexual connotations of birth control meant that, unlike family issues, it was an embarrassing topic. Many women regarded sex as so private an issue that they did not want to discuss it even with their own partners. Thus they were deeply reluctant to engage openly with any aspect of birth control strategy. The working-class women quoted below were typical in linking their decision to leave contraception to their husband to the embarrassment caused by the vulgar, sexual nature of the topic:

I think we all felt like that . . . I think in those days they used to leave it to the men, um, the women probably, you know, thought it was a bit embarrassing to (giggles) be thinking about that sort of—even thinking about having the sex (giggles) in a way. One didn't talk about it.[92]

I don't like talking about this thing [birth control], its a bit vulgar. But that's what they used to do, so you wouldn't have children . . . the men knew what to do—didn't need telling . . . you didn't talk about, er, you didn't talk about sex, you—you kept s-s-sex like to yourself, private.[93]

I'd've never've done it, no I think I were, ooh no, no . . . I just couldn't've done it . . . I've never been brought up that way. See, we never discussed, what went on in your bedroom was in your bedroom . . . he wouldn't come home and say smutty things to me . . . I don't know how James felt . . . it's a things as we never talked about . . . I couldn't've gone in a chemist so it were up to him . . . so he had to self-control.[94]

Middle-class women expressed similar sentiments. Indeed, concurrence in many middle-class as well as working-class homes that birth control was ideally a husband's responsibility, despite the considerable differences in material, economic, and social existences and the widely documented differences in domestic ideologies, should be interpreted as indicative of birth control's position as a sexual rather than domestic matter. Notions of female sexual respectability were allied in all communities to privacy, naivety, and passivity. Joanna, a secretary whose husband was a civil servant, like her working-class counterparts also left all the practicalities of birth control practice to her husband, and presented herself as too embarrassed to talk about it with anyone. The display of conjugal dynamics

[91] Stella, bc3ox#11. [92] Catherine, msf/kf/ht/#1. [93] Jennie, msf/kf/bl/#27.
[94] Lorna, msf/kf/bl/#25.

within the interview itself reflected the way in which her husband had taken responsibility for 'embarrassing' matters, and showed sensitivity to his wife by keeping his arrangements to himself and not forcing her to address issues that gave her discomfort:

MARK   She's shy, she's shy about that.
JOANNA   I never discussed it with anyone . . . Its too embarrassing now . . .
MARK   I think I've embarrassed Joanna.
JOANNA   Well, I'm not embarrassed exactly but (laughs) difficult to—this—talk about it . . .
MARK   We knew what each other wanted, I knew Joanna didn't want to get pregnant . . . I didn't discuss it.[95]

Appearing passive during sexual encounters was central to many women's notion of respectability.[96] Preparing for sex by taking control of contraception contravened this role. For many women then, as Sue Lees claimed remained the case after the 1960s, taking control of contraception forced a woman to question 'the patriarchal definition of her as innately responsive to male initiative, as reactive rather than pro-active' and 'conflicts with popular ideas of romantic spontaneity and implicitly labels them as slags'.[97] One woman courting in the 1950s 'felt terrible' going to a clinic because 'it was as if you enjoyed sex . . . I didn't ever discuss it. If I said I was using a contraceptive . . . wouldn't people think that I did really enjoy making love to my husband and wasn't that not quite nice?'[98] Lella Secor Florence reported the extent to which women were embarrassed by the need to insert caps, sometimes 'in the bedroom with her husband present'.[99] Angela linked her rejection of female methods to her 'prim and proper' attitude towards sex and her husband agreed, calling her 'puritanical':

ANGELA   I'm very prim and proper . . . that kind of thing I'm not very good or, err, certainly doing things like that to your body.
BERT   You're too puritanical about sexual relations. You're so, she's so innocent, ah, unbelievably innocent, she really is.[100]

Many women saw the articulation of sexual matters as embarrassing and vulgar, and resisted taking an active role in contraceptive responsibility for fear it would damage their respectability. Yet women's determination to leave the practicalities of birth control management to husbands incurred certain other costs. Sexual

[95] Mark and Joanna, msf/kf/ht/#22.

[96] Many women had found that rebutting male advances had been key to their appeal and respectability during courtship. What 'first attracted' the friend of one Mass-Observation panellist 'to his wife, was that when he tried to become too familiar she smacked his face, apparently it was his first rebuff'. Mass-Observation, DR 2751, reply to April 1944 Directive. On courtship see also Szreter and Fisher, 'Sexuality, Love and Marriage in England, 1918–1960'; Bourke, *Working-Class Cultures*, 30–1; Giles, ' "Playing hard to get" '; Gillis, *For Better, For Worse*, 267–84.

[97] Lees, *Sugar and Spice*, 199–200.   [98] 'In the Club', A&M: GC/105/45.

[99] Florence, *Progress Report on Birth Control*, 129   [100] Angela and Hugh, msf/kf/ht#18.

experiences were often described as having been marred by anxiety, and many remained fearful that birth control might not be used or might fail. However, women's determination to preserve an innocent and silent sexual persona was more powerful than any desire to improve sexual relations by taking fertility control into their own hands. Control of reproduction and the ability to control their own bodies was not an aim for most women in the 1930s and 1940s; indeed, it was actively rejected by many.[101]

A number of women did link their fear of pregnancy and the inadequacies of contraceptive methods to their lack of sexual satisfaction. Moya Woodside argued in 1946 that fear of pregnancy was the cause of much sexual maladjustment and 'destroyed' many marriage relationships.[102] For Lyn the 'real fear' of pregnancy 'overruled the sexual feelings'; June 'wouldn't climax' and couldn't 'let go' since she 'was always afraid' and Agatha got 'a nice feeling now and again' but not 'very often . . . because I was tense all the time, scared I was gonna 'ave a baby'.[103] Despite such experiences, women did not seek to improve sexual relations by taking responsibility for birth control and thereby lessening the fear of pregnancy. Rather than fuelling a female desire to take their fertility into their own hands, female sexual dissatisfaction did not produce any opposition to the male culture of contraception. In fact, this was due to women's sexual identity: the importance of remaining passive meant that, although sexual pleasure might be welcome, it could never be actively solicited. An understanding of women's sexual identity undermines the argument that women sought control of contraception as a step towards more fulfilling sexual experiences. Since women did not actively seek sexual pleasure and since they saw any attempt to do so a contravention of their sexual persona, many had a strong inclination to avoid any direct involvement in determining contraceptive strategy.

Women's notions of sexual passivity meant that few presented themselves as ever having sought out pleasurable sex.[104] This of course does not mean that women necessarily had unsatisfactory sex lives. For Marilyn, for example, it 'were the best thing'. She and her husband had a 'very good sex life'; it 'were exciting, very nice. I've missed it, you know in all these years.'[105] Rather, women, whether or not they had fulfilling or unfulfilling sexual experiences, were part of a culture which expected them to present sex as a conjugal duty and to use a language of sexual obligation rather than pleasure.[106] Women, especially among the working

---

[101] See also Cook, *The Long Sexual Revolution*, 111.

[102] Woodside, 'Health and Happiness in Marriage'. This was an initial summary of the survey, full results of which were published as *Patterns of Marriage*, with Eliot Slater, in 1951. E. L. Packer found that wives seeking marriage guidance usually expressed 'indifference and dislike of sexual intercourse': 'Aspects of Working-Class Marriage', 98.

[103] Lyn, msf/kf/bl/#1; June msf/kf/ht/#27; Agatha msf/kf/ht/#7.

[104] Judy Giles argues that women's self-representation in this period focused on 'femininity as apparently non-sexual': ' "Playing hard to get" ', 251.　　　　[105] Marilyn, msf/kf/bl/#7.

[106] Indeed, it is perhaps a mistake to present women who saw sex as a marital duty and women who 'enjoyed' it as at opposite ends of a spectrum: for some women the pleasure of sexual intercourse

classes, were rarely enthusiastic about describing their sexual lives. As Slater and Woodside found, comments about sexual enjoyment were frequently reserved: 'I do enjoy it', 'there's a certain amount of pleasure attached'.[107]

Doris rather grudgingly admitted having enjoyed sex, preferring to stress that she had to put up with it. Her testimony stands in sharp contrast to her husband's explicit enthusiasm:

IVOR   . . . when you have sex, the man comes climax, and the woman climax. Well when you climax—you don't climax—you stop before you climax, and that stops you having children. And that's something else you've learnt! (laughs) I don't think so!

DORIS   Yeah. You've got to be careful.

. . .

IVOR   One would probably climax before the other, like, you know, so, we always— recent years like—we always enjoyed sex, didn't we, Doris?

DORIS   Yeah (with emphasis), yeah. (pause) Part of married life which you gotta, you don't take for granted, but I mean, er—there's things you gotta put up with, isn't it?

. . .

So would you say it was something you enjoyed?

DORIS   Well, I did enjoy it, yeah. I can't say I didn't.[108]

Despite admitting that she had had 'her moments', Nellie also chose to stress that she was not a 'sexy' person:

Did you enjoy sex as well sometimes?

Not always, because I was not a sexy person.[109] But there were occasions, yes, I've had my moments, I'm not saying I haven't, but, er, there were times I did it out of duty, like . . .

---

was intimately connected to their perception that they dutifully provided their husbands with sexual access. One interviewee recalled that, despite being extremely tired after the birth of her first child, their sex life did not reduce in frequency as she 'still considered it my duty to love my husband, and I still wanted to': Angela and Hugh, msf/kf/ht/#18. One woman wrote to Marie Stopes for advice on 'how to live my married life naturally fulfilling wifely duties', without running the risk of pregnancy: Stopes, *Mother England*, 2. It is important to recognize women's commitment to indulging what they perceived as their husbands' sexual needs and desires. Letters to Marie Stopes, for example, reveal both women's recognition that abstinence could not be maintained for long periods of time, but also their positive acceptance of the sexual role demanded of wives, whatever their own personal or individual reaction to the experience: 'my husband is a normal man, he is wonderfully good to me and always has been, and I have been no Wife to him for two years. How he restrains himself I dont know, I am sorry my health is so poor for his sake because he is so kind': Stopes, *Mother England*, 68.

107   Slater and Woodside, *Patterns of Marriage*, 31–68. They found one-third of women 'always' experienced orgasm, and one-tenth never experienced it. Lee Rainwater grouped female responses to questions about sexual enjoyment into three categories: those who made very positive statements about enjoyment, those for whom enjoyment was not emphasized, and those who expressed negative attitudes. See Rainwater, 'Marital Sexuality in Four Cultures of Poverty', 461.

108   Doris and Ivor, bc3sw#29.

109   'Sexy' was almost universally used to mean sexual rather than sexually attractive.

By contrast, she presented her husband as 'a greedy so-and-so':

I mean, he used to say to me 'If God made anything better, he'd kept it to himself,' . . . he used to say to me, 'You never ask me for it?' I said 'I don't get a chance.' Which I didn't. My God, he well supplied me! More than what I wanted.[110]

Louisa also clearly had a satisfactory sex life, but had no access to a positive language of enjoyment which might describe what she had experienced:

Did you enjoy it?
I enjoyed it sometimes, sometimes you lose contact and don't enjoy it—just a waste of time, but more often than not I used to—nice feeling to have—unusual feeling.[111]

Some middle-class women expressed similar views. The notion that sexual intercourse was a marital obligation was particularly well developed in working-class narratives; nevertheless middle-class voices were just as concerned not to be seen to desire sex openly or independently of male seduction, despite the growing rhetoric of female pleasure in elite, bohemian, and sexological circles. Gay also had low expectations of sex within marriage and did not think to try and improve her experiences: 'I wasn't that enamoured of it . . . sex happened when he felt like it and . . . I didn't think I was missing out really because I wasn't—you know—I hadn't found anything to be madly keen about.'[112]

Many women saw sexual pleasure as an unpredictable by-product of intercourse, but not as a goal to be sought actively by couples or demanded by wives. It was important for wives to maintain a passive sexual identity in which they received the attentions of husbands but did not themselves play any active role in initiating sexual activity.[113] Indeed, some women found the notion that they might be seen to want, enjoy, or embrace sexual intercourse excruciating. A probation officer working with marriages in difficulty in the 1940s concluded that women's 'attitude in coition is one of passive endurance . . . a nice girl should not enjoy coition'.[114] Hubert classified his wife as 'frigid'. Yet she indicated that she had no other choice; to do anything more than tolerate his attentions was to 'behave like a loose woman':

People vary in their sexual responses, don't they? There was none with her at all. And she avoided contact as much as possible, kissing or anything like that, which I thought was due at first to modesty. There we are. Well I just had to accept it, I made my choice so I stood by it. (pause) . . . I learned—I read the necessary mo-methods . . . to rouse her in the first place by the hand, and to continue with the penis (pause). I learned that there was a sort of erection and the nipples are too, of course. But she seemed to restrain herself terribly.

How could you tell whether she had an orgasm?
Well, it's a sort of electric shock goes through the body. Don't know how else to describe it. Very similar to that.

---

[110] Nellie, bc3ox#19.   [111] Louisa, bc3ox#14.   [112] Gay, msf/kf/ht/#13.
[113] Holtzman, 'The Pursuit of Married Love', 45.
[114] Packer, 'Aspects of Working-Class Marriage', 99.

And did she enjoy that?

Must have done, I think. She never let on though . . . I faced her with the fact that she was—seemed to be totally uninterested. 'Well', as I told you, she said, 'Well, I'm not going to behave like a loose woman.' [115]

As a result, most women left all decisions about the timing and frequency of sex up to men. Almost all overt sexual advances were made by men. Indeed, husbands were well aware of their wives' inability make sexual requests and sought to decipher their unspoken desires. Colin, for example, spoke of his responsibility to work out his wives' wishes at the point when he wanted sex, as he knew that they saw it as their duty to appear available, even when they did not wish it:

Martha and Amy thought it was a woman's job to give a man sex. They would never say no, you know what I mean? So, I'd to say no for them. I knew when they . . . so I—I say no for them. But they always thought that if a man wanted sex, regardless of whether they enjoy it or not, they'd give the man sex and that's—thank God it's changing like you know. [116]

The fact that most women neither sought out sexual pleasure nor wished to be involved in initiating or controlling sexual activity is crucial to understanding their reluctance to take control of their own fertility and their satisfaction with a male-dominated contraceptive strategy. Far from making women's experience of sex more pleasurable, women saw an active role in birth control as brazen and indecent.[117] Women who were not prepared to be seen actively seeking sexual pleasure in fact saw it as advantageous to cede responsibility (and a degree of power) for contraception to men.[118] Consequently, the vast majority of women presented men's dominance of contraceptive decision-making as entirely in accord with their own preferences.

Much has been made of the impact of the link between women's preparedness, in middle-class circles at least, to embrace contraception and the rhetoric of mutual sexual pleasure emanating from sexologists in the early twentieth century and promoted by the marriage and sex manuals.[119] For women, the use of birth control, and in particular female methods, is seen as a crucial factor in their ability to achieve the sexual adjustment increasingly seen as necessary to a successful marriage. Indeed there were very occasional suggestions that the use of a female method of birth control had a positive impact on the enjoyment of sexual intercourse. Tim, who was born into a working-class family but became a qualified precision instrument maker and married a typist, insisted that both he and his wife

[115] Hubert, msf/kf/ht/#32.

[116] Colin, msf/kf/bl/#36. He married his first wife in 1947 and his second, following his first wife's death, in 1976.

[117] See also Thomas, 'The Medical Construction of the Contraceptive Career', 58–9, on similar difficulties for women in more recent history.

[118] Jan Pahl argues that 'being able to offload certain decisions . . . on to the other spouse can itself be a sign of power', Quoted in Murcot, ' "It's a Pleasure to Cook for Him" ', 89.

[119] See e.g. Collins, *Modern Love*, 96–8; Cook, *The Long Sexual Revolution*; Dyehouse, *Feminism and the Family in England*, 179–84; Ellen Holtzman, 'The Pursuit of Married Love', 40.

found the cap more 'satisfactory' than other types of contraception because it was the most 'intimate' method of birth control.[120] Gill, who took a certificate in social work at Manchester University during the Second World War, self-consciously echoed the language of sexology in explaining why she and her husband preferred the Dutch cap and why they employed French letters and withdrawal more reluctantly:

Oh, they're [condoms] a menace, aren't they? (laughs) Well, you've got to stop and fiddle about you see . . .

. . . it's the paraphernalia, isn't it? I think that's the really the thing, you know you've got the—you're not totally relaxed . . .

. . . you can put that [the cap] in before you see, it's much better than the French Letters somehow . . .

. . . I mean part of thing is that that you should really have the penis inside er after the sex act, shouldn't you? After the ejaculation. Oh, good grief I'm—these words sound like a medical dictionary or something (laughs).[121]

However, as is also widely recognized, the majority of marriage manuals were aimed at men and saw it as the husband's responsibility to educate his partner in sexual matters and 'awaken' her 'capacity' for sexual desire and feeling.[122] Rather than encouraging wives to seek out contraception as a means of improving sexual relations a clear message emanating from much of the contemporary written material on sexual relationships was that men needed to attend to their technique.[123] Responsibility for the quality of sexual encounters was placed on the shoulders of the husband and, indeed, women were further encouraged to abdicate responsibility for contraception, and the attendant improved sexual experience this might bring, precisely because so many husbands took these issues so seriously. Whereas most women did not feel entitled to sexual pleasure and merely welcomed it if it occurred, many men saw it as a goal to arouse their partner, and measured their own skill by their perception of their wife's orgasm. Lella Secor Florence found husbands who 'suffer in great anxiety if pleasure is not mutual'.[124] Phyllis's husband was 'very very patient' and would 'hold back until I had and there're some times I'd even have to er pretend I had them, you know, otherwise I'd think crikey, going to go on all night here and I couldn't'.[125] Frank similarly remembered how his relationship developed until 'you got to that stage then where you already knew er, er the sensitive parts to touch . . . Er, you knew by the

---

[120] Tim, msf/srss/bl/#19.   [121] Gill, msf/kf/bl/#48.

[122] Margaret Jackson, *The Real Facts of Life*, 160–7. See also K. White, *The First Sexual Revolution*, which concurs that 'the onus for the success of the sex act was placed on men' (p. 76).

[123] It was, however, recognized by some that 'unless both husband and wife have read the book . . . reading text-books on sex technique has not proved helpful in correcting sexual maladjustment'. See Packer, 'Aspects of Working-Class Marriage', 99.

[124] Florence, *Progress Report on Birth Control*, 217. See also L. Hall, *Hidden Anxieties*, 103–13.

[125] Phyllis, msf/kf/bl/#5.

reaction of your partner whether you were getting through to her or not . . . you didn't need to say anything y-you knew . . . No, no she never, she never had any complaints.'[126]

Men's desire to improve women's experience of sexual intercourse contributed significantly to their willingness to take responsibility for contraception. Many men realized that contraceptive use was advantageous not only because it might lessen their wives' fear of pregnancy and increase their sexual pleasure, but also because it would improve relations and increase the frequency with which they could request sex.[127] One man wrote to Marie Stopes in order to prevent his wife insisting upon abstinence:

She is not passionate in the least and she tells me if I left her altogether she would be better pleased . . . I feel that I need to co-habit with her every week or else I feel nervous and irritable . . . Could you advise me . . . because I don't think I could leave her alone for years, and I don't want to be the cause of bringing children into this world.[128]

Agatha described herself as indifferent to the pleasures of sex: 'I never thought anything of it, wouldn't 'ave worried me if I'd never 'ad it . . . you're kind of made to believe that er, it's wrong to do things and it puts you off.' Her husband, however, realised that sexual arousal and the use of withdrawal ensured an active sex life. He would 'fiddle about' which 'kind of worked you up so that you didn't mind what he did'.[129] As Lesley Hall has argued, we should not see the average man during this period as 'an insensitive oaf blinded to his wife's needs by his own impetuous desires', despite 'his construction . . . in contemporary works'.[130] Whereas women maintained a passive sexual identity and did not seek to improve their sex lives, men saw the attainment of good sexual relations as a goal to strive for, and viewed the use of contraception as an important means to that end, and as an essential part of a good marriage.

Finally, women often saw their ability to leave responsibility for contraception to their husbands not as an indication of their subordination, but rather as a liberating power. It was felt by interviewees that modern culture, which was seen to place contraceptive responsibility on women, was far from advantageous to them.[131]

---

126 Frank, msf/srss/bl/#16.

127 Hera Cook sees the use of withdrawal in this context. She claims that women's preferred method of contraception was abstinence, given their dislike of sex, and argues that men were only persuaded to use withdrawal when faced with their wives' refusal to have sex on any other terms: *The Long Sexual Revolution*, 117.   128 Stopes, *Mother England*, 14.

129 Agatha, msf/kf/ht/#7.   130 L. Hall, 'Impotent Ghosts', 62.

131 This is, of course, in sharp contrast to feminist work which has recognized that 'men exercise a considerable control over women's sexuality and reproductive processes': Elliot, *The Family*, 92–3. See also H. Roberts, 'Male Hegemony in Family Planning', 14. In contrast to much sociological literature, historical studies of women's sexuality and contraceptive use have been concerned not to portray women as victims. It is perhaps this 'political' desire to acknowledge women's active roles that motivates the insistence that women were the driving force behind increased contraceptive use, alongside historians' appreciation of the (relatively well known) work of the clinic movement, with its explicit agenda of concern for women's needs and rights. I am sympathetic to the need not simply to see women in the past as helpless victims of male oppression and I do not wish to neglect the ways

Many women were pleased not to have to concern themselves with the issue of contraception:

They were more careful in them days than what they are today, by what I hear of them like. *In what way, careful?* Well, I don't know—they sort of—they had—more responsible to what they was doing, you know, they—they draw back before anything like—they considered the girls, but today they don't consider the girls, only their own pleasure, that's my imagination of them, you know—but the fellas years ago used to be more considerate to the girls. That's how I found life, anyway.[132]

Some women in Britain in this period considered their husbands' control of contraception as giving them independence because they viewed birth control itself as a chore. Lorna focused on the trouble of organizing and using contraception. Her husband's role in using birth control was presented as welcome and helpful; it saved her a lot of 'bother':

I hadn't time to be bothered. Wasn't interested in it . . . well, there are—there's—there's the sheath and then there's the coil and the diaphragm—this is all I've learned lately . . . This last few years I've learnt more about contraception than I ever knew before. Because it didn't dominate my lifetime . . . that were left to James and he was determined we weren't having any more so he must've controlled hisself . . . Never bother, never bothered. I left it to him, no.[133]

Lella Secor Florence revealed that many women found using birth control a burden that they only managed 'off and on'. They portrayed the use of female methods as onerous rather than liberating, and tempting to neglect after an exhausting day: 'so many have said, "I was feeling nervy just then", or "I was not at all well", or "I was so overwrought with domestic worries" '.[134] The fact that among the middle classes female caps were more frequently adopted does not indicate that middle-class women increasingly recognized the benefits of being able to control their fertility themselves. When middle-class women adopted female methods of birth control it was often when faced with husbands who did not think it was their role to take responsibility for birth control:

I had a Dutch cap that's right . . . he wouldn't do anything because he said it was like eating a sweet with the paper on [pause] so there was no way he was going to do anything, so I went and had a Dutch cap fitted . . . I remember talking to him about that and he said 'certainly not' . . . I just thought, Oh well, I don't know, Oh dear, and I thought, well it's up to me.[135]

Those middle-class women who did take responsibility for birth control often presented the business as a tiresome burden. Naomi Mitchison felt 'it must be

---

which women found to influence contraceptive behaviour. However, the eagerness of some to dismiss the importance of the role of husbands is conceptually and empirically flawed.

[132] Elizabeth, bc3sw#12.   [133] Lorna, msf/kf/bl/#25.
[134] Florence, *Progress Report on Birth Control*, 140–3.   [135] Gay, msf/kf/ht/#13.

rather pleasant' 'to be spared the trouble of decision' and 'lazily' leave 'the man to take the precautions'.[136] Patrick's wife, a bookkeeper at the Post Office Savings Bank, is presented as having chosen to take responsibility for contraception in order that he be saved a chore. Patrick thought the responsibility should be his and saw his wife's action as part of her selfless approach to their marriage:

There was a Family Planning Association that Joan got in touch with . . . she said 'Well, the girls at the office are going to it and I think I ought to,' so she did and she was very happy with the treatment she got, 'cause eventually it became the thing to do and it was done in the right way, right place, with the right people. But err, she had—she started off with the cap and anti-sperm stuff, and we always used that.

. . .

I didn't send her out to find out, err, in fact, it was one of the things that I was bothered about and I'd said to her 'What are we going to do?' And she said 'Well, I'll ask the girls because I know they're getting something umm, from the Family Planning people'.

. . .

but she didn't mind putting a cap in, you see, funny woman, but she was like that, if it inconvenienced her it didn't matter, but as long as it didn't inconvenience me—and I think that sums her up very well.[137]

This rare instance of a middle-class woman apparently happy to use a cap and content to take full responsibility for developing a contraceptive strategy is presented as the action of a particularly self-sacrificing wife. She is depicted as choosing to relieve her husband of his expected duty, and as taking on one of his chores.

Others also recognized that birth control was a burden. Penny's doctor sought to ensure that contraception was used following two failures. Yet instead of suggesting female methods, he lectured the husband. As a busy mother this was one worry that she could do without and the husband could take on:

I talked to the doctor about it and he said 'You could [use] a cap, a Dutch Cap or something that you could use to put in', and he said 'You are a busy mother' . . . 'You will go to bed . . . and you will forget to put the cap in . . . and your husband will think that . . . you're still doing it.' He said . . . 'No, it's your husband's place to use the contraceptives not yours.'[138]

Some women regarded it as appropriate that men were burdened with arranging birth control; since sex was primarily perceived as a male pleasure, so the inconvenience of contraception should be theirs and theirs alone.[139] Marilyn was determined a male method should be used in order that her husband share at least some of the disadvantages of reproduction. 'Well he were enjoying hisself, weren't he?

---

[136] Mitchison, *Comments on Birth Control*, 17.　　[137] Patrick, msf/kf/ht/#16.

[138] Penny, msf/srss/ht/#20. See also McLaren, 'Illegal Operations', 802–4.

[139] One study of American couples in the 1960s also found some women who believed that 'since her husband is the only one who enjoys sex he should be the one to worry about contraception': Rainwater, *Family Design*, 240.

And it were his part . . . I mean I were having children and all t'pain and men get away with murder . . . Men have nothing—no, let them—they should see to it.'[140]

Many women saw male control of contraception as both appropriate and personally advantageous.[141] Despite fearing the failure of male methods of birth control, most women did not want to be able to control their fertility themselves. Most pertinently, they saw an active role in determining and implementing contraceptive strategy as a significant challenge to their notions of respectable female behaviour; a passive, non-interventionist, silent, and accepting sexual identity could not easily be squared with taking an active role in either discussing or implementing birth control.[142] Yet far from presenting themselves as having been at the 'mercy' of their husbands, who could decide whether or not to use contraception, women felt relieved at being spared such a chore. They did not present themselves as disempowered. Instead, they compared their situation favourably to that of their daughters and granddaughters.[143] The idea that modern women 'took control of their own bodies' was not seen as a great revolution for the better, but rather merely the result of the selfishness of modern men who refused to relieve their female partners of contraceptive burdens:

But all we knew about was French letters—up to the fella—you never heard much about what you could do with yourself, no pills then. And I wouldn't, I don't think I'd've taken them then. I prefer the man to help. I think they should do. The men are free today, aren't they? They rely on the girl having the pill, they don't do anything.[144]

'You're to stick up for yourself'[145]

Despite most women's acceptance of male authority over decision-making, and their determination to preserve a naive, innocent, and passive sexual identity, there were ways in which they could influence contraceptive practices. Although men were usually seen as having the ultimate power to determine birth control strategies, women had a spectrum of tactics—ranging from gentle cajoling to refusing sexual intercourse—through which they could articulate and effect their

---

[140] Marilyn, msf/kf/bl/#7.

[141] Jennifer Hirsch's research on Mexico has also highlighted the advantages perceived by women in having men take care of contraception. Many of her interviewees liked their husband to use withdrawal because 'you are not the only one worrying about it, he is also worrying about it. He needs to be attentive and alert. And it seems really nice to me, the idea that he would care about it too, and not just me.' Hirsch and Nathanson, 'Some Traditional Methods Are More Modern Than Others', 413.

[142] Some authors recognize that, in modern Britain, 'male control of sexuality is part of the social constitution of masculinity and femininity': Holland, Ramazanoglu, Sharpe, and Thomson, 'Pressured Pleasure', 250.

[143] By the 1970s, as Angus McLaren points out, women realized that the development of the Pill was 'at the price of assuming full responsibility for the inconveniences and risks involved', whereas withdrawal 'required a high level of male involvement': McLaren, *A History of Contraception*, 244.

[144] Louisa, bc3ox#14.   [145] Marilyn, msf/kf/bl/#7.

desires. However, these strategies were shaped by the need to preserve an image of sexual naivety. Many wives avoided talking too directly about the details of birth control use, preferring to use euphemistic language or leaving their desires vague, a technique which preserved their dignity but might not be understood.

Although in inter-war Britain male dominance of contraceptive decision-making was the norm, especially in working-class communities, there were frequent instances of extremely powerful, manipulative, and dominant wives adept at expressing themselves and getting their own way. Agatha would not have put up with a husband like her father, who wasn't careful: 'I'd 'ave told him . . . I should have given him a kick up the bum!'[146] Marilyn decided to 'stick up' for herself, refusing to use caps and making her husband continue to use withdrawal, much to his annoyance:

He kept complaining that it—it weren't the same. I said 'No, I know it's not the same', but I said 'I don't want to—I don't want no more children' . . . He had a friend and his wife, er, had got a cap. And he said 'Do you want to go?' I said 'No, I'm not going nowhere.' . . . No, you're—even though you're married and you love 'em you—you're to stick up for yourself, I mean you haven't to let 'em have all their own way. Or else, I mean, er, er, they'll just walk all over you, I weren't having that . . . Perhaps I were selfish but I don't think I were.[147]

Aafke Komter found that women's strategies were often cautious: 'they tried to get things changed . . . by hinting, grumbling and giving sly digs'.[148] Joanna Bourke recognizes the 'non-confrontational power' of 'placid sabotage' and presents women's use of 'indirect subversion', 'cajoling', and 'disdainful silence' in the early twentieth century as essential to understanding women's image in biographies as dominant in the household while at the same time appearing unassertive and acquiescent.[149] Catherine explicitly sought to guide her husband around to her point of view while appearing to accept his authority: 'I've always let him try and be there in charge. I don't think you should show—you can guide 'em round to what you want, can't you, gently?'[150]

Women's ability to 'stick up for themselves' was likely to increase as a marriage progressed. Wives who were sexually experienced, had used birth control, and had had children were more likely to have both stronger opinions and the confidence to express them. Later in marriage women were much more likely both to initiate discussion about birth control practice, and to cajole, manipulate, and persuade if their husbands proved unwilling either to use birth control as frequently as desired or to employ a particular method.

---

[146] Agatha, msf/kf/ht/#7.   [147] Marilyn, msf/kf/bl/#7.
[148] Komter, 'Hidden Power in Marriage', 204.
[149] Bourke, *Working-Class Cultures*, 78–81. On women's power within marriage, despite the apparent deference to their husbands' perspectives from a sociological perspective, see Luxton, *More Than a Labour of Love*, 43–79. Safilios-Rothschild also highlights some of the subtle ways in which power is exercised, finding that wives frequently successfully influenced their husbands while letting them, 'officially make the decisions': 'The Study of Family Power Structure', 541.
[150] Catherine, msf/kf/ht/#1.

Margaret recalled the start of her marriage, when she faced a husband 'more ignoranter than her'. She had no independent knowledge of birth control methods and, partly because of her age, she lacked the authority necessary to persuade her husband to act differently.[151] She speculated that later in marriage she might have found ways to influence him:

I couldn't do much about it. Well, a woman can't do much about it, can she? . . . That's why I had 'em children so quick, I think. And he was—I think he was ignoranter than me. If he'd've known—if we—if—I'd've known better to made him, he'd've had no choice, but I didn't, I was too young, see, love.[152]

Terence's wife did not intervene in their contraceptive strategy early in their marriage. Terence wanted one child only, but 'she weren't bothered really'. He used withdrawal and condoms and his wife was content to let the family grow; it 'just happened'. After the third pregnancy, however, her attitude changed, as did her assertiveness: 'it was wife's idea, she'd try something different'. 'She said . . . "We've got enough now, three, three's enough," . . . So it were wife's decision that . . . she went in the doctor's and . . . she went and got caps.'[153]

When women did want to communicate their desires with regard to contraception, the importance of maintaining a naive, innocent persona meant that many attempted to find neutral, non-sexual contexts in which to express them. For instance, women often made positive or negative statements about children and childbearing, or made comments about the burdens of a large family experienced by relatives and neighbours, in order to put pressure on a man to act. Gladys, for example, remembered 'grumbling, because I always seemed, I said once "I've either got a baby in the shawl or in my belly", so he had to be careful', although in practice sometimes 'he was that drunk . . . he didn't know what he was doing'.[154] Clare would not discuss birth control in any detail because it was one of her 'personal things'. However, she was able to tell both of her husbands when she wanted children:

It was never talked about, you'd discuss things if you wanted a child and as I say, I was quite a long while 'fore I fell for me second child—I would 'ave 'ad twins but I lost one of them. But personal things, you used to keep to yourself—your personal things.

Yeah. Would you talk to your husbands about those things?

No, everything was kept—everything was kept—or what word would you use?—you didn't discuss things like that.[155]

---

[151] A recent study of domestic workers in Rio de Janeiro also revealed a pattern of 'gradual change from a passive to an active attitude' towards contraception on the part of women. A sexual ideology framed contraception as a male concern during marriage or courtship and only later, when the determination to avoid pregnancy increased, and various contraceptives had been tried, would women seek actively to be involved or to change the views of their partners. See Pitanguy and De Mello E. Souza, 'Codes of Honour', 91.   [152] Margaret, bc3sw#13.

[153] Terence, msf/srss/bl/#15.   [154] Gladys, bc3sw#28.

[155] Clare, msf/kf/ht/#8. Clare married first in 1936 and then again in 1944 after her first husband's death in 1940.

It was often difficult for women to find non-sexual references or euphemisms which allowed them to maintain their naive self-image yet at the same time make their sexual or contraceptive wishes clear to their husbands. Women would tell their husbands to 'be careful', yet many men interpreted this in their own fashion. Sally, for example, spoke of the problems associated with using euphemistic language for 'withdrawal':

He laughed. He, he said 'Well, I've never heard that.' I said, 'You'll have to get off at Mill Hill for a long time.'[156] He said, 'All right.' I said 'You know what I mean?' He said 'Yes. I've worked with men, you know.' I said 'Yes, I know.' (laughs) No, we had a good laugh about it.[157]

Such exhortations were often effective, if subtle. Iris was probably typical of many women, quietly reminding their husbands to withdraw:

Was he co-operative about being careful?
Well, he never voiced an opinion one way or the other, but I used to say 'Watch what you're doing'.[158]

Some women did use more direct techniques to ensure their preferences were heard. However they chose those methods which required them neither to discuss sexual issues explicitly, nor to take on an amorous sexual persona. Some chose to refuse sex as it allowed them to influence contraceptive practice without appearing brazen. Rosie acknowledged her use of threats to ensure contraceptive use: 'He knew that it, that something had to happen—either that or he didn't have to have his sex.'[159] Similarly, when Doreen's sexual desires conflicted with her husband's she responded the 'diplomatic way', ensuring they went to bed at different times, or pretending she had a period when she did not.[160] Intercourse can be seen to have been permitted only on the condition that men promised to implement birth control.[161] Pru would say: ' "Well, you be jolly careful then if we have sex" . . . so he said "Yes, all right." He was very good like that.'[162] Norman recalled a friend who once 'tried to have sex' with his sleeping wife who woke up and said ' "You . . . you dare! . . . If I have another child, I'll pack up my job and you won't like that, will you?" '[163] Colin frequently failed to withdraw, or tried to kid his wife that he had, despite his wife's desire to avoid pregnancy. However, he also realized that if he did not employ contraception at least some of the time, 'she might've started developing headaches, she might've started saying I don't want sex, you see and I want, I'm not bothered, you know and things like that'.[164] Despite not being able to ensure the consistent use of birth control, his wife was able significantly to reduce her risk of pregnancy.

---

[156] Mill Hill was a train station in the Blackburn suburbs. Sally was therefore using one of the common euphemisms for withdrawal: getting off a train before the final destination.
[157] Sally, msf/kf/bl/#31.   [158] Iris, bc2#8.   [159] Rosie, bc1#2.
[160] Doreen, msf/kf/bl/#20; for a similar example, see Florence, *Progress Report on Birth Control*, 214.
[161] Cook, *The Long Sexual Revolution*, 117–21.   [162] Pru, msf/kf/ht/#12.
[163] Norman, msf/kf/ht/#17.   [164] Colin, msf/kf/bl/#36.

Finally, in order for wives to avoid addressing contraceptive issues directly, other authorities were sometimes called upon by women to ensure male action. Third parties were often used to impart a contraceptive message to a spouse.[165] Marilyn's mother told her son-in-law that 'he should've been more careful' after her daughter's second child, while Reg's own mother bought some condoms and gave them to her son.[166] When Nurse Fowles gave a lecture on birth control methods to forty 'young mothers', she reported their 'anxious' request 'that "the men" should be talked to'.[167] Angela was extremely anxious to avoid pregnancy and worried that the cap might easily slip out of place. She wanted her husband to carry on using condoms as well, which he felt were superfluous. She sought the doctor's assistance in prescribing the use of two methods simultaneously, and used his authority to back up her position:

ANGELA   I never felt very secure which is why.
HUGH   Why she insisted on me still wearing the condom.
ANGELA   Yeah, the G.P. said that we should, yeah, that's right, he did.[168]

Frank's wife similarly told him, ' "We've got to do what the doctor tells us to do otherwise there's no point in having a doctor." So er we just had to put up with it.'[169] When Penny's doctor 'had given him a lecture', 'he didn't make any fuss about it at all'. 'I think that sort of made his mind up that we'd got to be careful.'[170]

Women's abdication of responsibility for direct control of contraception did not leave them powerless. Although many strategies were subtle, indirect, and euphemistic, women succeeded in asserting their point of view, establishing that their expectations of male action were known, and exerting pressure on their husbands to act in accordance with their desires. In addition, women possessed the ultimate power to refuse to co-operate in having sexual intercourse if their reproductive aims were not met. In practice, this was a limited power, as most women did not feel able to deny their husbands sexual access regularly or for prolonged periods of time. However, such threats were far from hollow. While they might not force a husband to accept the wife's perspective, they were likely to increase the frequency with which contraception was used, or reduce the number of occasions on which pregnancy was risked.

'He just wanted what was best for me'[171]

By the inter-war period the expectation that most men would use some form of birth control was so widespread that women saw little need to take matters into their own

---

[165] See also W. Seccombe, 'Starting to Stop', 179.
[166] Marilyn, msf/kf/bl/#7; Reg msf/kf/bl/#36.
[167] Report of a meeting at Barton L.P. Club, Gloucester, 15 Oct. 1930, BL Add. MSS 58622.
[168] Angela and Hugh, msf/kf/ht/#18.   [169] Frank, msf/kf/bl/#16.
[170] Penny, msf/srss/ht/#20.   [171] Millie, bc3ox#21.

hands. In most households there was little conflict about whether or not birth control would ever be used, only disputes about when and how often. For many who wanted a small family but did not have a fixed number in mind, the general acknowledgement that the husband would use some form of birth control most of the time was sufficient. Despite not having control of the methods used, such women were content that their contraceptive aims would be met. Having just one or two fewer or more pregnancies than desired was an acceptable price to pay for the benefits of being absolved from the responsibility for day-to-day birth control practices.

The study of gender relations focuses on power relationships. While this perspective is crucial in highlighting the inequalities that shaped everyday lives, it fails to recognize the extent to which men and women were actively engaged in an attempt to please each other and work together. Marital relations were not simply a battle between individuals with entrenched positions and different interests. Co-operation, self-sacrifice, and solidarity were equally key to the everyday negotiation of marital roles. Certainly many women presented their relationships in this way. With regard to the use of birth control, women interpreted men's unilateral decision-making not as a form of arbitrary power but as a sign of love, consideration, and thoughtful anticipation of the wife's need to remain sexually withdrawn. The power of a man to adopt a contraceptive strategy silently, without embarrassing his wife, or perhaps even without consulting her, was welcomed and appreciated by many women, especially in working-class communities where the implicit nature of birth control decisions was carefully preserved. Eileen gave an extreme account of her husband's unilateral power. Until recently, she had not realized the contraceptive purpose behind his use of withdrawal:

So did you not talk to your husband about why he was coming out?
No, no, no, no, no (shouting)—don't talk to 'im about anything like that, no.
So would you say that was a decision that he made by himself?
Must 'ave bin . . .'e wouldn't go right through with it . . . what 'e did it for—I know now what 'e did it for, I didn't know then, but I know now—didn't want to have any children.

Rather than viewing this as a manifestation of his authority and her powerlessness, she interpreted both his actions and his silence on the matter as a symbol of his consideration for her.' 'E loved me . . . I couldn't 'ave any more children—'e wouldn't 'ave any more, 'e wouldn't go through with it.'[172] In the majority of households in all classes male responsibility for birth control was valued as gallant and considerate:

The reason I didn't use any contraception methods at all was because my husband did it always. It was the done thing. He wouldn't have dreamt of allowing you to. I don't mean to say we didn't have intercourse, we had it very frequently, but um nevertheless that was his side of the picture.[173]

[172] Eileen, msf/kf/bl/#12.
[173] A middle-class woman courting in the 1920s interviewed for 'In the Club', A&M: GC/105/23.

Other wives were defined as unfortunate if their husbands did not assume responsibility for contraception. One woman told Mass-Observation that, although 'my hubby's always very considerate and careful', she had heard other women complain that 'their husbands wouldn't leave them alone', who were 'terrified out of their wits'.[174] Far from stressing their own powerlessness, such stories revealed women's investment in a system of male control of contraception. By the inter-war period, strong cultural expectations put pressure on husbands to take an interest in birth control. Men, too, took considerable pride in their willingness to assume responsibility for contraception. Rather than using birth control only when their wives insisted, or selfishly seeing control of contraception as a power which ensured that their opinion upon the matter prevailed, they regarded the use of contraception as the duty of a good husband. Many husbands' sense of dignity, self-respect, and honour was satisfied by taking on this role. As one woman who wrote to Marie Stopes revealed, a husband felt 'somehow that he is to blame which of course he isnt any more than the woman' if pregnancy occurred, while some men earnestly wrote as they did not 'want to risk causing my wife any danger'.[175] Most women marrying during the 1920s and 1930s could confidently assume that their husbands would use some form of contraception.

Women recognized that they were at the mercy of husbands who had the power to determine contraceptive practice, but nevertheless were both proud and grateful if their husband proved considerate. While, as some historians have argued, this might have been the result of decades of pressure on the part of women to persuade or force husbands to use contraception, the conclusion remains that power to determine contraceptive practice was willingly entrusted to the husband.[176] That wives did not seek to oppose this state of affairs indicates that women had much invested in maintaining it. Male dominance of contraception relieved them of a chore, and allowed them to preserve their status as sexually naive, pure, and demure. Furthermore, in the majority of cases, the use of contraception by the husband was an aspect of married life they could take pride in.

'IT WAS THE MAN'S JOB':[177] MASCULINE IDENTITIES AND BIRTH CONTROL PRACTICES

Whereas most women wanted to remain divorced from sexual issues, including birth control, many men regarded contraceptive decision-making as an essential element of a husband's role. Moreover, in the 1920s, male use of contraception

---

[174] Mass-Observation, TC Family Planning 1944–49, Chelsea, TC3/2/A.

[175] Stopes, *Mother England*, 102, 108.

[176] Hera Cook argues that male use of birth control in the inter-war period indicates that 'by that time women had won the battle': Cook, *The Long Sexual Revolution*, 120.

[177] Ernest, bc3sw#2.

was not seen primarily as an action demanded by women, nor as one that men undertook in response to a perception of their wives' needs. Rather, men took responsibility for contraception because they saw it as their duty. By the 1920s, a stereotypical image of a brutal Victorian husband who would beat his wife and refuse to do anything to limit the size of the family had been constructed in British popular culture.[178] Regardless of the validity of such a 'bogeyman' figure, it served as an antitype that most men wished to distance themselves from. Comparing themselves favourably with their 'irresponsible' parents and grandparents, husbands in the inter-war period prided themselves on having taken responsibility for the size of their families. Some historians have therefore suggested that male responsibility for birth control should be seen as indicative of the emergence of the new 'companionate' man who was sensitive to his wife's desires and who behaved accordingly.[179] Here I will suggest otherwise: rather, a *range* of masculine identities arose in response to the image of the Victorian brute, all of which prized male responsibility for birth control. On the one hand, some men did define themselves using the contemporary terminology of companionateness and justi-fied their responsibility for birth control in terms of taking care of their wife's needs; however, even in the case of such a sensitized man, contraceptive decisions were often taken without discussion with his wife and according only to his own perceptions of her needs. On the other hand, there were men who rejected not only the image of the brutal, uncivilized Victorian husband, but also the ideal of the 'companionate' man, whom they considered insufficiently masculine and overly domesticated (a 'Mary Ann').[180] Rather, they described themselves as 'authoritarian' or 'old-fashioned'. Despite their self-consciously 'anti-modern' stance, they *did* take responsibility for contraception, but saw its use not as an act

[178] Attacks on the Victorian father are evident in elite autobiography, for example Samuel Butler's *The Way of all Flesh* (1903) and Edmund Gosse's *Father and Son* (1907). John Tosh cautions historians from seeing these works as evidence for Victorian relationships, and interprets them as examples of a twentieth-century construction of anti-Victorian values: *Manliness and Masculinities*, 139. Such invective against 'Victorianism' was rife among the Bloomsbury group: see Gardiner, *The Victorians*, 19–36. Twentieth-century histories were quick to supplement and reinforce this image: see e.g. Grisewood (ed.), *Ideas and Beliefs of the Victorians*. On the lower-middle class and descriptions of Victorian and Edwardian patriarchs see Thomas Crossland, *The Suburbans* (1905), and the discus-sion in Mort, 'Social and Symbolic Fathers and Sons', 361; Bingham, *Gender, Modernity and the Popular Press*, 169; L. Hall, 'Impotent Ghosts', 67. See also Kucich and Sadoff (eds.), *Victorian Afterlife*, for a range of essays on the centrality of images and constructions of the Victorian age as cen-tral to late twentieth-century consciousness. This research has found that by the end of the twentieth century personal narratives from a range of individuals also drew upon a negative construction of the Victorian family.

[179] Gittins, *Fair Sex*, 185; Cook, *The Long Sexual Revolution*, 119; L. Hall, 'Impotent Ghosts', 67–70.

[180] See also George Orwell's diary comment in 1936 that 'the woman continues to do all the housework . . . The man would lose his manhood if, merely because he was out of work, he became a "Mary Ann" ' (quoted in *Oxford English Dictionary*). Mary Ann also appears to have had associations with homosexuality and prostitution. See e.g. the 'autobiography' of Jack Saul, a professional prosti-tute, published in 1881 as *The Sins of the Cities of the Plain or The Recollections of a Mary-Anne*, as dis-cussed in Weeks, 'Inverts, Perverts, and Mary-Annes', 207.

of sensitivity towards the wife but as a fundamental right of men within marriage to decide on the limits to family size. Thus the act of taking responsibility for birth control could be framed as the act of a sensitive or companionate man, but could also be felt to illustrate men's position as controlling, masterly, and dominant.[181]

Almost all men used birth control, were expected to take responsibility for it, and were roundly criticized if they did not. The voices below come from two middle-class women and one working-class man:

I presume he—you see, it was years before the Pill, and it was just usual for the man to take precautions . . . everything was left to the man.[182]

You just had to rely on them being, er, being good . . . he would be careful . . . the men knew what to do, didn't need telling.[183]

Yes, it was the man's option to prevent the children, but, er . . . We were responsible, we took the responsibility of seeing that there were no conceptions, unwanted. It was the man—it was the man's job.[184]

The stigmatized historical stereotype of the brutal Victorian man who would not take care of his family placed much pressure on men to reject the indiscriminate use of male power in marriage and take responsibility for contraception. This does not mean, of course, that such a bogeyman Victorian figure ever really existed in the form in which he was presented after the First World War: indeed, recent work on the nineteenth-century family has significantly questioned the monolithic image of the Victorian father and re-evaluated the relationship between Victorian men and the home, their wives, and their children.[185] Historians have

---

[181] Keith Wrightson highlights the overlapping and complex behaviour expected of 'patriarchal' and 'companionate' unions and the fluidity of the terms in *English Society 1580–1680*, ch. 4. James Hammerton also urges historians to stop portraying patriarchal and companionate marriage as stark opposites: *Cruelty and Companionship*, 7. The dominance of these models in modern historiography is extremely misleading and implies that these models of marriage were clearly defined social realities. Despite the dominance of these terms in much contemporary source material, 'companionate' and 'patriarchal' are not stable categories and cannot be easily drawn upon to describe changing marriage relationships.   [182] Hilda, msf/kf/bl/#50.

[183] Jennie, msf/kf/bl/#27.   [184] Ernest, bc3sw#2.

[185] Martin Francis has reviewed the literature on men's domestic roles in the Victorian period (and after) in 'The Domestication of the Male?'. Some historians are revising our image of Victorian patriarchy. John Gillis argues that during the twentieth century men's active role as fathers actually declined rather than increased. The medicalization of pregnancy and childbirth and the rise of ideas about 'scientific motherhood' marginalized male roles, as revealed by the increasing tendency of divorce courts to assign the custody of children to the mother: Gillis, 'Bringing Up Father'. Ralph LaRossa argues that, despite the rise in the image of the involved father and a 'culture of daddyhood', in fact men's involvement in the lives of their children did not rise significantly during the twentieth century: 'Fatherhood and Social Change', 448–60. See also LaRossa, *The Modernization of Fatherhood*; Filene, 'The Secrets of Men's History'; Pleck, 'American Fathering in Historical Perspective'; Rotundo, *American Manhood*. John Tosh has drawn particular attention to the complexities of masculine identities in the Victorian period, and the continuities in debates about men's roles in the home then and now. He suggests that the balance between work and home life was as critical to the Victorian family as it was in twentieth-century marital and gender politics. Middle-class marriages, he argues, tended to strike a balance between the two supposedly opposite poles, with men, for example, more involved with their children than 'at any time before or since', but at the same

become increasingly aware that the 'Victorian father' was a stereotype that emerged early in the twentieth century as a 'portmanteau term' for all that was to be 'rejected' in the new century.[186] Material from individuals comparing past relationships with their own tells us very little about how their marriages differed in fact from those of their Victorian predecessors. Rather, it reveals the influence exerted by the image of the Victorian father on the boundaries of acceptable male behaviour in the twentieth century.[187]

The brutally bossy Victorian husband and father was a rhetorical stereotype against whom partners could be contrasted rather than a real description of social change.[188] This was revealed by Marilyn: she sought to demonize her husband, a hairdresser, categorizing his views as antiquated, and her own as acceptable, by labelling him Victorian. Yet she realized while speaking that to characterize him as Victorian was to suggest that he was violent and despotic. She therefore quickly revised her description to acknowledge that, far from being unacceptably old-fashioned, he was 'just like most men'. He did not fully conform to the Victorian tyrant– he was not violent and he also used birth control, albeit reluctantly:

> He were Victorian . . . the man was the man of the house. And, um, everybody else were like subservant [*sic*] to him, don't get me wrong, I weren't unhappy er—we good laugh . . . He never hit me, he weren't cruel and he were good with children . . . I can't complain, I could've done a lot worse, probably . . . I don't want you to think . . . that he were a monster. Er, he weren't. He were only like most men.[189]

Most men wished to distance themselves from the perceived insensitivities of their Victorian forebears. Most men therefore saw it as their role to take responsibility for birth control and the limitation of family size. Many women presented their husbands as newly considerate, in contrast to their own fathers'

---

time frequently 'inflexible' in imposing a rigid domestic regime: Tosh, *A Man's Place*. On the variety of Victorian fathers and the complexities of their relationships with wives and children, see also D. Roberts, 'The Paterfamilias of the Victorian Ruling Classes'. Jennifer Lloyd, 'Conflicting Expectations in Nineteenth-Century British Matrimony', refers to early Victorian ideals of marriage as indicating the rise of the 'companionate' marriage, as does Battan, 'The "Rights" of Husbands and the "Duties" of Wives'. For a lively revision of myths about the Victorian patriarch and the sexual double standard, see Sweet, *Inventing the Victorians*.

[186] Marcus Collins, *Modern Love*, 5, 30. We should be wary of accepting his conclusion, however, that the 'Victorians' reputation . . . was well earned'. John Tosh highlights the extent to which the 'label "Victorian"' reflects the dominance of a 'negative and simplified image of Victorian sexuality' to hold up against our own society. The Victorian world has become 'a past from which we are anxious to escape': *A Man's Place*, 195. Michael Mason also recognizes that 'modern understandings of Victorian attitudes' are in fact 'enduring prejudices' that originated and became 'deeply entrenched in the Edwardian period': *The Making of Victorian Sexuality*, 5, paraphrased in Bristow, 'Respecting Respectability', 286.

[187] *Viz* magazine's 'Victorian Dad' is an excellent example of the enduring impact of the image of the nineteenth-century authoritarian patriarch on the twentieth-century imagination.

[188] On the ways in which cultural understandings of men are reliant on social memories and cultural images of past husbands and fathers, see Haywood and Mac an Ghaill, *Men and Masculinities*, 46.

[189] Marilyn, msf/kf/bl/#7.

behaviour.[190] Nellie contrasted her husband, who was a train driver, with the 'old-fashioned' spouse like her father, who 'never used to think' and was happy to have 'eight or nine children'. This type of man 'couldn't care less whether their wives were pregnant or not. I mean, as I say, I will give my husband his due, 'cos he was very good like that . . . 'cos they were very old fashioned . . . as time went on things got more modern'.[191] Jennie, who had been a spinner before marriage, made an explicit contrast between the care shown by her husband, who had come round to the female point of view (they 'thought like us'), and the domineering fathers and spouses who she felt typified early generations and contributed to large families:

The husband in them days—in me mother's days—were very domineering and they always thought the women had to stay at home and have children while they went out drinking. Now as we grew up we knew a bit different than that so it didn't come to us . . . the men were—thought like us . . . they were more thought—more thoughtful—more thoughtful.[192]

Some historians have linked male birth control use with the rise of companionate unions, in which newly considerate men were prepared to respond to their wives' needs, and have characterized non-companionate men as indifferent or opposed to the use of contraception.[193] The argument boldly stated by Edward Shorter in 1973, but still broadly accepted, is that 'within companionate marriages, an emancipated woman might successfully persuade her husband to begin coitus interruptus' whereas in 'traditional marriages' the husband 'refuses to contain his sexual convenience'.[194] They chart a shift from marriages at the end of the nineteenth century and beginning of the twentieth century (particularly in 'traditional, low income, long-established working-class' areas), in which 'husband and wife had distinct and separate responsibilities, activities, interests and friendships', to one in which, by the late 1940s and 1950s, spouses organized their lives and domestic responsibilities together.[195] This is seen as having resulted in a sharing of childrearing, finances, household tasks, leisure, and social relationships, and a newly communicative relationship in which men listened to

---

[190] It is not entirely clear when this contrast emerged in working-class narratives. It is likely that it was concurrent with the debate about companionate marriage which appears to have been part of working-class marital negotiations during the inter-war period and after. An unfavourable image of the Victorian husband and father continued to dominate late twentieth-century popular culture, reinforcing this image in retrospective articulations, such as autobiographies and oral history testimony collected at the end of the twentieth century. [191] Nellie, bc3ox#19.

[192] Jennie, msf/kf/bl/#27.

[193] See e.g. Bott, *Family and Social Network*; Mogey, *Family and Neighbourhood*; Young and Willmott, *Family and Kinship in East London*; eid., *The Symmetrical Family*, 87–8; Rosser and Harris, *The Family and Social Change*; Klein, *Samples from English Cultures*, vols. i and ii; Degler, 'Women and the Family', 317; Smith, 'Family Limitation'; Wells, 'Family History and Demographic Transition'; Williamson, ' "Getting Off at Loftus" '; L. Hall, 'Impotent Ghosts', 67–70. [194] Shorter 'Female Emancipation', 631–2.

[195] Elliot, *The Family*, 80.

women's needs in areas such as contraception.[196] Certainly many men connected their use of contraception with a communicative relationship and a respect for their wives' desires. Bernard, a journalist, asserted his willingness to stop having children as soon as his wife requested it, regardless of his own desires: 'you're at the sticky end of it. . . . You say no, there it is, I didn't press anything on her to have any more. I mean, if my wife said no—she has the baby you know, not me.'[197] A 31-year-old wife living in Hampstead told Mass-Observation in 1984: 'My husband says, " Well, you've got to bring the children up, not me, you do what you want".'[198] Similarly, a 24-year-old man from Chelsea felt that 'if a woman doesn't want children, a man's got no right to make her have them'.[199] Men, just as much as women, might be 'disgusted with those men who don't care what happens to their wives'.[200] Charlie criticized his neighbour Bert, a brick-layer whose wife also worked in a fruit shop, who 'was one of them. I mean he never done it the same way, you know—he was a bit couth, he got in five daugh-ters didn't he and two sons . . . I never had the family he had—he would get into bed and forget about it'.[201] Similarly, Ernest, a trained engineer who married a nurse, distinguished himself from authoritarian men who were insensitive to their wives' opinions: 'you were protecting your partner . . . but there were some men that didn't give a damn, I mean they were getting seven, eight, nine, ten chil-dren. They didn't care . . . [they] were terrors, used to behave atrociously to their wives'.[202]

Believing that sensitivity and communication were necessary for the practice of successful contraception, both contemporary sources and later historians have argued that, in those marriages which remained traditional, patriarchal, non-companionate, and uncommunicative, female desires for smaller families were rarely achieved. Those men who did not see themselves as 'companionate', it was argued, were much less likely to use birth control.[203] In south Wales, for instance, Jaclyn Gier recognized that, in traditional unions, dominant men would enforce their perceived 'right to sex' without regard for the consequences: a 'system of patriarchal values' bolstered by Nonconformist religion 'asserted the male's conju-gal rights and encouraged female ignorance in matters relating to sexuality'.[204] Oral testimony initially appeared to support this view too, with old-fashioned,

---

[196] Men far more frequently used the language of companionship than women to describe their ideals of marital relations in Mass-Observation's 1947 survey. Mass-Observation, TC Family Planning 1944–49, Matrimony Questionnaire, 1947, TC3/3/A, B.

[197] Bernard, msf/jm/bl/#45.

[198] Mass-Observation, TC Family Planning 1944–49, Chelsea, TC3/2/A.

[199] Mass-Observation, TC Family Planning 1944–49, Hampstead, TC3/1/B.

[200] 34-year-old man, married in 1937, Mass-Observation, TC Family Planning 1944–49, Harlesden, TC3/1/B.   [201] Charlie, bc2#25.

[202] Ernest, bc3sw#2.

[203] Young and Willmott, *Family and Kinship*, 20–1; R. Hoggart, *The Uses of Literacy*, 30; Klein, *Samples from English Cultures*, i. 439.

[204] Gier, 'Miners' Wives', 79, 209–17; see also V. Hall, 'Contrasting Female Identities'.

non-companionate, and unreformed men being castigated for their refusal to use birth control:

Others are, uh, macho type of man in a family—only he was having children all the time, and didn't have a second thought about it, you know . . . (sighs) It wasn't always an act of, uh, love, if you like, I mean, the men were so—some of them had worked so hard, the only tonic they had was to go to a pub, have a few pints, then go home and screw the wife sort of thing. I mean it wasn't done by twos, not in working-class areas, and, uh, of course the women very often died in those days.[205]

At first sight this testimony seemed to support the argument that in families described as 'non-companionate', traditional, or old-fashioned only occasional, ineffective, and primitive attempts at contraception were employed by careless and uncommitted men. Large families were seen to reflect the lack of consideration men had for the suffering of their wives, and the inability of wives to alter the situation.[206] However, it is a mistake to link the use of birth control too simplistically with the rise of companionate marriage. The language of the 'Victorian' father who refused to use birth control served as a salutary example of unacceptable masculinity even for authoritarian husbands. Unlike men who thought of themselves as companionate though, they did not regard their control of contraception as an act of sensitivity towards their spouses. Rather, for them, male control of contraceptive use was valued as a statement of male power over family size, and the effective use of contraception as evidence of the natural efficacy of male dominance in marriage.[207]

In some decidedly 'non-companionate' unions, both spouses reported the husband's effective, regular adoption of birth control. By the inter-war period there is no irresolvable tension between unions represented as 'traditional' and the systematic adoption of birth control. Henry and Dee neither planned their family nor

[205] Norman, msf/kf/ht/#17.

[206] See also Williamson, ' "Getting Off at Loftus" ', 11–12; Collins, *Modern Love*, 107–8. The claim that the use of appliance methods increased during the twentieth century is also linked to changing gender relations. Ariès observed that, by the 1960s, withdrawal had become 'the archaic tool of a macho, phallocratic, and non-permissive society': Ariès, 'Two Successive Motivations for the Declining Birth Rate in the West'. *Population and Development Review*, 6 (1980), 648, quoted in Santow, 'Coitus Interruptus in the Twentieth Century', 768.

[207] This is not to argue that 'companionate' and 'traditional' marriages represented clearly defined or concrete social realities in the period; they should be viewed instead as vague constructions that were variously interpreted by individuals engaged in the process of negotiating conjugal relationships. Moreover it is important to pay attention to the complex connections between wider social forces, such as the changing position of women, and the parameters of debates about and models of marriage and male conjugal roles. Clearly, for example, changing attitudes towards women are likely to have affected the framing of the boundaries of acceptable behaviour even among men who ostensibly claimed to have ignored such developments and to have maintained 'traditional' relationships. Those men who used birth control while at the same time asserting that doing so was an example of their own patriarchal authority were plausibly reacting to the rhetoric of the companionate model despite their reactionary stance. Far from seeing 'companionate' and 'traditional' marriages as rigid or sharply opposed we should instead recognize the complex interaction between marriage values occasioned by a period of intense public debate and perceived social change.

discussed it, but saw it as the husband's role to use withdrawal and condoms regularly. Dee presented herself as having had nothing at all to do with this practice; indeed, when interviewed alone she failed to mention that condoms had been used and remained embarrassedly silent when the use of this method was discussed with them both together. Henry adopted a relatively segregated form of marriage and was adamant that the husband should have the final say in decision-making. He specifically rejected a model of marriage that was 'bombastic', cruel, or violent, but considered masculine power and male control as both appropriate and righteous:

DEE   It was a woman's place to look after the children and it's a man's place to bring the money in—that's the idea but, err, sometimes he'd take, 'em out for a walk or something like that, but . . . he never bothered much around the house—let me do these things. That's how it was those days . . . he'd go to the pub mostly.

HENRY   If we decide upon anything it still must be my final word, which is what the Bible says, you see, and we go by that, and Dee is quite content about that in you? . . . I mean she can still have her word in—if she don't [agree] and tell me if she thinks she's right and well then it's up to me then to see if she is right, then I'll change my mind then . . . The man is head of the household and that's how we follow and there's no finer way—providing it's done, as it should be done, in a loving way—not in a forceful, bombastic way, you know—being cruel and beating your wife and things, no, that's not it—must be done in a loving, kind way . . . if [she] for instance was crying out for another baby the man would readily oblige but, err, you would have to otherwise use your power—your will power to—if it's the withdrawal system like, it's a lot of will power—I was able to do it, there you are, that was it.[208]

Many men did not conform to the rigid images of the 'companionate' man or the 'authoritarian'. Instead, these models existed to frame the spectrum of possible male personas, and most men drew on aspects of both masculine types in the construction of their complex individual identities.[209] Far from being terms which accurately depict the social realities of marriages during the twentieth century, far from directly reflecting a simple change in family forms and marital relationships, 'companionateness' and 'old-fashionedness' served to provide men with a debate about sexual codes which they drew on in constructing their lives. Norman, a teacher, for example, presented himself as partially companionate; he chose condoms because he felt this made sex more enjoyable for his wife, and presented his use of birth control as part of his consideration for her. On the other hand, he also recognized the extent to which he took control of all decision-making. His choice of French letters, although framed as a benefit to his wife, was a unilateral one,

[208] Dee and Henry, bc2#27.
[209] On images of companionate and patriarchal husbands, see Bingham, *Gender, Modernity and the Popular Press*, 216–43; Collins, *Modern Love*, 92–9.

taken without discussion (thanks to her prudishness) and against her wishes: she did not like condoms. Norman revealed a complex identity that drew on both authoritarian and companionate models, presenting himself as a 'bully' who sought to make the decisions that suited his wife:

I think she was a bit prudish in some ways, I can't recall any long discussions on it [birth control], no, she left it to me. And I think she was pleased to leave it to me . . . I think it was—it was—women don't like the condoms, many don't—I don't . . . uh—I used to think it made it a little more enjoyable, uh, the woman didn't have to worry.

. . .

I was general manager . . . I admit to being quite guilty in that, I felt quite—I do feel quite guilty—I probably bullied her a good deal. Um, bullied her in the sense in that I made her decisions, we did what I wanted her to do.[210]

A food packing manager who wrote to Mass-Observation similarly hoped he was being considerate to his wife in using birth control, but worried that he had bullied her into the decision: 'we did not desire children . . . my wife I know likes children, but I have no special love for them. The thought does haunt me sometimes that I have persuaded my wife into a decision against her better judgement.'[211]

The fact that men wanted to take responsibility for birth control is best understood by examining the range of masculine identities available to men in the first half of the twentieth century. All men, regardless of the type of marriage they had or the sort of husband they believed themselves to be, saw birth control as their fundamental duty. Men who viewed themselves as companionate and sensitive saw their responsibility for birth control as part of a necessary consideration of their wives. Men who saw themselves as more authoritarian equally saw it as their responsibility, believing their control over contraceptive strategy to be a valid expression of male power over sex and family size in marriage.

The absence of class or regional differences in male contraceptive roles is striking. However, the construction of contraceptive responsibility as a male duty in the vast majority of families from all classes and in many regions of the country does not indicate uniformity in gender relations in Britain. Class- and region-specific codes continued to dominate British cultures and marital relationships. Despite the continued importance of class and regional divides, the idea that the husband would regularly use birth control and that he would take full responsibility for the management of a contraceptive strategy was integrated into a range of different family forms. By the inter-war period men in all classes and cultures of Britain united in using birth control, but in doing so expressed a variety of different gender identities.

---

[210] Norman, msf/kf/ht/#17.
[211] Mass-Observation, DR 2684, reply to March 1944 Directive.

CONCLUSION

Despite the earlier assumption that women were the driving force behind the radical decline in family size in Britain, this research has suggested that, at least between the 1920s and the 1950s, it was husbands, not wives, who rooted out birth control information, framed contraceptive strategies for the family, and put these into practice. Rather than this phenomenon being seen as a result of women being increasingly able to pressurize men to do their bidding, and thus as part of the beginnings of an attenuation of patriarchal power within marriage generally, men's influence over birth control was often presented by historical actors as symptomatic of a husband's unquestioned position as head of the household, just as much as it was an indication of his consideration of and sympathy for his wife's opinions and desires. There were some areas of marriage in which women were beginning to push for a redistribution of roles at the margins, in particular over issues such as housework. However, virtually none envisaged a fundamental redistribution of power, and most accepted men as the ultimate authority on most issues. In the case of birth control, they actively welcomed their husbands' dominance over decision-making, as it relieved them from the burdens of a role that would have forced them to play an unwanted proactive sexual role within marriage. Most women wanted to retain a passive, naive sexual persona, and saw their husbands' assumption of contraceptive responsibility as a sign that they cared for their wives and did not want to force them to discuss issues which they found unpleasant or embarrassing. While some women did accept that male responsibility for contraception could be detrimental to their enjoyment of intercourse, as they feared that their husbands might fail in attempts to protect them from pregnancy, this fear did not outweigh their desire to remain untroubled by the sexualized role that an active part in implementing the use of contraception would have required of them. This is not to argue that women had no influence over birth control issues; many wives found subtle ways to influence their husbands' strategies and express their desires. Most importantly, however, women felt that they did not need to take an active role. Husbands during this period saw it as part of their role as men to take responsibility for their wives' fertility and to show consideration for their sexual and reproductive needs. Moreover, such consideration was not confined to newly 'companionate' husbands. The debate about companionate marriage and the construction of the Victorian patriarch as an increasingly unacceptable model of masculinity should not trap us into thinking that marriages became more companionate during this period or that companionate marriages and the decline in family size were directly causally related. However, shifting birth control behaviour should be analysed within the context of debates about marital and gender relations. Debates about the male role provided men with a wide variety of messages and ways of responding to wider social shifts, for example, in the position of women. It is striking, however, that the resulting models of masculinity were united in constructing birth control as a male responsibility. Indeed, that alternative masculine codes all focused on the appropriateness of a husband's control of contraception might be interpreted as generating an overwhelming pressure on men which fuelled fertility change. While some men might represent their contraceptive responsibilities as part of their generation's increased respect for a wife's needs, men who viewed themselves as more 'traditional' or 'authoritarian' equally saw the management of family limitation strategies as their role, reformulating male use of birth control as a proper expression of a husband's natural dominance over all spheres of marriage.

Epilogue

I frequently hear it said, even by members associated with me in this business that this is purely a woman's question . . . For the vast mass of the working class people of this country, the man is as vitally concerned as the woman. There is a danger in concentrating too much on the woman and treating the man generally as a somewhat negligible quantity. There may be and doubtless there are occasions on which a woman is justified in deceiving her husband in this matter, but it is far better that contra-conception and conception should be the conscious regulated act of both parties. It is light we want on the subject not darkness nor even semi-darkness, and so I want to bring in the man.[1]

Most descriptions and historical analyses of the use of birth control in the twentieth century regarded the matter as a 'woman's question'. Women have been placed at the forefront of the dramatic increase in the use of birth control, either persuading husbands to use withdrawal or condoms, or taking matters into their own hands by insisting upon abstinence, turning to abortion, or adopting female methods such as caps. Birth control campaigners, whose voices dominated much of the debate over these issues in the twentieth century, have also consistently framed contraception as a women's issue. This increasing female control over contraceptive matters is seen to have culminated in the arrival of the Pill in 1961 and the legalization of abortion in 1967. In many historical accounts there is a teleological progression from the 1870s through to the 1960s: the era of the Pill becomes the end point in a narrative of women's desperate attempts to control their own bodies and divorce sex from reproduction.

My research has uncovered cultures of contraceptive practice which undermine this simple century-long progression. In the first half of the twentieth century it was primarily husbands, not wives, who took responsibility for birth control strategies. Class and regional differences notwithstanding, both husband and wife saw contraception as part of the male world, and a man's duty. Women were reluctant to take an active role in the management and enforcement of birth control strategy. This would have required them to engage with sexual information, demanded that they speak about sexual matters publicly in order to obtain appliances, entailed the awkwardness of discussing family limitation with their husbands, and compelled them to display a direct interest in coitus prior to the

[1] Councillor Reed (Battersea), Joint Meeting with Workers' Birth Control Group, 19 June (?1924), BL Add. MSS 58589.

act (for example, by inserting a female method of birth control). They regarded such activities as inappropriate transgressions of their passive and naive sexual personas.

These findings—that women were not incrementally taking control of contraception in the first half of the twentieth century, and that birth control strategies were generally led by men for the generations marrying in the first half of the twentieth century—raise some fundamental questions about the way in which we view the development of contraceptive cultures in modern Britain. We should no longer see the entire twentieth century as a series of increasingly successful attempts by women to determine their reproductive future. If by the late twentieth century women were playing a greater role in controlling their own fertility (as is generally assumed), and were not doing so in the 1930s and 1940s, then we need to locate and explain an extremely significant break in social practice. At some point, women came to discard their distaste for birth control issues, to cease valuing their husbands' role in relieving them of the full burden of contraception, and to embrace greater responsibility for these issues.

Research is needed to understand how women overcame their refusal to be involved in contraception. Most 'female' methods (caps, sponges, diaphragms, and pessaries) were widely distrusted and unpopular. The development of new forms of female reproductive technology, in particular the Pill, provided women with methods which were seen to be free from many of the disadvantages of earlier contraceptives. The Pill did not force women to adopt a sexual persona as older methods had. In regularly taking it, women did not have to anticipate sexual intercourse or appear to solicit it at any particular moment.[2] It appeared less artificial than innovations in birth control technology in the early century: the Pill was initially marketed as a 'natural' means of fertility control and was advertised as much for the treatment of menstrual and gynaecological problems as it was for preventing pregnancy.[3] The fact that it was taken independent of coitus and allowed sex to be spontaneous separated it from caps, which had required preparation immediately prior to intercourse and were thus seen to have inhibited the natural expression of sexual desire. Swallowing a pill desexualized the use of contraception and proved far more palatable than methods which demanded 'unhygienic', messy, inelegant, and awkward genital fumbling. In addition, it appeared to be a newly 'respectable' form of contraception: from its launch, it was subject to enormous media discussion and was openly debated on television and in newspapers in a way that was completely new. This gave it a reputable medical association and did much to erode the previous generation's associations of birth control with illicit sexual activity, smutty rubber shops and back-street abortions. Finally, the Pill was more accessible than earlier female methods, which had required either attendance at a birth control clinic or the luck to encounter a sympathetic, proactive doctor. Women were aware that the majority of their own GPs would be

[2] Marks, *Sexual Chemistry*, 195.   [3] Ibid. 5.

prepared to prescribe the Pill. Indeed, some women found themselves under pressure from their doctors to take it.[4]

However, it is possible to overestimate the role of the Pill in altering the gendered dynamics of contraceptive practices. Detailed research is needed to examine the ways in which changing attitudes towards female sexuality transformed women's attitudes towards birth control practices and responsibility. The Pill shared many of the disadvantages that were associated with earlier forms of contraception: it required women to obtain contraceptive advice regularly, submit to medical examination, detail their sexual histories, get regular repeat prescriptions, and remember to take it each day. The effort, expense, and embarrassment which put so many off using caps may have also remained a problem with the Pill. The idea that contraceptives might be dangerous harbingers of infection or carcinogens—a fear which had deterred women from using caps—also dogged the reception of the Pill.[5] Given that the Pill had some of the same disadvantages as earlier methods, we need to identify additional factors behind women's changing approach to birth control use. Women marrying in the 1930s and 1940s resisted taking an active role in the negotiation of contraceptive practices because this demanded that the wife display a sexual persona which made her appear overly sexualized or brazenly available. We need to explain how women became comfortable with the active sexual identity that the Pill might imply. It might be that the sexologists and family-planning campaigners, who had previously largely failed to convince women that they should take an active role in birth control use as a means to engineer more rewarding sexual experiences within their marriages, finally persuaded a receptive audience.[6] We should also look more broadly at the changing sexual culture of Britain, which from the post-war period onwards saw more frequent and open public discussions of sexual ethics and practices inside and outside marriage.[7]

---

[4] Cook, *The Long Sexual Revolution*, 280–1.

[5] Kristin Luker's study of women attending abortion clinics in the 1970s provides an excellent illustration of the disadvantages women faced in using the Pill, and the reasons why they often failed to do so and accidentally became pregnant. For these women, the Pill proclaimed their sexual availability and implied that they were 'looking to have sex'. They found clinic rigmarole intrusive and time-consuming, and disliked the Pill's side-effects: see Luker, *Taking Chances*, esp. 46.

[6] Throughout the second half of the twentieth century marriage advice literature continued to expand. Major new texts were produced, while the material from earlier in the century continued to be reprinted. Helena Wright, for example, produced a sequel to her 1930 *The Sex Factor in Marriage—Sex Fulfilment in Married Women* (later retitled *More About the Sex Factor in Marriage*)—in 1947; L. Hall, *Sex, Gender and Social Change*, 154. The 1960s and 1970s in particular saw a massive expansion in sex and marriage advice literature which received much broader coverage in the mass media than the earlier works of Stopes and her contemporaries. Cook discusses the impact of these works, especially Alex Comfort's *Sex in Society*, in its revised edition of 1963, in *The Long Sexual Revolution*, 282–8.

[7] This period saw, for example, the publication of the Kinsey Report, the debate on the decriminalization of homosexuality following the Wolfenden Report of 1956, and the relaxation of censorship after the unsuccessful attempt to prevent Penguin from publishing D. H. Lawrence's *Lady Chatterley's Lover* in 1960. On these and other developments, see L. Hall, *Sex, Gender and Social Change*, 150–70.

It seems probable, then, that the second half of the twentieth century witnessed a rise in women's direct involvement in birth control matters. New contraceptives such as the Pill were more popular than previous female methods, and women increasingly threw off their earlier reluctance to play any part in the negotiation of sexual activity. This is, however, in sharp contrast to the male-dominated contraceptive culture that has been revealed in this book: during the first half of the twentieth century a key element of a man's identity had been his control of sexual matters and his responsibility for the size and well-being of his family. Through the regular use of birth control, he had determined the frequency of sexual intercourse and taken charge of the welfare of his wife and her body. He might choose to protect her from pregnancy, or 'give' her a baby to love and look after. The rise of this new culture of contraception therefore requires us to explain not only why women were more and more involved, but also how men, accustomed to playing the primary role in contraceptive matters, accommodated this shift. Did the notion that birth control was a male duty wither away, or did men's earlier sense of responsibility coexist with, and adapt itself to, changing female roles and attitudes? We need to examine whether gendered roles were radically reformulated so that birth control became seen primarily as a wife's job, or whether men continued to play significant roles within new forms of relationship, in which birth control was openly negotiated by partners who saw contraception as a matter of joint concern.

It could be that men tended to divorce themselves from practical involvement in birth control and increasingly left responsibility for it to women. Some women complained that, by expecting them to be on the Pill, or to get an abortion in the case of an accident, men burdened their female partners with the sole responsibility for preventing pregnancy.[8] Such a scenario suggests that men might have relished the opportunity to abandon unsatisfactory and unreliable methods of contraception such as withdrawal and condoms, to avoid embarrassing encounters with contraceptive providers, and to be allowed to concern themselves solely with the pleasures of sex rather than its dangers or consequences. Hera Cook argues that sex and marriage manuals from the 1950s placed increasing sexual demands on the wife. She characterizes such material as spawning a 'libertine male sexual ethos', in which men were 'not responsible for their sexual actions' and saw women as 'wholly responsible for controlling sexual activity'.[9] However, given the importance of the duty to 'take care' of the wife in all sexual matters which many men felt up until the end of the 1940s, it is equally possible that, far from being grateful to women for taking more responsibility for contraceptive issues, men might have seen the increased use of female methods as a threat to their influence and role within a relationship.[10] As Linda Gordon suggests, Pill use was seen as a form

---

[8] See e.g. Greer, *Sex and Destiny*, 115–16; Hite, *The Hite Report: Women and Love*, 181–2. See also McLaren, *A History of Contraception*, 244.   [9] Cook, *The Long Sexual Revolution*, 242–4.
[10] Some initial responses to these questions are presented in Marks, *Sexual Chemistry*, 198–9.

of resistance to women's 'exploitation by men' and represented men's diminishing 'social power in the family'.[11]

However, it is far from clear that birth control became a predominantly female issue or that men's interest in birth control or preparedness to take responsibility for family limitation waned as significantly as is generally assumed. Given the dominance of 'male' methods and the centrality of male perspectives in framing contraceptive choices in the first half of the twentieth century, it is implausible to suggest that their interest in contraceptive issues simply collapsed. Clearly, older 'male' methods survived alongside these new female ones. This book has emphasized that, despite the rise of new reproductive technologies during the first half of the twentieth century—notably the latex disposable condom and the female cap—traditional methods remained an important element of everyday practice even among those who also used new appliances. Those marrying during the 1930s and 1940s frequently used various types of birth-control, switching between them as factors such as their motivation to avoid pregnancy shifted. Similarly, we should expect the use of multiple methods to have continued. Apparently high levels of Pill use, such as are indicated by the finding that by 1989 over 75 per cent of all women born between 1945 and 1959 had used the Pill at some time or other, can be misleading: many of these women may also have used other methods, and been on the Pill for varying periods of time.[12] Even after the 1960s, not only were condoms still widely used, but the extent of the use of withdrawal continued to surprise investigators in the 1970s, and other new technologies, notably vasectomy, also made significant gains.[13] Such practices might alert us to continuities in gendered roles and the persistence of forms of contraception for which men had traditionally taken responsibility.

We should not suppose that the rise of female methods would necessarily have provoked a decline in male responsibility. While new methods such as the Pill certainly gave women the option of taking their fertility into their own hands, we should not assume that they inevitably did. Men may have been instrumental in persuading their wives to try new reproductive technologies. Indeed, early critics of the Pill implied that women felt 'forced' to be on the Pill because men would presume they were.

The hypothesis should be explored that a culture was developing in which men and women saw it as their joint responsibility to take care of contraception, which would have required new forms of communication and negotiation within relationships. My research has highlighted that, up until the 1950s and 1960s, many married couples did not discuss birth control issues. This was both because it was seen as a man's responsibility and also because the act of planning was seen as cold, calculating, and an unnatural approach to family building. We might therefore

---

[11] Gordon, *Woman's Body, Woman's Right*, 412; see also Segal, *Straight Sex*, 10; Collins, *Modern Love*, 173.   [12] Cook, *The Long Sexual Revolution*, 268.
[13] L. Hall, *Sex, Gender and Social Change*, 177–8.

ask whether an increasing openness on the part of women to address issues surrounding birth control, and the end of sole male responsibility for it, made couples see birth control as a 'joint decision', and led them to newly open forms of communication about contraception which their parents' generation would have considered inappropriate. Certainly, by the 1960s, institutions such as the Family Planning Association began to present the successful use of birth control as the result of effective communication and active co-operation between husband and wife. They argued that new female methods such the Pill were unlikely to be successfully employed if only the wife was involved; bringing the husband into decision-making came to be seen as the way forward.[14]

The importance of male forms of contraception and of men as initiators of birth control use during the first half of the twentieth century challenges existing historical narratives of this period, and has the potential to revise our understanding of subsequent changes in contraceptive behaviour, particularly during the era of 'sexual revolution'. The increasingly significant role played by women in determining contraceptive strategy by the 1960s did not represent the culmination of their active attempts to limit the size of their families over the previous half-century. Rather, these developments were novel, and represented a sharp break with previous contraceptive practice. For those marrying in the 1930s and 1940s, birth control was the man's responsibility. This was reinforced by a sexual culture in which men knew more about contraception than women, male methods were predominantly used, and women did not wish to adopt the sexual persona that an active role in birth control strategy would have required of them. The story of how this male-dominated culture of contraception was transformed in the last half of the twentieth century is yet to be written, but to do so requires the sort of study produced here: personal understandings and experiences need to be placed at the forefront of the analysis of changing patterns of contraceptive behaviour. Intimate perspectives, which allow us access to the complex private meanings surrounding contraception, and to the way in which sexual and contraceptive behaviour is negotiated in the context of real relationships, can radically challenge and transform the understanding of major demographic and social changes.

---

[14] Cook, *The Long Sexual Revolution*, 277–8. Of course, those running clinics had from the outset seen birth control as a women's issue. For them, it was the idea that men should be allowed into clinics which was new.

APPENDIX

Oral History Respondents

Blackburn

Name	Ref. no.	Sex	dob	dom	aam	No. of children[a]	Main male occupation	Main place of residence	Contraceptive methods ever used[b]					
									Withdrawal	Condoms	Caps	Abstinence[c]	Pessaries	Abortion
Lyn	msf/kf/bl/#1	F	1907	1931	24	1	mill work (teacher)	Blackburn	y					
Iris	msf/kf/bl/#2	F	1914	1938	24	3	railway porter	Darwen	y	y				
Glynnis	msf/kf/bl/#4	F	1901	1924	23	5	plumber	Blackburn	y					
Phyllis	msf/kf/bl/#5	F	1921	1943	22	2	Paper mill (export clerk)	Reading						y
Laura	msf/kf/bl/#6	F	1923	1942	20	2	partly skilled factory work	Blackburn	y					
Marilyn	msf/kf/bl/#7	F	1914	1940	23	3	hairdresser (owned a salon)	Blackburn	y	y				
Maria	msf/kf/bl/#8	F	1917	1941	23	1	painter working for Blackburn council	Blackburn	y	y				y
Eva	msf/kf/bl/#9	F	1911	1932	21	2	owned shoe repair shop	Blackburn	y			y		
Lucy	msf/kf/bl/#10	F	1907	1931	24	1	grocer	Blackburn	y	y				
Eleanor	msf/kf/bl/#11	F	1907	1934	27	3	mechanic (coach builder)	Blackburn (London during the war)	y	y		y		
Eileen	msf/kf/bl/#12	F	1913	1943	30	1	partly skilled factory work	Blackburn	y					
Emily	msf/kf/bl/#13	F	1917	1938	21	2	electrical engineer	Blackburn (brief spell in Hitchin)	y	y				
Terence	msf/ssrs/bl/#15	M	1915	1939	24	3	decorator (self-employed)	Blackburn		y	y	y		
Frank	msf/ssrs/bl/#16	M	1919	1941	22	0	partly skilled labourer	Blackburn	y	y		y		y
Molly	msf/ssrs/bl/#17	F	1913	1939	26	2	bricklayer	Blackburn	y	y				
Maud	msf/kf/bl/#18	F	1912	1934	21	1	1st: warehouseman and despatch foreman; 2nd: cobbler	Blackburn						
Tim	msf/ssrs/bl/#19	M	1917	1947	29	3	watch repairer	Leyland	y	y	y			
Doreen	msf/kf/bl/#20	F	1922	1946	24	2	builder and foreman bricklayer	Blackburn	y	y	y			
Larry	msf/kf/bl/#20	M	1917	1946	29	2	builder and foreman bricklayer	Blackburn	y	y				
Rose	msf/kf/bl/#21	F	1928	1948	19	6	1st: unemployed 2nd: lorry driver	Blackburn						
Doris	msf/ssrs/bl/#22	F	1921	1945	24	3	foreman in an engineering works	Blackburn	y	y	y			
Jake	msf/ssrs/bl/#22	M	1922	1945	22	3	foreman in an engineering works	Blackburn	y	y	y			
Ed	msf/ssrs/bl/#23	M	1913	1937	24	2	carpenter	Blackburn	y	y	y			y
Arthur	msf/ssrs/bl/#24	M	1918	1942	24	1	JCB operator	Blackburn				y		
Lorna	msf/kf/bl/#25	F	1917	1939	21	2	factory worker (valve tester) later school caretaker	Blackburn	y			y		

Name	Code	Sex	dob	dom	aam	Final family size[a]	Occupation	Place						
Peter	msf/kf/bl/#26	M	1921	1940	19	3	cotton mill (stripper and grinder)	Blackburn						y
Elizabeth	msf/kf/bl/#26	F	1923	1947	24	1	milkman	Blackburn	y					
Jennie	msf/kf/bl/#27	F	1908	1930	22	1	sawmill worker	Blackburn	y					
Marian	msf/kf/bl/#28	F	1908	1939	30	1	colour-mixing in textile dyeing factory	Blackburn	y					
Mavis	msf/kf/bl/#29	F	1908	1929	21	6	long-distance lorry driver	Blackburn	y					
Sarah	msf/kf/bl#30	F	1906	1928	21	1	upholsterer	Bolton	y			y		
Sally	msf/kf/bl/#31	F	1908	1934	26	1	painter and decorator	Blackburn	y					y
Dick	msf/kf/bl/#32	M	1920	1953	28	3	clerk	Blackburn	y	y	y			
Jane	msf/kf/bl/#32	F	1925	1953	33	3	clerk	Blackburn	y	y	y			
Alistair	msf/kf/bl/#33	M	1927	1952	24	2	paper mill (supervisor)	Blackburn	y					
Christopher	msf/kf/bl/#34	M	1918	1947	29	3	army until 1952; building maintenance	Cumbria and Lancashire	y	y				y
Merlin	msf/kf/bl/#35	M	1908	1940	32	1	bus/tram driver	Blackburn	y	y				
Colin	msf/kf/bl/#36	M	1923	1947	24	3	plumber	Blackburn	y	y				
Felicity	msf/kf/bl/#37	F	1919	1954	34	2	claims assessor	Accrington						
Daphne	msf/jm/bl/#38	F	1912	1937	25	2	shopkeeper (confectioner)	Great Harwood						
Pearl	msf/kf/bl/#40	F	1915	never married	n/a	0	head teacher	Rochdale						
Mildred	msf/kf/bl/#41	F	1924	1947	22	0	teacher	Burnley						
Elma	msf/jm/bl/#42	F	1909	1933	24	1	policeman	Manchester	y					
Olive	msf/jm/bl/#44	F	1915	1951	37	0	undertaker	Standish	y				y	
Bernard	msf/jm/bl/#45	M	1907	1936	29	1	journalist (newspaper manager)	Blackburn						
Diana	msf/jm/bl/#45	F	1910	1936	26	1	journalist (newspaper manager)	Blackburn	y					
Maureen	msf/kf/bl/#46	F	1920	1943	22	2	sales rep (building trade)	Blackburn	y			y		
Nora	msf/jm/bl/#47	F	1920	1945	25	2	director of electrical retail business	Blackburn	y					
Gill	msf/kf/bl/#48	F	1920	1945	25	3	mill owner	Blackburn	y			y		
Enid	msf/kf/bl/#49	F	1909	1939	30	3	supervisor in textile mill	Blackburn	y					
Hilda	msf/kf/bl/#50	F	1914	1935	21	1	1st: sales director for pharmaceutical firm; 2nd: chartered accountant	Blackburn	y					

[a] Final family size, excluding stillbirths, stepchildren, adopted children.

[b] Only methods reportedly used are included. Any discrepancy between husband and wife in listing contraceptive practices is retained.

[c] Abstinence includes both those who reported a conscious reduction in coital frequency and those who avoided sex altogether. It does not include those whose testimony was ambiguous or contradictory.

dob date of birth

dom date of first marriage

aam age at first marriage

Hertfordshire

Name	Ref. no.	Sex	dob	dom	aam	No. of children[a]	Main male occupation	Main place of residence	Contraceptive methods ever used[b]					
									Withdrawal	Condoms	Caps	Abstinence[c]	Pessaries	Abortion
Catherine	msf/kf/ht/#1	F	1912	1941	29	1	watchmaker	Berkhamsted	y	y			y	y
Dougie	msf/kf/ht/#5	M	1919	1941	21	2	odd jobs then (eventually) chargehand (foreman) in chemicals factory	Berkhamsted	y	y				y
Rebecca	msf/kf/ht/#6	F	1903	1943	40	1	taxi driver	London						
Agatha	msf/kf/ht/#7	F	1910	1940	30	1	gardener	Surrey	y	y				
Clare	msf/kf/ht/#8	F	1912	1936	24	2	1st: milkman; 2nd: construction worker	Berkhamsted	y	y				
Esme	msf/kf/ht/#9	F	1921	1945	24	3	area sales manager	Sussex		y				y
Gerald	msf/kf/ht/#9	M	1919	1945	26	3	area sales manager	Sussex		y				y
Roger	msf/kf/ht/#10	M	1910	1938	27	1	chartered surveyor	Hertfordshire	y		y			y
Monica	msf/kf/ht/#11	F	1902	1933	30	4	RAF officer	military postings around the world					y	
Pru	msf/kf/ht/#12	F	1911	1935	24	2	bank securities	Newbury	y	y				
Gay	msf/kf/ht/#13	F	1928	1947	18	2	salesman	Tring			y			
Alf	msf/kf/ht/#14	M	1915	1938	23	2	sales assistant	London		y			y	
Heather	msf/kf/ht/#14	F	1916	1938	21	2	sales assistant	London		y			y	
Dennis	msf/kf/ht/#15	M	1915	1940	25	2	printer and compositor	Harpenden					y	
Patrick	msf/kf/ht/#16	M	1918	1941	23	3	clerk and auditor, salesman	East Ham			y			
Norman	msf/kf/ht/#17	M	1914	1944	30	1	teacher	London	y	y				
Angela	msf/kf/ht/#18	F	1924	1947	23	2	electrical engineer	Preston, Harpenden		y	y			
Hugh	msf/kf/ht/#18	M	1926	1947	20	2	electrical engineer	Preston, Harpenden		y	y			
Pam	msf/kf/ht/#19	F	1907	1932	24	0	mould maker in tyre factory	Harpenden				y		
Penny	msf/srss/ht/#20	F	1916	1938	21	3	rubber factory labourer	Harpenden	y	y				

			dob	dom	aam		occupation	place							
Joanna	msf/kf/ht/#22	F	1915	1947	32	0	civil servant	High Wycombe			y			y	
Mark	msf/kf/ht/#22	M	1917	1947	30	0	civil servant	High Wycombe			y			y	
Edmund	msf/kf/ht/#23	M	1910	1938	28	0	printer	Harpenden							
William	msf/kf/ht/#24	M	1902	1931	29	0	works manager	Dunstable	y		y			y	y
Bryan	msf/kf/ht/#25	M	1918	1947	28	2	rubber factory (machine operator became foreman)	St Albans			y			y	y
Humphrey	msf/kf/ht/#26	M	1914	1938	24	1	civil engineer and building surveyor	North London and Hertfordshire			y	y			
June	msf/kf/ht/#27	F	1914	1936	22	2	manager of chain of grocery stores	Yorkshire	y		y				y
Sam	msf/srss/ht/#28	M	1912	1941	29	1	articled clerk	Harpenden			y				y
Betty	msf/kf/ht/#31	F	1922	1948	26	2	head teacher	Brighton and Harpenden			y				y
Horace	msf/kf/ht/#31	M	1915	1948	33	2	head teacher	Brighton and Harpenden			y				y
Hubert	msf/kf/ht/#32	M	1911	1936	26	3	journalist then director agricultural engineering works	Leighton Buzzard	y		y	y	y		y
Judith	msf/kf/ht/#33	F	1931	1958	27	5	managing director of large grocery firm	St Albans	y	y					
Vera	msf/kf/ht/#34	F	1917	1949	32	3	dental mechanic	Harpenden		y	y				
Antonia	msf/kf/ht/#35	F	1928	1949	21	6	chartered accountant	St Albans		y	y	y			
Reg	msf/kf/ht/#36	M	1919	1942	21	4	film maker	Manchester	y		y			y	
Emma	msf/kf/ht/#37	F	1906	1936	30	3	research scientist	Harpenden		y	y			y	
Dora	msf/srss/ht/#38	F	1923	1945	22	2	mechanic	Radlett			y				
Grace	msf/srss/ht/#38	F	1922	1944	21	2	owned small motor-engineering business	Harpenden	y		y				

[a] Final family size, excluding stillbirths, stepchildren, adopted children.

[b] Only methods reportedly used are included. Any discrepancy between husband and wife in listing contraceptive practices is retained.

[c] Abstinence includes both those who reported a conscious reduction in coital frequency and those who avoided sex altogether. It does not include those whose testimony was ambiguous or contradictory.

dob   date of birth

dom   date of first marriage

aam   age at first marriage

Oxford

Name	Ref. no.	Sex	dob	dom	aam	No. of children[a]	Main male occupation	Main place of residence	Contraceptive methods ever used[b]					
									Withdrawal	Condoms	Caps	Abstinence[c]	Pessaries	Abortion
Annie	bc3ox#2	F	1905	1932	27	1	post office stamp counter	Oxford						
Gwen	bc3ox#3	F	1912	1935	23	1	compositor and printer	Oxford		y				
Vye	bc3ox#4	F	1919	1938	19	1	steel works inspector	Oxford	y	y				
Hilda	bc3ox#5	F	1918	1938	20	2	railway engineer	Oxford	y	y				
Hadyn	bc3ox#6	M	1910	1938	28	2	steel works (production line)	Oxford		y				
Fred	bc3ox#7	M	1915	1951	36	1	college cook	Oxford		y				
Vera	bc3ox#8	F	1910	1929	19	1	Co-op grocer	Oxford	y					
Gladys	bc3ox#9	F	1906	1932	26	6	Morris Motors	Oxford	y					
Rosaline	bc3ox#10	F	1913	1939	26	1	army medic (killed in 1941)	Oxford	y					
Stella	bc3ox#11	F	1906	1930	24	2	cobbler	Oxford						
Hetty	bc3ox#12	F	1914	1936	21	1	bus driver	Oxford			y		y	
Esther	bc3ox#13	F	1914	1938	24	2	self-employed painter and decorator	Oxford	y	y				y
Jack	bc3ox#13	M	1913	1938	25	2	self-employed painter and decorator	Oxford	y	y				y
Louisa	bc3ox#14	F	1908	1929	21	3	setter out (steel works)	Oxford	y	y				
Edward	bc3ox#15	M	1914	1937	23	2	general engineer (car plant)	Oxford	y					
Will	bc3ox#16	M	1907	1928	21	4	Morris Motors	Oxford	y					
Phyllis	bc3ox#17	F	1915	1937	21	2	steel works (check and template)	Oxford	y					
Margaret	bc3ox#18	F	1916	1940	24	2	hotel owner, chef, and catering manager	Oxford	y	y	y		y	y
Nellie	bc3ox#19	F	1920	1943	23	3	train driver	Oxford	y	y	y		y	
Doris	bc3ox#20	F	1920	1941	20	5	milkman	Oxford			y	y	y	
Millie	bc3ox#21	F	1902	1924	21	3	upholsterer	London, Oxford	y	y				
Nancy	bc3ox#22	F	1918	1939	21	2	pipe fitter—pressed steel	Oxford	y	y				
Rhonda	bc3ox#24	F	1905	1928	23	2	soldier before and during war, then in accounting department for Morris car works - unskilled clerical	Oxford	y					
Gladys	bc3ox#25	F	1908	1938	18	3	pressed steel inspector (print shop)	Oxford	y	y				

Name	Code	Sex	dob	dom	aam	Family size[a]	Occupation	Location				
William	bc3ox#25	M	1918	1938	30	3	pressed steel inspector (print shop)	Oxford	y			
Brenda	bc3ox#26	F	1908	1933	25	2	insurance salesman	Oxford	y			
Annie	bc3ox#27	F	1908	1929	21	2	self-employed painter and decorator	Oxford	y			
Ada	bc3ox#28	F	1911	1935	25	4	school textbook printer	Oxford	y		y	
Delia	bc3ox#29	F	1915	1938	22	3	foreman coppersmith at steel works	Oxford	y	y		
Joe	bc3ox#29	M	1915	1938	23	3	foreman coppersmith at steel works	Oxford	y	y		
Dorothy	bc3ox#30	F	1914	1937	21	2	pipe layer, Oxford waterworks	Oxford	y	y		
Arthur	bc3ox#30	M	1910	1937	25	2	pipe layer, Oxford waterworks	Oxford	y	y		
Hilda	bc3ox#31	F	1916	1939	23	2	security guard, steel works	Oxford	y			
Edna	bc3ox#32	F	1914	1936	21	2	steel works (piece work)	Oxford	y			
Richard	bc3ox#32	M	1914	1936	21	2	steel works (piece work)	Oxford	y			
John	bc3ox#33	M	1908	1933	24	5	printer	Oxford				
Sid	bc3ox#34	M	1906	1922	16	2	welder (car works)	Oxford				
Alfie	bc3ox#35	M	1908	1931	23	4	steel works (charge hand)	Wolverton	y			y
Arthur	bc3ox#36	M	1909	1936	27	4	steel works (foreman)	Oxford	y		y	
William	bc3ox#37	M	1902	1931	29	2	factory security guard	Oxford	y		y	y
Stanley	bc3ox#38	M	1911	1937	25	3	GWR (boilersmithing)	Oxford	y		y	y
Claire	bc3ox#39	F	1914	1938	24	1	Steel works (piece work, small tools)	Oxford	y	y		
Dick	bc3ox#39	M	1918	1938	28	1	Steel works (piece work, small tools)	Oxford	y			
Cecil	bc3ox#40	M	1915	1936	21	2	Steel works (panel beater)	Oxford	y			
Wyn	bc3ox#40	F	1916	1936	20	2	Steel works (panel beater)	Oxford	y			
Bertha	bc3ox#41	F	1912	1935	23	1	steel works (engineer)	Oxford	y			

[a] Final family size, excluding stillbirths, stepchildren, adopted children.

[b] Only methods reportedly used are included. Any discrepancy between husband and wife in listing contraceptive practices is retained.

[c] Abstinence includes both those who reported a conscious reduction in coital frequency and those who avoided sex altogether. It does not include those whose testimony was ambiguous or contradictory.

dob   date of birth

dom   date of first marriage

aam   age at first marriage

South Wales

Name	Ref. no.	Sex	dob	dom	aam	No. of children[a]	Main male occupation	Main place of residence	Contraceptive methods ever used[b]					
									Withdrawal	Condoms	Caps	Abstinence[c]	Pessaries	Abortion
Eva	bc1#1	F	1915	1933	18	2	construction worker (regularly unemployed)	Cardiff	y		y	y	y	
Rosie	bc1#2	F	1918	1939	21	5	miner	Abertillery		y			y	
Ivy	bc1#2	F	1913	1932	19	2	miner	Abertillery	y					
Nora	bc2#1	F	1900	1924	24	3	miner	Tonpentre	y					
Eileen	bc2#2	F	1899	1924	25	3	tin works	Pontyclun	y					
Muriel	bc2#3	F	1918	1938	20	7	miner	Pontllanfraith						y
Margaret	bc2#4	F	1901	1918	17	1	miner	Newbridge						
Mary-Jane	bc2#5	F	1919	1944	25	3	miner	Aberbargoed						
Eva	bc2#6	F	1909	1932	23	4	mechanic	Blackwood	y	y				
Iris	bc2#8	F	1914	1934	20	2	foreman steel director	Pontypridd	y					
Frances	bc2#9	F	1919	1936	17	6	miner	Newbridge						
Gwen	bc2#10	F	1917	1935	18	2	bus driver (x2)	Liswerry	y					
Thomas	bc2#11	M	1913	1933	20	8	professional boxer	Newport	y					
Dilys	bc2#13	F	1906	1926	20	6	postman	Swansea	y	y			y	y
Fred	bc2#14	M	1912	1934	22	1	railway booking office	Mountain Ash	y	y				
Violet	bc2#15	F	1907	1930	22	2	1st: railwayman; 2nd: merchant navy (sailor)	Penarth	y					
Kathleen	bc2#16	F	1910	1930	20	2	1st: miner; 2nd: owned green grocer's shop	Maesteg	y					
Tom	bc2#17	M	1906	1932	26	7	miner	Maesteg			y			
Thomas	bc2#18	M	1915	1953	38	1	miner	Maesteg		y				
Walter	bc2#20	M	1916	1940	21	7	cable layer	Penarth	y	y				
Maggie	bc2#21	F	1913	1937	23	2	bricklayer	Penarth		y			y	
Eileen	bc2#22	F	1900	1922	22	6	dockland coal supervisor	Penarth						
Edith	bc2#23	F	1908	1930	22	3	shop assistant, TB invalid	Penarth	y					
Ann	bc2#24	F	1912	1933	20	3	miner	Abertillery	y					
Ken	bc2#24	M	1913	1933	20	3	miner	Abertillery	y					
Charlie	bc2#25	M	1903	1936	33	2	boilerman	Penarth	y	y				
John	bc2#26	M	1920	1942	22	1	mechanic	Llanbradach	y					
Phyllis	bc2#26	F	1922	1942	21	1	miner then docker	Merthyr Tydfil	y				y	
Dee	bc2#27	F	1925	1939	24	2	miner then docker	Llanbradach	y					

Name	Code	Sex	dob	dom	aam	Family size[a]	Occupation	Place
Henry	bc2#27	M	1915	1939	24	3	mechanic	Merthyr Tydfil
Leslie	bc3sw#1	M	1915	1936	21	2	miner	Pontypridd
Ernest	bc3sw#2	M	1910	1936	26	5	fishmonger	Pontypridd
Charlie	bc3sw#3	M	1908	1933	24	2	miner	Pontypridd
Les	bc3sw#4	M	1918	1939	20	8	shepherd	Pontypridd
Beatrice	bc3sw#5	F	1914	1935	20	2	miner	Tonypandy
Jack	bc3sw#5	M	1914	1935	21	2	miner	Tonypandy
Doris	bc3sw#6	F	1915	1938	23	2	bricklayer	Pontypridd
Ern	bc3sw#8	M	1909	1936	27	2	miner	Porth
Walter	bc3sw#9	M	1908	1930	21	1	barber	Pontypridd
Claris	bc3sw#10	F	1911	1934	23	3	miner	Blaenavon
William	bc3sw#11	M	1911	1936	28	1	miner	Crumlin
Elizabeth	bc3sw#12	F	1918	1941	23	3	1st: unemployed (black market coal distribution); 2nd: factory foreman	Cardiff and Tredegar
Margaret	bc3sw#13	F	1921	1940	19	3	costermonger	Merthyr Tydfil
Aileen	bc3sw#14	F	1913	1932	19	8	carpenter	Caerphilly
Harriet	bc3sw#15	F	1915	1935	20	5	steel works	Pontypool
Edna	bc3sw#16	F	1899	1930	30	2	salesman (furniture)	Pontypool
Dolly	bc3sw#17	F	1911	1930	19	2	miner	Pontypool
Gwen	bc3sw#18	F	1914	1940	25	1	steel works	Pontypool
Betty	bc3sw#19	F	1912	1934	22	1	miner	Blaenavon
Gwendoline	bc3sw#22	F	1910	1931	21	3	foreman quarryman	Merthyr Tydfil
Hugh	bc3sw#23	M	1913	1934	21	4	miner	Senghenydd
Lilian	bc3sw#24	F	1913	1937	24	2	accountant	Pontypool
Rachel	bc3sw#25	F	1909	1930	21	2	miner	Blaenavon
Reenie	bc3sw#26	F	1916	1934	18	6	miner	Merthyr Tydfil
Gertrude	bc3sw#27	F	1902	1925	23	3	electrician	Aberdare
Gladys	bc3sw#28	F	1910	1930	20	3	miner	Troedyrhiw
Doris	bc3sw#29	F	1913	1936	23	2	inspector of engineering works	Pontypool
Ivor	bc3sw#29	M	1909	1936	27	2	inspector of engineering works	Pontypool

[a] Final family size, excluding stillbirths, includes stepchildren, adopted children.

[b] Only methods reportedly used are included. Any discrepancy between husband and wife in listing contraceptive practices is retained.

[c] Abstinence includes both those who reported a conscious reduction in coital frequency and those who avoided sex altogether. It does not include those whose testimony was ambiguous or contradictory.

dob   date of birth

dom   date of first marriage

aam   age at first marriage

Bibliography

MANUSCRIPT SOURCES

British Library Department of Manuscripts
  Marie C. Stopes Papers: BL Add. MSS 58589–58642
Archives and Manuscripts Collection at the Wellcome Library for the History and Understanding of Medicine:
  Family Planning Association Archives: A&M: SA/FPA
  Helena Wright Papers: A&M: PP/HRW
  Television History Workshop, 'In the Club: Birth Control This Century' transcripts: A&M: GC/105
  Marie C. Stopes Papers: A&M: PP/MCS
Mass-Observation Archive at the University of Sussex
  Topic Collection: Family Planning 1944–49: TC3
  File Reports: 3107 'The Ideal Family' 1949
                   2111 'Population Problems' 1944
  Directive Respondent: replies to March 1944 Directive, April 1944 Directive

OFFICIAL PUBLICATIONS

Birkett, Norman W., *see Report of the Inter-Departmental Committee on Abortion*
Campbell, Dame Janet, Cameron, Isabella, and Jones, Dilys M., 'High Maternal Mortality in Certain Areas', *Reports on Public Health and Medical Subjects*, 68, Ministry of Health (London: HMSO, 1932).
Lewis-Faning, E: *Report on an Enquiry into Family Limitation and its Influence on Human Fertility During the Past Fifty Years*, Papers of the Royal Commission on Population 1 (London: HMSO, 1949).
Ministry of Health, *Interim Report of Departmental Committee on Maternal Mortality and Morbidity* (London: HMSO, 1930).
—— *Final Report of Departmental Committee on Maternal Mortality and Morbidity* (London: HMSO, 1932).
—— *Report on Maternal Mortality in Wales* (London: HMSO, 1937).
—— *Report of the Inter-Departmental Committee on Abortion* (London: HMSO, 1939).
Rhondda Urban District Council, *Report of the Medical Officer of Health and School Medical Officer, for the Year 1935* (Ferndale, 1936).

JOURNALS AND NEWSPAPERS

Birth Control News
British Medical Journal
The Lancet
The New Generation
Western Mail

BOOKS, ARTICLES, AND THESES

ACCAMPO, ELINOR A., 'The Gendered Nature of Contraception in France: Neo-Malthusianism, 1900–1920', *Journal of Interdisciplinary History*, 34/2 (2003), 235–62.

ALEXANDER, SALLY, 'The Mysteries and Secrets of Women's Bodies: Sexual Knowledge in the First Half of the Twentieth Century', in Mica Nava and Alan O'Shea (eds.), *Modern Times: Reflections on a Century of English Modernity* (London: Routledge, 1996), 161–75.

ALTER, GEORGE, 'Theories of Fertility Decline: A Nonspecialist's Guide to the Current Debate', in John R. Gillis, Louise A. Tilly, and David Levine (eds.), *The European Experience of Declining Fertility, 1850–1970: The Quiet Revolution* (Cambridge, Mass.: Blackwell, 1992), 13–27.

AMIN, SAJEDA, and LLOYD, CYNTHIA B., 'Women's Lives and Rapid Fertility Decline: Some Lessons from Bangladesh and Egypt', *Population Research and Policy Review*, 21 (2002), 275–317.

ANDERSON, KATHRYN, and JACK, DANA C., 'Learning to Listen: Interview Techniques and Analyses', in Sherna Berger Gluck and Daphne Patai (eds.), *Women's Words. The Feminist Practice of Oral History* (New York: Routledge, 1991), 11–26.

ANDERSON, STUART, ' "The most important place in the history of British birth control": Community Pharmacy and Sexual Health in Twentieth Century Britain', *The Pharmaceutical Journal*, 266/7129 (2001), 23–9.

ANGIN, ZEYNEP, and SHORTER, FREDERIC C., 'Negotiating Reproduction and Gender During the Fertility Decline in Turkey', *Social Science and Medicine*, 47/5 (1998), 555–64.

ANON., 'Reflections of an Abortionist', *Family Planning*, 16/1 (1967); repr. in J. Medawar and D. Pyke (eds.), *Family Planning* (Harmondsworth: Penguin, 1971), 116–26.

ARCOTT, SHIRLEY, *Mothercraft and Maternity: Leicester's Maternity and Infant Welfare Services 1900–1948* (Leicester: Leicestershire Museums Arts & Records Service, 1997).

ARIÈS, PHILIPPE, 'On the Origins of Contraception in France', in O. Ranum and P. Ranum (eds.), *Popular Attitudes Towards Birth Control in Pre-Industrial France and England* (New York: Harper & Row, 1972), 10–20.

—— 'An Interpretation To Be Used for a History of Mentalities', in O. Ranum and P. Ranum (eds.), *Popular Attitudes Towards Birth Control in Pre-Industrial France and England* (New York: Harper & Row, 1972), 120–5.

Aristotle's Works (London: Shoe Land Publishing, n.d. [c.1850]).

ASHPLANT, TIMOTHY G., 'Anecdote as Narrative Resource in Working Class Life Stories', in Mary Chamberlain and Paul Thompson (eds.), *Narrative and Genre* (London: Routledge, 1998), 9–113.

ASKHAM, JANET, 'Telling Stories', *Sociological Review*, 30 (1982), 555–73.

—— *Identity and Stability in Marriage* (Cambridge: Cambridge University Press, 1984).

ATKINSON, JEAN, 'Gender Roles in Marriage and the Family: A Critique and Some Proposals', *Journal of Family Issues*, 8 (1987), 5–41.

AYRES, PAT, and LAMBERTZ, JAN, 'Marriage Relations, Money and Domestic Violence in Working-Class Liverpool, 1919–39', in Jane Lewis (ed.), *Labour and Love* (Oxford: Blackwell, 1986), 195–219.

BABER, KRISTINE M., 'Studying Women's Sexualities: Feminist Transformations', in Donna L. Sollie and Leigh A. Leslie (eds.), *Gender, Families and Close Relationships* (Thousand Oaks: Sage, 1994), 50–73.

BADEN-POWELL, ROBERT, *Rovering to Success* (London: Herbert Jenkins, 1922).

BANKS, J. A., *Prosperity and Parenthood: A Study of Family Planning among the Victorian Middle Classes* (London: Routledge & Kegan Paul, 1954).

—— *Victorian Values: Secularism and the Size of Families* (London: Routledge & Kegan Paul, 1981).

—— and BANKS, OLIVE, *Feminism and Family Planning in Victorian England* (Liverpool: Liverpool University Press, 1964).

BARRET-DUCROCQ, FRANÇOISE, *Love in the Time of Victoria*, trans. John Howe (London: Verso, 1991); 1st pub. as *L'Amour sous Victoria* (1989).

BATTAN, JESSE F., 'The "Rights" of Husbands and the "Duties" of Wives: Power and Desire in the American Bedroom 1850–1910', *Journal of Family History*, 24/2 (1999), 165–86.

BEALE, G. Courtenay, *Wise Wedlock: The Whole Truth* (1922; London: Health Promotion, 1930).

BEALE, OCTAVIUS CHARLES, *Racial Decay* (London: A. C. Fifield, 1911).

BECK-GERNSHEIM, ELISABETH, *Reinventing the Family: In Search of New Lifestyles*, trans. Patrick Camiller (Cambridge: Polity, 2002); 1st pub. as *Was kommt nach der Familie?* (Munich, 1998).

BECKMAN, LINDA J., 'Measuring the Process of Fertility Decision-Making', in Greer Litton Fox (ed.), *The Childbearing Decision: Fertility Attitudes and Behaviour* (Beverley Hills: Sage, 1982), 73–96.

BEED, TERENCE W., and STIMSON, ROBERT J. (eds.), *Survey Interviewing: Theory and Techniques* (Sydney: George Allen & Unwin, 1985).

BEIER, LUCINDA MCCRAY, ' "We were as green as grass": Learning about Sex and Reproduction in Three Working-Class Lancashire Communities, 1900–1970', *Social History of Medicine*, 16/3 (2003), 461–80.

BELL, COLIN, and NEWBY, HOWARD, 'Husbands and Wives: The Deferential Dialectic', in Diana Leonard and Sheila Allen (eds.), *Sexual Divisions Revisited* (Basingstoke: Macmillan, 1991), 25–44.

—— —— and ROBERTS, HELEN (eds.), *Social Researching: Politics, Problems, Practice* (London: Routledge & Kegan Paul, 1984).

BESANT, ANNIE, 'The Law of Population: Its Consequence and its Bearing upon Human Conduct and Morals' (1884), repr. in S. Chandrasekha (ed.), *A Dirty Filthy Little Book: The Writings of Charles Knowlton and Annie Besant on Reproductive Physiology and Birth Control and an Account of the Bradlaugh–Besant trial* (Berkeley and Los Angeles: University of California Press, 1981).

BIBBY, CYRIL, *Sex Education: A Guide for Parents, Teachers and Youth Leaders* (London: Macmillan, 1944).

BILLER, P. P. A., 'Birth Control in the West in the Thirteenth and Early Fourteenth Centuries', *Past and Present*, 94/0 (1982), 3–26.

BINGHAM, ADRIAN, *Gender, Modernity and the Popular Press in Inter-War Britain* (Oxford: Oxford University Press, 2004).

BLAKE, JUDITH, 'Are Babies Consumer Durables? A Critique of the Economic Theory of Reproductive Motivation', *Population Studies*, 22 (1968), 5–25.

BLAND, LUCY, *Banishing the Beast: English Feminism and Sexual Morality 1885–1915* (London: Penguin, 1995).

BLÉCOURT, WILLEM DE, 'Cultures of Abortion in The Hague in the Early Twentieth Century', in Franz X. Eder and Lesley Hall and Gert Hekma (eds.), *Sexual Cultures in Europe: Themes in Sexuality* (Manchester: Manchester University Press, 1999), 195–209.

BLEDSOE, CAROLINE, 'Contraception and "Natural" Fertility in America', in John B. Casterline, Ronald D. Lee, and Karen A. Foote (eds.), *Fertility in the United States: New Patterns, New Theories* (New York: Population Council, 1996), 297–324.

BOSANQUET, HELEN, *The Family* (1906: London: Macmillan, 1915).

BOTT, ELIZABETH, *Family and Social Network: Roles, Norms, and External Relationships in Ordinary Urban Families* (London: Tavistock, 1957).

BOURKE, JOANNA, *Working-Class Cultures in Britain, 1890–1960: Gender, Class and Ethnicity* (London: Routledge, 1994).

BRANNEN, JULIA, 'The Study of Sensitive Topics', *Sociological Review*, 36 (1988), 552–63.

BRIGGS, CHARLES L., *Learning How To Ask: A Sociolinguistic Appraisal of the Role of the Interview in Social Science Research* (Cambridge: Cambridge University Press, 1986).

BRISTOW, JOSEPH, 'Respecting Respectability: "Victorian Sexuality" and the Copulatory Imagination', *History Workshop Journal*, 41 (1996), 286–92.

British Medical Association, *Report of a Committee on Medical Aspects of Abortion* (London, 1936).

BROD, HARRY (ed.), *The Making of Masculinities: The New Men's Studies* (Winchester, Mass.: Allen & Unwin, 1987).

BRODIE, JANET FARRELL, *Contraception and Abortion in Nineteenth Century America* (Ithaca: Cornell University Press, 1994).

BROOKE, STEPHEN ' "A New World For Women"? Abortion Law Reform in Britain during the 1930s', *American Historical Review*, 106/2 (2001), 1–59.

—— 'Gender and Working Class Identity in Britain during the 1950s', *Journal of Social History*, 34/4 (2001), 773–95.

BROOKES, BARBARA, 'Women and Reproduction 1860–1939', in Jane Lewis (ed.), *Labour and Love: Women's Experience of Home and Family, 1850–1940* (Oxford: Blackwell, 1986), 149–71.

—— *Abortion in England 1900–1967* (London: Routledge, 1988).

—— 'Hygiene, Health and Bodily Knowledge, 1880–1940: A New Zealand Case Study', *Journal of Family History*, 28/2 (2003), 297–313.

BROWN, P. S., 'Female Pills and the Reputation of Iron as an Abortifacient', *Medical History*, 21 (1977), 291–304.

BULATAO, RUDOLFO A., and LEE, RONALD D. (eds.), *Determinants of Fertility in Developing Countries*, vol. i: *Supply and Demand for Children* (New York: Academic Press, 1983).

BURGESS, ERNEST W., and LOCKE, HARVEY J., *The Family from Institution to Companionship* (1945; 2nd edn. New York: American Book Company, 1960).

BURNETT, JACKY, 'Exposing "the Inner Life": The Women's Co-operative Guild's Attitude to "Cruelty" ', in Shani D'Cruze (ed.), *Everyday Violence in Britain, 1850–1950: Gender and Class* (Harlow: Pearson, 2000), 136–52.

BURNETT, JOHN, *Destiny Obscure: Autobiographies of Childhood, Education and the Family from the 1820s to the 1920s* (London: Routledge, 1982).

BUSFIELD, JOAN, and PADDON, MICHAEL, *Thinking about Children: Sociology and Fertility in Post-War England* (Cambridge: Cambridge University Press, 1977).

CALDWELL, JOHN C., 'Direct Economic Costs and Benefits of Children', in Rudolfo A. Bulatao and Ronald D. Lee (eds.), *Determinants of Fertility in Developing Countries*, vol. i: *Supply and Demand for Children* (New York: Academic Press, 1983), 458–93.

CALL, VAUGHN, SPRECHER, SUSAN, and SCHWARTZ, PEPPER, 'The Incidence and Frequency of Marital Sex in a National Sample', *Journal of Marriage and the Family*, 57 (1995), 639–52.

CAMPBELL, PATRICIA J., *Sex Education Books for Young Adults 1892–1979* (New York: R. R. Bowker, 1979).

CANNELL, C. F., 'Overview Response Bias and Interviewer Variability in Surveys', in Terence W. Beed and Robert J. Stimson (eds.), *Survey Interviewing: Theory and Techniques* (Sydney: George Allen & Unwin, 1985), 1–23.

CARLSSON, GÖSTA, 'The Decline of Fertility: Innovation or Adjustment Process', *Population Studies*, 20 (1966), 149–74.

CARTER, ANTONY T., 'Agency and Fertility: For an Ethnography of Practice', in Susan Greenhalgh (ed.), *Situating Fertility: Anthropology and Demographic Inquiry* (Cambridge: Cambridge University Press, 1995), 55–85.

CARTER, JULIAN B., 'Birds, Bees and Venereal Disease: Toward an Intellectual History of Sex Education', *Journal of the History of Sexuality*, 10/2 (2001), 213–49.

CARTER, MARION W., ' "Because he loves me": Husbands' Involvement in Maternal Health in Guatamala', *Culture, Health and Sexuality*, 4/3 (2002), 259–79.

CARTWRIGHT, ANN, *Parents and Family Planning Services* (London: Routledge & Kegan Paul, 1970).

—— *How Many Children?* (London: Routledge & Kegan Paul, 1976).

—— and MOFFETT, JOANNA, 'A Comparison of Results Obtained by Men and Women Interviewers in a Fertility Survey', *Journal of Bio-Social Science*, 6 (1974), 315–22.

CASTERLINE, JOHN B., LEE, RONALD D., and FOOTE, KAREN A. (eds.), *Fertility in the United States: New Patterns, New Theories* (New York: Population Council, 1996).

CHAMBERLAIN, MARY, and PAUL THOMPSON (eds.), *Narrative and Genre* (London: Routledge, 1998).

CHANDRASEKHA, S.(ed.), *A Dirty Filthy Little Book: The Writings of Charles Knowlton and Annie Besant on Reproductive Physiology and Birth Control and an Account of the Bradlaugh–Besant Trial* (Berkeley and Los Angeles: University of California Press, 1981).

CHARLES, ENID, *The Practice of Birth Control: An Analysis of the Birth-Control Experiences of Nine Hundred Women* (London: Williams & Norgate, 1932).

CHESSER, EUSTACE, *Love without Fear: A Plain Guide to Sex Technique for Every Married Adult* (London: Rich & Cowan, 1941).

—— *The Sexual, Marital and Family Relationships of the English Woman* (London: Hutchinson's Medical Publications, 1956).

CHINN, CARL, *They Worked All their Lives: Women of the Urban Poor in England 1880–1939* (Manchester: Manchester University Press, 1988).

CLARK, ANNA, 'Domesticity and the Problem of Wifebeating in Nineteenth-Century Britain: Working-Class Culture, Law and Politics', in Shani D'Cruze (ed.), *Everyday Violence in Britain, 1850–1950: Gender and Class* (Harlow: Pearson, 2000), 27–40.

CLARK, A. L., and WALLIN, P., 'The Accuracy of Husbands' and Wives' Reports of the Frequency of Marital Coitus', *Population Studies*, 18 (1964), 165–73.

CLARK, DAVID(ed.), *Marriage, Domestic Life and Social Change* (London: Routledge, 1991).

—— and HALDAN, DOUGLAS, *Wedlocked: Intervention and Research in Marriage* (Cambridge: Polity Press, 1990).

CLELAND, JOHN, and WILSON, CHRISTOPHER, 'Demand Theories of the Fertility Transition: An Iconoclastic View', *Population Studies*, 41 (1987), 5–30.

CLEPHANE, IRENE, *Towards Sex Freedom* (London: John Lane, 1935).

COALE, ANSLEY, 'The Demographic Transition Reconsidered', *International Population Conference, Liège*, vol. i: *Liège: International Union for the Scientific Study of Population* (1973), 53–71.

—— and WATKINS, SUSAN COTTS (eds.), *The Decline of Fertility in Europe* (Princeton: Princeton University Press, 1986).

COCKS, H. G., 'Saucy Stories: Pornography, Sexology and the Marketing of Sexual Knowledge in Britain, *c.* 1918–70', *Social History*, 29/4 (2004), 465–84.

COHEN, DEBORAH, 'Private Lives in Public Spaces: Marie Stopes, the Mothers' Clinics and the Practice of Contraception', *History Workshop Journal*, 35 (1993), 95–116.

COHEN, ESTELLE, ' "What the women at all times would laugh at": Redefining Equality and Difference, *circa* 1660–1760', *Osiris*, 12 (1977), 121–42.

COLDRICK, JACK, *Dr. Marie Stopes and Press Censorship of Birth Control: The Story of the Catholic Campaign against Newspaper Advertising in Ireland and Britain* (Belfast: Athol Books, 1992).

COLEMAN, DAVID, and SALT, JOHN, *The British Population: Patterns, Trends and Processes* (Oxford: Oxford University Press, 1992).

COLEMAN, PETER G., 'Ageing and Life History: The Meaning of Reminiscence in Late Life', in Shirley Dex (ed.), *Life and Work History Analyses: Qualitative and Quantitative Developments* (London: Routledge, 1991), 100–56.

COLLINS, MARCUS, *Modern Love: An Intimate History of Men and Women in Twentieth Century Britain* (London: Atlantic Books, 2003).

COMINOS, PETER T., 'Late Victorian Sexual Respectability and the Social System', pt. 1, *International Review of Social History*, 8/1 (1963), 18–48.

—— 'Late Victorian Sexual Respectability and the Social System', pt. 2, *International Review of Social History*, 8/2 (1963), 216–50.

CONNERTON, PAUL, *How Societies Remember* (Cambridge: Cambridge University Press, 1989).

COOK, HERA, *The Long Sexual Revolution: English Women, Sex, and Contraception, 1800–1975* (Oxford: Oxford University Press, 2004).

COURT, AUDREY, and WALTON, CYNTHIA, *1926–1991 Birmingham Made a Difference: The Birmingham Women's Welfare Centre, the Family Planning Association in Birmingham* (Birmingham: Barn Books, 2001).

COX, GLADYS, *Clinical Contraception* (1933; London: William Heinemann, 1937).

CRAFTS, N. F. R., 'Duration of Marriage, Fertility and Women's Employment Opportunities in England and Wales in 1911', *Population Studies*, 43 (1989), 325–35.

CRANE, SUSAN A., '(Not) Writing History: Rethinking the Intersections of Personal History and Collective Memory with Hans von Aufsess', *History and Memory*, 8 (1996), 7–29.

CROMWELL, RONALD E., and OLSEN, DAVID H. (eds.), *Power in Families* (New York: Sage, 1975).

CROTTY, MARTIN, *Making the Australian Male: Middle-Class Masculinity 1870–1920* (Sydney: Finch Publishing, 1996).

CUTTLER, WILLIAM III, 'Accuracy in Oral History Interviewing', in David Dunaway and Willa K. Baum (eds.), *Oral History: An Interdisciplinary Anthology* (Nashville Tenn.: American Association for State and Local History, 1984), 79–86.

DALY, KERRY, 'The Fit between Qualitative Research and Characteristics of Families', in J. F. Gilgun, Kerry Daly, and Gerald Handel (eds.), *Quantitative Methods in Family Research* (Newbury Park: Sage, 1992), 3–11.

DANIELS, E. S., *The Children of Desire: A Book on Practical Knowledge of Family Limitation* (London: George Standing, 1925).

D'ARCY, F., 'The Malthusian League and the Resistance to Birth Control Propaganda in Late Victorian Britain', *Population Studies*, 31/2 (1977), 429–30.

DARE, O. O., and CLELAND, O. O., 'Reliability and Validity of Survey Data on Sexual Behaviour', *Health Transition Review*, 4, supplement (1994), 93–110.

DAVEY, CLARE, 'Birth Control in Britain during the Inter-War Years: Evidence from the Stopes Correspondence', *Journal of Family History*, 13 (1988), 329–45.

DAVIES, ANDREW, *Leisure, Gender and Poverty: Working-Class Culture in Salford and Manchester, 1900–1939* (Buckingham: Open University Press, 1992).

DAVIES, MARGARET LLEWELYN, *Maternity: Letters from Working Women* (1915; London: Virago, 1978).

—— *Life As We Have Known It* (1931; London: Virago, 1977).

D'CRUZE, SHANI, 'Women and the Family', in June Purvis (ed.), *Women's History: Britain 1850–1945. An Introduction* (London: UCL Press, 1995), 51–83.

—— (ed.), *Everyday Violence in Britain, 1850–1950: Gender and Class* (Harlow: Pearson, 2000).

DEGLER, CARL, *At Odds: Women and the Family in America from the Revolution to the Present* (New York: Oxford University Press, 1980).

—— 'Women and the Family', in Michael Kammen (ed.), *The Past Before Us: Contemporary Historical Writing in the U.S.* (Ithaca: Cornell University Press, 1980), 308–473.

DENNIS, FERNANDO, HENRIQUES, NORMAN, and SLAUGHTER, CLIFFORD, *Coal Is Our Life: An Analysis of a Yorkshire Mining Community* (London: Tavistock, 1956).

DEVLIN, VIVIEN, *Motherhood from 1920 to the Present Day* (Edinburgh: Polygon, 1995).

DEX, SHIRLEY (ed.), *Life and Work History Analyses: Qualitative and Quantitative Developments* (London: Routledge, 1991).

DICKENS, STAN, *Bending the Twig* (Ilfracombe: Arthur H. Stockwell, 1975).

DIGBY, A., and STEWART, J. (eds.), *Gender, Health and Welfare* (London: Routledge, 1996), 143–66.

DODOO, F. NII-AMOO, EZEH, ALEX C., and OWUOR, TOM O., 'Some Evidence against the Assumption that Approval of Family Planning Is Associated with Frequency of Spouses' Discussion of the Subject', *Population Studies*, 55 (2001), 195–8.

—— LUO, YE, and PANAYOTOVA, EVELINA, 'Do Male Reproductive Preferences Really Point to a Need to Refocus Fertility Policy?', *Population Research and Policy Review*, 16 (1997), 447–55.

DOUGLAS, MARGARET, 'Women, God and Birth Control: The First Hospital Birth Control Clinic, Abertillery, 1925', *Llafur, Journal of Welsh Labour History*, 16 (1995), 110–22.

DRAPER, ELIZABETH, *Birth Control in the Modern World* (Harmondsworth: Penguin, 1965).

DRYSDALE, C. V., *The Small Family System: Is It Injurious or Immoral?* (London: A. C. Fifield, 1913).

DUBERMAN, MARTIN BAUML, VICINUS, MARTHA, and CHAUNCEY, GEORGE JR. (eds.), *Hidden from History: Reclaiming the Gay and Lesbian Past* (Harmondsworth: Penguin, 1991).

DUDGEON, MATTHEW R., and INHORN, MARCIA C., 'Men's Influences on Women's Reproductive Health: Medical Anthropological Perspectives', *Social Science and Medicine*, 59 (2004), 1379–95.

DUNAWAY, DAVID, and BAUM, WILLA K. (eds.), *Oral History: An Interdisciplinary Anthology* (Nashville, Tenn.: American Association for State and Local History, 1984).

DUNCAN-SMITH, KATE, and HAMILTON, PAULA (eds.), *Memory and History in Twentieth Century Australia* (Oxford: Oxford University Press, 1994).

DYEHOUSE, CAROL, *Feminism and the Family in England 1880–1939* (Oxford: Blackwell, 1989).

EASTERLIN, RICHARD A., and CRIMMINS, EILEEN M., *The Fertility Revolution: A Supply–Demand Analysis* (Chicago: University of Chicago Press, 1985).

EBERWEIN, ROBERT, *Sex Ed.: Film, Video, and the Framework of Desire* (New Brunswick: Rutgers University Press, 1999).

EDER, FRANZ X., HALL, LESLEY, and HEKMA, GERT (eds.), *Sexual Cultures in Europe: Themes in Sexuality* (Manchester: Manchester University Press, 1999).

EDGELL, LINDA, 'Couples Whom Nothing Seems To Suit', in Stephen Killick (ed.), *Contraception in Practice* (London: Martin Dunitz, 2000), 241–51.

EDGELL, STEPHEN, *Middle-Class Couples: A Study of Segregation, Domination and Inequality in Marriage* (London: Allen & Unwin, 1980).

ELDERTON, ETHEL M., *Report on the English Birth-Rate*, pt. 1: *England North of the Humber* (London: Dulau, 1914).

ELLIOTT, FAITH ROBERTSON, *The Family: Change or Continuity?* (Atlantic Highlands, NJ: Humanities Press International, 1986).

ENGLAND, L. R., 'Little Kinsey: An Outline of Sex Attitudes in Britain', *Public Opinion Quarterly*, 13 (1949–50), 587–600.

EYLES, LEONORA, *Commonsense about Sex* (London: Victor Gollancz, 1933).

Family Planning Association, *Abortion in Britain: Proceedings of a Conference Held by the Family Planning Association at the University of London University on 22 April, 1966* (London: Pitman Medical Publishing, 1966).

FAULKNER, EVELYN, "Powerless to prevent him": Attitudes of Married Working-Class Women in the 1920s and the Rise of Sexual Power', *Local Population Studies*, 49 (1992), 51–61.

FEATHERSTONE, SIMON, 'Jack Hill's Horse: Narrative Form and Oral History', *Oral History*, 19 (1991), 59–62.

FENTRESS, JAMES, and WICKHAM, CHRIS, *Social Memory* (Oxford: Blackwell, 1992).

FERRAROTTI, FRANCO, *The End of Conversation: The Impact of Mass Media on Modern Society* (New York: Greenwood Press, 1988).

FILENE, PETER, 'The Secrets of Men's History', in Harry Brod (ed.), *The Making of Masculinities: The New Men's Studies* (Winchester, Mass.: Allen & Unwin, 1987), 103–20.

Finch, Janet, ' "It's great to have someone to talk to": The Ethics and Politics of Interviewing Women', in Colin Bell and Helen Roberts (eds.), *Social Researching: Politics, Problems, Practice* (London: Routledge & Kegan Paul, 1984), 70–87.

—— and Mason, Jennifer, *Negotiating Family Responsibilities* (London: Tavistock/Routledge, 1993).

—— and Summerfield, Penny, 'Social Reconstruction and the Emergence of Companionate Marriage, 1945–59', in David Clark (ed.), *Marriage, Domestic Life and Social Change* (London: Routledge, 1991), 7–32.

Fisher, Kate, ' "Clearing Up Misconceptions": The Campaign to Set Up Birth Control Clinics in South Wales in the Inter-War Years', *Welsh Historical Review*, 18 (1998), 103–29.

—— 'An Oral History of Birth Control Practice, *c.*1925–50: A Study of Oxford and South Wales', D.Phil. thesis, University of Oxford, 1997 (1998).

—— 'Women's Experiences of Abortion before the 1967 Act', in Ellie Lee (ed.), *Abortion Law and Politics Today* (London: Macmillan, 1998), 27–42.

—— ' "Didn't stop to think, I just didn't want another one": The Culture of Abortion in Interwar South Wales', in Franz X. Eder, Lesley Hall, and Gert Hekma (eds.), *Sexual Cultures in Europe: Themes in Sexuality* (Manchester: Manchester University Press, 1999), 213–32.

—— ' "She was quite satisfied with the arrangements I made": Gender and Birth Control in Britain 1930–1950', *Past and Present*, 169 (2000), 161–93.

—— 'Uncertain Aims and Tacit Negotiation: Birth Control Practices in Britain, 1925–50', *Population and Development Review*, 26/2 (2000), 295–317.

—— and Szreter, Simon, ' "They prefer withdrawal": The Choice of Birth Control in Britain, 1918–1950', *Journal of Interdisciplinary History*, 34/2 (2003), 263–91.

Florence, Lella Secor, *Birth Control on Trial* (London: George Allen & Unwin, 1930).

—— *Our Private Lives* (London: George G. Harrap, 1944).

—— *Progress Report on Birth Control* (London: William Heinemann, 1956).

Folbre, Nancy, 'Of Patriarchy Born: The Political Economy of Fertility Decisions', *Feminist Studies*, 9 (1983), 261–84.

Foucault, Michel, *The History of Sexuality*, vol. i: *An Introduction* (Harmondsworth: Penguin, 1981).

Fox, Bonnie (ed.), *Family Bonds and Gender Divisions: Readings in the Sociology of the Family* (Toronto: Canadian Scholars' Press, 1988).

Fox, Greer Litton (ed.), *The Childbearing Decision: Fertility Attitudes and Behaviour* (Beverley Hills: Sage, 1982).

Francis, Martin, 'The Domestication of the Male? Recent Research On Nineteenth- and Twentieth-Century British Masculinity', *The Historical Journal*, 45/3 (2002), 637–52.

Frank, Deborah I., and Scanzoni, John, 'Sexual Decision-Making: Its Development and Dynamics', in Greer Litton Fox (ed.), *The Childbearing Decision: Fertility Attitudes and Behaviour* (Beverley Hills: Sage, 1982), 51–72.

Frankenberg, Ronald, *Communities in Britain: Social Life in Town and Country* (Harmondsworth: Penguin, 1966).

Friedlander, Dov, Okun, Barbara S., and Segal, Sharon, The Demographic Transition Then and Now: Processes, Perspectives, and Analyses', *Journal of Family History*, 24/4 (1999), 493–533.

Fryer, Peter, *The Birth Controllers* (London: Secker & Warburg, 1965).

FULLER, EVELYN, *On the Management of a Birth Control Centre* (London: Society for the Provision of Birth Control Clinics, 1926).

GAIR, J. P., *Sexual Science: Sexual Knowledge for the Young Woman* (London: Anglo-Eastern, 1921).

GALLICHAN, WALTER M., *A Text-Book of Sex Education: For Parents and Teachers* (London: T. Werner Laurie, 1919).

GAMARNIKOW, EVA, MORGAN, DAVID, PURVIS, JUNE, and TAYLORSON, DAPHNE (eds.), *The Public and the Private* (London: Heinemann, 1983).

GAMSON, JOSHUA, 'Rubber Wars: Struggles over the Condom in the United States', *Journal of the History of Sexuality*, 1 (1990), 262–82.

GARDINER, JOHN, *The Victorians: An Age in Retrospect* (London: Hambledon & London).

GARRETT, EILIDH, and REID, ALICE, 'Thinking of England and Taking Care: Family Building Strategies and Infant Mortality in England and Wales, 1891–1911', *International Journal of Population Studies*, 1 (1995), 69–102.

—— —— SCHÜRER, K., and SZRETER, S., *Changing Family Size in England and Wales: Place, Class and Demography, 1881–1911* (Cambridge: Cambridge University Press, 2001).

GEDI, NOA, and ELAM, YIGAL, 'Collective Memory—What Is It?', *History and Memory*, 8 (1996), 30–50.

GEPPERT, ALEXANDER C. T., 'Divine Sex, Happy Marriage, Regenerated Nation: Marie Stopes's Marital Manual *Married Love* and the Making of a Best-Seller, 1918–1955', *Journal of the History of Sexuality*, 8/3 (1998), 389–433.

GERVAIS, DIANE, and GAUVREAU, DANIELLE, 'Women, Priests, and Physicians: Family Limitation in Quebec, 1940–1970', *Journal of Interdisciplinary History*, 34/2 (2003), 293–314.

GIER, JACLYN, 'Miners' Wives: Gender, Culture and Society in the South Wales Coalfields 1919–1930', Ph.D. thesis, Northwestern University, 1993.

GILES, JUDY, ' "Playing hard to get": Working-Class Women, Sexuality and Respectability in Britain, 1918–40', *Women's History Review*, 1/2 (1992), 239–55.

GILGUN, JANE F., DALY, KERRY, and HANDEL, GERALD (eds.), *Quantitative Methods in Family Research* (Newbury Park: Sage, 1992).

GILLESPIE, D. L., 'Who Has the Power? The Marital Struggle', *Journal of Marriage and the Family*, 33 (1971), 445–58.

GILLIS, JOHN R., *For Better, For Worse: British Marriages, 1600 to the Present* (New York: Oxford University Press, 1985).

—— 'Gender and Fertility Decline among the British Middle Classes', in John R. Gillis, Louise A. Tilly, and David Levine (eds.), *The European Experience of Declining Fertility, 1850–1970: The Quiet Revolution* (Cambridge, Mass.: Blackwell, 1992), 31–47.

—— 'Bringing Up Father: British Paternal Identities, 1700 to the Present', *Masculinities*, 3/3 (1995), 1–27.

—— TILLY, LOUISE, and LEVINE, DAVID (eds.), *The European Experience of Declining Fertility, 1850–1970: The Quiet Revolution* (Cambridge, Mass.: Blackwell, 1992).

—— —— —— Introduction in eid. (eds.), *The European Experience of Declining Fertility, 1850–1970* (Cambridge, Mass.: Blackwell, 1992), 1–9.

GINSBURG, FAYE, and RAPP, RAYNA (eds.), *Conceiving the New World Order: The Global Politics of Reproduction* (Berkeley and Los Angeles: University of California Press, 1995).

GITTINS, DIANA, 'Women's Work and Family Size Between the Wars', *Oral History*, 5 (1977), 84–100.

—— *Fair Sex: Family Size and Structure 1900–1939* (London: Hutchinson, 1982).

GLUCK, SHERNA, 'What's So Special About Women? Women's Oral History', in David Dunaway and Willa K. Baum (eds.), *Oral History: An Interdisciplinary Anthology* (Nashville, Tenn.: American Association for State and Local History, 1984), 221–37.

—— and PATAI, DAPHNE (eds.), *Women's Words: The Feminist Practice of Oral History* (New York: Routledge, 1991).

GODWIN, DEBORAH, and SCANZONI, JOHN, 'Couple Decision-Making: Commonalties and Differences Across Issues and Spouses', *Journal of Family Issues*, 10 (1989), 291–319.

GOLDTHORPE, J. H., LOCKWOOD, D., BECHOFFER, F., and PLATT, J., *The Affluent Worker in the Class Structure* (Cambridge: Cambridge University Press, 1968).

GORDON, LINDA, *Woman's Body, Woman's Right: Birth Control in America* (Harmondsworth: Penguin, 1977).

GORER, GEOFFREY, *Exploring English Character* (London: Cresset Press, 1955).

—— *Sex and Marriage in England Today: A Study of the Views and Experiences of the Under-45s* (London: Thomas Nelson, 1971).

GRADDOL, DAVID, and SWANN, JOAN, *Gender Voices* (Oxford: Blackwell, 1989).

GRAY, HERBERT, *Sex Teaching* (London: National Sunday School Union, 1930).

GRAY, NIGEL, *The Worst of Times: An Oral History of the Great Depression in Britain* (Aldershot: Wildwood House, 1985).

GRAY, RONALD, with LERIDON, HENRI, and SPIRA, ALFRED (eds.), *Biomedical and Demographic Determinants of Reproduction* (Oxford: Clarendon Press, 1993).

GREEN, PENNY, 'Taking Sides: Partisan Research in the 1984–1985 Miners' Strike', in Dick Hobbs and Tim May (eds.), *Interpreting the Field: Accounts of Ethnography* (Oxford: Clarendon Press, 1993), 99–119.

GREEN, T. L., 'Sex Education and Social Biology', *Health Education Journal*, 3 (1945), 43.

GREENHALGH, SUSAN, 'Anthropology Theorizes Reproduction: Integrating Practice, Political, Economic, and Feminist Perspectives', in ead. (ed.), *Situating Fertility: Anthropology and Demographic Inquiry* (Cambridge: Cambridge University Press, 1995), 3–28.

—— (ed.), *Situating Fertility: Anthropology and Demographic Inquiry* (Cambridge: Cambridge University Press, 1995).

—— 'The Social Construction of Population Science: An Intellectual, Institutional, and Political History of Twentieth Century Demography', *Comparative Studies in Society and History*, 38/1 (1996), 26–66.

GREER, GERMAINE, *Sex and Destiny: The Politics of Human Fertility* (London: Picador, 1984).

GRELE, RONALD J., 'Movement without Aim: Methodological and Theoretical Problems in Oral History', in id. (ed.), *Envelopes of Sound: The Art of Oral History* (New York: Praeger, 1991), 127–9.

—— (ed.), *Envelopes of Sound: The Art of Oral History* (New York: Praeger, 1991), 127–9.

GRIER, J., 'Eugenics and Birth Control: Contraceptive Provision in North Wales, 1918–1929', *Social History of Medicine*, 11/3 (1998), 443–58.

GRISEWOOD, HARMAN (ed.), *Ideas and Beliefs of the Victorians: A Historical Revaluation of the Victorian Age* (London: Sylvan Press, 1949).

HACKER, HELEN MAYER, 'The New Burdens of Masculinity', *Marriage and Family Living*, 19/3 (1957), 227–33.

HAIRE, NORMAN, *How I Run My Birth Control Clinic* (London: Cromer Welfare Clinic, 1929), repr. from *Proceedings of Second International Congress of World League for Sexual Reform*, Copenhagen, July 1928.

HALBWACHS, MAURICE, *The Collective Memory* (New York: Harper & Row, 1980); 1st pub. as *La Mémoire collective* (1950).

HALL, LESLEY A., ' "Somehow very distasteful": Doctors, Men and Sexual Problems between the Wars', *Journal of Contemporary History*, 20 (1985), 553–74.

—— *Hidden Anxieties: Male Sexuality, 1900–1950* (Oxford: Polity, 1991).

—— 'Forbidden by God, Despised by Men: Masturbation, Medical Warnings, Moral Panic and Manhood in Great Britain, 1850–1950', *Journal of the History of Sexuality*, 2/3 (1992), 365–87.

—— 'Impotent Ghosts from No Man's Land, Flappers' Boyfriends, or Crypto-Patriarchs? Men, Sex and Social Change in 1920s Britain', *Social History*, 21/1 (1996), 54–70.

—— 'Marie Stopes and her Correspondents: Personalising Population Decline in an Era of Demographic Change', in Robert A. Peel (ed.), *Marie Stopes, Eugenics and the English Birth Control Movement* (London: Galton Institute, 1997), 27–48.

—— *Sex, Gender and Social Change in Britain since 1880* (London: Palgrave Macmillan, 2000).

—— 'A Suitable Job for a Woman: Women Doctors and Birth Control to the Inception of the NHS', in Anne Hardy and Lawrence Conrad (eds.), *Women and Modern Medicine* (Amsterdam: Rodolphi, 2000), 127–47.

HALL, RUTH, *Marie Stopes: A Biography* (London: André Deutsch, 1977).

—— (ed.), *Dear Dr. Stopes: Sex in the 1920s. Letters to Marie Stopes* (London: André Deutsch, 1978).

HALL, VALERIE GORDON, 'Contrasting Female Identities: Women in Coal Mining Communities in Northumberland, England, 1900–1939', *Journal of Women's History*, 13/2 (2001), 107–31.

HAMILTON, PAULA, 'The Knife Edge: Debates about History and Memory', in Kate Duncan-Smith, and Paula Hamilton (eds.), *Memory and History in Twentieth Century Australia* (Oxford: Oxford University Press, 1994), 9–32.

HAMMERTON, JAMES A., *Cruelty and Companionship: Conflict in Nineteenth Century Married Life* (London: Routledge, 1992).

HANSON, S. M. H., and BOZETT, F. W. (eds.), *Dimensions of Fatherhood* (Beverley Hills: Sage, 1985).

HARCOURT, WENDY (ed.), *Power, Reproduction and Gender: The Intergenerational Transfer of Knowledge* (New Jersey: Zed Books, 1997).

HARDY, ANNE, and CONRAD, LAWRENCE (eds.), *Women and Modern Medicine* (Amsterdam: Rodolphi, 2000).

HARDY, G., *How to Prevent Pregnancy* (Paris: G. Hardy, n.d. [?1916]).

HARRIS, CHRISTOPHER, *The Family and Industrial Society* (London: George Allen & Unwin, 1983).

HARRIS, JOSÉ, *Private Lives, Public Spirit: A Social History of Britain, 1870–1914* (Oxford: Oxford University Press, 1993).

HARTMANN, BETSY, *Reproductive Rights and Wrongs: The Global Politics of Population Control and Contraceptive Choice* (New York: Harper & Row, 1987).

HARTMANN, HEIDI I., 'The Family as the Locus of Gender, Class, and Political Struggle: The Example of Housework', *Signs: Journal of Women in Culture and Society*, 6 (1981), 366–94.

HARVEY, BRETT, *The Fifties: A Woman's Oral History* (New York: HarperCollins, 1993).

HATCHER, R., et al. (eds.), *Contraceptive Technology* (New York: Irvington, 1994).

HAYWOOD, CHRIS, and MAC AN GHAILL, MÁIRTÍN, *Men and Masculinities: Theory, Research and Social Practice* (Buckingham: Open University Press, 2003).

HEISE, LORI, L., 'Beyond Acceptability: Reorienting Research on Contraceptive Choice', in T. K. Sundari Ravindran, Marge Berer, and Jane Lottingham (eds.), *Beyond Acceptability: Users' Perceptives on Contraception* (London: Reproductive Health Matters/WHO, 1997), 6–14.

HEISS, JEROLD (ed.), *Family Roles and Interaction: An Anthology* (Chicago: McNally College, 1976).

HIGGINS, NATALIE, 'The Changing Expectations and Realities of Marriage in the English Working-Class, 1920–1960', Ph.D. thesis, University of Cambridge, 2002.

HIMES, NORMAN, 'Charles Knowlton's Revolutionary Influence on the English Birth-Rate', *New England Journal of Medicine*, 99/10 (1928), 461–5.

—— 'Birth Control in Historical and Clinical Perspective', repr. from *The Annals of the American Academy of Political and Social Science*, 2598 (1932), 1–17.

—— *Medical History of Contraception* (London: Allen & Unwin, 1936).

—— *Practical Birth-Control Methods* (London: George Allen and Unwin, 1940).

—— and HIMES, VERA C., 'Birth Control for the British Working Classes: A Study of the First Thousand Cases to Visit an English Birth Control Clinic', *Hospital Social Service*, 19 (1929), 578–617.

HIRSCH, JENNIFER S., and NATHANSON, CONSTANCE A., 'Some Traditional Methods Are More Modern than Others: Rhythm, Withdrawal and the Changing Meanings of Sexual Intimacy in Mexican Companionate Marriage', *Culture, Health & Sexuality*, 3/4 (2001), 413–28.

HITE, SHERE, *The Hite Report. Women and Love: A Cultural Revolution in Progress* (London: Viking, 1998).

HOBBS, DICK, and MAY, TIM (eds.), *Interpreting the Field: Accounts of Ethnography* (Oxford: Clarendon Press, 1993).

HOGGART, LESLEY, 'The Campaign for Birth Control in Britain in the 1920s', in A. Digby and J. Stewart (eds.), *Gender, Health and Welfare* (London: Routledge, 1996), 143–66.

HOGGART, RICHARD, *The Uses of Literacy* (1957; Harmondsworth: Penguin, 1958).

HOLLAND, JANET, and RAMAZANOGLU, CAROLINE, 'Power and Interpretation in Researching Young Women's Sexuality', in Mary Maynard and June Purvis (eds.), *Researching Women's Lives from a Feminist Perspective* (London: Taylor & Francis, 1994), 125–48.

—————— and SHARPE, SUE, *Wimp or Gladiator: Contradictions in Acquiring Masculine Sexuality* (London: Tufnell Press, 1993).

——————— and THOMSON, RACHEL, 'Pressured Pleasure: Young Women and the Negotiation of Sexual Boundaries', in Stevi Jackson and Sue Scott (eds.), *Feminism and Sexuality: A Reader* (Edinburgh: Edinburgh University Press, 1996), 248–62.

——————— *The Male in the Head: Young People, Heterosexuality and Power* (London: Tufnell Press, 1998).

——— SCOTT, SUE, SHARPE, SUE, and THOMSON, RACHEL, ' "Don't die of ignorance"; I Nearly Died of Embarrassment: Condoms in Context', in Stevi Jackson and Sue Scott (eds.), *Feminism and Sexuality: A Reader* (Edinburgh: Edinburgh University Press, 1996), 117–29.

HOLLAND, RAMAZANOGLU, C., SHARPE, S., AND THOMSON, R., 'Reputations: Journeying into Gendered Power Relations', in Jeffrey Weeks and Janet Holland (eds.), *Sexual Cultures* (London: Macmillan, 1996), 239–59.

HOLLOS, MARIDA, and LARSEN, ULLA, 'Which African Men Promote Smaller Families and Why: Marital Relations and Fertility in a Pare Community in Northern Tanzania', *Social Science and Medicine*, 58 (2004), 1733–49.

HOLTZMAN, ELLEN, 'The Pursuit of Married Love: Women's Attitudes Towards Sexuality and Marriage in Great Britain, 1918–1939', *Journal of Social History*, 16 (1982), 29–52.

HOMANS, HILARY (ed.), *The Sexual Politics of Reproduction* (Aldershot: Gower, 1985).

HOOPER, NURSE M. R., *The Voice of Experience* (1938; 2nd edn. London: Birth Control Advisory Bureau, 1941, repr.1944); copy in Mass-Observation, TC Family Planning 1944–1949, Birth Control Leaflets and Booklets, TC3/2/E, 9.

HOW-MARTYN, EDITH, *The Birth Control Movement in England* (London: John Bale/Danielsson, 1930).

HUMPHRIES, STEVE, *A Secret World of Sex, Forbidden Fruit: The British Experience 1900–1950* (London: Sidgwick & Jackson, 1988).

—— and GORDON, PAMELA, *A Labour of Love: The Experience of Parenthood in Britain, 1900–1950* (London: Sidgwick & Jackson, 1993).

—— —— *A Man's World: From Boyhood to Manhood, 1900–1960* (London: BBC Books, 1996).

—— MACK, JOANNA, and PERKS, ROBERT, *A Century of Childhood* (London: Sidgwick & Jackson, 1988).

HUNT, ALAN, 'The Great Masturbation Panic and the Discourses of Moral Regulation in Nineteenth and Early Twentieth Century Britain', *Journal of the History of Sexuality*, 8/4 (1998), 575–615.

ITTMAN, KARL, *Work, Gender and Family in Victorian England* (Basingstoke: Macmillan, 1995).

JACKSON, MARGARET, *The Real Facts of Life* (London: Taylor & Francis, 1994).

JACKSON, MARK (ed.), *Infanticide: Historical Perspectives on Child Murder and Concealment, 1550–2000* (Aldershot: Ashgate, 2002).

JACKSON, STEVI, and SCOTT, SUE (eds.), *Feminism and Sexuality: A Reader* (Edinburgh: Edinburgh University Press, 1996).

JOFFE, CAROLE, *The Regulation of Sexuality: Experiences of Family Planning Workers* (Philadelphia: Temple University Press, 1986).

JOHNSON, RICHARD, McLENNAN, GREGOR, SCHWARZ, BILL, and SUTTON, DAVID (eds.), *Making Histories: Studies in History-Writing and Politics* (London: Hutchinson, 1982).

JONES, GRETA, 'Marie Stopes in Ireland: The Mother's Clinic in Belfast, 1936–47', *Social History of Medicine*, 5 (1992), 257–77.

JORDAN, TERRY, *Agony Columns* (London: MacDonald/Optima, 1988).

KAMMEN, MICHAEL (ed.), *The Past Before Us: Contemporary Historical Writing in the US* (Ithaca: Cornell University Press, 1980).

KARRA, MIHIRA V., STARK, NANCY N., and WOLF, JOYCE, 'Male Involvement in Family Planning: A Case Study Spanning Five Generations of a South Indian Family', *Studies in Family Planning*, 28/1 (1997), 24–34.

KERR, MADELINE, *The People of Ship Street* (London: Routledge & Kegan Paul, 1958).

KERTZER, DAVID I., 'Political-Economic and Cultural Explanations of Demographic Behaviour', in Susan Greenhalgh (ed.), *Situating Fertility: Anthropology and Demographic Enquiry* (Cambridge: Cambridge University Press, 1995), 29–52.

KILLICK, STEPHEN (ed.), *Contraception in Practice* (London: Martin Dunitz, 2000).

KIMMEL, MICHAEL, S. (ed.), *Changing Men: New Directions in Research on Men and Masculinity* (Newbury Park: Sage, 1987).

—— and MESSNER, MICHAEL A., *Men's Lives* (1989; 3rd edn. Boston: Allyn & Bacon, 1998).

KLEIN, JOSEPHINE, *Samples from English Cultures*, vol. i: *Three Preliminary Studies: Aspects of Adult Life in England*; vol. ii: *Child-Rearing Practices* (London: Routledge & Kegan Paul, 1965).

KNIGHT, PATRICIA, 'Women and Abortion in Victorian and Edwardian England', *History Workshop Journal*, 4 (1977), 57–69.

KNODEL, J., and VAN DE WALLE, E., 'Lessons from the Past: Policy Implications of Historical Fertility Studies', *Population and Development Review*, 5 (1979), 220–37; repr. in Ansley, J. Coale and Susan Cotts Watkins (eds.), *The Decline of Fertility in Europe* (Princeton: Princeton University Press, 1986), ch. 10.

KOHLER, HANS-PETER, *Fertility and Social Interaction: An Economic Perspective* (Oxford: Oxford University Press, 2001).

KOMTER, AAFKE, 'Hidden Power in Marriage', *Gender and Society*, 3 (1989), 187–216.

KOWAL, DEBORAH, 'Coitus Interruptus (Withdrawal)', in R. Hatcher et al. (eds.), *Contraceptive Technology* (New York: Irvington, 1994), 341–6.

KRANICHFELD, MARION L., 'Rethinking Family Power', *Journal of Family Issues*, 8 (1987), 42–56.

KUCICH, JOHN, and SADOFF, DIANNE F. (eds.), *Victorian Afterlife: Postmodern Culture Rewrites the Nineteenth Century* (Minneapolis: University of Minnesota Press, 2000).

KUHN, ANNETTE, *Cinema, Censorship and Sexuality, 1909–1925* (London: Routledge, 1988).

LAING, STUART, *Representations of Working-Class Life, 1957–1964* (London: Macmillan, 1986).

LANGFORD, C. M. *Birth Control Practice and Marital Fertility in Great Britain* (London: Population Investigation Committee, 1976).

—— 'Birth Control Practice in Great Britain: A Review of the Evidence from Cross-Sectional Surveys', in Michael Murphy and John Hobcraft (eds.), *Population Research in Britain*, supplement to *Population Studies*, 45 (1991), 49–68.

LAQUEUR, THOMAS, *Making Sex: Body and Gender from the Greeks to Freud* (Cambridge, Mass.: Harvard University Press, 1990).

—— 'Simply Doing It', review of Roy Porter and Lesley Hall, *The Facts of Life*, *London Review of Books*, 22 Feb. 1996, 12.

LAROSSA, RALPH, *Conflict and Power in Marriage: Expecting the First Child* (Beverley Hills: Sage, 1977).

—— 'Fatherhood and Social Change', in Michael S. Kimmel and Michael A. Messner (eds.), *Men's Lives* (1989; 3rd edn. Boston: Allyn & Bacon, 1995), 448–60.

—— *The Modernization of Fatherhood: A Social and Political History* (Chicago: University of Chicago Press, 1997).

—— and REITZES, DONALD, 'Gendered Perceptions of Father Involvement in Early Twentieth-Century America', *Journal of Marriage and the Family*, 57 (1995), 223–9.

LASLETT, BARBARA, and RAPOPORT, RHONA, 'Collaborative Interviewing and Interactive Research', *Journal of Marriage and the Family*, 37 (1975), 968–77.

LATHAM, MELANIE, *Regulating Reproduction: A Century of Conflict in Britain and France* (Manchester: Manchester University Press, 2002).

LEAP, NICKY, and HUNTER, BILLIE, *The Midwife's Tale: An Oral History from Handywoman to Professional Midwife* (London: Scarlet Press, 1993).

LEATHARD, AUDREY, *The Fight for Family Planning* (London: Macmillan, 1980).

LEE, NANCY HOWELL, *The Search for an Abortionist* (Chicago: University of Chicago Press, 1969).

LEE, RAYMOND M., *Doing Research on Sensitive Topics* (London: Sage, 1993).

LEES, SUE, *Sugar and Spice: Sexuality and Adolescent Girls* (London: Penguin, 1993).

LEONARD, DIANA, *Sex and Generation: A Study of Courtship & Weddings* (London: Tavistock, 1980).

—— and ALLEN, SHEILA (eds.), *Sexual Divisions Revisited* (Basingstoke: Macmillan, 1991).

LESTHAEGHE, RON, 'On the Social Control of Human Reproduction', *Population and Development Review*, 6 (1980), 527–48.

—— and SURKYN, JOHAN, 'Cultural Dynamics and Economic Theories of Fertility Change', *Population and Development Review*, 14 (1988), 1–45.

LEVINE, DAVID, review of Michael Teitelbaum, *The British Fertility Decline: Demographic Transition in the Crucible of the Industrial Revolution*, *Journal of Social History*, 19 (1986), 720–1.

—— *Reproducing Families: The Political Economy of English Population History* (Cambridge: Cambridge University Press, 1987).

—— 'Moments in Time: A Historian's Context of Declining Fertility', in John R. Gillis, Louise A. Tilly, and David Levine (eds.), *The European Experience of Declining Fertility, 1850–1970, The Quiet Revolution* (Cambridge, Mass.: Blackwell, 1992), 326–38.

LEWIS, JANE, 'The Ideology and Politics of Birth Control in Inter-War England', *Women's Studies International Quarterly*, 2 (1979), 33–48.

—— *The End of Marriage? Individualism and Intimate Relations* (Cheltenham: Edward Elgar, 2001).

—— (ed.), *Labour and Love: Women's Experience of Home and Family, 1850–1940* (Oxford: Blackwell, 1986).

LEYDESDORFF, SELMA, PASSERINI, LUISA, and THOMPSON, PAUL (eds.), *Gender and Memory: International Yearbook of Oral History and Life Studies* (Oxford: Oxford University Press, 1996).

LINDSEY, BEN B., and EVANS, WAINWRIGHT, *The Companionate Marriage* (New York; Boni & Liverwright, 1927).

LIU, WILLIAM T. (ed.), *Family and Fertility: Proceedings of the Fifth Notre Dame Conference on Population* (Notre Dame: University of Notre Dame Press, 1966).

LLOYD, JENNIFER, 'Conflicting Expectations in Nineteenth-Century British Matrimony: The Failed Companionate Marriage of Effie Gray and John Ruskin', *Journal of Women's History*, 11/2 (1999), 86–109.

LOANE, M. E., *From their Point of View* (London: Edward Arnold, 1908).

LOUDON, IRVINE, *Death in Childbirth: An International Study of Maternal Care and Maternal Mortality 1800–1950* (Oxford: Clarendon Press, 1992).

LUKER, KRISTIN, *Taking Chances: Abortion and the Decision not to Contracept* (Berkeley and Los Angeles: University of California Press, 1975).

LUMMIS, TREVOR, 'The Historical Dimension of Fatherhood: A Case Study 1890–1914', in Lorna McKee and R. O'Brien (eds.), *The Father Figure* (London: Tavistock, 1982), 43–56.

LUNBECK, ELIZABETH, 'American Psychiatrists and the Modern Man, 1900–1920', *Men and Masculinities*, 1/1 (1998), 58–86.

LUXTON, MEG, *More Than a Labour of Love: Three Generations of Women's Work in the Home* (Toronto: The Women's Press, 1980).

—— 'Two Hands for the Clock: Changing Patterns in the Gendered Division of Labour in the Home', in Bonnie Fox (ed.), *Family Bonds and Gender Divisions. Readings in the Sociology of the Family* (Toronto: Canadian Scholars' Press 1988), 403–20.

McCANCE, R. A., LUFF, M. C., and WIDDOWSON, E. E., 'Physical and Emotional Periodicity in Women', *The Journal of Hygiene*, 37/4 (1937), 571–611.

McDONALD, GERALD, W., 'Family Power: The Assessment of a Decade of Theory and Research', 1970–79', *Journal of Marriage and the Family*, 42 (1980), 841–54.

McINTOSH, TANIA, ' "An Abortionist City": Maternal Mortality, Abortion and Birth Control in Sheffield, 1920–1940', *Medical History*, 44 (2000), 75–96.

MACINTYRE, SALLY, ' "Who Wants Babies?" The Social Construction of "Instincts" ', in Diana Leonard and Sheila Allen (eds.), *Sexual Divisions Revisited* (Basingstoke: Macmillan, 1991), 1–24.

McKEE, LORNA, and O'BRIEN, MARGARET, 'Interviewing Men: Taking Gender Seriously', in Eva Gamarnikow, David Morgan, June Purvis, and Daphne Taylorson (eds.), *The Public and the Private* (London: Heinemann, 1983), 147–61.

—— and O'BRIEN, R. (eds.), *The Father Figure* (London: Tavistock, 1982).

McKIBBIN, ROSS, *Classes and Cultures: England 1918–1951* (Oxford: Oxford University Press, 1998).

MACKINNON, ALISON, 'Were Women Present at the Demographic Transition? Questions from a Feminist Historian to Historical Demographers', *Gender and History*, 7 (1995), 222–40.

McLAREN, ANGUS, 'Women's Work and Regulation of Family Size', *History Workshop Journal*, 4 (1977), 70–81.

—— *Birth Control in Nineteenth-Century England* (New York: Holmes & Meier, 1978).

—— review of J. A. Banks, *Victorian Values: Secularism and the Size of Families*, *Victorian Studies*, 26 (1983), 234–5.

—— *Reproductive Rituals: The Perception of Fertility in England from the Sixteenth Century to the Nineteenth Century* (London: Methuen, 1984).

—— *A History of Contraception from Antiquity to the Present Day* (Oxford: Blackwell, 1990).

—— 'Illegal Operations: Women, Doctors and Abortion, 1886–1939', *Journal of Social History*, 26 (1993), 797–816.

—— ' "Not a Stranger: A Doctor": Medical Men and Sexual Matters in the Late Nineteenth Century', in Roy Porter and Mikulas Teich (eds.), *Sexual Knowledge, Sexual Science: The History of Attitudes to Sexuality* (Cambridge: Cambridge University Press, 1994), 267–83.

MARCH, NORAH, *Towards Racial Health: A Handbook for Parents, Teachers and Social Workers on the Training of Boys and Girls* (London: George Routledge, 1915).

—— *Sex Knowledge with a Special Chapter on Birth Control* (London: W. Foulsham, n.d. (?1920)).

MARKS, LARA, *Metropolitan Maternity: Maternal and Infant Welfare Services in Early Twentieth Century London* (Amsterdam: Rodolphi, 1996).

MARKS, LARA, *Sexual Chemistry: A History of the Contraceptive Pill* (New Haven: Yale University Press, 2001).

MASON, MICHAEL, *The Making of Victorian Sexual Attitudes* (Oxford: Oxford University Press, 1994).

—— *The Making of Victorian Sexuality* (Oxford: Oxford University Press, 1995).

Mass-Observation, *Britain and her Birth-Rate* (London: John Murray, 1945).

MATERNOWSKA, M. CATHERINE, 'A Clinic in Conflict: A Political Economy Case Study of Family Planning in Haiti', in Andrew Russell, Elisa J. Sobo, and Mary S. Thompson (eds.), *Contraception Across Cultures: Technologies, Choices, Constraints* (Oxford: Berg, 2000), 103–26.

MAYNARD, MARY, and PURVIS, JUNE (eds.), *Researching Women's Lives from a Feminist Perspective* (London: Taylor & Francis, 1994).

MAYNES, MARY JO, 'The Contours of Childhood: Demography, Strategy, and Mythology of Childhood in French and German Lower-Class Autobiographies', in John R. Gillis, Louise A. Tilly, and David Levine (eds.), *The European Experience of Declining Fertility, 1850–1970* (Cambridge, Mass.: Blackwell, 1992), 101–24.

MESSER, ELLEN, and MAY, KATHRYN, *Back Rooms: Voices from the Illegal Abortion Era* (New York: St Martin's Press, 1988).

MISHLER, ELLIOT, *Research Interviewing: Context and Narrative* (Cambridge, Mass.: Harvard University Press, 1986).

MITCHELL, W. J. T. (ed.), *On Narrative* (Chicago: University of Chicago Press, 1981).

MITCHISON, NAOMI, *Comments on Birth Control* (London: Faber & Faber, 1930).

MOGEY, J. M., *Family and Neighbourhood: Two Studies in Oxford* (Oxford: Oxford University Press, 1956).

MONTGOMERY, MARK R., and CASTERLINE, JOHN B., 'Social Learning, Social Influence, and New Models of Fertility', in John B. Casterline, Ronald D. Lee, and Karen A. Foote (eds.), *Fertility in the United States: New Patterns, New Theories* (New York, Population Council, 1996), 297–324.

MOORE, SUSAN M., and ROSENTHAL, DOREEN A., 'Contemporary Youths' Negotiations of Romance, Love, Sex, and Sexual Disease', in Victor C. de Munck (ed.), *Romantic Love and Sexual Behaviour* (Westport: Praeger, 1998), 233–46.

MORT, FRANK, *Dangerous Sexualities: Medico-Moral Politics in England since 1830* (London: Routledge & Kegan Paul, 1987).

—— 'Social and Symbolic Fathers and Sons in Postwar Britain', *Journal of British Studies*, 38/3 (1999), 353–84.

MORTON-WILLIAMS, JEAN, *Interviewer Approaches* (Aldershot: Dartmouth, 1993).

MOSER, C. A., *Survey Methods in Social Investigation* (London: Heinemann, 1958).

MUNCK, VICTOR C. DE (ed.), *Romantic Love and Sexual Behaviour* (Westport: Praeger, 1998).

MUNDIGO, AXEL I., 'Reconceptualizing the Role of Men in the Post-Cairo Era', *Culture, Health & Sexuality*, 2/3 (2000), 323–37.

—— PHILLIPS, J. F., and CHAMRATRITHIRONG, A., 'Determinants of Contraceptive Use Dynamics: Research Needs on Decisions and Choice', *Journal of Biosocial Science*, 11 (1989), 9–16.

MURCOTT, ANNE, ' "It's a pleasure to cook for him": Food, Mealtimes and Gender in Some South Wales Households', in Eva Gamarnikow, David Morgan, June Purvis, and Daphne Taylorson (eds.), *The Public and the Private* (London: Heinemann, 1983), 78–90.

Murphy, Michael, and Hobcraft, John (eds.), *Population Research in Britain: A Supplement to Population Studies 45* (1991).

National Birth-Rate Commission [National Council for Public Morals], *The Declining Birth-Rate: Its Causes and Effects* (London: Chapman & Hall, 1916).

—— *Problems of Population and Parenthood, Being the Second Report of and the Chief Evidence Taken by the National Birth-Rate Commission, 1918–1920* (London: Chapman & Hall, 1920).

—— *Medical Aspects of Contraception* (London: Martin Hopkinson, 1927).

Nava, Mica, and O'Shea, Alan (eds.), *Modern Times: Reflections on a Century of English Modernity* (London: Routledge, 1996).

Neushul, Peter, 'Marie C. Stopes and the Popularization of Birth Control Technology', *Technology and Culture*, 39/2 (1998) 245–72.

Newman, Lucile F. (ed.), *Women's Medicine: A Cross-Cultural Study of Indigenous Fertility Regulation* (New Brunswick: Rutgers University Press, 1985).

Noonan, John T. Jr., *Contraception: A History of its Treatment by the Catholic Theologians and Canonists* (Cambridge, Mass.: Harvard University Press, 1966).

Nott, James, *Music for the People: Popular Music and Dance in Interwar Britain* (Oxford: Oxford University Press, 2002).

O'Neil, Gilda, *My East End: Memories of Life in Cockney London* (Harmondsworth: Penguin, 1999).

Oppenheim-Mason, Karen, and Taj, Anju Malhotra, 'Differences between Women's and Men's Reproductive Goals in Developing Countries', *Population and Development Review*, 13 (1987), 611–38.

Packer, E. L., 'Aspects of Working-Class Marriage', *Pilot Papers*, 2/1 (1947), 92–104.

Padfield, Maureen, and Procter, Ian, 'The Effect of Interviewer's Gender on the Interviewing Process: A Comparative Enquiry', *Sociology*, 30/2 (1996), 355–66.

Parish, T. N., 'A Thousand Cases of Abortion', *Journal of Obstetrics and Gynaecology*, 39 (1935), 1107–41.

Parkes, Alan S., and King, Dee, 'The Mothers' Clinic', *Journal of Biosocial Science*, 6 (1974), 163–82.

Parry, L. A., *Criminal Abortion* (London: John Bale/Danielsson, 1932).

Passerini, Luisa, 'Work Ideology and Consensus under Italian Fascism', *History Workshop*, 8 (1979), 82–108.

Paul, Leslie, *First Love: A Journey* (London: SPCK, 1977).

Peel, J., 'The Manufacture and Retailing of Contraceptives in England', *Population Studies*, 17 (1963), 113–25.

—— and Carr, Griselda, *Contraception and Family Design: A Study of Birth Planning in Contemporary Society* (Edinburgh: Churchill Livingstone, 1975).

Peel, Robert, A. (ed.), *Marie Stopes, Eugenics and the English Birth Control Movement* (London: Galton Institute, 1997).

Pendergast, Tom, *Creating the Modern Man: American Magazines and Consumer Culture 1900–1950* (Columbia: University of Missouri Press, 2000).

Perks, Rob (ed.), *The Oral History Reader* (London: Routledge, 1998).

Pierce, Rachel M., and Rowntree, Griselda, 'Birth Control in Britain, Part I', *Population Studies*, 15 (1961), 3–31.

PIERCE, RACHEL M., and ROWNTREE, GRISELDA, 'Birth Control in Britain, Part II: Contraceptive Methods used by Couples Married in the Last Thirty Years', *Population Studies*, 15 (1961), 121–59.

PITANGUY, JACQUELINE, and DE MELLO E. SOUZA, CECILIA, 'Codes of Honour: Reproductive Life Histories of Domestic Workers in Rio de Janeiro', in Wendy Harcourt (ed.), *Power, Reproduction and Gender: The Intergenerational Transfer of Knowledge* (New Jersey: Zed Books, 1997), 72–97.

PLATT, JENNIFER, 'Some Problems in Measuring the Jointness of Conjugal Role-Relationships', *Sociology*, 3 (1969), 287–97.

PLECK, JOSEPH H., 'American Fathering in Historical Perspective', in Michael S. Kimmel (ed.), *Changing Men: New Directions in Research on Men and Masculinity* (Newbury Park: Sage, 1987), 83–97.

POHLMAN, EDWARD, *The Psychology of Birth Planning* (Cambridge, Mass.: Schenkman, 1969).

POLLACK, SCARLETT, 'Sex and the Contraceptive Act', in Hilary Homans (ed.), *The Sexual Politics of Reproduction* (Aldershot: Gower, 1985), 64–77.

POLLAK, R. A., and WATKINS, SUSAN, 'Cultural and Economic Approaches to Fertility: Proper Marriage or Mésalliance?', *Population and Development Review*, 19 (1993), 467–96.

Popular Memory Group, 'Popular Memory: Theory, Politics, Method', in Richard Johnson, Gregor McLennan, Bill Schwarz, and David Sutton (eds.), *Making Histories: Studies in History-Writing and Politics* (London: Hutchinson, 1982), 205–52.

PORTELLI, ALESSANDRO, 'The Peculiarities of Oral History', *History Workshop*, 12 (1981), 96–107.

—— *The Death of Luigi Vastulli and Other Stories: Form and Meaning in Oral History* (New York: State University of New York Press, 1991).

—— *The Battle of Valle Giulia: Oral History and the Art of Dialogue* (Madison: University of Wisconsin Press, 1997).

PORTER, ROY, and HALL, LESLEY, *The Facts of Life: The Creation of Sexual Knowledge in Britain, 1650–1950* (New Haven: Yale University Press, 1995).

—— and TEICH, MIKULÁŠ (eds.), *Sexual Knowledge, Sexual Science: The History of Attitudes to Sexuality* (Cambridge: Cambridge University Press, 1994), 267–83.

POTTER, ROBERT G. JR., SAGI, PHILIP C., and WESTOFF, CHARLES F., 'Improvement of Contraception during the Course of Marriage', *Population Studies*, 16/2 (1962), 160–74.

POTTS, MALCOLM, DIGGORY, PETER, and PEEL, J., *Abortion* (Cambridge: Cambridge University Press, 1977).

PURVIS, JUNE (ed.), *Women's History, Britain 1850–1945: An Introduction* (London: UCL Press, 1995).

RAINWATER, LEE, *And the Poor Get Children; Sex, Contraception, and Family Planning in the Working Class* (Chicago: Quadrangle Books, 1960).

—— *Family Design: Marital Sexuality, Family Size and Contraception* (Chicago: Aldine, 1965).

—— 'Marital Sexuality in Four Cultures of Poverty', *Journal of Marriage and the Family*, 26/4 (1964), 457–66.

RANUM, O., and RANUM, P. (eds.), *Popular Attitudes Towards Birth Control in Pre-Industrial France and England* (New York: Harper & Row, 1972).

RAVINDRAN, T. K. SUNDARI, BERER, MARGE, and LOTINGHAM, JANE (eds.), *Beyond Acceptability: Users' Perceptives on Contraception* (London: Reproductive Health Matters, WHO, 1997).

REAY, BARRY, *Rural England: Labouring Lives in the Nineteenth Century* (Basingstoke: Palgrave, 2004).

REEVES, MAUD PEMBER, *Round About a Pound a Week* (1913; London: Virago, 1979).

REGAN, LESLIE J., *When Abortion Was a Crime: Women, Medicine, and Law in the United States, 1867–1973* (Berkeley and Los Angeles: University of California Press, 1997).

RICHARDSON, ANGELIQUE, *Love and Eugenics in the Late Nineteenth Century: Rational Reproduction and the New Woman* (Oxford: Oxford University Press, 2003).

RILEY, JOHN WINCHELL, and WHITE, MATILDA, 'The Use of Various Methods of Contraception', *American Sociological Review*, 5/6 (1940), 890–3.

RILEY, NANCY E., 'Research on Gender in Demography: Limitations and Constraints', *Population Research and Policy Review*, 17 (1988), 521–38.

RISMAN, BARBARA J., and SCHWARTZ, PEPPER (eds.), *Gender in Intimate Relationships: A Micro Structural Approach* (Belmont, Calif.: Wandsworth, 1989).

ROBERTS, D., 'The Paterfamilias of the Victorian Ruling Classes', in A. S. Wohl (ed.), *The Victorian Family* (London: Croom Helm, 1978), 59–81.

ROBERTS, ELIZABETH, 'Working Wives and their Families', in Theo Barker and Michael Drake (eds.), *Population and Society in Britain 1850–1980* (London: Batsford, 1982), 140–71.

—— *A Woman's Place: An Oral History of Working-Class Women, 1890–1940* (Oxford: Blackwell, 1984).

—— *Women and Families: An Oral History, 1940–1970* (Oxford: Blackwell 1995).

ROBERTS, HELEN, 'Male Hegemony in Family Planning', in ead. (ed.), *Women, Health and Reproduction* (London: Routledge & Kegan Paul, 1981), 1–17.

—— (ed.), *Women, Health and Reproduction* (London: Routledge & Kegan Paul, 1981).

ROBINSON, CAROLINE HADLEY, *Seventy Birth Control Clinics* (Baltimore: Williams & Wilkins, 1930).

ROGERS, A. J. LAURENCE, 'An Army Experiment in Sex Education', *Health Education Journal*, 4 (1946), 183–6.

ROGERS, EVERETT, *Communication Strategies for Family Planning* (New York: The Free Press, 1973).

ROPER, MICHAEL, and TOSH, JOHN (eds.), *Manful Assertions: Masculinity in Britain since 1800* (London: Routledge, 1991).

ROSE, JONATHAN, *The Intellectual Life of the British Working Classes* (New Haven: Yale University Press, 2001).

ROSE, JUNE, *Marie Stopes and the Sexual Revolution* (London: Faber & Faber, 1992).

ROSEN, RAYE HUDSON, and BENSON, TWYLAH, 'The Second-Class Partner: The Male Role in Family Planning Decisions', in Greer Litton Fox (ed.), *The Childbearing Decision: Fertility Attitudes and Behaviour* (Beverley Hills: Sage, 1982), 97–124.

ROSS, ELLEN, *Love and Toil: Motherhood in Outcast London, 1870–1918* (Oxford: Oxford University Press, 1993).

ROSS, JOHN A., and FRANKENBERG, ELIZABETH, *Findings from Two Decades of Family Planning Research* (New York: Population Council, 1993).

ROSSER, COLIN, and HARRIS, CHRISTOPHER, *The Family and Social Change: A Study of Family and Kinship in a South Wales Town* (London: Routledge & Kegan Paul, 1965).

ROTUNDO, ANTHONY E., *American Manhood: Transformations in Masculinity from the Revolution to the Modern Era* (New York: Basic Books, 1993).

RUSSELL, ANDREW, SOBO, ELISA J., and THOMPSON, MARY S. (eds.), *Contraception Across Cultures: Technologies, Choices, Constraints* (Oxford: Berg, 2000).

RUSSELL, BERTRAND, *Marriage and Morals* (London: George Allen & Unwin, 1929).

SAFILIOS-ROTHSCHILD, CONSTANTINA, 'The Study of Family Power Structure: A Review 1960–1969', *Journal of Marriage and the Family*, 32 (1970), 539–52.

—— 'A Macro- and Micro-Examination of Family Power and Love: An Exchange Model', *Journal of Marriage and Family*, 38 (1976), 355–62.

SAGI, PHILIP C., POTTER, ROBERT G. JR., and WESTOFF, CHARLES, 'Contraceptive Effectiveness as a Function of Desired Family Size', *Population Studies*, 15/3 (1962), 291–6.

SAMUEL, RAPHAEL, and THOMPSON, PAUL (eds.), *The Myths We Live By* (London: Routledge, 1990).

SANTOW, GIGI, 'Coitus Interruptus in the Twentieth Century', *Population and Development Review*, 19 (1993), 767–92.

—— 'Coitus Interruptus and the Control of Natural Fertility', *Population Studies*, 49/1 (1995), 19–43.

SAUER, R., 'Infanticide and Abortion in Nineteenth Century Britain', *Population Studies*, 32/1 (1978), 81–93.

SCANZONI, JOHN, *Sex Roles, Life Styles and Childbearing: Changing Patterns in Marriage and the Family* (New York: The Free Press, 1975).

—— and SZINORACZ, MAXIMILIANE, *Family Decision-Making: A Developmental Sex Role Model* (Beverley Hills: Sage, 1980).

SCHARLIEB, MARY, and SIBLY, ARTHUR, F., *Youth and Sex: Dangers and Safeguards for Girls and Boys* (London and Edinburgh: T. C. & E. C. Jack/T. Nelson & Sons, 1919).

SCHNEIDER, JANE, and SCHNEIDER, PETER, 'Demographic Transitions in a Sicilian Rural Town', *Journal of Family History*, 9 (1984), 245–72.

SCHNEIDER, PETER, and SCHNEIDER, JANE, 'Coitus Interruptus and Family Respectability in Catholic Europe: A Sicilian Case Study', in Faye Ginsburg, and Rayna Rapp (eds.), *Conceiving the New World Order: The Global Politics of Reproduction* (Berkeley and Los Angeles: University of California Press, 1995), 177–94.

SCHOFIELD, A. T., and VAUGHAN-JACKSON, PERCY, *What a Boy Should Know* (London: Cassell, 1912).

SCHOFIELD, MICHAEL, *The Sexual Behaviour of Young People* (London: Allen Lane, 1968).

SCHUMAN, HOWARD, and PRESSER, STANLEY, *Questions and Answers in Attitude Surveys: Experiments on Question Form, Wording and Content* (New York: New York Academic Press, 1981).

SECCOMBE, KAREN, 'Assessing the Costs and Benefits of Children: Gender Comparisons among Childfree Husbands and Wives', *Journal of Marriage and the Family*, 53 (1991), 191–202.

SECCOMBE, WALLY, 'Starting to Stop: Working-Class Fertility Decline in Britain', *Past and Present*, 126 (1990), 151–88.

—— *Weathering the Storm, Working-Class Families from the Industrial Revolution to the Fertility Decline* (London: Verso, 1993).

SEGAL, LYNNE, *Slow Motion: Changing Masculinities, Changing Men* (London: Virago, 1990).

—— *Straight Sex: The Politics of Pleasure* (London: Virago, 1994).

SHORTER, EDWARD, 'Female Emancipation, Birth Control, and Fertility in European History', *American Historical Review*, 78/3 (1973), 605–40.

SIGAL, C., *Weekend in Dinlock* (London: Secker & Warburg, 1960).

SLATER, ELIOT, and WOODSIDE, MOYA, *Patterns of Marriage: A Study of Marriage Relationships in the Urban Working Classes* (London: Cassell, 1951).

SLIM, HUGO, and THOMPSON, PAUL, *Listening for a Change: Oral Testimony and Development* (London: Panos, 1993).

SLOAN, DOUGLAS G., 'The Extent of Contraceptive Use and the Social Paradigm of Modern Demography', *Sociology*, 17 (1983), 380–7.

SMITH, DANIEL SCOTT, 'Family Limitation, Sexual Control and Domestic Feminism in Victorian America', *Feminist Studies*, 1 (1973), 40–57.

SOBO, ELISA, J., *Choosing Unsafe Sex: AIDS—Risk Denial among Disadvantaged Women* (Philadelphia: University of Pennsylvania Press, 1995).

SOLLIE, DONNA L., and LESLIE, LEIGH A. (eds.), *Gender, Families and Close Relationships* (Thousand Oaks: Sage, 1994).

SOLOWAY, RICHARD, *Birth Control and the Population Question in England 1870–1930* (Chapel Hill: University of North Carolina Press, 1982).

SPBCC (Society for the Provision of Birth Control Clinics), *Birth Control and Public Health: A Report on Ten Years' Work of the Society for the Provision of Birth Control Clinics* (London, 1932).

SPILLANE, WILLIAM H., and RYSER, PAUL E., *Male Fertility Survey: Fertility Knowledge, Attitudes and Practices of Married Men* (Cambridge, Mass.: Ballinger, 1975).

STANLEY, LIZ, *Sex Surveyed, 1949–1994. From Mass-Observation's 'Little Kinsey' to The National Survey and the Hite Reports* (London: Taylor & Francis, 1995).

STEARNS, PETER N., *Be a Man! Males in Modern Society* (New York: Holmes & Meier, 1990).

STOPES, MARIE, C., *Married Love* (1918; London: Putnam, 1940).

—— *Wise Parenthood. The Treatise on Birth Control for Married People: A Practical Sequel to 'Married Love'* (London: Putnam, 1918)

—— *Contraception. Birth Control: Its Theory, History and Practice* (1923; London: G. P. Putnam, 1932).

—— *Mother England. A Contemporary History: Self-Written by Those Who Have No Historian* (London: John Bale & Sons/Danielsson, 1929).

—— *Preliminary Notes on Various Technical Aspects of the Control of Conception Based on the Analysed Data from Ten Thousand Cases attending the Pioneer Mothers' Clinic London* (London: Mothers' Clinic for Constructive Birth Control, 1930).

STRANGE, JULIE-MARIE 'The Assault on Ignorance: Teaching Menstrual Etiquette in England, *c.* 1920s to 1960s', *Social History of Medicine*, 14 (2001), 247–65.

STYCOS, MAYONE J., BACK, KURT, and HILL, REUBEN, 'Problems of Communication Between Husband and Wife on Matters Relating to Family Limitation', *Human Relations*, 9/2 (1956), 207–15.

SUSSMAN, MARVIN B., 'Family Interaction and Fertility', in William T. Liu (ed.), *Family and Fertility: Proceedings of the Fifth Notre Dame Conference on Population* (Notre Dame: University of Notre Dame Press, 1966), 101–11.

SUTTON, MAUREEN, *'We Didn't Know Aught': A Study of Sexuality, Superstition and Death in Women's Lives in Lincolnshire during the 1930s, '40s and '50s* (Stamford: Paul Watkins, 1992).

SWANSON, JANICE M., 'Men and Family Planning', in S. M. H. Hanson and F. W. Bozett (eds.), *Dimensions of Fatherhood* (Beverley Hills: Sage, 1985), 21–48.

SWEET, MATTHEW, *Inventing the Victorians* (London: Faber & Faber, 2001).

SZRETER, SIMON, 'The Genesis of the Registrar-General's Social Classification of Occupations', *British Journal of Sociology*, 35 (1984), 522–46.

—— 'The Official Representation of Social Classes in Britain, United States and France: The Professional Model and "les cadres" ', *Comparative Studies in Society and History*, 35 (1993), 285–317.

—— *Fertility, Class and Gender in Britain, 1860–1940* (Cambridge: Cambridge University Press, 1996).

—— and FISHER, K., 'Sexuality, Love and Marriage in England, 1918–1960' (forthcoming; provisional title).

TAIT, LAWSON, *Diseases of Women and Abdominal Surgery*, vol. i (Leicester: Richardson, 1889).

TEBBUTT, MELANIE, *Women's Talk? A Social History of Gossip in Working Class Neighbourhoods, 1880–1960* (Aldershot: Scolar Press, 1995).

THOMAS, HILARY, 'The Medical Construction of the Contraceptive Career', in Hilary Homans (ed.), *The Sexual Politics of Reproduction* (Aldershot: Gower, 1985), 45–63.

THOMAS, JAMES, and WILLIAMS, A. SUSAN., 'Women and Abortion in 1930s Britain: A Survey and its Data', *Society for the Social History of Medicine*, 11/2 (1997), 282–309.

THOMPSON, PAUL, *The Edwardians: The Remaking of British Society* (London: Weidenfeld & Nicolson, 1975).

—— *The Voice of the Past: Oral History* (1978; Oxford: Oxford University Press, 1988).

—— 'Oral History and the Historian', *History Today*, 33 (1983), 24–8.

THOMSON, ALISTAIR, 'Putting Popular Memory Theory into Practice in Australia', in Rob Perks (ed.), *The Oral History Reader* (London: Routledge, 1998), 300–10.

TILLY, LOUISE A., and SCOTT, JOAN W., *Women, Work and Family* (London: Routledge, 1989).

TOLSON, A. J., *The Limits of Masculinity* (London: Tavistock, 1977).

TONE, ANDREA, 'Contraceptive Consumers: Gender and the Political Economy of Birth Control in the 1930s', *Journal of Social History*, 29 (1996), 485–506.

TONKIN, ELIZABETH, *Narrating Our Pasts: The Social Construction of Oral History* (Cambridge: Cambridge University Press, 1992).

TOSH, JOHN, *A Man's Place: Masculinity and the Middle-Class Home in Victorian England* (New Haven: Yale University Press, 1999).

—— *Manliness and Masculinities in Nineteenth-Century Britain* (Harlow: Pearson, 2005).

TSUI, AMY ONG, 'The Dynamics of Contraceptive Use', *Journal of Biosocial Science*, 11, supplement (1989), 1–7.

TURNER, CHRISTOPHER, 'Conjugal Roles and Social Networks: A Re-examination of an Hypothesis', *Human Relations*, 20 (1967), 121–30.

UDRY, J. RICHARD, 'Coitus as Demographic Behaviour', in Ronald Gray, Henri Leridon, and Alfred Spira (eds.), *Biomedical and Demographic Determinants of Reproduction* (Oxford: Clarendon Press, 1993), 85–97.

USBORNE, CORNELIE, *Cultures of Abortion in Weimar Germany* (Oxford: Oxford University Press, forthcoming).

VAN DE KAA, D. J., 'Anchored Narratives: The Story and Findings of Half a Century of Research into the Determinants of Fertility', *Population Studies*, 50 (1996), 389–432.

VAN DE VELDE, THEODOOR H., *Ideal Marriage: Its Physiology and Technique* (1928; London: William Heinemann Medical Books, 1947).

—— *Fertility and Sterility in Marriage: Their Voluntary Promotion and Limitation*, trans. Stella Browne (New York: Random House, 1931; 1st pub. in German, 1929).

VAN DE WALLE, ETIENNE, 'Fertility Transition, Conscious Choice, and Numeracy', *Demography*, 29 (1992), 487–502.

WALDRON, THERESA, 'Cervical Cap: Effective, Convenient, But Overlooked', *Contraceptive Technology Update*, 11 (1990), 49–54.

WARD, TONY, 'Legislating for Human Nature: Legal Responses to Infanticide, 1860–1938', in Mark Jackson (ed.), *Infanticide: Historical Perspectives on Child Murder and Concealment, 1550–2000* (Aldershot: Ashgate, 2002), 249–69.

WATKINS, SUSAN COTTS, 'If All We Knew About Women Was What We Read in *Demography*, What Would We Know?', *Demography*, 30 (1993), 551–77.

—— and DANZI, ANGELA D., 'Women's Gossip and Social Change: Childbirth and Fertility Control among Italian and Jewish Women in the United States, 1920–1940', *Gender and Society*, 9 (1995), 469–90.

—— SPECTOR, ANN ROSEN, and GOLDSTEIN, ALICE, 'Family Planning Patterns among Jewish and Italian Women in the United States, 1900–1940', unpublished paper presented at the Social Science History Association meetings, New Orleans, October, 1991.

WATTS RICHARD, J., *Power in Family Discourse* (Berlin: Mouton de Gruyter, 1991).

WEATHERHEAD, LESLIE, D., *The Mastery of Sex through Psychology and Religion* (1931; 17th edn. Gateshead upon Tyne: SCM Press, 1954).

WEBB, SIDNEY, and WEBB, BEATRICE, *Industrial Democracy* (1898; 2nd edn. London: Longman Green & Co., 1987).

WEEKS, JEFFREY, *Sex, Politics and Society: The Regulation of Sexuality since 1800* (1989; London: Longman, 1981).

—— 'Inverts, Perverts, and Mary-Annes: Male Prostitution and the Regulation of Homosexuality in England in the Nineteenth and Early Twentieth Centuries', in Martin Bauml Duberman, Martha Vicinus, and George Chauncey Jr. (eds.), *Hidden from History: Reclaiming the Gay and Lesbian Past* (Harmondsworth: Penguin, 1991), 195–211.

WEIR, J. G., 'Lay Abortionists', in Family Planning Association, *Abortion in Britain* (London: Pitman Medical Publishing, 1966), 39–42.

WELLER, ROBERT H., 'The Employment of Wives, Dominance, and Fertility', *Journal of Marriage and the Family*, 30 (1968), 437–42.

WELLS, ROBERT V., 'Family History and Demographic Transition', *Journal of Social History*, 9 (1975), 1–19.

WEST, PETER, *Fathers, Sons and Lovers: Men Talk about their Lives from the 1930s to Today* (Sydney: Finch Publishing, 1996).

WESTOFF, C. F., POTTER, R. G., and SAGI, P. C., 'Some Estimates on the Reliability of Survey Data on Family Planning', *Population Studies*, 15 (1961), 52–69.

WETLESEN, TONE SCHOU, *Fertility Choices and Constraints: A Qualitative Study of Norwegian Families* (Oslo: Solum Forlag, 1991).

WHITE, HAYDEN, 'The Value of Narrativity in the Representation of Reality', in W. J. T. Mitchell (ed.), *On Narrative* (Chicago: University of Chicago Press, 1981), 1–23.

WHITE, KEVIN, *The First Sexual Revolution: The Emergence of Male Heterosexuality in Modern America* (New York: New York University Press, 1993).

WILE, IRA S., *Sex Education* (London: Andrew Melrose, 1913).

WILLIAMS, SUSAN A., *Women and Childbirth in the Twentieth Century: A History of the National Birthday Trust Fund 1928–93* (London: Sutton Publishing, 1997).

WILLIAMSON, MARGARET, ' "Getting Off at Loftus": Sex and the Working-Class Woman, 1920–1960', *Family and Community History*, 3/1 (2000), 5–17.

WOHL, A. S. (ed.), *The Victorian Family* (London: Croom Helm, 1978).

WOOD, CLIVE, and SUITTERS, BERYL, *The Fight for Acceptance: A History of Contraception* (Guildford: Billing & Sons, 1970).

WOODS, ROBERT, 'Debate: Working-Class Fertility Decline in Britain', *Past and Present*, 134 (1992), 200–11.

—— *The Demography of Victorian England and Wales* (Cambridge: Cambridge University Press, 2000).

WOODSIDE, MOYA, 'Health and Happiness in Marriage', *Health Education Journal*, 4 (1946), 147–8.

—— 'Attitudes of Women Abortionists', *Family Planning*, 12 (1963), 31–9.

—— 'The Woman Abortionist', in Family Planning Association, *Abortion in Britain* (London: Pitman Medical Publishing, 1966), 35–8.

WOOLF, MYRA, *Family Intentions: An Enquiry Undertaken for the General Register Officer* (London: OPCS, Social Survey Division, HMSO, 1971),

—— and PEGDEN, SUE, *Families Five Years On: A Survey Carried Out on Behalf of Population Statistics Division of the Office of Population Censuses and Surveys* (London: OPCS, Social Survey Division, HMSO, 1976).

WOOLF, ROWENA, 'Changes', in Family Planning Association, *Abortion in Britain* (London: Pitman Medical Publishing, 1966), 70–2.

WRIGHT, HELENA, *The Sex Factor in Marriage* (1930; London: National Marriage Guidance Council and the Family Planning Association, 1955).

—— *More About the Sex Factor in Marriage* (London: Williams & Norgate, 1954); 1st pub. as *Sex Fulfilment in Married Women* (1947).

WRIGHTSON, KEITH, *English Society 1580–1680* (London: Hutchinson, 1982).

YOUNG, MICHAEL, and WILLMOTT, PETER, *Family and Kinship in East London* (London: Routledge & Kegan Paul, 1957).

—— —— *The Symmetrical Family* (London: Routledge & Kegan Paul, 1973).

YOW, VALERIE R., *Recording Oral History* (London: Sage, 1994).

ZIMMERMAN, MARY, 'Experiencing Abortion as a Crisis: The Impact of Social Context', in Barbara J. Risman, and Pepper Schwartz (eds.), *Gender in Intimate Relationships: A Micro Structural Approach* (Belmont, Calif.: Wandsworth Publishing, 1989), 132–7.

ZWEIG, F., *The Worker in an Affluent Society: Family Life and Industry* (London: Heinemann, 1961).

Index